The New Sabin;

Entries 8444-11225

The New Sabin;
Books Described by Joseph Sabin and His
Successors, Now Described Again on the
Basis of Examination of Originals,
and Fully Indexed by Title, Subject,
Joint Authors, and Institutions and Agencies

by

Lawrence S. Thompson

Entries 8444-11225

Volume IV

The Whitston Publishing Company
Troy, New York

1977

PREFACE

This fourth volume of The New Sabin contains titles from Lyle Wright's bibliography of American Fiction, 1774-1900. Subsequent volumes will contain the remaining titles from the Wright bibliography. Nearly all entries correspond to the Wright entries, but in a few cases editions have been identified which are more satisfactory for the student. All editions described here are available on microfiche from the Lost Cause Press of Louisville, and thus this volume represents a guide to pre-1900 American fiction in print.

While Wright's indexes are exemplary within their defined scope, the index to this volume represents a considerable expansion. All of the elements in Wright's indexes are included, but there are also many additional "secondary entries" and, most important, subject entries and analytical entries for titles of short stories. Thus we have here a guide to the subject matter of eighteenth and nineteenth century American Fiction, with special emphasis on local, regional, and historical themes. In addition, it is an index to short stories in non-serial publications. The importance of this policy of indexing has been brought home in a striking manner to the compiler, who has been able to identify several titles which should have been included in his bibliography of The Kentucky Novel (1953).

The first two volumes of The New Sabin contain a good many titles of pre-1900 American fiction which do not appear here. However, the cumulative index which will be provided for the first five volumes will identify them in the same manner in which the titles in this volume are indexed. Further, some pseudonyms and analytical entries for short stories not in the indexes of single volumes will be in the cumulative index.

Lawrence S. Thompson
Lexington, Kentucky
March, 1977

LAWRANCE ROGER THOMPSON
(1906–1973)

A

8444 [Abbot, Anne Wales] ed.
Autumn leaves. Original pieces in prose and verse...
Cambridge [Mass.] J. Bartlett, 1853.
vi p., 1 l., 200 p.   18 1/2 cm.
Prefatory note signed: Anne W. Abbot.

8445 Abbott, Charles Conrad, 1843-1919.
A colonial wooing. By Charles Conrad Abbott. Philadelphia, J. B. Lippincott company, 1895.
241 p.   18 1/2 cm.

8446 Abbott, Charles Conrad, 1843-1919.
The hermit of Nottingham. A novel, by Charles Conrad
Abbott. Philadelphia, J. B. Lippincott company, 1898.
332 p.   18 1/2 cm.

8447 Abbott, Charles Conrad, 1843-1919.
When the century was new. A novel, by Charles Conrad
Abbott, M. D. Philadelphia, J. B. Lippincott company,
1897.
275 p.   18 1/2 cm.
"Story of old Nottingham." - Dedication.

8448 [Abbott, L   A   ] b. 1813.
Seven wives and seven prisons; or, Experiences in the life
of a matrimonial monomaniac. A true story, written by
himself. New York, The author, 1870.
x,[11]-205 p. incl. front., plates.   17 1/2 cm.

8449 Abbott, Lyman, 1835-1922.
Laicus; or. The experiences of a layman in a country
parish. By Lyman Abbott. New York, Dodd & Mead. 1872.
[3], 6-358 p.   19 cm.

8450 Abbott, Mrs. Mary Perkins (Ives) 1851-1904.
       Alexia, by Mary Abbott. Chicago, A. C. McClurg and
    company, 1889.
       vi, [7]-177 p.   18 cm.

8451 Abrams, Albert, 1863-1924.
       Scattered leaves from a physician's diary. By Albert
    Abrams... St. Louis, M., Fortnightly press co., 1900.
       1 p. l., 59 p. port.   24 1/2 cm.

8452 Abrams, Albert, 1863-1924.
       Transactions of the Antiseptic club, reported by Albert
    Abrams... New York, E. B. Treat [etc., etc.] 1895.
       206 p. incl. front, illus., plates.   21 cm.

8453 Abrojal, Tulis, pseud.
       An index finger [a story] by Tulis Abrojal ... New
    York, R. F. Fenno & company, 1898.
       382 p.   19 cm.

8454 Ackerman, A   W
       The price of peace. A story of the times of Ahab, king of
    Israel. By A. W. Ackerman. Chicago, A. C. McClurg and
    company, 1894.
       viii, [9]-390 p.   19 1/2 cm

8455 Acklan, William Hayes.
       Sterope: the veiled Pleiad, by Wm. Hayes Acklan ...
    Washington, Gibson bros., 1892.
       300 p   20 cm.

8456 [Adams, Charles]
       The adventures of my Cousin Smooth. By Timothy
    Templeton. Of Tewksbury [pseud.] New York and Auburn,
    Miller, Orton & Mulligan [etc., etc.] 1856.
       iv, 236 p.   19 1/2 cm.

8457 Adams, Charles Abel, 1854-
       An ocean special. New York, The Author, 1900.
       250 p. pl.   16 cm.

8458 [Adams, Francis Colburn]

The life and adventures of ... Roger Sherman Potter:
together with an accurate ... account of his great achieve-
ment in politics, diplomacy, and war ... Illustrated by
Huber ... By Pheleg Van Trusedale [pseud.] New York,
Stanford & Delisser, 1858.
viii, 9-522 p. plates. 19 cm.

8459 Adams, Francis Colburn.
Manuel Pereira; or, The sovereign rule of South Carolina.
With views of southern laws, life, and hospitality. By F. C.
Adams ... London, Clarke, Beeton, & co.; Washington,
Buell & Blanchard [etc., etc.] 1854.
1 p. l., [v]-xiii, 388 p. 18 cm.
The operations of the S. C. law for incarceration of free
men of color brought within her limits.

8460 Adams, Francis Colburn.
Our world; or, The slaveholder's daughter ... New York
and Auburn, Millor, Orton & Mulligan, 1855.
3 p. l., 597 p. front., plates. 19 cm.

8461 Adams, Francis Colburn.
Siege of Washington, D. C., written expressly for little
people. By F. Colburn Adams ... 26 illustrations.
Illustrated by A. W. Waud. New York, Dick & Fitzgerald
[1867]
1 p. l., 130 p. front. (port.) illus., plates. 18 x
14 1/2 cm.

8462 Adams, Francis Colburn.
The Von Toodleburgs; or, The history of a very distinguished
family. By F. Colburn Adams ... Philadelphia, Claxton,
Remsen & Haffelfinger, 1868.
vi, [9]-290 p. plates, 20 cm.

8463 [Adams, Mrs. H   A   ]
Dawn, [A novel] Boston, Adams & company; London,
Trübner & co., 1868.
[3], 6-404 p. 19 cm.

8464 Adams, Harriet A   "Mrs. J. S. Adams," d. 1885
Allegories of life. By Mrs. J. S. Adams. Boston, Lee

3

& Shepard; New York, Lee, Shepard, & Dillingham, 1872.
2p. l. , [7]-93 p.   21 1/2 cm.

8465 [Adams, Henry] 1838-1918.
... Democracy, an American novel. New York, H. Holt
and company, 1880.
1 p. l. , 374 p.   17 1/2 cm. (Leisure-hour series.
no. 112)
Variously attributed by different authorities to Henry
Adams, John Hay and Clarence King. cf. W. R. Thayer,
Life of John Hay, 1915, v. 2, p. 58-59. The authorship of
Adams is affirmed by the publisher Henry Holt in the
Unpartisan review, no. 29, Jan.-Mar. 1921, p. 156; and
Literary review, Dec. 24, 1920.

8466 [Adams, James Alonzo]
Colonel Hungerford's daughter. Story of an American
girl. By Grapho [pseud.] ... Chicago, C. H. Kerr &
company, 1896.
1 p. l. , 5-304 p.   20 cm.

8467 Adams, John Stowell, d. 1893.
Sam Squab, the Boston boy: containing a sketch of his
early life, and wonderful adventures. By John S. Adams ...
Boston [Redding & co. ,] 1844.
48 p.   21 1/2 cm.

8468 [Adams, John Turvill] 1805-1882.
The knight of the golden melice, a historical romance, by
the author of "The lost hunter" ... New York, Derby &
Jackson; Cincinnati, W. H. Derby & co. , 1857.
2 p. l. , [9]-473 p.   19 cm.
Published also under title: The white chief among the
red men.

8469 [Adams, John Turvill] 1805-1882.
The lost hunter. A tale of early times ... New York,
Derby & Jackson; Cincinnati, H. W. Derby, 1856.
xvi, [17]-462 p.   18 1/2 cm.

8470 [Adams, Nehemiah] 1806-1878.
Bertha and her baptism. By the author of Agnes and the

little key; or, Bereaved parents instructed and comforted.
Boston, S. K. Whipple and company, 1857.
    viii, [9]-209 p.   20 cm.

8471 [Adams, Nehemiah] 1806-1878.
    Catharine. By the author of "Agnes and the little key."
Boston, J. E. Tilton and company; London, Knight and son,
1859.
    192 p.   19 1/2 cm.

8472 [Adams, Nehemiah] 1806-1878.
    The sable cloud: a southern tale, with northern comments.
By the author "A south-side view of slavery" ... Boston,
Ticknor and Fields, 1861.
    iv, 275 p.   18 cm.

8473 Adams, Oscar Fay, 1855-1919.
    The archbishop's unguarded moment and other stories, by
Oscar Fay Adams ... Boston, L. C. Page and company
(incorporated) 1899.
    6 p. l., 11-270 p. front.   19 1/2 cm.
    CONTENTS. -The archbishop's unguarded moment. -The
evolution of a bishop. Why the bishop left Rye beach. -The
trials of a retired bishop. -A night with William of Wykeham. -
The discontented bishop. -The serious dilemma of the Bishop
of Oklaho.

8474 Adams, William Taylor, 1822-1897.
    Living too fast; or, The confessions of a bank officer,
by William T. Adams (Oliver Optic.) ... Boston, Lee and
Shepard [1904]
    351 p. incl. front., illus. plates.   19 cm.
First published, 1876.

8475 Ade, George, 1866-1944.
    Artie. A story of the streets and town, by George Ade,
Pictures by John T. McCutcheon. Chicago, H. S. Stone &
co., 1896.
    2 p. l., 192 [1] p. plates.   16 1/2 cm.

8476 Ade, George, 1866-1944.
    Doc' Horne: a story of the streets and town, by George

Ade ... Pictures by John T. McCutcheon. Chicago and New York, H. S. Stone and company, 1899.
2 p. l. , 292 p. , 1 l. front. , illus. 17 cm.
"Rewritten in part from a series of articles that first appeared in the Chicago record."-Verso of t. -p.
"Second impression."

8477 Ade, George, 1866-1944.
Fables in slang; illustrated by C. J. Newman. Chicago and New York, H. S. Stone & co. , 1900.
4 p. l. , 201 p. illus. 17 cm.

8478 Ade, George, 1866-1944.
More fables, by George Ade ... Illustrated by Clyde J. Newman. Chicago & New York, H. S. Stone and company, 1900.
4 p. l. , 218 p. , 1 l. illus. 15 1/2 cm.
Title-page in red and black, printed on two pages facing each other within one ornamental border.

8479 Ade, George, 1866-1944.
Pink Marsh. A story of the streets and town, by George Ade ... Pictures by John T. McCutcheon. Chicago & New York, H. S. Stone & co. , 1897.
2 p. l. , 197 p. front. , plates. 17 1/2 cm.

8480 Adler, Cyrus, 1863-
Told in the coffee house. Turkish tales. Collected and done into English by Cyrus Adler and Allan Ramsay. New York, The Macmillan company; London, Macmillan & co. , ltd. , 1898.
viii, 174 p. 15 cm.

8481 Adsonville; or, Marrying out. Albany, S. Shaw, 1824.
viii, 280 p. 16 cm.

8482 Agnus, Felix, 1839-
A woman of war, and other stories. By Felix Agnus. Baltimore, The American job printing office, 1895.
180 p. 20 1/2 cm.
CONTENTS. - Noel of 1864. -A woman of war. -The gunner of "Lady Davis."-A sacred trust.

8483 Aiken, Clementine Edith.
        The days we live in. A story of society. By C. E. A. ...
    Boston, W. F. Brown & company, 1876.
        478 p. front, 2 pl.   19 1/2 cm.

8484 Albert, Bessie.
        How Bob and I kept house. A story of Chicago hard times.
    By Bessie Albert. New York, The Authors' publishing
    company [c1880]
        65 p.   17 x 14 cm. (On cover: Satchel series, no 28).

8485 [Alcott, Louisa May] 1832-1888.
        ... A modern Mephistopheles. Boston, Roberts brothers,
    1877.
        290 p.   17 cm. (No name series)

8486 Alcott, Louisa May, 1832-1888.
        Moods. By Louisa M. Alcott ... 2d ed. Boston, Loring,
    1865.
        v, [7]-297 p.   19 cm.

8487 Alcott, Louisa May, 1832-1888.
        Work: a story of experience. By Louisa M. Alcott ...
    Boston, Roberts brothers, 1873.
        3 p. l., 443 p. illus.   18 cm.
        First edition.

8488 Alden, Isabella (Macdonald) "Mrs. G. R. Alden," 1841-
        By way of the wilderness, by "Pansy" (Mrs. G. R.
    Alden) and Mrs. C. M. Livingstone ... Boston, Lothrop
    publishing company [1899]
        394 p. front.   19 1/2 cm.
8489 See p. 424.
8490 Alden Joseph, 1807-1885.
        Alice Gordon. Or, The uses of orphanage. By Joseph
    Alden ... With ten illustrations. New York, Harper &
    brothers [1847]
        198 p. incl. front., plates.   17 cm. (On cover:
    Harper's Fireside library)

8491 Alden, Joseph, 1807-1885.
        The old revolutionary soldier. By Joseph Alden ...

New York, Gates & Stedman, 1848.
vi, [7]-152 p. front. , 4 pl.   15 cm.
Added t. -p. , illus.

8492 Alden, William Livingstone, 1837-1908.
Domestic explosives and other sixth column fancies.
(From the New York Times.) By W. L. Alden. New York,
Lovell, Adam, Wesson & company, 1877.
2 p. l. , [3]-334 p.   18 1/2 cm.
Published also under titles: The comic liar and The
coming girl.

8493 Alden, William Livingston, 1837-1908.
Shooting stars as observed from the "sixth column" of the
Times, by W. L. Alden. New York, G. P. Putnam's sons,
1878.
iv, [5]-224 p. front. , plates.   17 1/2 cm.

8494 [Alden], W[illiam] Livingston, 1837-1908.
Told by the colonel. By W. L. Livingston. Illustrated
by Richard Jack and Hal Hurst. New York, J. S. Tait
& sons [c1893]
iii, 176 p. incl. illus, plates.   19 1/2 cm.

8495 Aldrich, Anne Reeve, 1866-1892.
The feet of love. By Anne Reeve Aldrich ... New York,
Worthington co. , 1890.
290 p. incl. front. (port.) plates.   19 cm.

8496 Aldrich, Anne Reeve, 1866-1892.
A village Ophelia, by Anne Reeve Aldrich. New York,
G. W. Dillingham co. , 1899.
1 p. l. , 5-188 p.   20 cm.
CONTENTS. - A village Ophelia. -A story of the Vere de
Vere. - A lamentable comedy. -An African discovery. -An
evening with Callender.

8497 Aldrich, Thomas Bailey, 1836-1907.
Daisy's necklace: and what came of it. (A literary episode.)
By T. B. Aldrich ... New York, Derby & Jackson: Cincinnati, H. W. Derby & co. , 1857.
viii, [9]-225 p. , 1 l.   19 cm.

8498 Aldrich, Thomas Bailey, 1836-1907.
    Marjorie Daw and other people. Boston, New York:
Houghton, Mifflin and company, The Riverside Press,
Cambridge [n.d.]
    243 p.   20 cm.

8499 Aldrich, Thomas Bailey, 1836-1907.
    A midnight fantasy, and The little violinist. By T. B.
Aldrich. Illustrated. Boston, J. R. Osgood and company,
late Ticknor & Fields, and Fields, Osgood & co., 1877.
    3 p. l., [11]-96 p. incl. 1 illus., 3 pl. front.   12 1/2 cm.

8500 Aldrich, Thomas Bailey, 1836-1907, ed.
    Out of his head. A romance ... [Also, Paul Lynde's sketch
book] Ed. by Thomas Bailey Aldrich. New York, Carleton,
1862.
    1 p. l., [v]-viii, [2], [11]-226 p. · 19 cm.

8501 Aldrich, Thomas Bailey, 1836-1907.
    Père Antoine's date palm. By Thomas Bailey Aldrich.
Cambridge [Eng.] Welch, Bigelow, and company, 1866.
    20 p.   20 1/2 x 15 1/2 cm.
    Title vignette.

8502 Aldrich, Thomas Bailey, 1836-1907.
    ... Prudence Palfrey. A novel. Boston, J. R. Osgood
and company, 1874.
    vi, [7]-311 p. front.   18 cm.
    Author's name at head of t.-p.

8503 Aldrich, Thomas Bailey, 1836-1907.
    Two bites at a cherry, with other tales, by Thomas
Bailey Aldrich. Boston and New York, Houghton, Mifflin
and company, 1894.
    3 p. l., 269 p. 18 cm.
    CONTENTS.-Two bites at a cherry.-"For bravery on the
field of battle."-The Chevalier de Resseguier.-Goliath.-
My cousin the colonel.-A Christmas fantasy, with a moral.-
Her dying words.

8504 Aleck and Pete; or, 'The hand of the diligent maketh rich.' Saint
Louis, S. W. book and publishing co., 1870

16 p.   15 1/2 cm.

8505 Alexander, Sigmund B
   A moral blot. A novel. By Sigmund B. Alexander ...
  Boston, Arena publishing company, 1894.
   4 p. l. , 233 p.   20 cm.

8506 All for her; or, St. Jude's assistant. A novel. By * * * * ?
  ... New York, G. W. Carleton & co. , 1877.
   429 p.   19 cm.
  An edition published in 1883 has title: A cruel secret.

8507 All for him. A novel. By * * * * ? Author of "All for her"
  ... New York, G. W. Carleton & co. [etc. , etc.] 1877.
   1 p. l. , [5]-376 p.   19 cm.

8508 [Allen, Elizabeth Ann (Chase) Akers] 1832-1911.
   The triangular society. Leaves from the life of a Portland family. Portland, Hoyt, Fogg & Donham, 1886.
   381 p.   20 cm.

8509 [Allen, Henry Francis]
   The key of industrial co-operative government. By
  Pruning Knife [pseud.] St. Louis, Mo. , The author, 1886.
   133 p. front. (port.) illus.   22 cm.

8510 [Allen, Henry Francis]
   A strange voyage. A revision of The key of industrial
  co-operative government. An interesting and instructive
  description of life on Planet Venus. By Pruning Knife
  [pseud.] St. Louis, Mo. , The Monitor publishing company,
  1891.
   xi, 226 p.   16 cm.

8511 Allen, James Lane, 1849-1925.
   Aftermath. Part second of "A Kentucky cardinal. " By
  James Lane Allen ... New York, Harper & brothers, 1896.
   2 p. l. , 135 p.   15 1/2 cm. (On cover: Harper's little
  novels)

8512 Allen, James Lane, 1849-1925.
   The bride of the mistletoe ... New York, The Macmillan

company, 1909.
190 p.   19 cm.

8513 Allen, James Lane, 1849-1925.
The choir invisible ... New York, Macmillan, 1917.
361 p.   17 cm.

8514 Allen, James Lane, 1849-1925.
John Gray: A Kentucky tale of the olden time ...
Philadelphia, J. B. Lippincott company, 1893.
218 p. front.   20 cm.

8515 Allen, James Lane, 1849-1925.
The mettle of the pasture. New York, The Macmillan
company, 1903.
448 p.   20 cm.

8516 Allen, James Lane, 1849-1925.
The reign of law, a tale of the Kentucky hemp fields ...
with illustrations by Harry Fenn and J.C. Earl. New York,
The Macmillan company, 1900.
385 p. illus.   20 1/2 cm.

8517 Allen, James Lane, 1849-1925.
Summer in Arcady: a tale of nature ... New York,
Macmillan and co.; London, Macmillan & co., ltd., 1896.
170 p.   20 cm.

8518 Allen, James Lane, 1849-1925.
Two gentlemen of Kentucky, by James Lane Allen. New
York and London, Harper & brothers, 1899.
2 p. l., 73 p. front.   16 1/2 x 9 cm. [Little books by
famous writers]
This story is taken from the author's book, "Flute and
violin."

8519 Allen, Martha.
Day-dreams. By Martha Allen ... Philadelphia, Lippincott,
Grambo, and co., 1852.
viii, [13]-154 p.   18 cm.

8520 Allen, Richard.

Miss Eaton's romance. A story of the New Jersey shore, by Richard Allen. New York, Dodd, Mead and company [c1890]
300 p. 19 cm.

8521 [Allen, Samuel A   ]
My own home and fireside: being illustrative of the specu-lations of Martin Chuzzlewitt and co., among the "wenom of the walley of Eden." By Syr [pseud.] Philadelphia, J. W. Moore; [etc., etc.] 1846.
iv, 5-384 p. 19 1/2 cm.

8522 Allerton, James Martin.
Hawk's Nest; or, The last of the Cahoonshees. A tale of the Delaware valley and historical romance of 1690. By James M. Allerton. Port Jervis, N. Y., The gazette book & job print [c1892]
2 p. l., [4]-246, [6] p. front. (port.) 22 1/2 cm.

8523 Allyn, Eunice Gibbs.
One thousand smiles [by] Eunice Gibbs Allyn. Dubuque, Iowa, Press M. S. Hardie [1898]
4 p. l., [11]-90 p. 18 cm.

8524 Altsheler, Joseph Alexander, 1862-1919.
In circling camps; a romance of the civil war, by Joseph A. Altsheler ... New York, D. Appleton and company, 1900.
vi, 419 p. 19 1/2 cm.

8525 Altsheler, Joseph Alexander, 1862-1919.
The last rebel ... Philadelphia & London, J. B. Lippincott company, 1900.
219 p., illus. 20 cm.
Of a Confederate colonel after the war.

8526 Amelia; or, The faithless Briton. An original American novel, founded upon recent facts. To which is added, Amelia; or, Malevolence defeated: and Miss Seward's monody on Major Andre. Boston, W. Spotswood, and C. P. Wayne, 1798.
1 p. l., 61, 22 p. front. 12 cm.

8527 Amelia Sherwood; or, Bloody scenes at the California gold mines,

with a narrative of the tragic incidents on a voyage to San
Francisco. Richmond, Barclay & co. , 1850.
32 p. incl, front.   22 1/2 cm.
Front. printed on both sides.

8528 American coin; a novel ... By the author of "Aristocracy."
New York, D. Appleton and company, 1889.
213 p.   19 cm.   (On cover: Appletons' town and country
library, no. 31)

8529 [Ames, Mrs. Eleanor Maria (Easterbrook)] 1831-1908.
Libra: an astrological romance. By Eleanor Kirk [pseud.]
Brooklyn, E. Kirk [1896]
4 p. l. , [3]-270 p. illus.   18 1/2 cm.

8530 Ames, Mrs. Eleanor Maria (Easterbrook) 1831-1908.
Up Broadway, and its sequel. A life story. By Eleanor
Kirk [Nellie Ames] New York, Carleton [etc. , etc.] 1870.
2 p. l. , 7-271 p.   18 1/2 cm.

8531 Ames, Mrs. Mary (Clemmer) 1839-1884.
Eirene; or, A woman's right. By Mary Clemmer Ames ...
New York, G. P. Putnam & sons, 1871.
3 p. l. , 219 p.   23 cm.

8532 Ames, Mrs. Mary (Clemmer) 1839-1884.
His two wives, by Mary Clemmer Ames ... New York,
Hurd and Houghton, 1875.
vi. 585 p.   19 cm.

8533 [Amory, John H   ]
Alnomuc; or, The golden rule, a tale of the sea. With
twenty-four engravings. Salem, D. B. Brooks and brother;
Cleveland, O. , Jewett, Proctor, and Worthington, 1837.
144 p. front. , plates.   15 1/2 cm.

8534 Anderson, C   H
Armour; or, What are you going to do about it ? By C. H.
Anderson ... New York, W. B. Smith & co. [c1881]
272 p. incl front.   20 cm.

8535 Anderson, Mrs. Finley.

A woman with a record. A novel, by Mrs. Finley Anderson. New York, G. W. Dillingham co., 1896.
223 p.   20 1/2 cm.

8536 Anderson, Florence.
Zenaida. By Florence Anderson. Philadelphia, J. B. Lippincott & co., 1858.
374 p.   19 cm.

8537 Anderson, Nephi.
Added upon. A story. By Nephi Anderson ... Salt Lake City, Utah, Deseret news publishing company, 1898.
140 p.   19 1/2 cm.

8538 Andrews, Jessie Agnes.
Eteocles: a tale of Antioch. By Jessie Agnes Andrews ... New York [A. D. F. Randolph and co.] 1889.
3 p. 1., [v]-vi, [7]-135 p.   18 1/2 cm.

8539 Anna Archdale; or, The Lowell factory girl. And other tales. Boston, F. Gleason [185-?]
1 p. 1., [7]-100 p.   26 cm.
Reprinted from the Flag of our union, Ladies' national magazine, and Graham's magazine.
CONTENTS. -Anna Archdale; or, The Lowell factory girl. - The innkeeper's wife: a tale of the revolution._ A washing day experience. -Annie Sinclair; or, The fourth of July sail. - Lilias Atherton; or, The rescue. - The fairy fountain. -A picnic of olden time. - The bachelor at home. - The prima donna. -The scientific angler. -The widow's lesson. -The generous lovers. -The volunteer's return. -The Lady Blanche. -The captive maiden.

8540 Annals of the Empire City, from its colonial days to the present. By a New Yorker. Tale 1, The quadroon; or, New York under the English ... New York, J. F. Trow, printer, 1852.
238 p.   18 1/2 cm.

8541 Appleton, Emily.
Alice Mannering; or, The nobleman's son. A tale of London, by Emily Appleton. Boston, Gleason's publishing

hall, 1845.
   1 p. 1. , [5]-54 p.   23 1/2 cm.

8542 ... The Arab wife. A romance of the Polynesian seas. New
   York, D. Appleton and company, 1878.
      156 p.   16 1/2 cm. (On cover: Appletons' new handy-
   volume series.   13)
      Series title also at head of t. -p.

8543 [Archer, Geroge W   ]
      More than she could bear; a story of the Gachupin war in
   Texas, A. D. 1812-13. By Hesper Bendbow [pseud.] ...
   Philadelphia, Claxton, Remsen & Haffelfinger, 1872.
      1 p. 1. , vii-xvi, 17-439 p.   19 1/2 cm.

8544 Argyle, Anna, pseud. ?
      Olive Lacey: a tale of the Irish rebellion of 1798. By
   Anna Argyle ... Philadelphia, J. B. Lippincott & co. , 1874.
      365 p.   19 cm.

8545 Argyle, Archie, pseud. ?
      Cupid's album. By Archie Argyle. New York, M.
   Doolady; St. Louis, M. B. Cullen, 1866.
      2 p. 1. , vi, [7]-332 p.   18 cm.

8546 [Arkell, William J   ]
      Napoleon Smith. Author, a well-known New-Yorker. New
   York, The Judge publishing company, 1888.
      202 p.   19 cm.
      Cover-title: Napoleon Smith. A novel by W. J. Arkell and
   A. T. Worden. 4th ed. New York, 1889.

8547 Armstrong, William, 1856-1942.
      An American nobleman; a story of the Canaan wilderness,
   by William Armstrong. Chicago, F. J. Schulte & company
   [c1892]
      277 p. front. , plates.   20 cm.

8548 Armstrong, William, 1856-1942.
      Cleopatra's daughter. Romance of a branch of roses,
   by William Armstrong ... Boston, De Wolfe, Fiske & co. , 1889.
      2 p. 1. , [9]-226 p.   19 cm.

8549 Armstrong, William, 1856-1942.
Thekla: a story of Viennese musical life. By William
Armstrong. Philadelphia, J. B. Lippincott company, 1887.
239 p.   19 cm.

8550 [Arnold, Alexander Streeter] 1828-
The Benson family. A story for old and young. By the
author of "Uncle Timothy Taber" ... Central Falls, R. I.,
E. L. Freeman, 1869.
xi, [13]-196 p.   20 1/2 cm.

8551 Arnold, Augustus C   L
The signet of King Solomon; or, The Templar's daughter.
By Aug. C. L. Arnold ... To which is added a memoir of
Elizabeth Aldworth, the female freemason. And a Masonic
prologue ... New York. Macoy & Sickels: Atlanta, Ga.,
McPherson & co., 1860.
vi, [7]-307 p. front. (port.) illus.   19 cm.

8552 [Arnold, Josephine]
Bachelors and butterflies. A midsummer diversion. By
Allis Arnould [pseud.] New York, W. B. Smith & co.
[c1882]
194 p.   17 1/2 cm. (On cover: Satchel series, no. 40)

8553 Arrest, confession and suicide of Almira Cathcart; who having
hitherto eluded all efforts to capture her, was arrested last
week in Cincinnati: and after writing her confession, in which
she acknowledges inveigling thirteen beautiful young ladies,
she poisoned herself with prussic acid, which she had con-
cealed in one of her ear rings ... Philadelphia, C. W.
Alexander, c1869.
1 p. 1., 19-62 p. incl. 2 pl., port.   24 cm.

8554 [Arrington, Alfred W   ] 1810-1867.
The lives and adventures of the desperadoes of the Southwest: containing an account of the duelist and dueling ... By
Charles Summerfield [pseud.] New York, W. H. Graham,
1849.
iv, [5]-98 p.   24 cm.

8555 Arthur, Timothy Shay, 1809-1885.

Agnes; or, The possessed. A revelation of mesmerism. By T. S. Arthur ... Philadelphia, T. B. Peterson [c1848] 4, 9-116 p. 24 cm.

8556 Arthur, Timothy Shay, 1809-1885.
The angel and the demon: a tale of modern spiritualism. By T. S. Arthur. Philadelphia, J. W. Bradley, 1858. 2 p. 1., 7-311 p. 19 1/2 cm.

8557 Arthur, Timothy Shay, 1809-1885.
The bar-rooms at Brantley; or, The great hotel speculation. By T. S. Arthur ... Philadelphia, Porter & Coates [c1877]
vi, 7-437 p. incl. front. 19 1/2 cm

8558 Arthur, T[imothy] S[hay] 1809-1885.
The beautiful widow. By T. S. Arthur ... Philadelphia, Carey and Hart, 1847. 2 p. 1., [13]-103 p. 24 cm.

8559 Arthur, Timothy Shay, 1809-1885.
Bell Martin; or, The heiress. An American story of real life. By T. S. Arthur ... Philadelphia, Burgess & Zieber, 1843. 32 p. 31 1/2 cm [The American novelist's library. No. 1]

8560 Arthur, Timothy Shay, 1809-1885.
Cast adrift. By T. S. Arthur ... Philadelphia, J. M. Stoddart & co.; New York, W. Gibson, jr. [etc., etc.] 1873. 2 p. 1., 7-364 p. front., plates. 19 cm.

8561 Arthur, Timothy Shay, 1809-1885.
Danger; or, Wounded in the house of a friend. By T. S. Arthur ... Philadelphia, J. M. Stoddart & co.; Chicago, Western publishing house; [etc., etc., c1875] 334 p. front., plates. 19 1/2 cm.

8562 Arthur, Timothy Shay, 1809-1885.
Friends and neighbours; or, Two ways of living in the world. Edited by T. S. Arthur. Philadelphia, H. C. Peck & T. Bliss, 1856.

vi 7-300 p. front.   19 cm.

8563   Arthur, Timothy Shay, 1809-1885.
          The good time coming. By T. S. Arthur. Philadelphia,
       J. W. Bradley, 1855.
          308 p. front.   19 cm.

8564   Arthur, Timothy Shay, 1809-1885.
          ... Growler's income tax. By T. S. Arthur. [New York,
       Francis & Loutrel, printer, 1864]
          4 p.   22 cm. (Loyal publication society ... [Pamphlets]
       no. 57)
          Caption title.
          Another issue is without names of printers at foot of p. 4.

8565   Arthur, Timothy Shay, 1809-1885.
          The hand but not the heart; or, The life-trials of Jessie
       Loring. By T. S. Arthur. New York, Derby & Jackson,
       1858.
          317 p.   19 cm.

8566   Arthur, Timothy Shay, 1809-1885.
          Heart-histories and life-pictures. By T. S. Arthur.
       New York, C. Scribner, 1853.
          vi, [9]-350 p. front.   17 1/2 cm.
          Added t.-p. engr.

8567   Arthur, Timothy Shay, 1809-1885.
          Home-heroes, saints, and martyrs. By T. S. Arthur.
       Philadelphia, J. B. Lippincott & co., 1865.
          296 p. front.   18 cm.

8568   Arthur, T[imothy] S[hay] 1809-1885.
          Illustrated temperance tales. By T. S. Arthur ...
       Philadelphia, J. W. Bradley, 1850.
          320 p. front. (port.) plates.   23 cm.

8569   Arthur, Timothy Shay, 1909-1885.
          Insubordination; or, The shoemaker's daughters: an
       American story of real life. By T. S. Arthur ... Phila-
       delphia, T. B. Peterson, 1848.
          104 p.   24 cm.

8570 Arthur, Timothy Shay, 1809-1885.
        Lessons in life, for all who will read them. By T. S.
    Arthur. Philadelphia, Lippincott, Grambo & co., 1851.
        215 p.   16 cm.

8571 Arthur, T[imothy] S[hay] 1809-1885.
        Lizzy Glenn; or, The trials of a seamstress. By T. S.
    Authur ... Philadelphia, B. Peterson and brothers [c1859]
        1 p. 1., 21-253 p. front.   18 1/2 cm.

8572 Arthur, Timothy Shay, 1809-1885.
        The mother's rule; or, The right way and the wrong way.
    Ed. by T. S. Arthur. Philadelphia, H. C. Peck & T. Bliss,
    1856.
        vi, 7-300 p. front.   18 1/2 cm.

8573 Arthur, Timothy Shay, 1809-1885.
        The old man's bride. By T. S. Arthur. New York, C.
    Scribner, 1853.
        vi, 7-347 p. front.   17 cm.
        Added t.-p., engr.

8574 Arthur, Timothy Shay, 1809-1885.
        Orange blossoms, fresh and faded. By T. S. Arthur ...
    Philadelphia. J. M. Stoddart & co.: New York, W. Gibson,
    jr., 1871.
        415 p. front. (port.) plates.   19 1/2 cm.

8575 Arthur, Timothy Shay, 1809-1885.
        Our homes : their cares and duties, joys and sorrows.
    Ed. by T. S. Arthur. Philadelphia, H. C. Peck & T.
    Bliss, 1856.
        vi, 7-300 p. front.   18 1/2 cm.

8576 Arthur, Timothy Shay, 1809-1885.
        Rising in the world; or, A tale for the rich and poor.
    By T. S. Arthur ... New York, Baker & Scribner, 1848.
        198 p.   25 1/2 cm.

8577 Arthur, Timothy Shay, 1809-1885.
        Sketches of life and character. By T. S. Arthur ...
    Philadelphia, J. W. Bradley, 1850.

416 p. front. (port.) plates.   23 1/2 cm.

8578 Arthur, Timothy Shay, 1809-1885.
        Sparing to spend; or, The Loftons and Pinkertons. By
     T. S. Arthur. New York, C. Scribner, 1853.
        358 p. front.   17 1/2 cm.
        Added t.-p., engr.

8579 Arthur, T[imothy] S[hay] 1809-1885.
        Stories for young housekeepers. By T. S. Arthur.
     Philadelphia, Lippincott, Grambo & co., 1851.
        212 p.   16 cm.

8580 Arthur, Timothy Shay, 1809-1885.
        Sweethearts and wives; or, Before and after marriage.
     By T.S. Arthur ... New-York, Harper & brothers, 1843.
        iv, [5]-163, 12p.   16 cm.
        Publisher's advertisements: 12 p. at end.

8581 Arthur, Timothy Shay, 1809-1885.
        Temperance tales; by T. S. Arthur ...   Philadelphia,
     E. Ferrett & co., 1844.
        2 v. in 1. front.   19 cm.

8582 Arthur, Timothy Shay, 1809-1885.
        Ten nights in a bar-room, and what I saw there. By
     T. S. Arthur. Philadelphia, J. W. Bradley, 1854.
        240 p. front.   19 cm.

8583 [Arthur, Timothy Shay] 1809-1885.
        Three years in a man-trap. By the author of "Ten nights
     in a bar-room." Philadelphia, J. M. Stoddart & co., 1872.
        364 p. front., plates.   18 1/2 cm.

8584 Arthur, T[imothy] S[hay] 1809-1885.
        Twenty years ago, and now. By T. S. Arthur. Phila-
     delaphia, J. W. Bradley, 1860.
        307 p.   19 cm.

8585 Arthur, T[imothy] S[hay] 1809-1885.
        The village doctors, and other tales. By T. S. Arthur.
     Philadelphia, Godey & McMichael, 1843.

72 p.   19 1/2 cm.

8586 Arthur, Timothy Shay, 1809-1885.
       The wedding guest: a friend of the bride and bridegroom.
       Ed. by T. S. Arthur. Philadelphia, H. C. Peck & T. Bliss,
       1856.
       vi, 7-300 p. front.   19 cm.

8587 Asheton, Francis.
       A modern Cressida, by Francis Asheton; and On the
       church steps, by Sarah C. Hallowell. Philadelphia, J. B.
       Lippincott & co. , 1875.
       94 p. front.   22 1/2 cm.
       Reprint from Lippincott's magazine.

8588 Ashland, Aria.
       Muscoma; or, Faith Campbell. A romance of the revolution.
       By Aria Ashland. Boston, Hotchkiss & co. , 1848.
       2 p. 1. , [9]-100 p. incl. pl.   26 cm.

8589 Astor, William Waldorf Astor, 1st viscount, 1848-1919.
       Sforza, a story of Milan, by William Waldorf Astor ...
       New York, C. Scribner's sons, 1889.
       ix, 282 p.   19 cm.

8590 Astor, William Waldorf Astor, 1st viscount, 1848-1919.
       Valentino. An historical romance of the sixteenth cen-
       tury in Italy, by William Waldorf Astor. New York, C.
       Scribner's sons, 1885.
       vii, 325 p.   19 1/2 cm.

8591 Atherton, Mrs. Gertrude Franklin (Horn) 1857-1948.
       American wives and English husbands. A novel by
       Gerturde Atherton ... New York, Dodd, Mead and company,
       1898.
       3 p. 1. , 338 p.   19 cm.

8592 Atherton, Mrs. Gertrude Franklin (Horn)] 1857-1948.
       His fortunate grace. By Gertrude Atherton ... New
       York, D. Appleton and company, 1897.
       3 p. 1. , 210 p.   17 1/2 cm.

8593 Atherton, Mrs. Gertrude Franklin [Horn] 1857-1948.
        Hermia Suydam. [By] Gertrude Franklin Atherton ...
New York, San Francisco [etc. , The Current literature
publishing co. c1889]
        207 p.   19 cm.

8594 [Atherton, Mr. Gerturde Franklin (Horn)] 1857-1948.
        What dreams may come. A romance by Frank Lin
[pseud.] Chicago, New York [etc.] Belford, Clarke and co.
[c 1888]
        102 p.   19 1/2 cm.

8595 Atherton, Mrs. Gerturde Franklin (Horn) 1857-1948.
        A whirl asunder. By Gerturde Atherton ... New York
and London, F. A. Stokes company [c1895]
        192 p.   14 1/2 cm.

8596 Athey, Henry.
        With gyves of gold. A novel. By Henry Athey and
A. Herbert Bowers. New York, G. W. Dillingham co. ,
1898.
        2 p. 1. , vii-viii, 9-274 p.   19 cm.

8597 Atlantic tales. A collection of stories from the Atlantic monthly.
Boston, Ticknor and Fields, 1866.
        2 p. 1. , 479 p.   19 cm.
        CONTENTS. -My double; and how he undid me, by E. E.
Hale. -The diamond lens, by F. J. O'Brien. -Life in the
iron-mills, by Miss R. B. Harding. -The pursuit of knowledge under difficulties, by Gail Hamilton [pseud.]-A raft
that no man made, by R. T. S. Lowell. -Why Thomas was
discharged, by G. Arnold. -Victor and Jacqueline, by Caroline
Chesebro. -Elkanah Brewster's temptation, by C. Nordhoff. -
The queen of the red chessmen, by Lucretia P. Hale. -Miss
Lucinda, by Rose Terry. -The Denslow palace, by J. D.
Whelpley. -Fried Ell's daughter, by B. Taylor. -A half-life
and half a life, by Miss E. H. Appleton. -The man without
a country, by E. E. Hale.

8598 Augustin, George.
        Romances of New Orleans. By Geo. Augustin ... New
Orleans, L. Graham & son, 1891.

214 p.   19 cm.

8599 [Augustin, Marie]
Le Macandal. Épisode de l'insurrection des noirs à St.
Domingue. Par Tante Marie [pseud.] Nouvelle-Orléans,
Impr. G. Müller, 1892.
2 p. l. , [5]-112 p.   24 cm.

8600 Austin, Mrs. Jane (Goodwin) 1831-1894.
Betty Alden: the first born daughter of the Pilgrims, by
Jane G. Austin ... Boston and New York, Houghton,
Mifflin and company, 1891.
xii, 384 p.   18 1/2 cm.

8601 Austin Mrs. Jane (Goodwin) 1831-1894.
Cipher; a romance ... By Jane G. Austin. New York,
Sheldon & company, 1869.
175 p. front. , plates.   24 cm.

8602 Austin, Mrs. Jane (Goodwin) 1831-1894.
David Aldens' daughter, and other stories of colonial
times, by Jane G. Austin ... Boston and New York,
Houghton, Mifflin and company, 1892.
viii p. , 1 l. , 316 p.   18 cm.

8603 [Austin, Mrs. Jane (Goodwin)] 1831-1894.
Dora Darling; the daughter of the regiment. Boston,
J. E. Tilton and company, 1865.
370 p. plates.   18 cm.
Added t.-p. , illus.

8604 Austin, Mrs. Jane (Goodwin) 1831-1894.
Dr. Le Baron and his daughters; a story of the Old Colony,
by Jane G. Austin ... [10th thousand] Boston and New York,
Houghton, Mifflin and company, 1901.
viii, 460 p.   18 cm.

8605 [Austin, Mrs. Jane (Goodwin)] 1831-1894.
... Mrs. Beauchamp Brown ... Boston, Roberts brothers,
1880.
viii, [9]-319 p.   17 1/2 cm. (No name series. [2d series
v. 4])

8606 [Austin, Mrs. Jane (Goodwin)] 1831-1894.
    ... A nameless nobleman ... Boston, J. R. Osgood and company, 1881.
      vi, 369 p. 17 1/2 cm. (Round-robin series)
    Published anonymously.

8607 Austin, Mrs. Jane (Goodwin) 1831-1894.
    Nantucket scraps: being the experiences of an off-islander, in season and out of season, among a passing people, by Jane G. Austin. Boston, J. R. Osgood and company, 1883.
      vi. 354 p. 17 1/2 cm.

8608 Austin, Mrs. Jane (Goodwin) 1831-1894.
    The shadow of Moloch mountain. By Jane G. Austin ... New-York, Sheldon & company, 1870.
      1 p. 1., [5]-142 p. illus. 23 1/2 cm.

8610 Austin, John Osborne, 1849-1918.
    The journal of William Jefferay, gentleman. Born at Chiddingly, old England ... 1591; died at Newport, New England ... 1675. Being some account of divers people, places and happenings, chiefly in New England. A diary that might have been. Edited by John Osborne Austin ... Limited ed. [Providence, R. I., Press of E. L. Freeman & sons] 1899.
      x, 189 p. front. (col. coat of arms) pl. 20 1/2 cm.

8611 Austin, Maude Mason.
    'Cension. A sketch from Paso Del Norte, by Maude Mason Austin ... New York, Harper & brothers, 1896 [1895]
      4 p. 1., 159 p. front, plates. 15 cm. (On cover: Harper's little novels)

8612 Authors club, New York.
    The first book of the Authors club; Liber scriptorum ... New York, The Authors club, 1893.
      xvi p., 1 1., 588, [4] p. 33 1/2 cm.
    Title in red and black; head and tail pieces; initials.
    "The only edition. Two hundred and fifty-one copies printed." This copy unnumbered.
    Contains 109 articles by different authors, each signed

with pen and ink.

    Preface signed: Rossiter Johnson, John Denison Champlin, George Cary Eggleston, editing committee.

8613 The autobiography of a married woman. No girlhood. New York, S. A. Rollo & co., 1859.
      334 p. 19 cm.

8614 Averill, Charles E
      The pirates of Cape Ann; or, The freebooter's foe. A tale of land and water. By Charles E. Averill ... Boston, F. Gleason [1848]
      ·1 p. 1., [7]-100 p. 25 1/2 cm.

8615 Avery, M   A
      The rebel general's loyal bride: a true picture of scenes in the late civil war. By M. A. Avery. Springfield, Mass., W. J. Holland and company, 1873.
      417 p. front., plates. 19 1/2 cm.

8616 Avery, Samuel Putnam, 1822-1904.
      Mrs. Partington's carpet-bag of fun. With 150 engravings ... By S. P. Avery. New York, Garrett & co., 1854.
      vi, [7]-300 p. front., illus. 17 1/2 cm.

8617 Avery-Stuttle, Mrs. Lilla Dale, 1855-1933.
      Making home happy. Battle Creek, Mich., Chicago [etc], Review & Herald pub. co., 1898.
      206 p. illus. 16 cm.

8618 Avery-Stuttle, Mrs. Lilla Dale, 1855-1933.
      Making home peaceful; sequel to "Making home happy," by Mrs. L. D. Avery-Stuttle ... Battle Creek, Mich., Home life publishing co.-limited [1899]
      232 p. incl. front. (port.) illus., plates. 10 1/2 x 14 cm.

8619 Aztec revelations; or, Leaves from the life of the fate doomed. An auto-biography of an early adventurer in Mexico. Tr. by an officer of the army. Oquawaka, Ill., J. B. & E. II. N. Patterson, 1849.
      96 p. 18 1/2 cm.

8620 Baars, F[red] D
      The story of the seas. A romance in reality of a sailor's
life, by F. D. Baars. Arkadelphia, Ark., Baars & Neeley
[c1896]
      265 p. front. (port.) plates.   22 1/2 cm.

8621 Babcock, Mrs. Bernie (Smade) 1868–
      The daughter of a Republican, by Bernie Babcock. Chicago,
The New voice press, 1900.
      115 [1] p. illus.   20 cm.

8622 Babcock, Mrs. Bernie (Smade) 1868–
      The martyr; a story of the great reform, by Bernie
Babcock ... Illustrated by Frank Beard. Chicago, New
voice press, 1900.
      178 p. front. (port.) illus.   17 x 10 cm.

8623 Babcock, Rufus, 1798–1875.
      The emigrant's mother: a true story of the last fifty years,
for the old and the young ... With a prefatory authentication.
By Rufus Babcock, D. D. New York, Sheldon & company,
1871.
      viii, [9]–144 p. front., plates.   15 1/2 cm. (On cover:
Good girl's library)

8624 Bache, Anna.
      The fire-screen, or Domestic sketches. By Mrs. Anna
Bache ... Philadelphia, W. J. & J. K. Simon; New York,
R. Carter, 1841.
      viii p., 2 1., [13]–191 p.   19 1/2 cm.

8625 Bache, Richard Meade.
      Under the palmetto in peace and war. By Richard Meade
Bache. Philadelphia, Claxton, Remsen, & Haffelfinger,
1880.
      106 p.   17 1/2 cm.

8626 Bacheller, Irving, 1859–1950, ed.
      Best things from American literature, edited by Irving

Bacheller ... New York, The Christian herald, 1899.
416 p. front., illus. (incl. ports., facsims.) 22 cm.

8627 Bacheller, Irving, 1859-1950.
Eben Holden; a tale of the north country, by Irving Bacheller
... Boston, Lothrop publishing company [c1900]
vii p., 1 1., 432 p. 18 1/2 cm.

8628 Bacheller, Irving, 1859-1950.
The master of silence. A romance, by Irving Bacheller.
New York, C. L. Webster & co., 1892.
176 p. 18 1/2 cm. (Half-title: Fiction, fact, and fancy
series)

8629 Bacheller, Lois H
The Dabney will, by L. H. Bacheller. New York, Warner
& Brownell, 1900.
232 p., 1 1. 18 cm.

8630 [Bachman, Maurice A   ]
Prejudice? A novel by Ovidius [pseud.] Illustrated by
H. D. Bame. New York, M. A. Bachman [1900]
4 p. 1., 92 pp. illus., pl. 14 cm.

8631 [Bacon, Delia Salter] 1811-1859.
The bride of Fort Edward, founded on an incident of the
revolution. New-York, S. Colman, 1839.
2 p. 1., [vii]-viii p., 2 1., [13]-174 p. 19 1/2 cm.

8632 [Bacon, Delia Salter] 1811-1859.
Tales of the Puritans. The regicides.-The fair Pilgrim.-
Castine. New-Haven, A. H. Maltby; New-York, G. and C.
and H. Carvill, and J. Leavitt; [etc., etc.] 1831.
2 p. 1., [13]-300 p. 19 cm.

8633 Bacon, Edgar Mayhew, 1855-
The pocket piece; short stories and sketches by American
authors. 1st series, no. 1, by Edgar Mayhew Bacon. New
York, Walbridge & co., [c1891]
4 p. 1., [7]-128 p. 14 1/2 cm.
CONTENTS.-The Toddville raffle.-Zenas Smith's ride to
Roxbury.-Squaring an old account.-McRotty's van.-Uncle

Sunday. -The historian of the future.

8634 Bacon, Mrs. Eugenia (Jones) 1840-
Lyddy: a tale of the old South, by Eugenia J. Bacon. New
York, Continental publishing co., 1898.
237 p. 19 cm.

8635 Bacon, Josephine Dodge (Daskam) 1876-
Smith college stories. Ten stories by Josephine Dodge
Daskam. New York, C. Scribner's sons, 1900.
5 p. l., 343 p. 19 1/2 cm.
CONTENTS. -The emotions of a sub-guard. -A case of
interference. -Miss Biddle of Bryn Mawr. -Biscuits ex
machina. -The education of Elizabeth. -A family affair. -A
few diversions. -The evolution of Evangeline. -At commence-
ment. -The end of it.

8636 Bedeau, Adam, 1831-1895.
The vagabond: by Adam Badeau ... New York, Rudd &
Carleton, 1859.
xi p., 1 l., [15]-368 p. 19 1/2 cm.

8637 Baffled schemes. A novel. Boston, Loring, 1867.
159 p. 23 cm.

8638 Bagby, Albert Morris, 1859-
"Miss Träumerei." A Weimar idyl, by Albert Morris
Bagby. Boston, Lamson, Wolffe, and company, 1895.
2 p. l., [7]-292 p. 19 cm.

8639 [Bagby, George William] 1828-1883.
... What I did with my fifty millions. By Moses Adams
[pseud.] Ed. from the posthumous ms. by Caesar Maurice ...
Philadelphia, J. B. Lippincott & co., 1874.
128 p. 19 cm.
At head of t. -p.: For Virginians only.

8640 Bailey, Mrs. Alice Ward, 1857-
Mark Heffron. A novel, by Alice Ward Bailey. New York,
Harper & brothers, 1896.
1 p. l., 354 p. 19 cm.

8641 Bailey, James Montgomery, 1841–1894.
England from a back-window; with views of Scotland and
Ireland. By J. M. Bailey ... Boston, Lee & Shepard;
New York, C. T. Dillingham, 1879.
475 p. 20 cm.

8642 Bailey, James Montgomery, 1841–1894.
Life in Danbury: being a brief but comprehensive record
of the doings of a remarkable people, under more remarkable
circumstances, and chronicles in a most remarkable manner,
by the author, James B. Bailey, "The Danbury news man";
and carefully compiled with a pair of eight-dollar shears, by
the compiler. Boston, Shepard and Gill, 1873.
303 p. front. (port.) 17 1/2 cm.

8643 Bailey, James Montgomery, 1841–1894.
Mr. Philips' goneness. By James M. Bailey ... Boston,
Lee and Shepard; New York, C. T. Dillingham, 1879.
v, 7–179 p. 18 cm.

8644 Bailey, Nathan J
Johnsville in the olden time, and other stories. By
Nathan J. Bailey. New York, Printed by E. O. Jenkins'
sons, 1884.
255 p. 24 1/2 cm.

8645 Baily, T[homas] L
In the pine woods. By Rev. T. L. Baily. New York,
American tract society [c1893]
304 p. front., plates. 19 cm.

8646 Bainbridge, William Folwell, b. 1843.
Self-giving; a story of Christian missions. Boston, D.
Lothrop [c1883]
521 p. front. 20 cm.

8647 ... The baked head, and other tales ... New York, G. P.
Putnam & co., 1856.
309 p. 19 1/2 cm. (Putnam's library of choice stories)
Lettered on cover: Putnam's story library.
CONTENTS. –Story of the baked head. –The wolf in sheeps
clothing. –Elkanah Smithers, jun. –Infatuation. –An ordeal. –

A royal whim.-A story of Sweden.-Major O'Shaughnessy's
adventure on the duke's moor.-A cock-fight in the Havana.-
Angelica Staggers.-The fall of the Janissaries.-Leaves from
the diary of a law clerk.-The golden guillotine.-Edward
Drysdale.-The story of the unfinished picture.

8648 Baker, Beth.
    Mystery Evans. By Beth Baker. Boston, De Wolfe,
Fiske & co. , 1890.
      256 p.   18 cm.

8649 [Baker, Mrs. Harriette Newell (Woods)] 1815-1893.
    Juliette; or, Now and forever. By Mrs. Madeline Leslie
[pseud.] Boston, Lee and Shepard, 1869.
      416 p.   18 1/2 cm. (Half-title: Home life [series, v. 4])

8650 [Baker, Mrs. Harriette Newell (Woods)] 1815-1893.
    Ten millions; or, Uncle Jacob's legacy. By Mrs.
Madeline Leslie [pseud.] ... Boston, I. Bradley & co.
[c1888]
      305 p. front.   18 cm.

8651 Baker, Mary Marsh.
    Ruby Dana. A novel, by Mary Marsh Baker. New York,
J. B. Alden, 1890.
      2 p. 1. , [7]-287 p.   19 1/2 cm.

8652 [Baker, William Elliott Smith]
    The battle of Coney Island; or, Free trade overthrown.
A scrap of history written in 1900. By an eye witness.
Philadelphia, J. A. Wagenseller, 1883.
      116 p.   19 1/2 cm.
    Published anonymously.

8653 Baker, William Mumford, 1825-1883.
    Carter Quarterman. A novel. By William M. Baker ...
Illustrated by Elias J. Whitney. New York, Harper &
brothers, 1876.
      3 p. 1. , [13]-158 p. front. , illus.   23 1/2 cm.

8654 [Baker, William Mumford] 1825-1883.
    Colonel Dunwoddie, millionaire. New York, Harper &

brothers, 1878.

    2 p. 1. , [vii]-viii, [9]-187 p.   24 cm. (On cover:
Harper's library of American fiction, no. 5)

    Published anonymously.

8655 [Baker, William Mumford] 1825-1883.

    ... His majesty, myself ... Boston, Roberts brothers,
1880.

    vi, [7]-290 p.   17 cm. (Half-title: No name series.
[2d series, v. 3])

    Series title also at head of t. -p.

    Published anonymously.

8656 [Baker, William Mumford] 1825-1883.

    Inside: a chronicle of secession. By George F. Harrington
[pseud.] With illustrations by Thomas Nast. New York,
Harper & brothers, 1866.

    vi, [7]-223 p. illus.   23 1/2 cm.

8657 [Baker, William Mumford] 1825-1883.

    The making of a man. By the author of "His majesty,
myself" ... etc. ... Boston, Roberts brothers, 1884.

    iv, [7]-322 p.   18 cm.

8658 Baker, William Mumford, 1825-1883.

    Mose Evans: a simple statement of the singular facts of
his case, by William M. Baker ... New York, Hurd &
Houghton, 1874.

    3 p. 1. , 317 p.   18 1/2 cm.

8659 Baker, William Mumford, 1825-1883.

    The new Timothy. [A novel] by Wm. M. Baker ... New
York, Harper & brothers, 1870.

    6, [vii]-x, [11]-344 p.   19 cm.

8660 Baker, William Mumford, 1825-1883.

    The Virginians in Texas. A story for young old folks
and old young folks, by William M. Baker ... New York,
Harper & brothers, 1878.

    2 p. 1. , [9]-169 p.   24 cm. (On cover: Harper's library
of American fiction, no. 11)

    Originally published in Harper's monthly.

8661 Baker, William Mumford, 1825-1883.
       A year worth living: a story of a place and of a people one cannot afford not to know, by William M. Baker ... Boston, Lee and Shepard; New York, C. T. Dillingham, 1878.
       2 p. 1., 3-325 p.   20 cm.
       "A portion of this book was published in 'The Christian at work', of New York."

8662 Balch, William Stevens, 1806-1887.
       A peculiar people; or, Reality in romance, By William S. Balch ... Chicago, H. A. Sumner & company, 1881.
       3 p. 1., xi-xii, 13-452 p.   18 1/2 cm.

8663 [Baldwin, Mrs. A   E   Corey]
       On the battery; or, Mildred's dishes. A story of New York city and other places ... New York, The author, 1879.
       vi, 7-208 p. front., plates.   17 1/2 cm.

8664 Baldwin, Eugene F
       Doctor Cavallo, by Eugene F. Baldwin and Maurice Eisenberg ... Peoria, Ill. [Press of J. W. Franks & sons] 1895.
       317 p.   19 cm.

8665 Baldy, Alice Montgomery.
       The romance of a Spanish nun. By Alice Montgomery Baldy. Philadelphia, J. B. Lippincott company, 1891
       2 p. 1., 3-199 p.   19 cm. (On cover: American novels)

8666 Balestier, Wolcott, 1861-1891.
       A victorious defeat. A romance, by Wolcott Balestier. New York, Harper & brothers, 1886.
       2 p. 1., [3]-349 p. front., plates.   17 1/2 cm.

8667 Ball, Walter Savage, ed.
       Amherst life. Selections from the undergraduate publications at Amherst college. Ed. by Walter Savage Ball. Illustrated by William Cary Duncan. Amherst, W. C. Howland, 1896.
       xii p., 1 1., 139 p. incl. front, illus.   17 1/2 cm.

8668 [Ballou, Clara E   ]
      Ethelind. By "Carlottah" [pseud.] ... New York, J. S.
Ogilvie & company [c1885]
      179 p.   18 1/2 cm.

8669 [Ballou, Maturin Murray] 1820-1895.
      ... The adventurer; or, The wreck on the Indian Ocean.
A land and sea tale. By Lieutenant Murray [pseud.] ...
Boston, F. Gleason, 1848.
      3 p. 1., [11]-100 p. incl. pl.   24 cm.
      At head of t.-p.: A prize tale.
      Reprinted from The flag of our Union.

8670 [Ballou, Maturin Murray] 1820-1895.
      Fanny Campbell, the female pirate captain. A tale of
the revolution. By Lieutenant Murray [pseud.] Boston,
F. Gleason, 1845.
      2 p. 1., [9]-100 p. incl. plates.   24 cm.

8671 Ballou, Maturin Murray, 1820-1895.
      Red Rupert, the American bucanier. A tale of the Spanish
Indies, by Lieutenant Murray [pseud.] Boston, Gleason's
publishing hall, 1845.
      2 p. 1., [7]-54 p.   23 cm.

8672 [Ballou, Maturin Murray] 1820-1895.
      The Turkish spies Ali Abubeker Kaled, and Zenobia
Marrita Mustapha; or, The Mohammedan prophet of 1854.
A true history of the Russo-Turkish war. By Lieutenant
Murray [pseud.] ... Baltimore, Philadelphia [etc.] A. R.
Orton, 1855.
      2 p. 1., [17]-267 p. front., illus. 22 cm.
      Added t.-p., illus, in color.
      On cover: The great-book. Turkish spies, or Mohammedan
prophet of 1854.
      CONTENTS.-The prophet.-The Circassian slave.-The
life and confessions of Don Hernandez Romez de Arago.-
The twin brothers.-The two sisters.-The robbers.-The
adventures of a medical student.-Madame Le Hocq.

8673 Bandelier, Adolph Francis Alphonse, 1840-1914.
      The delight makers, by Adolf F. Bandelier. New York,

Dodd, Mead and company [c1890]
iv, 490 p.   19 1/2 cm.

8674   Bangs, John Kendrick, 1862-1922.
        The booming of Acre Hill, and other reminiscences of
urban and suburban life, by John Kendrick Bangs.   Illustrations by C. Dana Gibson.   New York and London,
Harper & brothers, 1900.
        6 p. 1., 265, [1] p. front., pl.   18 cm.
        These stories have appeared in the Ladies' home journal,
the Woman's home companion, and the various publications of
Messrs. Harper & brothers.
        CONTENTS. -The booming of Acre Hill. -The strange
misadventures of an organ. -The plot that failed. -The base
ingratitude of Barkis, M. D. -The utilitarian Mr. Carraway. -
The book sales of Mr. Peters. -The valor of Brinley. -
Wilkins -The mayor's lamps. -The balance of power. -
Jarley's experiment. -Jarley's thanksgiving. -Harry and Maude
and I-also James. -An affinitive romance. -Mrs. Upton's
device.

8675   Bangs, John Kendrick, 1862-1922.
        Coffee and repartee, by John Kendrick Bangs ...   New
York, Harper & brothers, publishers, 1893.
        viii, 123 p. incl. front., illus.   14 cm.   (On cover:
Harper's black & white series)

8676   Bangs, John Kendrick, 1862-1922.
        The dreamers; a club.   Being a more or less faithful
account of the literary exercises of the first regular meeting
of that organization, reported by John Kendrick Bangs, with
illustrations by Edward Penfield.   New York and London,
Harper & brothers, 1809.
        vii, [1] p., 1 1., 246 [1] p. front., plates.   18 cm.

8677   Bangs, John Kendrick, 1862-1922.
        The enchanted typewriter, by John Kendrick Bangs;
illustrated by Peter Newell.   New York and London, Harper
& brothers, 1899.
        v, [1] p., 1 1., 170 p., 1 1. front. plates.   17 cm.

8678   Bangs, John Kendrick, 1862-1922.

Ghosts I have met and some others. By John Kendrick
Bangs. With illustrations by Newell, Frost, & Richards.
New York and London, Harper & brothers, 1898.
5 p. 1., 190 [1] p. front., plates. 17 cm.

8679 Bangs, John Kendrick, 1862-1922.
A house-boat on the Styx; being some account of the divers
doings of the associated shades. By John Kendrick Bangs
... New York, Harper & brothers, 1896.
viii, 171 p. front., plates. 17 1/2 cm.

8680 Bangs, John Kendrick, 1862-1922.
The idiot, by John Kendrick Bangs ... New York, Harper
& brothers, 1895.
vi, 115 p. front., plates. 16 1/2 cm.

8681 Bangs, John Kendrick, 1862-1922.
The Idiot at home, by John Kendrick Bangs; illustrated
by F. T. Richards. New York and London, Harper &
brothers, 1900.
ix, 313, [1] p. incl. plates. front. (port.) 18 cm.

8682 [Bangs, John Kendrick] 1862-1922.
Mr. Bonaparte of Corsica. New York, Harper & brothers,
1895.
xii, 265 p. incl. front., illus. 17 cm.
Illustrated by H. W. McVickar.

8683 Bangs, John Kendrick, 1862-1922.
Paste jewels, being seven tales of domestic woe, by
John Kendrick Bangs ... New York and London, Harper &
brothers, 1897.
vi p., 2 1., [3]-202 p. front. 17 1/2 cm.
CONTENTS. -The emancipation of Thaddeus. -Mr. Bradley's
jewel. -Unexpected pomp at the Perkins's. -An object-lesson. -
The Christmas gift of Thaddeus. -A strange banquet. -Jane.

8684 Bangs, John Kendrick, 1862-1922.
Peeps at people, being certain papers from the writing of
Anne Warrington Witherup [pseud.] Collected by John
Kendrick Bangs ... with illustrations by Edward Penfield.
New York and London, Harper & brothers, 1899.

5 p. 1., 3-184, [1] p. front., plates.   18 cm.

8685   Bangs, John Kendrick, 1862-1922.
          The pursuit of the house-boat; being some further account
       of the divers doings of the associated shades, under the
       leadership of Sherlock Holmes, esq.; by John Kendrick Bangs,
       illustrated by Peter Newell. New York, Harper & brothers,
       1897.
          1 p. 1., viii, 204 p. front., plates.   17 1/2 cm.

8686   Bangs, John Kendrick, 1862-1922.
          A rebellious heroine. A story. By John Kendrick Bangs.
       Illus. by W. T. Smedley. New York, Harper & brothers,
       1896.
          4 p. 1., 225 p. front., plates.   18 cm.

8687   Bangs, John Kendrick, 1862-1922.
          Three weeks in politics, by John Kendrick Bangs ... New
       York, Harper and brothers, 1894.
          4 p. 1., 82 p. front., plates.   13 1/2 cm. (On cover:
       Harper's black & white series)

8688   Bangs, John Kendrick, 1862-1922.
          Toppleton's client; or, A spirit in exile. By John Kendrick
       Bangs. New York, C. L. Webster & company, 1893.
          viii, 269 p.   19 cm.

8689   Bangs, John Kendrick, 1862-1922.
          The water ghost and others, by John Kendrick Bangs ...
       New York, Harper & brothers, 1894.
          4 p. 1., 296 p. incl. plates. front.   18 cm.
          CONTENTS.-The water ghost of Harrowby hall.-The
       spectre cook of Bangletop.-The speck of the lens.-A midnight
       visitor.-A quicksilver Cassandra.-The ghost club.-A
       psychical prank.-The literary remains of Thomas Bragdon.

8690   Banks, Charles Eugene, 1852-1932.
          In Hampton roads; a dramatic romance, by Charles
       Eugene Banks and George Cram Cook. Chicago and New
       York, Rand, McNally & company, [1899]
          288 p.   19 1/2 cm.

8691 Banks, Mary Ross, 1846–
　　　Bright days in the old plantation time. By Mary Ross
　　　Banks. Illus. by James H. Moser. Boston, Lee and
　　　Shepard; New York, C. T. Dillingham, 1882.
　　　3 p. l., 266 p. front., plates.　20 cm.

8692 [Barber, Harriet Boomer]
　　　Wrecked, but not lost. A novel. By Faith Templeton
　　　[pseud.] ... Philadelphia, J. B. Lippincott & co., 1880.
　　　327 p.　19 cm.

8693 [Barber, Joseph] of New York.
　　　War letters of a disbanded volunteer. Embracing his
　　　experiences as honest old Abe's bosom friend and unofficial
　　　adviser ... New York, F. A. Brady, 1864.
　　　312 p. front.　19 cm.

8694 Barbour, Sarah G
　　　Spiders and rice pudding. By Sarah G. Barbour. New
　　　York, The Authors' publishing company [c1879]
　　　88 p.　18 x 15 1/2 cm.　(On cover: Satchel series
　　　[no. 18])

8695 [Barclay, Mrs. Cornelia S　　　　　]
　　　Mrs. Singleton. New York, The Authors' publishing
　　　company [c1880]
　　　174 p.　17 x 14 cm.　(On cover: Satchel series [no. 24])
　　　Published anonymously.

8696 [Barclay, George Lippard]
　　　... "Little Cuba;" or, Circumstantial evidence. Being a
　　　true story of love, war, and startling adventures. The
　　　massacre of the young students! Shooting the men found
　　　on the American ship "Virginius." Spanish deeds of blood-
　　　chilling atrocity! ... Philadelphia, Barclay & co., [1873]
　　　1 p. l., [19]-94 p. incl. plates. pl.　24 cm.

8697 Bardeen, Charles William, 1847-1924.
　　　... Commissioner Hume; a story of New York schools, by
　　　C. W. Bardeen ... Syracuse, N. Y., C. W. Bardeen, 1899.
　　　3 p. l., [5]-210 p.　17 1/2 cm.　(On cover: Standard
　　　teachers' library)

A sequel to Roderick Hume; the story of a New York teacher.
Published originally as a serial in the School bulletin.

8698 Barker, Benjamin.
  The bandit of the ocean; or, The female privateer. A
  romance of the sea. By Benjamin Barker ... New York,
  R. M. De Witt [186-?]
    1 p. l., [7]-115, [1] p.   23 cm.
    L. C. copy imperfect? All before t.-p. wanting?

8699 Barker, B[enjamin]
  Blackbeard; or, The pirate of the Roanoke. A tale of
  the Atlantic, By B. Barker ... Boston, F. Gleason, 1847.
    1 p. l., [5]-50 p.   23 cm.

8700 Barker, Benjamin.
  Ellen Grafton, the lily of Lexington; or, The bride of
  liberty. A romance of the revolution, by Benjamin Barker ...
  Boston, Gleason's publishing hall, 1846.
    2 p. l., [9]-100 p. incl. plates.   24 cm.

8701 Barker, Benjamin.
  Mary Morland; or, The fortunes and misfortunes of an
  orphan. By Benjamin Barker ... Boston, Gleason's
  publishing hall, 1845.
    46 p.   23 1/2 cm.
    Illustrated cover.

8702 Barker, Benjamin.
  The Sea Serpent; or, The queen of the coral cave. A
  romance of the ocean. By B. Barker ... Boston, F.
  Gleason, 1847.
    1 p. l., [7]-100 p.   26 cm.

8703 Barker, Mrs. Laura Cooke.
  Society silhouettes; collection of short stories, by
  Laura Cooke Barker. Cleveland, The Helman-Taylor
  company, 1898.
    2 p. l., [7]-271 p.   18 cm.
    CONTENTS. -A search for sensations. -The senator's
  wooing. -Keeping up appearances. -The touch of nature. -

Barbara's emancipation. -A twentieth century romance.

8704　Barlow, David Hatch.
　　　　The Howards: a tale founded on facts.　By D. H. Barlow
　　　... Philadelphia, Getz & Buck, 1851.
　　　　45 p.　18 1/2 cm.

8705　[Barnard, Charles] 1838-1920.
　　　　Farming by inches; or, "With brains, sir" ...　Boston,
　　　Loring [c1869]
　　　　123 p.　20 1/2 cm.

8706　Barnard, Charles, 1838-1920.
　　　　Gardening for money.　How it was done, in flowers,
　　　strawberries, vegetables.　By Charles Barnard.　Boston,
　　　Loring [c1869]
　　　　345 p.　20 cm.
　　　　CONTENTS. -My ten-rod farm: or, How I became a florist. -
　　　The strawberry garden.　How it was planted, what it cost,
　　　what come of it, financially and sentimentally. -Farming by
　　　inches; or, "With brains, sir."

8707　Barnard, Charles, 1838-1920.
　　　　Knights of to-day; or, Love and science.　By Charles
　　　Barnard.　New York, C. Scribner's sons, 1881.
　　　　3 p. l., 256 p.　17 1/2 cm.
　　　　CONTENTS. -A sanitary measure. -Under high pressure. -
　　　Applied science. -Love and a lantern. -Put yourself in her
　　　place. -The wreck of the Pioneer.

8708　[Barnard, Charles] 1838-1920.
　　　　My ten-rod farm; or, How I became a florist.　By Mrs.
　　　Maria Gilman [pseud.]　Boston, Loring, 1869.
　　　　119 p.　20 1/2 cm.

8708　[Barnard, Charles] 1838-1920.
　　　　The soprano: a musical story.　By Jane Kingsford [pseud.]
　　　Boston, Loring [c1869]
　　　　179 p.　20 1/2 cm.

8710　Barnes, Charlotte Mary Sanford, 1819?-1863.
　　　　Plays, prose and poetry.　By Charlotte M. S. Barnes

... Philadelphia, E. H. Butler & co., 1848.
viii p., 4 1., [13]-489 p., 1 1.   19 cm.
CONTENTS. -Octavia Bragaldi; or, The confession. -
Fugitive pieces. -The forest princess; or, Two centuries ago. -
The heart? or the soul? A series of tales.

8711 Barnes, Euphemia.
Ellen Durand. By Euphemia Barnes. Cincinnati, Moore,
Wilstach, Keys & co., 1855.
vii, [9]-228 p.   19 cm.

8712 Barnes, James, 1866-1936.
A Princetonian; a story of undergraduate life at the
College of New Jersey, by James Barnes, class of '91 ...
New York [etc.] G. P. Putnam's sons, 1896.
viii p., 1 1., 431 p. front., 2 pl.   18 cm.

8713 Barnes, Josiah.
The old inn; or, The travellers' entertainment. By
Josiah Barnes, sen. New-York, J. C. Derby; Boston,
Phillips, Sampson & co., [etc., etc.] 1855.
viii, 9-360 p.   18 1/2 cm.

8714 Barnes, Willis.
Dame Fortune smiled. The doctor's story. By Willis
Barnes. Boston, Arena publishing company, 1896.
335 p.   20 cm.

8715 [Barnitz, William Tell]
The recluse of the Conewaga; or, The little valley of the
Blue spring. A legend of Adams county. By W. T. B., a
junior of Dickinson ... Carlisle, E. Cornman, printer,
1853.
85 (i. e. 86) p.   23 cm.
Error in paging: p. 86 numbered 85.

8716 Barns, Charles Edward.
Digby: chess professor. By Charles Edward Barns. New
York, Fracker & company, 1889.
5 p. 1., 15-152 p.   20 1/2 cm.
T. -p. illus.

8717 Barns, Charles Edward.
    A disillusioned occultist. A drama-novel. By Charles
Edward Barns ... New York, W. Fracker & company,
1889.
    5 p. 1., 15-146 p.   20 1/2 cm.

8718 Barns, Charles Edward.
    A Venetian study in black and white. By Charles Edward
Barns. New York, W. Fracker & co., 1889.
    6 p. 1., 15-172 p.   20 1/2 cm.
    T.-p. illus.

8719 Barnum, Mrs. Frances Courtenay (Baylor) 1848-1920.
    On both sides. A novel. By Frances Courtenay Baylor.
8th ed. Philadelphia, J. B. Lippincott company, 1887.
    1 p. 1., 478 p.   18 1/2 cm.

8720 Barr, Mrs. Amelia Edith (Huddleston) 1831-1919.
    The beads of Tasmer, by Amelia E. Barr ... With
illustrations by Warren B. Davis. New York, R. Bonner's
sons, 1891.
    2 p. 1., [7]-895 p. plates.   19 cm. (On cover: Ledger
library, no. 45)

8721 Barr, Mrs. Amelia E[dith (Huddleston)] 1831-1919.
    Bernicia, by Amelia E. Barr ..., New York, Dodd, Mead
and company, 1895.
    3 p. 1., 306 p.   18 cm.

8722 Barr, Mrs. Amelia Edith (Huddleston) 1831-1919.
    A border shepherdess: a romance of Eskdale, by Amelia
E. Barr ... New York, Dodd, Mead & company [c1887]
    2 p. 1., 325 p.   18 cm.

8723 Barr, Mrs. Amelia Edith (Huddleston) 1831-1919.
    Christopher, and other stories ... New York, Phillips
and Hunt; Cincinnati, Cranston and Stowe, 1888.
    352 p.   20 cm.
    CONTENTS.-Christopher.-Crowther and the thirsk.-The
master of Rushen.-Rex Macarthy.-"Our Joe."-Jonathan
Yeadon's justification.-Seed by the wayside.-The heart of
Sam Naylor.

8724 Barr, Mrs. Amelia E[dith (Huddleston)] 1831-1919.
          Feet of clay, by Amelia E. Barr... New York, Dodd,
      Mead & company [c1889]
              2 p. 1. , 369 p.   18 1/2 cm.

8725 Barr, Mrs. Amelia Edith (Huddleston) 1831-1919.
          The flower of Gala Water. A novel. By Mrs. Amelia
      E. Barr... With illustrations by C. Kendrick. New York,
      R. Bonner's sons, 1895.
              2 p. 1./, 7-392 p.   20 cm.   (The choice series,
      no. 119)

8726 Barr, Mrs. Amelia Edith (Huddleston) 1831-1919.
          Friend Olivia, by Amelia E. Barr. New York, Dodd,
      Mead and company, 1898.
              3 p. 1. , 455 p. front.   19 cm.

8727 Barr, Mrs. Amelia Edith (Huddleston) 1831-1919.
          Girls of a feather; a novel. By Mrs. Amelia E. Barr ...
      With illustrations by J. O. Nugent. New York, R. Bonner's
      sons, 1893.
              2 p. 1. , [7]-366 p. plates.   20 cm.   (The choice series,
      no. 97)

8728 Barr, Mrs. Amelia Edith (Huddleston) 1831-1919.
          The household of McNeil, by Amelia E. Barr. New
      York, Dodd, Mead and company, 1890.
              2 p. 1. , [9]-327 p. front.   18 1/2 cm. [The Ajax
      series, no. 31]

8729 Barr, Mrs. Amelia Edith (Huddleston) 1831-1919.
          I, thou and the other one; a love story, by Amelia E.
      Barr. New York, Dodd, Mead and company, 1898.
              3 p. 1. , 354 p. front. , plates   19 1/2 cm.

8730 Barr, Mrs. Amelia Edith (Huddleston) 1831-1919.
          Jan Vedder's wife, by Amelia E. Barr. New York, Dodd,
      Mead & company, [1885]
              2 p. 1. , 329 p.   17 1/2 cm.

8731 Barr, Mrs. Amelia E[dith (Huddleston)] 1831-1919.
A knight of the nets, by Amelia E. Barr. New York,
Dodd, Mead and company, 1896.
3 p. 1., 314 p.   20 cm.

8732 Barr, Mrs. Amelia E[dith (Huddleston)] 1831-1919.
The lone house, by Amelia E. Barr ... New York, Dodd,
Mead & company [c1893]
235 p.   19 cm.

8733 Barr, Mrs. Amelia Edith (Huddleston) 1831-1919.
The maid of Maiden lane; a sequel to "The bow of orange
ribbon". A love story, by Amelia E. Barr ... New York,
Dodd, Mead and company, 1900.
2 p. 1., 338 p. col. front., plates.   19 1/2 cm.

8734 Barr, Mrs. Amelia Edith (Huddleston) 1831-1919.
Master of his fate, by Amelia E. Barr ... New York,
Dodd, Mead & company [c1888]
2 p. 1., 293 p.   18 cm.
Published also under title "In spite of himself."
cf. Allibone's dictionary supplement.

8735 Barr, Mrs. Amelia Edith (Huddleston) 1831-1919.
The mate of the "Easter Bell", and other stories. By
Amelia E. Barr ... New York, R. Bonner's sons, [c1893]
2 p. 1., 7-347 p. plates.   19 cm. (The choice series ...
no. 80)
CONTENTS. -The mate of the "Easter Bell". -The harvest
of faith and constancy. -Consequences of a mistake. -Agnes
Stirling. -A horse for a wife. -A tale of two brothers. -
Romance of two pictures. -The story of a wedding. -A discovered life. -The true Delzel. -Earning one's capital. -A
brave girl. -Just as it happened. -The druid's moss. -"I
meant no harm."-The hero of Saltham Pit. -Only Jones. -
The "blue Wesley tea-pot". -Not for gold. -One pair of
gloves. -A dishonored bill. -The belle of the Orkney Isles. -
Nap Fontaine's duel. -Tom Burleson's love affair. -Davie's
shoulder-straps. -More than two at a bargain. -Housewife
and wife. -Only my lord's brother. -The gypsy lady. -The
saving of Eshold. -"It's guid to be honest and true."

8736   Barr, Mrs. Amelia E[dith (Huddleston)] 1831-1919.
        Mrs. Barr's short stories. By Amelia E. Barr ...
New York, R. Bonner's sons [c1892]
        2 p. 1., 7-335 p. plates.   19 cm. (The choice series,
no. 53).
        CONTENTS. -Femmetia. -Marring for money. -Out of
Egypt. -John Taggert's trial. -The Forsyth will case. -
Luck. -Mary's marriage. -"Only this once."-A southern
temper. -A man and his own way. -A romance of labor. -
A faithful woman. -Kate Dalrymple. -With her eyes open. -
James Macharg's temper. -"I don't care."-The Kennedy's
good fortune. -Paid in his own coin. -Roy of Airlie. -The
Udaler's daughter. -How I said "Yes."-Smitten with re-
morse. -Ike Brennan's watch. -Sold for naught. -A young
man saved. -"Anything for peace."-The good-for-nothing. -
The parents' mistake. -The ruined house. -"For better,
for worse."

8737   Barr, Mrs. Amelia Edith (Huddleston) 1831-1919.
        Prisoners of conscience, by Amelia E. Barr. New
York, The Century co., 1897.
        5 p. 1., 240 p. front., plates.   19 1/2 cm.
A story of Shetland.

8738   Barr, Mrs. Amelia Edith (Huddleston) 1831-1919.
        Remember the Alamo, by Amelia E. Barr ... New
York, Dodd, Mead & company [c1888]
        2 p. 1., 431 p.   17 1/2 cm.

8739   Barr, Mrs. Amelia Edith (Huddleston) 1831-1919.
        A rose of a hundred leaves; a love-story, by Amelia E.
Barr ... New York, Dodd, Mead and company, 1891.
        238 p. front., illus.   19 1/2 cm.

8740   Barr, Mrs. Amelia E[dith (Huddleston)] 1831-1919.
        A singer from the sea, by Amelia E. Barr ... New York,
Dodd, Mead & company [c1893]
        iv, 346 p.   19 cm.

8741   Barr, Mrs. Amelia E[dith (Huddleston)] 1831-1919.
        A sister to Esau, by Amelia E. Barr... New York,
Dodd, Mead & company [c1891]
        2 p. 1., 341 p.   19 1/2 cm.

8742 Barr, Mrs. Amelia Edith (Huddleston) 1831-1919.
The squire of Sandal-Side; a pastoral romance, by Amelia
E. Barr ... New York, Dodd, Mead and company, [c1887]
342 p. 17 1/2 cm.

8743 Barr, Mrs. Amelia Edith (Huddleston) 1831-1919.
Stories of life and love, by Amelia E. Barr ... New York,
The Christian herald [c1897]
320 p. 15 cm. (On cover: The Christian herald library)

8744 Barr, Mrs. Amelia Edith (Huddleston) 1831-1919.
Trinity bells; a tale of old New York, by Amelia E. Barr
... illustrated by C. M. Relyea ... New York, J. F.
Taylor and company, 1899.
viii, 278 p. front., plates. 20 cm.

8745 Barr, Mrs. Amelia Edith (Huddleston) 1831-1919.
Was it right to forgive? A domestic romance, by Amelia
E. Barr. Chicago and New York, H. S. Stone and company,
1899.
2 p. 1., 294 p., 1 1. 19 cm.

8746 Barr, Mrs. Amelia Edith (Huddleston) 1831-1919.
Winter evening tales. By Amelia E. Barr ... New York,
The Christian herald [c1896]
320 p. 15 cm. (On cover: The Christian herald library)

8747 Barrell, George, jr.
Bubbles of fiction. By George Barrell, jr. New-York,
Dewitt & Davenport, 1852.
viii, [9]-300 p. 19 cm.

8748 Barrington, Charles F
Nancy Waterman; or, Woman's faith triumphant. A
story of New York City. New York, Samuel French, (c1853)
100 p., illus. 20 cm.

8749 Barrow, Elizabeth N., 1869-
The fortune of war; being portions of many letters and
journals written to and for her cousin Mistress Dorothea
Engel ... by Katherine ... Patison, during ... the time of
the struggle for the independence of the colonies, these

writings have been condensed and arranged ... by
Elizabeth N. Barrow. New York, H. Holt and company,
1900.
    1 p. l. , 268 p.   19 1/2 cm.

8750 Barry, John Daniel, 1866-
    The intriguers. A novel, by John D. Barry. New York,
D. Appleton and company, 1896.
    2 p. l. , 295 p.   18 1/2 cm. (Half-title: Appletons'
town and country library, no. 203)

8751 Barry, John Daniel, 1866-
    Mademoiselle Blanche: a novel, by John D. Barry.
New York & London, J. Lane, 1904.
    3 p. l. , 330 p.   20 cm. (Half-title: Canvas-back
library of popular fiction, vol I)

8752 [Bartlett, Napier] 1836-1877.
    Clarimonde: a tale of New Orleans life, and of the present
war. By a member of the N. O. Washington artillery.
Richmond [Va.] M. A. Malsby, 1863.
    79 p.   19 1/2 cm.
    Ascribed to Napier Bartlett. cf. Library of southern
literature, v. 15, p. 25; T. McCaleb. The Louisiana book,
1894, p. 98; L. C. McVoy and R. B. Campbell. A
bibliography of fiction by Louisianians.

8753 [Bartol, Mary]
    Honor May [a story] Boston, Ticknor and Fields, 1866.
    2 p. l. , 404 p.   18 cm.
    Published anonymously.

8754 Barton, K
    Io: a tale of the olden fane. By K. Barton ... New York,
D. Appleton & company, 1851.
    251 p.   18 1/2 cm.

8755 Barton, William Eleazar, 1861-1930.
    A hero in homespun. A tale of the loyal South, by William
E. Barton ... Boston, New York and London, Lamson,
Wolffe and company, 1897.
    xiii, 393 p. front. , 9 pl.   20 1/2 cm.

8756 [Batchelder, Eugene] 1822–1878.
A romance of the sea serpent, or, The ichthyosaurus.
[By Wave, pseud.] Also, a collection of the ancient and
modern authorities, with letters from distinguished
merchants and men of science. Cambridge [Mass.] J.
Bartlett, 1849.
2 p. l. , 172 p. illus.   17 cm.

8757 [Bates, Fanny D   ]
My sister Kitty; a story of election day. Boston, Lee
and Shepard, 1881.
1 p. l. , 232 p.   15 cm.

8758 Baylor, Frances Courtenay, 1848–1920.
Behind the Blue Ridge: a homely narrative ... Philadelphia, J. B. Lippincott company, 1887.
313 p.   20 cm.
Of Virginia mountaineers.

8759 Baylor, Frances Courtenay, 1848–1920.
Claudia Hyde: a novel ... Boston and New York,
Houghton, Mifflin and company, 1894.
442 p.   20 cm.
An Englishman farms in Virginia.

8760 Baylor, Frances Courtenay, 1848–1920.
The ladder of fortune ... Boston and New York,
Houghton, Mifflin and company, 1899.
352 p. [1] p.   20 cm.
From California to Paris.

8761 [Beal, Nathan Stone Reed]
Diamond leaves from the lives of the Dimond family. By
an old, old bachelor ... Macedon, N. Y. , Pub. by the
author, 1872.
viii p. , 2 l. , [13]-384 p.   19 1/2 cm.

8762 Bean, Fannie.
Col. Judson of Alabama; or, a southerner's experience
at the North. By F. Bean ... New York, United States
book company [c1892]
197 p.   19 cm.

8763 The beautiful Jewess Rachel Mendoza, her lamentable
      connection with the dark and eventful career of Charles
      Bernard otherwise called "Prince Charles" ... Phila-
      delphia, E. E. Barclay, 1853.
          1 p. 1. , 7-39 p. front. , illus.   22 1/2 cm.
          Prefatory note signed: B. T.

8764 Beebe, Carrie D
          Violets. By Carrie D. Beebe. Middletown, N. Y. ,
      "Banner of liberty" publishing house, 1873.
          384 p.   19 1/2 cm.

8765 [Beebe, Charles Washington]
          Edmund Dawn; or, Ever forgive. By Ravenswood
      [pseud.] New York, G. W. Carleton & co.; [etc. , etc.]
      1873.
          2 p. 1. , [7]-301 p.   18 1/2 cm.

8766 Beecher, Charles, 1815-1900.
          The incarnation; or, Pictures of the Virgin and her Son.
      By Charles Beecher ... with an introductory essay, by
      Mrs. Harriet Beecher Stowe. New York, Harper & brothers,
      1849.
          ix p. , 1 1. , [13]-227 p.   17 1/2 cm.
          "Mary at the cross ... by Mrs. Harriet Beecher Stowe"
      (poem): p. [225]-227.

8767 [Beecher, Eunice White (Bullard)] "Mrs. Henry Ward Beecher,"
      1813-1897.
          From dawn to daylight; or, The simple story of a western
      home. By a minister's wife. New York, Derby & Jackson,
      1859.
          vii, 9-339 p.   19 cm.

8768 Beecher, Henry Ward, 1813-1887.
          ... Norwood; or, Village life in New England. By Henry
      Ward Beecher. New York, C. Scribner & company, 1868.
          1 p. 1. , [v]-xi, 549 p.   19 cm.
          At head of title: [From the New York Ledger]

8769 Behind the curtain. A tale of Elville ... Dansville, N. Y. ,
      J. R. Trembly; New York, G. P. Putnam & co. , 1853.

1 p. 1. , [11]-442 p.   18 cm.

8770 Belisle, Orvilla S
        The arch bishop; or, Romanism in the United States.
        By Orvilla S. Belisle ... 4th ed. Philadelphia, W. W.
        Smith, 1855.
            xiii, [1], 15-408 p. incl. front. , plates.   18 cm.

8771 Bell, Lilian Lida, "Mrs. A. H. Bogue," 1867-1929.
        The expatriates; a novel, by Lilian Bell. New York and
        London, Harper & brothers, 1900.
            2 p. 1. , 431, [1] p.   19 1/2 cm.

8772 Bell, Lilian Lida, "Mrs. A. H. Bogue," 1867-1929.
        The love affairs of an old maid, by Lilian Bell ... New
        York, Harper & brothers [1893]
            viii p. , 1 1. , 188 p.   18 cm.

8773 Bellamy, Edward, 1850-1898.
        The blindman's world and other stories, by Edward
        Bellamy, with a prefactory sketch by W. D. Howells.
        Boston and New York, Houghton, Mifflin and company,
        1898.
            xiii p. , 1 1. , 415, [1] p.   19 1/2 cm.
            CONTENTS. -The blindman's world. -An echo of Antietam. -
        The old folks' party. -The cold snap. -Two days' solitary
        imprisonment. -A summer evening's dream. -Potts's
        painless cure. -A love story reversed. -Deserted. -Hooking
        watermelons. -A positive romance. -Lost. -With the eyes
        shut. -At Pinney's ranch. -To whom this may come.

8774 Bellamy, Edward, 1850-1898.
        The Duke of Stockbridge; a romance of Shays' rebellion,
        by Edward Bellamy ... New York, Boston [etc.] Silver,
        Burdett and company, 1900.
            xi p. , 1 1. , 371 p.   front. , plates.   20 1/2 cm.

8775 Bellamy, Edward, 1850-1898.
        Equality, by Edward Bellamy ... New York, D.
        Appleton and company, 1897.
            viii, 412 p.   19 1/2 cm.
            Sequel to "Looking backward."

8776 Bellamy, Edward, 1850-1898.
    Miss Ludington's sister; a romance of immortality, by
    Edward Bellamy ... Boston, J. R. Osgood and company,
    1884.
        2 p. 1. , 260 p.   17 1/2 cm.

8777 Benedict, Frank Lee, 1834-1910.
    John Worthington's name. A novel. By Frank Lee
    Benedict ... New York, Harper & brothers, 1874.
        2 p. 1. , [7]-197 p.   23 1/2 cm.

8778 [Benedict, Frank Lee] 1834-1910.
    Miss Van Kortland. A novel. By the author of "My
    daughter Elinor". New York, Harper & brothers, 1870.
        1 p. 1. , [5]-180 p.   24 cm.

8779 Benedict, Frank Lee, 1834-1910.
    Mr. Vaughan's heir: A novel ... New York, Harper &
    brothers, 1875.
        199 p.   20 cm.
    Printed in double cols.

8780 [Benedict, Frank Lee] 1834-1910.
    My daughter Elinor. A novel. New York, Harper &
    brothers, 1869.
        1 p. 1. , 7-257 p.   24 cm.
    Published anonymously.

8781 Benedict, Frank Lee, 1834-1910.
    St. Simon's niece. A novel. By Frank Lee Benedict ...
    New York, Harper & brothers, 1875.
        189 p.   24 cm. [Harper's library of select novels]

8782 [Benham, George Chittenden]
    A year of wreck. A true story by a victim. New York,
    Harper and brothers, 1880.
        472 p.   20 cm.

8783 Benjamin, Samuel Greene Wheeler, 1837-1914.
    The choice of Paris; a romance of the Troad. By S. G. W.
    Benjamin ... New York, Hurd and Houghton, 1870.

v p., 1 1., 342 p.   16 1/2 cm.

8784 Bennett, Emerson, 1822-1905.
      The fair rebel: a tale of colonial times. By Emerson
      Bennett ... Cincinnati, H. M. Rulison, 1853.
      1 p. 1., [5]-98 p.   24 cm.

8785 Bennett, Emerson, 1822-1905.
      The female spy: or, Treason in the camp. A story of the
      revolution. By Emerson Bennett ... Cincinnati, L. Stratton
      [c1851]
      112 p.   24 cm.
      Sequel: Rosalie Du Pont.

8786 Bennett, Emerson, 1822-1905.
      ... Intriguing for a princess. An adventure with Mexican
      banditti. By Emerson Bennett ... Philadelphia, J. W.
      Bradley, 1859.
      1 p. 1., 5-96 p.   17 cm. (Bradley's railroad library [no. 3])

8787 Bennett, Emerson, 1822-1905.
      The league of the Miami. By Emerson Bennett ... New
      ed., enl. and rev. by the author. Cincinnati, U. P. James
      [1860]
      2 p. 1., [9]-116 p.   23 1/2 cm.

8788 Bennett, Emerson, 1822-1905.
      The orphan's trials; or, Alone in a great city. By
      Emerson Bennett ... Philadelphia, T. B. Peterson &
      brothers [c1874]
      1 p. 1., 7-302 p.   18 1/2 cm.

8789 Bennett, Emerson, 1822-1905.
      The renegade. A historical romance of border life.
      By Emerson Bennett ... Cincinnati, Robinson & Jones,
      1848.
      iv, [9]-138 p.   23 cm.
      A later ed. has title: Ella Barnwell.

8790 [Bennett, Mary E   ]
      Poems and tales, by Mary Campbell, Mary Mel, etc.,
      noms de plume of M. E. B. New York, T. W. Strong,

1851,
    viii, [9]-160 p.   19 cm.

8791 Benson, Blackwood Ketcham, 1845-
      Who goes there? The story of a spy in the civil war, by
      B. K. Benson. New York, The Macmillan company; London.
      Macmillan & co., ltd., 1900.
          xviii p., 1 1., 485 p.   illus. (maps)
          19 1/2 cm.

8792 Benton, Kate A
      Geber, a tale of the reign of Harun al Raschid, Khalif
      of Bagdad ... New York, Frederick A. Stokes company
      [1900]
          487 p.   19 cm.

8793 Bergengren, Mrs. Anna (Farquhar) 1865-
      The professor's daughter, by Anna Farquhar. New
      York, Doubleday & McClure co., 1899.
          324 p.   20 1/2 cm.

8794 Berkley, Cora.
      The Beauforts; a story of the Alleghanies. By Cora
      Berkley. Philadelphia, P. F. Cunningham, 1866.
          170 p.   15 cm.

8795 Berkley, Cora.
      The Hamiltons; or, Sunshine in storm. By Cora Berkley.
      New York, E. Dunigan & brother, 1856.
          216 p.   15 1/2 cm.

8796 [Berry, Mrs. Martha Eugina]
      Bella; or, The cradle of liberty. A story of insane
      asylums. By Mrs. Eugenia St. John [pseud.] Boston, N.
      D. Berry, 1874.
          351 p.   19 1/2 cm.

8797 Bickford, L[uther] H
      Phyllis in Bohemia, by L. H. Bickford & Richard Stillman
      Powell [pseud.] Illustrations by Orson Lowell. Chicago
      and New York, H. S. Stone & co., 1897.
          2 p. 1., iii, 5-233 p. front., 2 pl.   17 1/2 cm.

8798 Bickley, Charles Powell.
Garnelle, or The rover's oath of blood. An exciting tale
of the ocean and the land [and other stories] By Charles
Powell Bickley. New York, Garrett & co., 1853.
111 p.   23 1/2 cm.
CONTENTS. -Garnelle; or, The rover's oath of blood.
By C. P. Bickley. -The six stages of punishment; or, The
victim of a vitiated society. By E. F. Roberts. -The
Lapland rat; or, The loss of the Royal George.
The first story "Garnelle" was published in 1877, under
title: The rover's oath.

8799 [Bickley, Lloyd Wharton] 1801-1855.
The aristocrat: an American tale. By the author of "Zoe",
etc. ... Philadelphia, Key & Biddle, 1833.
2 v.   17 1/2 cm.

8800 Biddle, Anthony Joseph Drexel, 1874-
Word for word and letter for letter; a biographical
romance, by A. J. Drexel Biddle. Illustrated by Edward
Holloway. London, Gay and Bird; Philadelphia, Drexel
Biddle, 1898.
207 p. illus.   20 cm.
Binder's title: A biographical romance.

8801 Bien, Hermann M   1831-1895.
Ben-Beor; a story of the Anti-Messiah, in two divisions.
Pt. 1. Lunar intaglios. The man in the moon, a counterpart
of Wallace's "Ben-Hur." Pt. 2. Historical phantasmagoria.
The wandering gentile, a companion romance to Sue's
"Wandering Jew." By H. M. Bien ... Baltimore, I.
Friedenwald co., 1891.
ix, 528 p.   18 1/2 cm.

8802 [Bierce, Ambrose] 1842-
The fiend's delight. By Dod Grile [pseud.] ... New York,
A. L. Luyster, 1873.
197 p., 1 1.   18 1/2 cm.
Reprinted mainly from various California journals.

8803 Bigelow, Harriet Hamline.
The curse entailed. By Harriet Hamline Bigelow ...

Boston, Wentworth and compnay; Cleveland, O. , I. I.
Bigelow, 1857.
xiv, 545 p. front.   19 1/2 cm.

8804 Bigelow, Jacob, 1787-1879.
The wars of the gulls; an historical romance. In three
chapters ... New-York, Pub. at the Dramatic repository,
Shakespeare gallery, 1812.
36 p.   19 1/2 cm.
Published anonymously.
A Federalist satire by Jacob Bigelow and Nathan Hale.

8805 [Bird, Robert Montgomery] 1806-1854.
Sheppard Lee. Written by himself ... New-York, Harper
& brothers, 1836.
2 v.   19 1/2 x 12 1/2 cm.

8806 [Birdsall, Eliza R   M   ]
Dora Raymond; or, Truth triumphant. By Azile [pseud.]
... Binghampton [N. Y.] Daily republican office, 1863.
32 p.   22 1/2 cm.

8807 The birthday gifts: a story for wives. New York, Sutton,
Bowne & co. , 1867.
1 p. 1. , 14 p.   15 1/2 x 12 cm.

8808 The black crook, a most wonderful history. Now being performed with immense success in all the principal theatres
throughout the United States. Philadelphia, Barclay & co.
[c1866]
1 p. 1. , 29-148 p. 4 col. plates.   23 1/2 cm.

8809 Blackbeard. A page from the colonial history of Philadelphia
... New-York, Harper & brothers, 1835.
2 v.   18 1/2 cm.

8810 Blackwell, Mrs. Antoinette Louisa (Brown) 1825-1921.
The island neighbors. A novel of American life. By
Antoinette Brown Blackwell ... New York, Harper &
brothers, 1871.
viii p. , 1 1. , [11]-140 p. incl. front. , illus. , plates.
24 cm.

In double columns.

8811　Blake, Mrs. Lillie (Devereux) 1835–
　　　　Fettered for life; or, Lord and master. A story of today.
　　　By Lillie Devereux Blake ... New York, Sheldon & company,
　　　1874.
　　　　vi, [7]–379 p.　　18 1/2 cm.

8812　Blake, Mrs. Lillie (Devereux) 1835–
　　　　Rockford; or, Sunshine and storm. By Mrs. Lillie
　　　Devereux Umsted ... New York, Carleton, 1863.
　　　　1 p. 1., [5]–308 p.　　18 cm.

8813　[Blauvelt, Mrs. Issac Remsen]
　　　　The yoke and burden. New York, United States publishing
　　　company, 1869.
　　　　4 p. 1., 401 p.　　19 1/2 cm.

8814　Bleecker, Ann Eliza (Schuyler) 1752–1783.
　　　　The history of Maria Kittle. By Ann Eliza Bleecker.
　　　In a letter to Miss Ten Eyck. Hartford, Printed by E.
　　　Babcock, 1797.
　　　　70 p.　　16 1/2 cm.

8815　Bloomfield, Obadiah Benjamin Franklin, pseud.
　　　　The life and adventures of Obadiah Benjamin Franklin
　　　Bloomfield, M. D., a native of the United States of America,
　　　now on the tour of Europe. Interspersed with episodes, and
　　　remarks, religious, moral, public spirited, and humorous.
　　　Written by himself ... Philadelphia, Published for the
　　　proprietor. 1818.
　　　　xi, 210 p.　　18 cm.
　　　　Copyrighted by Edward Franklin.

8816　[Blox, John E　　　　　]
　　　　Justo Ucundono, prince of Japan. By Philalethes [pseud.]
　　　Baltimore, J. Murphy & co.; [etc., etc.] 1854.
　　　　1 1., xvi, [25]–343, [1] p.　　20 cm.

8817　Boaz, Ben, pseud.
　　　　The winged chariot; an allegory [and other stories] by Ben
　　　Boaz ... Cincinnati, A. B. Volney, 1858.

iii, 4-300 p. front., pl.   18 1/2 cm.
CONTENTS.-The winged chariot: an allegory.-The way the
world goes.-The wheel of fortune; or, The ups and downs of
life.-Autobiography of Ben Boaz.-The fallen angel.-Light from
heaven; or, The great revival of 1858.-Conclusion.

8818 Bolton, Mrs. Sarah (Knowles) 1841-1916.
The present problem. [A temperance story] By Sarah
K. Bolton. New York, G. P. Putman's sons, 1874.
2 p. 1., [7]-167 p.   19 cm.

8819 [Bonn, Alexander Kerr]
An original, laughable and comical tale of Hughie Morrison,
the Scottish emigrant ... By Bramble Brae [pseud.] ...
Baltimore, Printed by Sherwood & co., 1846.
35 p.   21 1/2 x 12 1/2 cm.

8820 Borgia, Experience, pseud.
The confessions of a magdalen, or, Some passages in the
life of Experience Borgia, in letters to Forgiveness Mande-
ville, esq. ... New-York, Printed for the publisher, 1831.
31 p.   20 cm.

8821 Bosher, Mrs. Kate Lee (Langley) 1865-
"Bobbie", by Kate Cairns [pseud.] Richmond, Va.,
Presses of B. F. Johnsen publishing co., 1899.
134 p. front., illus.   21 cm.

8822 Boston two hundred years ago, or The romantic story of Miss
Ann Carter (daughter of one of the first settlers,) and the
celebrated Indian chief, Thundersquall; with many
humorous reminiscences and events of olden time.
Boston, 1830,
16 p. incl. front.   30 cm.
Cover-title: Boston in 1630.

8823 Botsford, Edmund, 1745-1819.
The spiritual voyage, performed in the ship Convert,
under the command of Captain Godly-fear, from the port of
Repentance-unto-Life, to the haven of Felicity on the
continent of Glory. An allegory. By Edmund Botsford ...
Harrisburg, Re-printed for D. Barnes, 1828.

126 p.   11 cm.
English edition published, London, 1821.

8824 [Botsford, Mrs. Margaret] fl. 1812-1828.
      The reign of reform or Yankee Doodle court. By a lady.
Baltimore, Printed for the authoress, 1830.
      iv, [5]-146 p.   15 cm.
      "Dialogue between Col. Hardfare, and Maj. Dauntless,
(two revolutionary patriots)." An attack on Jackson's
administration.

8825 [Bourne, George] 1780-1845.
      Lorette. The history of Louise, daughter of a Canadian
nun, exhibiting the interior of female convents ... 2d ed.
New York, C. Small, 1834.
      2 p. l., [ix]-xv, [17]-208 p. front.   15 1/2 cm.
      Added t.-p., engr.
      Published anonymously.

8826 [Bouton, John Bell] 1830-1902.
      Round the block. An American novel ... New York [etc.]
D. Appleton and company, 1864.
      468 p. front., plates.   19 cm.
      Published anonymously.

8827 [Bowen, Mrs. Sue (Petigru)] 1824-1875.
      Busy moments of an idle woman ... New York [etc.] D.
Appleton & company, 1854.
      285 p.   18 1/2 cm.
      Published anonymously.
      CONTENTS.-Edith.-An every-day life.-The widow.-Old
maidism versus marriage.-An episode in the life of a
woman of fashion.

8828 [Bowen, Mrs. Sue (Petigru)] 1824-1875.
      Lily. A novel, by the author of "The busy moments of an
idle woman." New York, Harper & brothers, 1855.
      2 p. l., [13]-330 p.   19 1/2 cm.

8829 [Bowen, Mrs. Sue (Petigru)] 1824-1875.
      Sylvia's world [and] Crimes which the law does not reach.
By the author of "Busy moments of an idle woman" ... New

York, Derby & Jackson, 1859.
384 p.   18 cm.

8830 B[ower], Mrs. E[lla] E
      Leaves from a bad girl's diary. By E. E. B. Chicago,
      Owens publishing company, 1884.
      83 p.   17 1/2 x 13 cm.

8831 Bowline, Charley, pseud.
      The iron tomb, or The mock count of New York. A local
      tale, written in scenes, with a free hand, especially for
      the readers of the 'Uncle Sam' ... by Charley Bowline.
      Boston, G. H. Williams [c1852]
      1 p. 1., [7]-100 p. incl. pl.   25 cm.

8832 Bowman, Jacob L
      You and me; or, Sketches for both of us ... By Hans
      Patrick Le Connor (Jacob L. Bowman.) St. Louis, Mo.,
      G. Knapp & co., printers, 1867.
      viii, [9]-288 p. front. (port.)   18 cm.

8833 Boyesen, Hjalmar Hjorth, 1848-1895.
      Gunnar; a tale of Norse life, by Hjalmar Hjorth Boyesen ...
      Boston, J. R. Osgood and company, 1874.
      292 p.   15 1/2 cm.

8834 Boyesen, Hjalmar Hjorth, 1848-1895.
      A Norseman's pilgrimage. By Hjalmar Hjorth Boyesen ...
      New York, Sheldon & company, 1875.
      4, [7]-301 p.   17 1/2 cm.

8835 Brace, John Pierce, 1793-1872.
      The fawn of the pale faces; or, Two centuries ago. By J.
      P. Brace. New-York, D. Appleton & company, 1853.
      2 p. 1., [7]-288 p.   18 1/2 cm.

8836 Brace, John Pierce, 1793-1872.
      Tales of the devils. By J. P. Brace ... Hartford, S.
      Andrus and son, 1847.
      iv, [5]-277 p.   15 cm.

8837 Bradbury, Osgood.

Isabelle; or, The emigrant's daughter. A tale of
Boston and the West. By Osgood Bradbury, esq. [Also, The
rescued maiden. By S. Nelson] Boston, F. Gleason, 1848.
1 p. l., [7]-100 p.   24 1/2 cm.

8838 Bradford, Sarah Elizabeth (Hopkins) "Mrs. J. M. Bradford,"
b. 1818.
The Linton family; or, The fashion of this world. By
Sarah H. Bradford ... New York, Pudney & Russell, 1860.
5 p. l., [13]-320 p.   19 1/2 cm.

8839 Brady, James Topham, 1815-1869.
A Christmas dream. By James T. Brady. Illus. by
Edward S. Hall. New York, C. A. Alvord, 1860.
35 p. illus.   19 cm.
Added t.-p., engraved.

8840 [Bragg, Henry A   ]
Tekel; or, Cora Glencoe. A novel ... By Braganza
[pseud.] Philadelphia, J. B. Lippincott & co., 1870.
vi, 7-463 p.   19 cm.

8841 [Brainard, John Gardiner Calkins] 1796-1828.
Fort Braddock letters; or, A tale of the French and
Indian wars, in America, at the beginning of the eighteenth
century. Worcester [Mass.] Dorr & Howland, 1827.
vi, [7] 90 p.   14 1/2 cm.
Originally published in the "Connecticut mirror."

8842 Brazelton, Mrs. Ethel Maude (Colson)
The story of a dream, by Ethel Maude Colson. Chicago,
C. H. Kerr & company, 1896.
304 p.   18 cm.

8843 [Brice, James F   ]
Castler Crosier. A romance. By an American. Annapolis,
Printed by W. M. M'Neir, 1827.
79 p.   21 cm.

8844 Brierwood, Frank, pseud. ?
Mabel Clifton. A novel. By Frank Brierwood ... Philadelphia, Claxton, Remsen & Haffelfinger, 1869.

viii, 9-304 p.   18 1/2 cm.

8845 [Briggs, Charles Frederick] 1804-1877.
          The adventures of Harry Franco: a tale of the great panic
          ... New York, F. Saunders, 1839.
          2 v.   19 cm.
          Published anonymously.

8846 [Briggs, Mrs. Emily Edson] 1831-1910.
          Ellen Parry; or, Trials of the heart. By Olivia [pseud.] ...
          New York, D. Appleton & co.; Philadelphia, G. S. Appleton,
          1850.
          1 p. 1. , [9]-186 p.   19 cm.

8847 Bright, Mrs. A[manda] M[etcalf]
          The three Bernices; or, Ansermo of the crag. By Mrs.
          A. M. Bright ... Philadelphia, Claxton, Remsen &
          Haffelfinger, 1869.
          xii, 13-380 p.   19 cm.

8848 Brisbane, Abbott Hall, d. 1861.
          Ralphton; or, The young Carolinian of 1776. A romance
          on the philosophy of politics. By A. H. Brisbane. Charles-
          ton, Burges and James, printers, 1848.
          xi, 242 p.   19 x 12 cm.

8849 Brisbane, William Henry, ca. 1803-1878.
          Amanda: a tale for the times. By W. H. Brisbane ...
          Philadelphia, Merrihew & Thompson, printers, 1848.
          51 p.   15 cm.

8850 Brisée ... [A novel] Philadelphia, J. B. Lippincott & co.,
          1862.
          255 p.   19 cm.

8851 Bristed, Charles Astor, 1820-1874.
          The upper ten thousand: sketches of American society.
          By C. Astor Bristed. New York, Stringer & Townsend,
          1852.
          274 p. front. , plates.   20 1/2 cm.

8852 Brittan, Harriet G   1823-1897.

Shoshie, the Hindoo Zenana teacher. By Miss Harriette G. Brittan ... New York, T. Whittaker [c1873]
4 p. 1., 7-222 p. front., plates.   18 cm.

8853 Brooks, Mrs. Maria (Gowen) 1795-1845.
Idomen; or, The vale of Yumuri. By Maria del Occidente [pseud.] New-York, S. Colman, 1843.
xxiii, 236 p.   16 cm.

8854 Brother Mason, the circuit rider; or, Ten years a Methodist preacher ... Cincinnati, H. M. Rulison; Philadelphia, Quaker City publishing house, 1855.
v, [7]-310 p. front.   19 1/2 cm.

8855 Brotherhead, Alfred Paxton.
Himself his worst enemy; or, Philip Duke of Wharton's career ... Philadelphia, J. B. Lippincott, Co., 1871.
374 p.   20 cm.

8856 Brougham, John, 1810-1880.
The Bunsby papers (2d series) Irish echoes. By John Brougham ... With designs by McLenan. New York, Derby & Jackson; Cincinnati, H. W. Derby & co., 1856.
1 p. 1., viii, 9-298 p. front.   18 1/2 cm.
Added t.-p., illus.

8857 Brown, Alice, 1857-
The day of his youth, by Alice Brown. Boston and New York, Houghton, Mifflin and company, 1897.
1 p. 1., 143, [1] p.   18 cm.

8858 Brown, Alice, 1857-
Tiverton tales, by Alice Brown. Boston and New York, Houghton, Mifflin and company, 1899.
3 p. 1., 339, [1] p.   19 cm.
CONTENTS. -Dooryards.-A March wind.-The mortuary chest.-Horn-o' the moon.-A stolen festival.-A last assembling.-The way of peace.-The experience of Hannah Prime.-Honey and myrrh.-A second marriage.-The flat-iron lot.-The end of all living.

8859 [Brown, Charles Brockden] 1771-1810.

61

Edgar Huntly; or, Memoirs of a sleep-walker. By the author of Arthur Mervyn, Wieland,-Ormond, & c. ... Philadelphia: Printed by H. Maxwell, No. 3 Letitia court, and sold by Thomas Dobson, Asbury Dickins, and the principal booksellers. 1799.
    3 v.   19 1/2 cm.
    Introduction signed: C. B. B.
    "Death of Cicero": v. 3, 48 p. at end.

8860 Brown, Charles Brockden, 1771-1810.
    Ormond; or, The secret witness. By Charles Brockden Brown. [Uniform ed.] New York, Philadelphia [etc.] W. Taylor & co., 1846.
    144 p.   23 1/2 cm. (On cover: Library of standard romance, no. 2)

8861 [Brown, Charles Brockden] 1771-1810.
    Wieland; or, The transformation. An American tale... New York, Printed by T. & J. Swords, for H. Caritat, 1798.
    2 p. 1., 298 p.   17 1/2 cm.
    "Advertisement" signed: C. B. B.

8862 [Brown, James E   ]
    ... Mose Skinner's bridal tour, and other sketches. Boston, New England news company [c1871]
    21 p.   18 cm.

8863 [Brown, James E   ]
    Mose Skinner's great world's jubilee and humstrum con-vulsion. Illustrated. Boston [New England news company] 1872.
    21 p.   18 1/2 cm.

8864 [Brown, James E   ]
    Our great peace festival and pow-wow; to be held in Boston, June 1869 ... Boston, Printed by W. Richardson, 1869.
    21 p.   19 cm.
    On cover: Mose Skinner's grand peace jubilee.
    These sketches appeared originally in the "Wide world" Newspaper.

8865 [Brown, James E   ]
  Recollections of a lazy life. By Mose Skinner [pseud.]
... Boston, Printed by W. Richardson, 1869.
  23 p.   19 cm.

8866 [Brown Nathan] 1807-1886.
  The history of Magnus Maharba and the Black Dragon.
  By Kristofur Hadmus [pseud.] From the original manu-
  scripts. New York, Printed for the proprietor, 1867.
  1 p. 1., 105 p.   17 1/2 cm.
  Allegorical account of Abraham Lincoln and the civil war.

8867 [Brown, Nathan] 1807-1886.
  Ae histori ov Magnus Maha'rba and ae Blak Dragun.
  Bai Kristofur Kadmus [pseud.] ... Nû-York, Printed for
  ae Filolojikal gemána, 1866.
  1 p. 1., ii, [3], 122 p.   17 cm.
  Text on p. [3] of cover.
  Spelling is phonetic throughout.
  Allegorical account of Abraham Lincoln and the Civil war.

8868 [Brown, Nathan] 1807-1886.
  Zyx and his fairy: or, The soul in search of peace.
  New-York, Brown and Duer, 1867.
  2 p. 1., [7]-72 p.   17 1/2 cm.

8869 Brown, Mrs. Phoebe (Hinsdale) 1783-1861.
  The tree and its fruits, or, Narratives from real life.
  By Mrs. P. H. Brown. New York, E. Collier, 1836.
  142 p. incl. front.   15 1/2 cm.
  Title vignette.

8870 Brown, Thurlow Weed, d. 1866.
  ... Minnie Herman; or, The night and its morning ... By
  Thurlow W. Brown ... 5th thousand. Auburn and Buffalo,
  Miller, Orton & Mulligan, 1854.
  472 p. front. (port.) plates.   19 1/2 cm.

8871 Brown, Thurlow Weed, d. 1866.
  Why I am a temperance man: a series of letters to a friend.
  Together with Tales and sketches from real life, and Hearth-
  stone reveries. By Thurlow W. Brown ... Auburn, Derby

and Miller; Buffalo, Derby, Orton and Mulligan; [etc., etc.]
1853.
    viii, [9]-384 p. front. (port.) plates.   20 cm.

8872 Brown, Walter W
    Money don' make 'ristercrats. A story. By Walter W.
Brown ... Nashville, Tenn., Printed for the author,
1893.
    29 p.   16 1/2 cm.

8873 Brown, William Perry.
    A sea-island romance. A story of South Carolina after the
war. By William Perry Brown. New York, J. R. Alden,
1888.
    2 p. 1., 9-161 p.   19 1/2 cm.

8874 [Browne, Charles Farrar] 1834-1867.
    Artemus Ward; his travels ... with comic illustrations by
Mullen. New York, Carleton [etc., etc.] 1865.
    231 p. plates.   19 cm.
    Added t.-p., illustrated.
    CONTENTS.-pt. I. Miscellaneous.-pt. II. Among the
Mormons.

8875 [Browne, Charles Farrar] 1834-1867.
    Artemus Ward in London, and other papers. With comic
illustrations by J. H. Howard. New York, G. W. Carleton
& co.; London, S. Low, son & co., 1867.
    vi p., 2 1., [11]-229 p. incl. front. plates.   19 cm.
(Half-title: Comic books by Artemus Ward ... III ...)

8876 [Browne, Charles Farrar] 1834-1867.
    Artemus Ward's panorama. (As exhibited at the Egyptian
hall, London) Ed. by his executors, T. W. Robertson and
E. P. Hingston. With thirty-four illustrations. New York,
G. W. Carleton; [etc., etc.] 1869.
    vii, [8]-213 p. illus.   19 cm.

8877 Browne, John Ross, 1817-1875.
    An American family in Germany. By J. Ross Browne ...
Illustrated by the author. New York, Harper & brothers,
1866.

1 p. 1., [v]-xiv, [15]-381 p.   illus.   19 1/2 cm.
CONTENTS.-An American family in Germany.-A whirl
through Algeria.-A visit to the salt-mines of Wieliczka.

8878 Browne, John Ross, 1817-1875.
      Crusoe's island: a ramble in the footsteps of Alexander
Selkirk. With sketches of adventure in California and Washoe.
By J. Ross Browne ... New York, Harper & brothers, 1864.
      vii, [9]-436 p. illus.   20 cm.
      CONTENTS.-Crusoe's island.-A dangerous journey.-
Observations in office.-A peep at Washoe.

8879 Browne, John Ross, 1817-1875.
      The land of Thor. By J. Ross Browne ... Illustrated by
the author. New York, Harper & brothers, 1867.
      vii, [9]-542 p. illus.   19 1/2 cm.
      Describes Russia, Sweden, Norway and Iceland.

8880 Browne, John Ross, 1817-1875.
      Yusef; or, The journey of the Fungi: A crusade in the East.
By J. Ross Browne ... New-York, Harper & brothers, 1853.
      1 p. 1., xii, [13]-421 p. illus.   19 1/2 cm.

8881 Browne, Lida Briggs.
      Words that burn. A romance, by Lida Briggs Browne.
Utica, N. Y., D. B. Briggs, 1900.
      2 p. 1., 366 p. front (port.)   19 1/2 cm.

8882 Browne, Walter Scott.
      Andrew Bentley; or, How he retrieved his honor ... A
story of the civil war founded on facts. By Walter Scott
Browne. Camden, N. J., A. C. Graw [c1900]
      3 p. 1., [13]-311 p. incl. plates. front., port.   20 cm.
      Portrait of author, 15 x 10, affixed to blank leaf.

8883 Brownell, Mrs. Gertrude (Hall) 1863-
      April's sowing [by] Gertrude Hall ... New York, McClure,
Phillips & co., 1900.
      ix, 282, [1] p. front., illus.   20 cm.

8884 Brownell, Mrs. Gertrude (Hall) 1863-
      Far from to-day. By Gertrude Hall ... Boston, Roberts

brothers, 1892.
>1 p. l. , 291 p.   18 cm.
>CONTENTS. -Tristiane. -Sylvanus. -The sons of Philemon. -
>Theodolind. -Servirol. -Shepherds.

8885 Brownell, Mrs. Gertrude (Hall) 1863-
>Foam of the sea, and other tales. By Gertrude Hall ...
>Boston, Roberts brothers, 1895.
>5 p. l. , [9]-299 p.   18 cm.
>CONTENTS. -Foam of the sea. -In Battlereagh house. -
>Powers of darkness. -The late returning. -The wanderers. -
>Garden deadly.

8886 Brownson, Orestes Augustus, 1803-1876.
>Charles Elwood; or, The infidel converted. By O. A.
>Brownson. Boston, C. C. Little and J. Brown, 1840.
>xi, 262 p.   18 cm.
>"I am willing the public should take the book as an account
>... of my own former unbelief and present belief."-Pref.

8887 [Brownson, Sarah M   ]
>Marian Elwood; or, How girls live. By one of themselves.
>New York, E. Dunigan & brother, 1859.
>360 p.   18 cm.

8888 Bruce, Mrs. E   M
>A thousand a year. By Mrs. E. M. Bruce. Boston, Lee
>& Shepard, 1866.
>263 p.   16 1/2 cm.

8889 Buchanan, Harrison, Gray.
>Asmodeus; or, Legends of New York. Being a complete
>exposé of the mysteries, vices and doings, as exhibited by
>the fashionable circles of New York... By Harrison Gray
>Buchanan... Facts without fiction. New York, Munson &
>co. , 1848.
>96 p.   23 cm.

8890 Buckingham, Emma May.
>A self-made woman; or, Mary Idyl's trials and triumphs.
>By Emma May Buckingham ... New York, S. R. Wells,
>1873.

343 p.   18 1/2 cm.

8891 Buckley, Mrs. Maria L
        Amanda Willson; or, The vicissitudes of life. By Mrs.
     Maria L. Buckley ... New York, The author, 1856.
        iv, [5]-40 p. front. (port.)   23 cm.

8892 Buckley, Mrs. Maria L
        Edith Moreton; or, Temperance versus intemperance.
     By Mrs. Maria L. Buckley ... Philadelphia, Pub. for the
     author, 1852.
        48 p.   19 cm.

8893 Bunce, Oliver Bell, 1828-1890.
        A bachelor's story, by Oliver Bunce. New York, Rudd
     & Carleton, 1859.
        247 p.   19 cm.

8894 [Bunce, Oliver Bell] 1828-1890.
        Bensley: a story of to-day. By the author of "Life before
     him." New York, J. G. Gregory, 1863.
        221 p.   17 1/2 cm.

8895 [Bunce, Oliver Bell] 1828-1890.
        Life before him. A novel ... New York, W. A. Townsend
     & company, 1860.
        vii, 9-401 p.   18 1/2 cm.

8896 Bunkley, Josephine M
        ... The testimony of an escaped novice from the Sisterhood
     of St. Joseph, Emmettsburg, Maryland, the mother-house
     of the Sisters of charity in the United States. By Josephine M.
     Bunkley. New York, Harper & brothers, 1855.
        xii, [13]-338 p. incl. illus. (plans) pl.   20 1/2 cm.
        At head of title: Miss Bunkley's book.

8897 Bunner, Henry Cuyler, 1855-1896.
        Love in old cloathes, and other stories. B. H. C. Bunner.
     Illustrated by W. T. Smedley, Orson Lowell, and André
     Castaigne. New York, C. Scribner's sons, 1896.
        5 p. 1., 217 p. illus., 12 pl. (incl. front.)   19 1/2 cm.
        CONTENTS.-Love in old cloathes.-A letter and a para-

graph. -"As one having authority."-Crazy wife's ship. -
French for a fortnight. -The red silk handkerchief. -Our
aromatic uncle.

8898 Bunner, Henry Cuyler, 1855-1896.
      More "Short sixes," by H. C. Bunner, illustrated by C.
J. Taylor. New York, Keppler & Schwarzmann, 1894.
      4 p. l., 229 p. illus., port.   19 1/2 cm.
      CONTENTS. -The cumbersome horse. -Mr. Vincent Egg
and the wage of sin. -The ghoollah. -Cutwater of Seneca. -Mr.
Wick's aunt. -What Mrs. Fortescue did. -"The man with the
pink pants. "-The third figure in the cotillion. -"Samantha
Boom-de-ay. "-My dear Mrs. Billington.

8899 Bunner, Henry Cuyler, 1855-1896.
      Zadoc Pine, and other stories, by H. C. Bunner. New
York, C. Scribner's sons, 1891.
      4 p. l., 256 p.   18 1/2 cm.
      CONTENTS. -The Zadoc Pine labor union. -Natural
selection: a romance of Chelsea village and East Hampton
town. -Casperl. -A secondhand story. Mrs. Tom's spree. -
Squire Five-Fathom.

8900 Burckett, Florence.
      Wildmoor. A novel. By Florence Burckett ... Phila-
delphia, J. B. Lippincott & co., 1875.
      464 p.   19 cm.

8901 Burdett, Charles, b. 1815.
      The second marriage; or, A daughter's trials. A domestic
tale of New York. By Charles Burdett ... New York, C.
Scribner, 1856.
      238 p.   18 1/2 cm.

8902 Burdett, Charles, b. 1815.
      Three per cent a month; or, The perils of fast living. By
Charles Burdett ... New York, Derby & Jackson; Cincinnati,
H. W. Derby & co., 1856.
      3 p. l., ix-xii, [13]-395 p.   19 cm.

8903 Burgwyn, Collinson Pierrepont Edward, 1852-1915.
      The Huguenot lovers, a tale of the Old Dominion. By

C. P. E. Burgwyn ... Richmond, Va., Published by the
author, 1889.
4 p. 1., 219 p.   18 cm.

8904 Burnett, Mrs. Frances (Hodgson) 1849-1924.
His Grace of Osmonde; being the portions of that nobleman's
life omitted in the relation of his lady's story presented to the
world of fashion under the title of A lady of quality, by Frances
Hodgson Burnett. New York, C. Scribner's sons, 1897.
xl, 465 p.   19 cm.

8905 Burnett, Mrs. Frances (Hodgson) 1849-1924.
In connection with the De Willoughby claim, by Frances
Hodgson Burnett. New York, C. Scribner's sons, 1899.
2 p. 1., 445 p.   19 1/2 cm.

8906 Burnett, Mrs. Frances (Hodgson) 1849-1924.
A lady of quality; being a most curious, hitherto unknown
history, as related to Mr. Isaac Bickerstaff but not presented
to the world of fashion through the pages of The Tatler, and
now for the first time written down. New York, C. Scribner's
sons, 1896.
xi, 303 p.   19 cm.
A companion volume: His Grace of Osmonde.

8907 Burnett, Mrs. Frances (Hodgson) 1849-1924.
Louisiana, by Frances Hodgson Burnett ... New York,
C. Scribner's sons, 1880.
vii, 163 p. front.   19 cm.
Frontispiece wanting.

8908 Burnett, Mrs. Frances (Hodgson) 1849-1924.
The one I knew the best of all; a memory of the mind of a
child, by Frances Hodgson Burnett. Illustrated by Reginald
B. Birch. New York, C. Scribner's sons, 1893.
xv, [1], 325 p. incl. front., illus.   19 1/2 cm.

8909 Burnett, Mrs. Frances (Hodgson) 1849-1924.
. The pretty sister of José, by Frances Hodgson Burnett ...
New York, C. Scribner's sons, 1889.
3 p. 1., 127 p. front., plates.   19 1/2 cm.

8910 Burnett, Mrs. Frances (Hodgson) 1849-1924.
Surly Tim, and other stories, by Frances Hodgson Burnett.
New York, Scribner, Armstrong & co. , 1877.
4 p. 1. , 270 p.   17 cm.
"All these stories first appeared in Scribner's monthly,
except 'Seth', which was published in Lippincott's magazine."
CONTENTS. -"Surly Tim." A Lancashire story. -"Le
Monsieur de la petite dame."-Smethurstses.-One day at Arle.-
Esmeralda.-Mère Giraud's little daughter.-Lodusky.-"Seth."

8911 Burnett, Mrs. Frances (Hodgson) 1849-1924.
That lass o' Lowrie's. A Lancashire story. By Frances
Hodgson Burnett. New York, Scribner, Armstrong & co.
[1877]
269 p.   18 cm.

8912 Burnett, Mrs. Frances (Hodgson) 1849-1924.
Through one administration. By Frances Hodgson Burnett ... Boston, J. R. Osgood and company, 1883.
1 p. 1. , 564 p.   19 1/2 cm.

8913 Burnham, Mrs. Clara Louise (Root) 1854-1927.
Dr. Latimer; a story of Casco bay, by Clara Louise
Burnham. Boston and New York, Houghton, Mifflin and
company, 1893.
2 p. 1. , 384 p.   18 cm.

8914 Burnham, Mrs. Clara Louise (Root) 1854-1927.
A great love. By Clara Louise Burnham. Boston and
New York, Houghton, Mifflin and company, 1898.
2 p. 1. , 309 p.   17 1/2 cm.

8915 Burnham, Mrs. Clara Louise (Root) 1854-1927.
The wise woman, a novel, by Clara Louise Burnham.
Boston and New York, Houghton, Mifflin and company, 1895.
2 p. 1. , 430 p.   18 cm.

8916 Burnham, George P.
A hundred thousand dollars in gold. How to make it. A
practical narrative, suggesting how to use, and not abuse it;
how to gain, and how to lend it... [A novel] by Capt. George
P. Burnham... Springfield, Mass., W. J. Holland, 1875.

xiv p., 1 1., 17-407 p. incl. front., illus., plates.
20 1/2 cm.

8917 Burnham, George Pickering 1814-1902.
Gleanings from the portfolio of the "Young 'un" [pseud.]
A series of humorous sketches. Illustrated by Hitchcock.
3d ed ... Boston, R. B. Fitts & co., 1849.
viii, [7]-142 p. front., illus., plates.   19 cm.
Dedication signed: Geo. P. Burhham.
"Appeared in the New York 'Spirit of the times,' in the
Philadelphia 'Saturday courier,' Gleason's 'Flag of our union,'
in the 'American union,' Boston, and other well-known
journals."-Pref.

8918 [Burton, Mrs. Henry S   ]
Who would have thought it? A novel ... Philadelphia,
J. B. Lippincott & co., 1872.
438 p.   18 cm.
Published anonymously.

8919 [Burton, Warren] 1800-1866.
The district school as it was. By one who went to it.
[3d] rev. ed. Boston, Phillips, Sampson and company, 1850.
x, [11]-206 p. front.   17 cm.
"First published in 1833 ... A second and larger ed. was
issued in New York."

8920 [Burts, Robert] d. 1839.
The scourge of the ocean; a story of the Atlantic. By an
officer of the U. S. navy ... Philadelphia, Carey and Hart,
1847.
2 p. 1., [9]-109 p.   24 cm.

8921 [Burts, Robert] d. 1839.
The sea-king: a nautical romance. By the author of the
"Scourge of the ocean." Ed. and completed by the editor of
"Valerie" ... Philadelphia, A. Hart, 1851.
2 p. 1., 11-203 p.   23 1/2 cm.

8922 The Buttonwoods; or, The refugees of the revolution. A
Historical sketch ... By the author of "Legends of revolution." The "Forest inn," &c. &c. Philadelphia,

71

M. E. Harmstead, 1849.
    95 p.   25 cm. (On cover: Legends of the revolution,
no. 1)

8923 [Byrn, Marcus Lafayette]
        The rambles of Fudge Fumble, or The love scrapes of
      a lifetime. By the author of the "Arkansaw doctor" ...
      New York, F. A. Brady, 1860.
        2 p. 1., 232 p. plates.   19 1/2 x 12 cm.

8924 [Byrn, Marcus Lafayette]
        Rattlehead's chronicles: or, A little experience with old
      maids and young maids; old bachelors, fools, and drunkards;
      quack doctors, men of science, and the world at large. By
      David Rattlehead [pseud.] Philadelphia, Lippincott, Grambo,
      & co.; New York, Long & brother; [etc., etc.] 1852.
        xi, [13]-175 p. front. (port.) plates.   20 1/2 cm.

                                  C

8925 Cable, George Washington, 1844-1925.
           Dr. Sevier, by George W. Cable ...   Boston, J. R.
        Osgood and company, 1885.
           473 p.   19 1/2 cm.

8926 Cable, George Washington, 1844-1925.
           The Grandissimes; a story of Creole life, by George W.
        Cable ... New York, C. Scribner's sons, 1880.
           ix, 448 p.   19 cm.
           First edition.

8927 Cable, George Washington, 1844-1925.
           John March, Southerner ... New York, Charles
        Scribner's sons, 1894.
           513 p.   20 cm.

8928 Cable, George Washington, 1844-1925.

Madame Delphine, by George W. Cable ... New York,
C. Scribner's sons, 1881.
2 p. 1., iii-iv, 125 p.   18 cm.
First edition.

8929 Cable, George Washington, 1844-1925.
Old Creole days. By George W. Cable. New York,
C. Scribner's sons, 1897.
viii, 234 p.   20 cm.
CONTENTS. -Café des Exiles. -Belles Demoiselles
Plantation. -"Posson Jone' ". -Jean-Ah Poquelin. -'Tite
Poulette. -'Sieur George. -Madame Délicieuse.

8930 Cable, George Washington, 1844-1925.
Strong hearts. By George W. Cable. New York, C.
Scribner's sons, 1899.
4 p. 1., 3-214 p.   18 cm.
CONTENTS. -The solitary. -The taxidermist. -The entomologist.

8931 [Cabot, Arthur Winslow]
Two gentlemen of Gotham, by C. & C. New York, Cassell
& company, limited [c1887]
2 p. 1., 344 p.   17 1/2 cm.
"C. & C.", pseud. of Arthur W. Cabor and Howard Coghill.

8932 Caldwell, John H   b. 1820.
The Thurstons of the old Palmetto state: or, Varieties of
southern life. Illustrated in the fortunes of a distinguished
family of South Carolina. By Rev. John H. Caldwell ...
New-York, J. Russell, 1861.
1 p. 1., [vii]-viii, [9]-406 p.   19 cm.

8933 [Cameron, Reb]
Salted with fire. By H. M. Le Grange [pseud.] ... New
York, E. J. Hale & son, 1872.
177 p.   19 1/2 cm.

8934 Campbell, Jane C
American evening entertainments; or, Tales of city
and country life. By Jane C. Campbell ... New York,
J. C. Derby; Boston, Phillips, Sampson & co.; [etc.,
etc.] 1856.

2 p. 1., [9]-353 p.   19 cm.
Published also under title: The money maker and other
tales.
  CONTENTS. -Money-maker, -Christine. -Catharine Clayton. -
Paul Talbot. -Robert Dunning. -Blanche Acheson. -Farmer's
daughter. -The seamstress. -The first step. -A wife's love. -
Lazy philanthropy.

8935 [Campbell, Mrs. Juliet H   (Lewis)] 1823-
  Eros and Anteros; or, The bachelor's ward. By Judith
Canute [pseud.] New York, Rudd & Carleton, 1857.
  xii, 13-360 p.   18 1/2 cm.

8936 [Cannon, Charles James] 1800-1860.
  Ravellings from the web of life. By Grandfather Greenway
[pseud.] New York [etc.] D. & J. Sadlier & co. [1855]
  1 p. 1., [vii]-xii, [13]-364 p.   19 cm.

8937 Cannon, Susan.
  Maidee, the alchemist; or, Turning all to gold, by Susan
Cannon. New York, M. Doolady, 1871.
  2 p. 1., [7]-249 p.   19 1/2 cm.

8938 Canty, Samuel.
  The chipboy of the dry dock. A local moral story. By
Samuel Canty.... New York, Printed and pub. for the
author, 1855.
  112 p.   24 cm.

8939 Capron, Carrie.
  Helen Lincoln: a tale. By Carrie Capron. New York,
Harper & brothers, 1856.
  308 p.   19 1/2 cm.

8940 Captain Le Diable, pseud.
  Historical sketch of the third annual conquest of Florida.
[By] Captain Le Diable ... Port Royal, S. C., 1864.
  19 p.   18 cm.
  A humorous narrative, apparently written by a Union
officer.

8941 Carey, Charles.

The lady of the green and blue; or, The magic figure head.
By Charley Carey ... Boston, G. H. Williams, 1847.
103 p.   26 cm.

8942 Carpenter, William Henry, 1813-1899.
Claiborne the rebel. A romance of Maryland, under the
proprietary. By W. H. Carpenter ... New York, Philadelphia [etc.] E. Ferrett & co.; [etc., etc.] 1845.
104 p.   22 1/2 cm.

8943 Carpenter, William H[enry] 1813-1899.
Ruth Emsley, the betrothed maiden. A tale of the Virginia
massacre. By Wm. H. Carpenter ... Philadelphia, A. Hart,
1850.
1 p. 1., 9-130 p.   19 1/2 cm.

8944 Carter, John Henton.
The log of Commodore Rollingpin: his adventures afloat
and ashore. By John H. Carter ... New York, G. W.
Carleton & co.; [etc., etc.] 1874.
258 p. incl. front., illus.   19 cm.

8945 Carter, St. Leger Landon.
Nugae, by Nugator; or, Pieces in prose and verse. By
St. Leger L. Carter. Baltimore, Printed by Woods and
Crane, 1844.
iv, [5]-215 p.   16 cm.

8946 Cary, Alice, 1820-1871.
The bishop's son. A novel, by Alice Cary. New York,
G. W. Carleton & co.; [etc., etc.] 1867.
2 p. 1., 7-416 p.   19 cm.

8947 Cary Alice, 1820-1871.
Clovernook; or, Recollections of our neighborhood in
the West. [1st-] 2d series. By Alice Carey [!] New York,
Redfield, 1852, 1853.
2 v. front., pl.   18 cm.
Collections of short stories.

8948 Cary, Alice, 1820-1871.
Hagar, a story of to-day. By Alice Carey [!] ... New

York, Redfield, 1852.
    2 p. 1. , [iii]-vi, [13]-300 p.   19 cm.
"Second edition.

8949 Cary, Alice, 1820-1871.
    Married, not mated; or, How they lived at Woodside and
Throckmorton Hall. By Alice Cary ... New York, Derby
& Jackson; Cincinnati, H. W. Derby, 1856.
    2 p. 1. , [13]-425 p.   19 cm.

8950 Casseday, Davis B
    The Hortons: or, American life at home. By Davis B.
Casseday. Philadelphia, J. S. Claxton; New York, D.
Appleton & co. , [etc. , etc.] 1866.
    viii, [5]-362 p.   18 1/2 cm.

8951 The catastrophe; a tale of the nineteenth century. Lowell, Rand
& Southmayd, 1833.
    18 p.   15 1/2 cm.

8952 Cate, E[liza] Jane, 1812-1884.
    A year with the Franklins; or, To suffer and be strong.
By E. Jane Cate. New York, Harper & brothers, 1846.
    276 p.   15 1/2 cm.

8953 Catherwood, Mrs. Mary (Hartwell) 1847-1902.
    The lady of Fort St. John, by Mary Hartwell Catherwood
... Boston and New York, Houghton, Mifflin and company,
1891.
    vii p. , 1 1. , 284 p.   18 cm.
    A story of Acadia.

8954 Catherwood, Mrs. Mary (Hartwell) 1847-1902.
    Old Kaskaskia [a novel] by Mary Hartwell Catherwood ...
Boston and New York, Houghton, Mifflin and company,
1893.
    2 p. 1. , 200 p.   18 Cm.

8955 Catherwood, Mrs. Mary (Hartwell) 1847-1902.
    The romance of Dollard, by Mary Hartwell Catherwood ...
New York, The Century co. [1889]
    3 p. 1. , 206 p. front. , plates.   20 cm.

8956 Catherwood, Mrs. Mary (Hartwell) 1847-1902.
The white islander, by Mary Hartwell Catherwood ... New York, The Century co., 1893.
viii p., 2 1., 164 p. incl. front., plates.   20 cm.

8957 Catherwood, Mrs. Mary (Hartwell) 1847-1902.
A woman in armor. By Mary Hartwell. New York, G. W. Carleton & co.; London, S. Low, son & co., 1875.
2 p. 1., [9]-196 p. front., plates.   18 1/2 cm.
Includes also "Old Gargoyle" and "The man who 'hadn't time'."

8958 Cazneau, Jane Maria (McManus) 1807-1878.
Eagle Pass; or, Life on the border, by Cora Montgomery [pseud.] New York, Putnam, 1852.
188 p.   18 cm.

8959 Celadon, pseud.
The golden age: or, Future glory of North America, discovered by an angel to Celadon, in several entertaining visions. Vision 1 ... By Celadon. [n.p.] 1785.
16 p.   17 1/2 cm.

8960 Chamberlain, Charles, jr.
Put to the test; a novel, by Charles Chamberlain, jr. ... New York, II. L. Ilinton, 1874.
1 p. 1., [vii]-xi, [13]-362 p.   17 1/2 cm.

8961 Chamberlain, Charles, jr.
The servant-girl of the period the greatest plague of life. What Mr. and Mrs. Honeydew learned of housekeeping, by Charles Chamberlain, jr. New York, J. S. Redfield, 1873.
215 p.   18 1/2 cm.

8962 Chamberlain, Nathan Henry, 1830 (ca.)-1901.
The autobiography of a New England farm-house; a book, by N. H. Chamberlain. New York, Carleton, 1865.
365 p.   19 cm.

8963 Chambers, Robert William, 1865-1933.
The conspirators, a romance. New York, Harper & brothers company, 1900.

266 p.   illus.   19 cm.

8964   Chambers, Robert William, 1865-1933.
         The haunts of men, by Robert W. Chambers ... New York,
       Frederick A. Stokes company [c1898]
         5 p. 1., 3-302 p.   19 cm.
         CONTENTS.-The god of battles.-Pickets.-An inter-
       national affair.-Smith's battery.-Ambassador extraordinary.-
       Yo espero.-Collector of the port.-The whisper.-The little
       misery.-Enter the queen.-Another good man.-Envol.
         Imperfect: p. 3-4 wanting.

8965   Chambers, Robert William, 1865-1933.
         The mystery of choice, by Robert W. Chamber ... New
       York, D. Appleton and company, 1897.
         1 p. 1., v-ix, 288 p.   16 1/2 cm.
         CONTENTS.-The purple emperor.-Pompe funèbre.-The
       messenger.-The white shadow.-Passeur.-A matter of
       interest.-Envoi.

8966   Chambers, Robert William, 1865-1933.
         The red republic; a romance of the commune, by Robert
       W. Chambers ... New York [etc.] G. P. Putnam's sons,
       1895.
         viii, 475 p.   20 cm.
         Third of the trilogy: "Lorraine," "Ashes of empire,"
       "The red republic."

8967   The Chameleon; or, The mysterious cruiser! By an old salt,-
       author of "The meteor". [Also, Arnold; or, The British
       spy, signed J. H. I.] New York, Smith, Adams & Smith,
       1848.
         96 p.   23 1/2 cm.

8968   Chandler, Joseph R[ipley] 1792-1880.
         The Beverly family; or, Home influence of religion ...
       by Joseph R. Chandler. Philadelphia, P. F. Cunningham
       & son, 1875.
         viii, 9-166 p.   15 cm.

8969   The Chap-book.
         Stories from the Chap-book; being a miscellany of curious

and interesting tales, histories, &c; newly composed by many
celebrated writers, and very delightful to read. Chicago,
Printed for H. S. Stone & company, 1896.
   5 p. 1., 5-241 p., 1 1.   18 cm.
   On cover: Chap-book stories.
   CONTENTS.-Bates, K. Whither thou goest. An impassable
gulf.-Boyce, N. In a garden.-Channing, G. E. Oreste's
patron.-Cummings, E. The appeal to Anne.-Dorsey, A. V.
The dead oak.-Holloway, W., jr. The making of Monsieur
Lescarbot's ballad.-Lefevre, E. On the brink.-Leland, A.
A woman's life. "When the King comes in."-Pool, M. L.
Mandany's fool.-Ross, C. The way to Constantinople.-
Thanet, Octave [pseud.] The old partisan.

8970 Chapin, Sallie F   (Moore)
        Fitz-Hugh St. Clair, the South Carolina rebel boy: or,
     It is no crime to be born a gentleman. Philadelphia,
     Claxton, Remsen and Haffelfinger, 1872.
        252 p. illus.   19 cm.

8971 [Chaplin, Heman White]
        Five hundred dollars, and other stories of New England
     life. By C. H. W. Boston, Little, Brown and company,
     1887.
        305 p.   20 cm.

8972 [Chaplin, Mrs. Jane (Dunbar)] 1819-1884.
        The convent and the manse. By Hyla [pseud.] ... Boston,
     J. P. Jewett & company; Cleveland, Proctor & Worthington;
     [etc., etc.] 1853.
        iv, [5]-242 p.   19 cm.

8973 Chaplin, Mrs. Jane (Dunbar) 1819-1884.
        Out of the wilderness. By Mrs. Jane Dunbar Chaplin.
     Boston, H. A. Young & co., 1870.
        1 p. 1., [v]-vi, [7]-330 p.   19 cm.
        Published as a serial in the "Watchman and reflector."

8974 Charfield-Taylor, Hobart Chatfield, 1865-
        Two women & a fool, by H. C. Chatfield-Taylor; with
     pictures by C. D. Gibson. Chicago, Stone & Kimball, 1895.

3 p. 1., 232 p. 1 1. front., plates.   17 1/2 cm.
Imperfect: 4 plates wanting.

8975 Chellis, Mary Dwinell.
          ... Bill Drock's investment. By Mary Dwinell Chellis
       ... Boston, H. A. Young & co., [c1869]
          2 p. 1., 337 p. front., plates.   17 1/2 cm. (Added
       t.-p.: The standard series of temperance tales [v. 1])
          Series title also at head of t.-p.
          Added t.-p., engr.

8976 Chellis, Mary Dwinell.
          Father Merrill ... By Mary Dwinell Chellis ...
       Boston, I. P. Warren [c1872]
          1 p. 1., 410 p. front., plates.   18 cm. (Added
       t.-p.: $500 prize series of illustrated books)
          Added t.-p. in red and black.

8977 Chellis, Mary Dwinell.
          The hermit of Holcombe. By Mary Dwinell Chellis ...
       Boston, H. A. Young & co., [c1871]
          336 p. front., plates.   17 1/2 cm. (Added t.-p.:
       The standard series of temperance tales [v. 4])
          Added t.-p., engraved.

8978 Chellis, Mary Dwinell.
          ... Mark Dunning's enemy. By Mary Dwinell Chellis
       ... Boston, H. A. Young & co., [c1870]
          1 p. 1., 363 p. front., plates.   17 cm. (Added t.-p.:
       The standard series of temperance tales [v. 3])
          Series title also at head of t.-p.
          Added t.-p., engr.

8979 Chellis, Mary Dwinell.
          Molly's Bible ... Boston, H. A. Young & Co., 1870.
          404 p. illus.

8980 Chellis, Mary Dwinell.
          ... The old doctor's son. By Mary Dwinell Chellis ...
       Boston, H. A. Young & co., [c1870]
          2 p. 1., 354 p. front., plates.   17 1/2 cm. (Added
       t.-p.: The standard series of temperance tales [v.2])

Series title also at head of t. -p.
Added t. -p. , engr.

8981 Chellis, Mary Dwinell.
Out of the fire. By Mary Dwinell Chellis ... New York,
National temperance society and publication house, 1869.
420 p. front. , plates. 17 cm.

8982 Chellis, Mary Dwinell.
The temperance doctor. By Mary Dwinell Chellis ...
New York, National temperance society and publication
house, 1868.
370 p. front. 16 1/2 cm.

8983 Chellis, M[ary] D[winell]
Wealth and wine. By Miss M. D. Chellis ... New York,
National temperance society and publication house, 1874.
iv, 5-337 p. front. 17 1/2 cm.

8984 Cheney, Mrs. Harriet Vaughan (Foster)
The rivals of Acadia, an old story of the New world.
Boston, Wells and Lilly, 1827.
2 p. 1. , [13]-271 p. 18 cm.

8985 Chesebro', Caroline, 1825-1873.
The children of light; a theme for the time, by Caroline
Chesebro'. New-York, Redfield, 1853.
374 p. 19 1/2 cm.

8986 Chesebro', Caroline, 1825-1873.
The foe in the household. By Caroline Chesebro' ...
Boston, J. R. Osgood and company, 1871.
114 p. 23 1/2 cm.

8987 Chesebro', Caroline, 1825-1873.
Peter Carradine; or, The Martindale pastoral, by Caroline
Chesebro' ... New York, Sheldon & company; Boston,
Gould & Lincoln, 1863.
vi, [7]-399 p. 19 1/2 cm.

8988 Chesebro', Caroline, 1825-1873.
Philly and Kit; or, Life and raiment, by Caroline

Chesebro' ... New York, Redfield, 1856.
342 p.   18 1/2 cm.

8989 Child, Mrs. Lydia Maria (Francis) 1802-1880.
       Autumnal leaves: tales and sketches in prose and rhyme.
       By L. Maria Child ... New York, Boston, C. S. Francis
       & co. , 1857.
       365 p.   17 1/2 cm.

8990 Child, Mrs. Lydia Maria (Francis) 1802-1880.
       The coronal. A collection of miscellaneous pieces,
       written at various times. By Mrs. Child ... Boston,
       Carter and Hendee, 1832.
       3 p. l. , [v]-vi, 285 p.   front.   17 x 10 cm.

8991 Child, Mrs. Lydia Maria (Francis) 1802-1880.
       Fact and fiction: a collection of stories. By L. Maria
       Child ... New York, C. S. Francis & co.; Boston, J. H.
       Francis, 1846.
       282 p.   18 1/2 cm.
       CONTENTS. -The children of Mount Ida -The youthful
       emigrant. -The quadroons. - The Irish heart. -A legend of the
       apostle John. -The beloved tune. -Elizabeth Wilson. -The
       neighbour-in-law. -She waits in the spiritland. -A poet's
       dream of the soul. -The black Saxons. -Hilda Silfverling. -
       Rosenglory. -A legend of the Falls of St. Anthony. -The
       brothers.

8992 [Child, Mrs. Lydia Maria (Francis)] 1802-1880.
       Hobomok, a tale of early times. By an American ...
       Boston, Cummings, Hilliard & co. , 1824.
       iv, [5]-188 p.   17 1/2 cm.

8993 Child, Mrs. Lydia Maria (Francis) 1802-1880.
       Philothea. A romance ... By Mrs. Child ... 2d ed.
       Boston, Otis, Broaders & company, 1839.
       2 p. l. , [vi]-viii, [9]-284 p.   19 cm.

8994 [Child, Mrs. Lydia Maria (Francis)] 1802-1880.
       The rebels; or, Boston before the revolution. By the
       author of Hobomok ... Boston, Cummings, Hilliard,
       and company, 1825.

vi, [7]-304 p.   18 1/2 cm.

8995 Child, Mrs. Lydia Maria (Francis) 1802-1880.
          A romance of the republic, by L. Maria Child. Boston,
     Ticknor and Fields, 1867.
          2 p. 1. , 442 p.   18 1/2 cm.

8996 Childe, Edward Vernon, 1804-1861.
          Edward Vernon; my cousin's story. By E. V. Childe ...
     New York, Harper & brothers, 1848.
          194 p.   19 cm.

8997 Chiles, Rosa Pendleton.
          Down among the crackers. By Rosa Pendleton Chiles.
     Cincinnati, The Editor publishing co. , 1900.
          vi p. , 1 1. , 328 p.   22 1/2 cm.

8998 Choat, J   F
          George Welding; or, Crime and its consequences ... By
     Rev. J. F. Choat ... Cincinnati, H. M. Rulison [1859]
          cover-title, 3-32 p. illus.   22 1/2 cm.

8999 The Christian Indian; or, Times of the first settlers ...
          The first of a series of American tales. New York,
     Collins & Hannay [etc.] 1825.
          251 p.   19 cm.

9000 A chronicle of Louisiana: being an account of one of the wars
     of Don Diego Rosa, called IIe, of the iron arm, the last
     Catholic governor of that province. Paraphrased from the
     Spanish of the learned doctor Frai Pedro Prado [pseud.]
     New-York, Linen & Fennell, 1838.
          xiv, [13]-87 p. front. , pl.   23 cm.

9001 [Church, Pharcellus] 1801-1886.
          Mapleton; or, More work for the Maine law ... Boston,
     Jenks, Hickling and Swan, 1853.
          vi, [7]-432 p.   19 cm.

9002 Churchill, Winston, 1871-1947.
          The celebrity, an episode, by Winston Churchill. New
     York, London, The Macmillan co. , 1898.

3 p. 1. , 302 p.   19 cm.

9003 Churchill, Winston, 1871-1947.
       Richard Carvel, by Winston Churchill ... With illustra-
       tions by Carlton T. Chapman and Malcolm Fraser. New
       York, London, The Macmillan company, 1899.
       xiii, 538 p. front. , plates.   20 cm.

9004 Clack, Mrs. Louise.
       Our refugee household, by Mrs. Louise Clack ... New
       York, Blelock & co. , 1866.
       226 p.   17 1/2 cm.

9005 Claremont; or, The undivided household. Philadelphia,
       Parry and McMillan, 1857.
       viii, [9]-206 p.   19 1/2 cm.

9006 [Clark, Charles Heber] 1841-1915.
       Out of the hurly-burly; or, Life in an odd corner. By
       Max Adeler [pseud.] with nearly four hundred illustrations
       by Arthur B. Frost, Fred B. Schell, Wm. L. Sheppard
       and Ed. B. Bensell. Philadelphia, "To-day" publishing
       company, 1874.
       398 p. incl. front. , illus. , plates.   19 cm.
       Added t. -p. , illus.

9007 Clark, George Edward.
       Seven years of a sailor's life. By George Edward Clark.
       "Yankee Ned" ... Boston, Adams & company, [1867]
       6 p. 1. , [11]-358 p. ix pl. (incl. front.)   19 1/2 cm.

9008 [Clark, John A   ]
       A young disciple. A novel. New York, W. B. Smith & co.
       [c1882]
       441 p.   19 1/2 cm.

9009 Clark, S   W
       From the sublime to the ridiculous. By S. W. Clark, ...
       Chicago, Ill. , 1875.
       101 p.   19 cm.

9010 Clark, S   W

Happy home, woman's rights, and divorce, by S. W.
Clark, Minneapolis ... Chicago, Ill., 1875.
45 p. illus.   19 1/2 cm.

9011 [Clark, William Adolphus] 1825-1906.
Agnes Farriday; or, The harlot's friend ... New York,
F. A. Brady [1869]
301 p. front.   19 1/2 cm.

9012 Clark, Willis Gaylord, 1808-1841.
The literary remains of the late Willis Gaylord Clark.
Including the Ollapodiana papers, the Spirit of life, and a
selection from his various prose and poetical writings.
Edited by Lewis Gaylord Clark. New York, Burgess,
Stringer & co., 1844.
480 p.   23 cm.
"Memoir of Willis Gaylord Clark": p. [5]-16.

9013 [Clarke, E   G   H   ]
Lovers and thinkers. A novel. By Hewes Gordon [pseud.]
... New York, Carleton, 1865.
1 p. 1., 5-287 p.   19 cm.

9014 Clarke, Mrs. Henry Steele.
"Their children." By Mrs. Henry Steele Clarke ...
Boston, D. Lothrop & co., [1875]
414 p. front., plates.   18 cm.

9015 Clay, Josephine Russell.
Some little of the angel still left; a novel, by Mrs. J. M.
Clay ... Cincinnati, R. Clarke & co., 1893.
242 p.   19 1/2 cm.

9016 Clay, Josephine Russell.
Uncle Phil; a novel, by Mrs. John M. Clay ... 2d and rev.
ed. New York [etc.] The Abbey press [c1901]
271 p. port.   20 1/2 cm.

9017 Claytor, Graham, 1852-
Pleasant Waters: a story of southern life and character.
By Graham Claytor ... Philadelphia, J. B. Lippincott
company, 1888.

215 p.   18 cm.

9018 Claytor, Graham, 1852–
         Wheat and tares. A novel. By Graham Claytor ... Phila-
      delphia, J. B. Lippincott company, 1889.
         2 p. l., 7-273 p.   19 cm.

9019 Cleary, Kate M
         Like a gallant lady, by Kate M. Cleary ... Chicago.
      Way & Williams, 1897.
         3 p. l., 292 p., 1 l.   18 cm.

9020 Clemens, Jeremiah, 1814–1865.
         Bernard Lile; an historical romance, embracing the periods
      of the Texas revolution, and the Mexican war. By the Hon.
      Jeremiah Clemens. Philadelphia, J. B. Lippincott & co.,
      1856.
         2 p. l., ix-xii, [13]-287 p.   19 cm.

9021 Clemens, Jeremiah, 1814–1865.
         Mustang Gray: a romance. By the Hon. Jeremiah
      Clemens ... Philadelphia. J. B. Lippincott & co., 1858.
         vii. 13-206 p.   18 1/2 cm.

9022 Clemens, Jeremiah, 1814–1865.
         The rivals: a tale of the times of Aaron Burr and Alexander
      Hamilton. By Hon. Jere. Clemens ... Philadelphia,
      J. B. Lippincott & co., 1860.
         1 p. l., v-xi, 13-286 p.   19 1/2 cm.
         Published in 1900 under title: An American colonel.

9023 Clemens, Jeremiah, 1814–1865.
         Tobias Wilson: a tale of the great rebellion. By Hon. Jere.
      Clemens. Philadelphia. J. B. Lippincott & co., 1865.
         viii, 9-328 p.   18 cm.

9024 [Clemens, Samuel Langhorne] 1835–1910.
         The American claimant, by Mark Twain [pseud.] New
      York, C. L. Webster & co., 1892.
         4 p. l., xi-xv, 17-277 p. incl. front., illus. 21 cm.

9025 [Clemens, Samuel Langhorne] 1835–1910.

A book for an hour, containing choice reading and character sketches. A curious dream, and other sketches, rev. and selected for this work by the author Mark Twain [pseud.] Also, examples of microscopic printing, being the smallest type matter ever printed-reducing the contents of a newspaper sheet to less than a single page of this book. New York [Ennis brothers, printers] 1873.

    63, [1] p.   22 1/2 cm.

Advertising matter, containing illustrations, interspersed.

Illustrated blue paper covers, with title: Fun, fact, and fancy: a collection of original comic sketches ...

Contains Mark Twain's Curious dream, My late senatorial secretaryship, The new crime, Back from "Yurrup", More distinction, A, self-made man (1st edition)

9026 [Clemens, Samuel Langhorne] 1835-1910.

The celebrated jumping frog of Calaveras County, and other sketches. By Mark Twain [pseud.] Edited by John Paul [pseud.] New York, C. H. Webb, 1867.

    198 p.   17 1/2 cm.

Not the first issue according to M. Johnson's Bibliography of Mark Twain, 1910, p. 2.

9027 Clemens, Samuel Langhorne, 1835-1910.

The innocents abroad; or, The new Pilgrim's progress; being some account of the steamship Quaker City's pleasure excursion to Europe and the Holy land; with descriptions of countries, nations, incidents, and adventures as they appeared to the author ... By Mark Twain (Samuel L. Clemens) ... Hartford, American publishing company; [etc., etc.] 1869.

    xviii, [19]-651 p. front., illus., plates.   22 cm.

9028 [Clemens, Samuel Langhorne] 1835-1910.

The man that corrupted Hadleyburg, and other stories and essays, by Mark Twain [pseud.] ... New York and London, Harper & bors., 1900.

    5 p. 1., 398 p. front., plates, port.   20 1/2 cm.

CONTENTS. -That man that corrupted Hadleyburg. -My début as a literary person. - From the "London times" of 1904. -At the appetitecure. -My first lie, and how I got out of it. -Is he living or is he dead ?-The Esquimau maiden's

romance. -How to tell a story. -About play-acting. -Concerning
the Jews. -Stirring times in Austria. -The Austrian Edison
keeping school again. -Travelling with a reformer. -Private
history of the "Jumping frog" story. -My boyhood dreams.

9029 [Clemens, Samuel Langhorne] 1835-1910.
Merry tales, by Mark Twain [pseud.] New York, C. L.
Webster & co., 1892.
vi p., 1 1., 9-209 p.   18 1/2 cm.   (Half-title: Fiction,
fact, and fancy ser.)
First edition.
CONTENTS. -The private history of a campaign that failed. -
The invalid's story. -Luck. -The captain's story. -A curious
experience. -Mrs. McWilliams and the lightning. -Meister-
schaft.

9030 [Clemens, Samuel Langhorne] 1835-1910.
The £ 1,000,000 bank-note, and other new stories, by
Mark Twain [pseud.] New York, C. L. Webster & company,
1893.
3 p. 1., 9-260 p. front.   20 cm.
CONTENTS. -The £ 1,000,000 bank-note. -Mental tele-
graphy. -A cure for the blues. -The enemy conquered. -
About all kinds of ships. -Playing courier. -The German
Chicago. -A petition to the Queen of England. -A majestic
literary fossil.

9031 [Clemens, Samuel Langhorne] 1835-1910.
Personal recollections of Joan of Arc. By the Sieur Louis
de Conte [pseud.] (her page and secretary) Freely translated
out of the ancient French into modern English from the
original unpublished manuscript in the national archives of
France, by Jean François Alden. Illustrated from original
drawings by F. V. Du Mond ... New York, Harper &
brothers, 1896.
xiv p., 1 1., 461 p. incl. front. plates.   19 1/2 cm.

9032 Clemens, Samuel Langhorne, 1835-1910.
Punch, brothers, punch! and other sketches. By Mark
Twain [pseud.] New York, Slote, Woodman & co. [1878]
140 p. illus.   16 cm.
First edition?

CONTENTS. -Punch, brothers, punch! -Speech on the weather at the New England society's seventy-first annual dinner. -Rogers. -Map of Paris (with map)-Random notes of an idle excursion. -Speech at a dinner of the Knights of St. Patrick. -An encounter with an interviewer. -The loves of Alonzo Fitz Clarence, etc. -Canvasser's tale.

9033 [Clemens, Samuel Langhorne] 1835-1910.
The stolen white elephant, etc. , by Mark Twain [pseud.]
Boston, J. R. Osgood and company, 1882.
306 p.   17 1/2 cm.
First edition.

9034 [Clemens, Samuel Langhorne] 1835-1910.
Tom Sawyer abroad. Tom Sawyer, detective, and other stories, etc. , etc; by Mark Twain [pseud.] ... New York, Harper & brothers, 1896.
vii, 410 p. front. , illus. , plates.   20 cm.

9035 Clemens, Samuel Langhorne 1835-1910.
A true story, and The recent carnival of crime. By Mark Twain [pseud.] Boston, J. R. Osgood and company, 1877.
92 p. incl. front. , plates.   12 1/2 cm. [Vest-pocket series of standard and popular authors]
First edition.

9036 Cleveland, Cecilia Pauline, 1850-
The story of a summer; or, Journal leaves from Chappaqua. By Cecilia Cleveland. New York, G. W. Carleton & co.; [etc. , etc] 1874.
274 p. incl. front. , illus. plates.   15 cm.

9037 Cleveland, Cynthia E[loise]
His honor; or, Fate's mysteries. A thrilling realistic story of the United States army. By Cynthia E. Cleveland ... New York, The American news company, 1889.
258 p. front. , plates.   20 cm.

9038 [Cleveland, Cynthia Eloise]
See-saw, or Civil service in the departments. By one of'm ... Detroit, Mich. , F. B. Dickerson & co. , 1887.

226 p.   21 cm.

9039 Cleveland, Rose Elizabeth, 1846-1918.
          The long run, by Rose Elizabeth Cleveland. Detroit, Mich.,
      F. B. Dickerson & co., 1886.
          1 p. l., 9-146 p.   19 cm.

9040 Clewline, Frank, pseud.
          The Nautilus, or, The American privateer. A tale of
      land and sea during the last war. By Frank Clewline
      [pseud.] Boston, F. Gleason, 1847
          1 p. l., [5]-50 p.   23 cm.

9041 [Clift, William] b. 1817.
          The Tim Bunker papers; or, Yankee farming. By Timothy
      Bunker [pseud.] ... With illustrations by Hoppin. New York,
      O. Judd and company [c1868]
          314 p. incl. front. plates.   19 1/2 cm.

9042 Cline, A   J
          Henry Courtland; or, What a farmer can do. By A. J.
      Cline. Philadelphia, J. B. Lippincott & co., 1870.
          398 p.   19 1/2 cm.

9043 Clinton, Park.
          Glanmore: a romance of the revolution, by Park Clinton.
      New York, Stearns and company [c1853]
          102 p.   24 cm.
          Cover-title: Glanmore, the bandit of Saratoga lake.

9044 [Clippinger, John Albert]
          Sam Johnson: the experience and observations of a rail-
      road telegraph operator. By Samson [pseud.] New York,
      W. J. Johnston, 1878.
          177 p.   20 cm.

9045 Clouston, Mrs. [Adella] Octavia, 1864-
          What would the world think? A novel. By Octavia
      Clouston ... New York, The Dodworth publishing house
      [c1897]
          2 p. l., 7-283 p.   20 cm.

9046 [Chute, Oscar]
  The blessed bees, by John Allen [pseud.] New York,
  G. P. Putnam's sons, 1878.
    169 p.   17 cm.

9047 Coakley, Timothy Wilfred.
  Keef; a life-story in nine phases, by Timothy Wilfred
  Coakley. With illustrations by Ritchie. Boston, C. E.
  Brown & co., 1897.
    2 p. l., 151, [1] p. front., plates.   17 1/2 cm.

9048 Coale, Mrs. James Carey.
  The cottage by the sea, by Mrs. James Carey Coale.
  Baltimore, J. Murphy & company, 1896.
    186 p.   19 cm.

9049 Cobb, Cyrus, 1834-1903.
  The veteran of the Grand army. A novel. By the brothers
  Cobb... Boston, C. and D. Cobb, 1870.
    384 p. front.   20 cm.

9050 Cobb, Sylvanus, 1823-1887.
  The child of the bay; or, The old sailor's protégé. A tale
  of England, India, and the ocean. By Sylvanus Cobb, jr.
  Boston, F. Gleason, 1852.
    1 p. l., [7]-100 p.   24 1/2 cm.

9051 Cobb, Sylvanus, 1823-1887.
  The Golden Eagle; or, The privateer of '76. A tale of
  the revolution. By Sylvanus Cobb, jr. Boston, F. Gleason,
  1850.
    1 p. l., [7]-100 p.   25 1/2 cm.

9052 Cobbe, William Rosser, d. 1907.
  Doctor Judas. A portrayal of the opium habit, by William
  Rosser Cobbe ... Chicago, S. C. Griggs and company, 1895.
    320 p.   19 1/2 cm.

9053 Cochran, Katherine Madison.
  Poise; or, From reveille to retreat. An army story.
  By Mrs. M. A. Cochran ... Cincinnati, The Robert Clarke
  company, 1896.

194 p. illus. 21 cm.

9054 Cocke, James R
      Blind leaders of the blind: the romance of a blind lawyer.
      By James R. Cocke ... Boston, Lee and Shepard, 1896.
      487 p. front. (port.) 19 1/2 cm.

9055 [Codman, John] 1814-1900.
      Sailors' life and sailors' yarns, by Captain Ringbolt
      [pseud.] New York, C. S. Francis & co.; Boston, J. H.
      Francis, 1847.
      4 p. 1., [13]-252 p. 17 1/2 cm.

9056 [Coe, Mrs. Caroline L (Capron)] 1831-
      The charity "boom". By the author of "Me" ... Fair
      ed. [New York] Hahnemann hospital free bed fund associ-
      ation, 1880.
      70 p. incl. front., plates. 18 cm.

9057 Coffin, Charles Carleton, 1823-1896.
      Caleb Krinkle. A story of American life, by Charles
      Carleton Coffin, "Carleton" ... Boston, Lee and Shepard;
      New York, Lee, Shepard, and Dillingham, 1875.
      vii, 500 p. 19 cm.
      Published in 1894 under title: Dan of Millbrook.

9058 Coffin, Charles Carleton, 1823-1896.
      Daughters of the revolution and their times, 1769-1776;
      a historical romance by Charles Carleton Coffin. Boston
      and New York, Houghton, Mifflin and company [c1895]
      vii p., 2 1., 387 p. front., illus., plates, ports. 20 cm.
      "Ninth thousand."

9059 [Coffin, Robert Barry] 1826-1886.
      Castles in the air, and other phantasies. By Barry
      Gray [pseud.] ... New York, Hurd and Houghton, 1871.
      x, 352 p. 18 1/2 cm.
      These stories appeared originally in "Harper's monthly
      magazine", "Harper's bazaar", and other magazines.
      CONTENTS.-Castles in the air.-Broken sheaves and
      bitter almonds.-Wild oats and apple-blossoms.-Around
      the mahogany.-Musidora and my southern maid.-Model

yound ladies.

9060 [Coffin, Robert Barry] 1826-1886.
   Matrimonial infelicities, with an occasional felicity, by
way of contrast. By an irritable man. To which are added,
as being pertinent to the subject, My neighbors, and Down
in the valley. By Barry Gray [pseud.] New York, Hurd
and Houghton; Boston, E. P. Dutton and company, 1865.
   1 p. 1., [v]-x, 269 p.   19 cm.

9061 [Coffin, Robert Barry] 1826-1886.
   My married life at Hillside. By Barry Gray [pseud.]
New York, Hurd and Houghton, 1865.
   3 p. 1., [v]-xv, 290 p. plates.   19 cm.
   Added t.-p., illustrated.

9062 [Coffin, Robert Barry] 1826-1886.
   Out of town. A rural episode, by Barry Gray [pseud.] ...
New York, Hurd and Houghton, 1866.
   x, 311 p. front., plates.   19 cm.

9063 Coggeshall, William Turner, 1824-1867.
   Easy Warren and his contemporaries: sketched for home
circles, by William Turner Coggeshall. New York,
Redfield, 1854.
   viii p., 1 1., [11]-332 p.   19 cm.
   Short stories.

9064 Cogswell, Frederick Hull, 1859-1907.
   The regicides. A tale of early colonial times, by Frederick Hull Cogswell. New York, Colonial publishing co.,
1896.
   363, vi p.   19 cm.

9065 [Cohen, Alfred J   ] 1861-1928.
   His own image. A novel, by Alan Dale [pseud.] ...
New York, G. W. Dillingham co., 1899.
   1 p. 1., 5-310 p.   20 cm.

9066 [Cohen, Alfred J   ] 1861-1928.
   ... Jonathan's home, by Alan Dale [pseud.] ... Bristol,
J. W. Arrowsmith; London, Simpkin, Marshall & co., 1885.

iv, 160 p.   16 1/2 cm. (Arrowsmith's Bristol
library, v. 7)

9067 Colburn, Mrs. Frona Eunice Wait (Smith) 1859-
          Yermah the Dorado, by Frona Eunice Wait [pseud.] ...
       San Francisco, W. Doxey, 1897.
          vi, 350 p. front. (double map)   19 1/2 cm.

9068 [Cole, Cornelius] 1822-1924.
          California three hundred and fifty years ago. Manuelo's
       narrative, tr. from the Portuguese, by a pioneer. San
       Francisco, S. Carson & co.; New York, C. T. Dillingham,
       1888.
          333 p. front.   20 cm.
          Preface signed: Escritor [pseud.]

9069 Cole, Cyrus.
          The auroraphone. A romance, by Cyrus Cole. Chicago,
       C. H. Kerr & company, 1890.
          249 p.   18 1/2 cm.

9070 [Cole, William Morse] 1866-
          An old man's romance; a tale, written by Christopher
       Craigie [pseud.] Boston, Copeland and Day, 1895.
          3 p. 1., 215 p.   15 1/2 cm.

9071 Coleman, William Macon, 1838-
          The wandering Jew in America. A novel, by William
       Macon Coleman. Washington, D. C., J. G. Hester
       [c1875]
          iv, [5]-57 p.   22 1/2 cm.

9072 Colesworthy, D[aniel] C[lement] 1810-1893.
          The old bureau, and other tales. By D. C. Colesworthy
       ... Boston, Antique book store, 1861.
          iv. [5]-408 p.   19 1/2 cm.

9073 Collingwood, Herbert Winslow, 1857-
          Andersonville violets. A story of northern and southern
       life, by Herbert W. Collingwood. Boston, Lee and Shepard;
       New York, C. T. Dillingham, 1889.
          vii, 270 p.   19 cm.

9074 [Collins, Clarence B   ]
　　　 Tom and Joe. Two farmer boys in war and peace and love.
　　 A Louisiana memory. Richmond, Va., E. Waddey, 1890.
　　　　 259 p. front. (port.)   20 cm.
　　　 Author's name on back of cover.

9075 [Collins, J   L   ]
　　　 Queen Krinaleen's plagues; or, How a simple people were
　　 destroyed. A discourse in the twenty-second century, by
　　 "Jonquil" [pseud.] ... New York, American news company,
　　 1874.
　　　　 151 p.   17 1/2 cm.

9076 [Collins, J   L   ]
　　　 Was she engaged? By "Jonquil" [pseud.] Philadelphia,
　　 J. B. Lippincott & co., 1871.
　　　　 339 p.   18 1/2 cm.

9077 Collins, Mrs. Jane S
　　　 Free at last. By Mrs. Jane S. Collins ... Pittsburgh,
　　 Press of Murdoch, Keer & co., 1896.
　　　　 208 p. incl plates, ports. front.   18 1/2 cm.

9078 Collins, P   V
　　　 A country romance. By P. V. Collins ... Milwaukee,
　　 Wis., J. H. Yewdale & sons co., 1896.
　　　　 5 p. l., 138 p. incl. front., illus., plates.   15 x 12 cm.
　　　 Advertising medium of the J. I. Case threshing machine co.

9079 Colter, [Hattie E   ] "Mrs. J. J. Colter."
　　　 A gentle benefactress, by Mrs. J. J. Colter ... Boston,
　　 D. Lothrop company [c1892]
　　　　 2 p. l., 9-329 p. front., plates.   19 1/2 cm.

9080 Colter, [Hattie E   ] "Mrs. J. J. Colter."
　　　 Medoline Selwyn's work. By Mrs. J. J. Colter ... Boston,
　　 I. Bradley & co. [c1889]
　　　　 395 p.   18 cm.

9081 Coltharp, Jeannette Downes.
　　　 Burrill Coleman, colored. A tale of the cotton fields.
　　 By Jeannette Downes Coltharp. Franklin, O., The Editor

publishing company, 1896.
315 p.　　19 cm.

9082　Colton, Arthur Willis, 1868-
Bennie Ben Cree; being the story of his adventure to
southward in the year '62, by Arthur Colton.　New York,
Doubleday & McClure co. , 1900.
4 p. 1. , 138 p.　　16 1/2 cm.

9083　Colville, William Wilberforce Juvenal, 1862-1917.
Dashed against the rock, a romance of the coming age, by
W. J. Colville ... Boston, Colby & Rich, 1894.
310 p.　6 diagr.　　19 1/2 cm.

9084　Comer, Mrs. Cornelia Atwood (Pratt)
A book of martyrs, by Cornelia Atwood Pratt.　New York,
C. Scribner's sons, 1896.
6 p. 1. , [3]-179 p.　　16 1/2 cm.　(On cover: The
ivory series)
Reprinted in part from various periodicals.
CONTENTS. -Witherle's freedom. -Serene's religious
experience; an inland story. -An instance of chivalry. -
A consuming fire. -An unearned reward. -Hardesty's
cowardice. -"The honor of a gentleman. "-Rivals. -At the
end of the world.

9085　Comer, Mrs. Cornelia Atwood (Pratt)
The daughter of a stoic, by Cornelia Atwood Pratt.　New
York, Macmillan and co. ; London, Macmillan & co. , ltd. ,
1896.
2 p. 1. , 179 p.　　17 1/2 cm.

9086　Comfield, Mrs. Amelia Stratton.
Alida; or, Miscellaneous sketches of occurrences during
the late American war.　Founded on fact.　By an unknown
author.　New York, Printed for the author, 1841.
vii, 222 p. , 1 1. incl. front.　　16 cm.

9087　Comfort, Will Levington, 1878-
Trooper tales; a series of sketches of the real American
private soldier, by Will Levington Comfort.　New York,
Street & Smith [c1899]

ix p. , 1 1. , [13]-248 p. front. , plates.   18 1/2 cm.
CONTENTS. -The new recruit in the black cavalry. -The
silent trooper. -The degeneration of Laddie. -Toreador the
game one. -The wooing of Benito. -Two women and a soldier. -
Red Brennan of the Seventh. -A soldier of misfortune. -
Shadow and the Cherub. -Back to San Anton'. -The voice in
the fourth cell. -The good which was in him. -The aberration
of Private Brown. -The last cell to the right. -The fever's
fifth man. -The story of a cavalry horse. -A soldier and a man.

9088 [Comins, Elizabeth Barker]
The Hartwell farm. By Laura Caxton [pseud.] Illustrated
by the author. Boston, Loring [c1871]
200 p. front. , plates.   19 cm.

9089 Commelin, Anna Olcott.
Not in it. By Anna Olcott Commelin ... New York,
Fowler & Wells co. ; [etc. , etc. c1897]
iv, [5]-96 p.   20 cm.

9090 Comstock, William, 1804-1882.
The life of Samuel Comstock, the terrible whaleman. Containing an account of the mutiny, and massacre of the officers
of the ship Globe, of Nantucket; with his subsequent adventures, and his being shot at the Mulgrave Islands. Also,
Lieutenant Percival's voyage in search of the survivors.
Boston, J. Fisher, 1840.
xvi, 115 p. illus.   19 cm.

9091 Cone, John A[lbert] 1860-1928.
A musical reformation, by John A. Cone. New York
[etc.] The Abbey press [1900]
95 p.   20 1/2 cm.
CONTENTS. -A musical reformation. -"My escape from
suicide."-A strange adoption. -Mr Brett's excursion. -A
spoiled story. -A natural conclusion. -The new minister. -
His "week off. "
"Five of the stories in this volume originally appeared
in 'The Lewiston Jounral'. "

9092 The confessions of a convict. Edited by Julian Hawthorne.
Illustrations from life. Philadelphia, R. C. Hartranft,

1893.
    288 p. incl. front., illus., plates.   19 1/2 cm.
    Introduction signed "19,759."
    "The other side," introduction signed S. P.: p. [225]-288.

9093 Connelly, Emma M
    Tilting at windmills, a story of the Blue Grass country;
by Emma M. Connelly ... Boston, D. Lothrop company
[c1888]
    439 p. incl. front.   19 cm.

9094 Connelly, Emma M
    Under the surface. By Emma M. Connelly. Philadelphia,
J. B. Lippincott & co., 1873.
    332 p.   19 cm.

9095 Converse, Clarence Conyers.
    Mr. Isolate of Lonelyville, by C. C. Converse. New
York, R. H. Russell, 1899.
    2 p. 1., 3-140 p. illus.   22 1/2 cm.

9096 Converse, Florence, 1871-
    The burden of Christopher, by Florence Converse.
Boston and New York, Houghton, Mifflin and company, 1900.
    5 p. 1., [3]-315, [1] p.   19 cm.

9097 Converse, Florence, 1871-
    Diana Victrix: a novel, by Florence Converse. Boston and
New York, Houghton, Mifflin and company, 1897.
    viii, 362 p.   18 1/2 cm.

9098 Converse, James Booth, 1844-1914.
    Uncle Sam's Bible; or, Bible teachings about politics,
by James B. Converse ... Chicago, The Schulte publishing
company, [1899]
    230 p. col. front.   20 cm.

9099 Conway, Clara L
    Life's promise to pay. A novel. By Clara L. Conway ...
Philadelphia, J. B. Lippincott & co., 1876.
    294 p.   19 cm.

9100 Conway, Katherine Eleanor, 1853-1927.
    The way of the world and other ways; a story of our set,
by Katherine E. Conway. Boston, The Pilot publishing
company, 1900.
        3 p. l., 251 p.   20 cm.

9101 Conway, Moncure Daniel, 1832-1907.
    ... Prisons of air, by Moncure D. Conway ... New York,
J. W. Lovell company [c1891]
        270 p.   19 cm. (American authors' series, no. 35)

9102 Conway, William B
    The cottage on the cliff; a tale of the revolution. By
William B. Conway ... Ebensburg, Pa., J. Morgan, 1838.
        v, [7]-144 p.   14 1/2 cm.

9103 [Cook, Mrs. Mary Louise (Redd)]
    Ante bellum. Southern life as it was. By Mary Lennox
[pseud.] Philadelphia, J. B. Lippincott & co., 1868.
        vii, 9-322 p.   19 1/2 cm.

9104 Cooke, John Esten, 1830-1886.
    Canolles: the fortunes of a partisan of '81, by John Esten
Cooke. Detroit, E. B. Smith & company, 1877.
        313 p.   19 cm.

9105 Cooke, John Esten, 1830-1886.
    Doctor Vandyke. A novel. By John Esten Cooke ... New
York, D. Appleton and company, 1872.
        142 p. front., plates.   23 1/2 cm.

9106 Cooke, John Esten, 1830-1886.
    Ellie; or, The human comedy. By John Esten Cooke ...
With illustrations after designs by Strother. Richmond [Va.]
A. Morris, 1855.
        1 p. l., 576 p. front., plates.   19 1/2 cm.
        Added t.-p., engraved.

9107 [Cooke, John Esten] 1830-1886.
    ... Fanchette. By one of her admirers. Boston, J. R.
Osgood and company, 1883.
        iv, 369 p.   17 1/2 cm. (Round-Robin series. [v. 15])

9108　Cooke, John Esten, 1830-1886.
　　　　　Henry St. John, gentleman, of "Flower of Hundreds," in
　　　the county of Prince George, Virginia. A tale of 1774-'75 ...
　　　By John Esten Cooke ... New York, Harper & brothers,
　　　1859.
　　　　　xv, [17]-503 p.　　　20 cm.
　　　　　Published also under title: Bonnybel Vane.

9109　Cooke, John Esten, 1830-1886.
　　　　　The last of the foresters; or, Humors on the border; a
　　　story of the old Virginia frontier. By John Esten Cooke ...
　　　New-York, Derby & Jackson; Cincinnati, H. W. Derby &
　　　co., 1856.
　　　　　vi, [7]-419 p.　　　19 1/2 cm.

9110　Cooke, John Esten, 1830-1886.
　　　　　Mr. Grantley's idea, by John Esten Cooke ... New York,
　　　Harper & brothers, 1879.
　　　　　1 p. l., [7]-154 p.　　　13 cm. (On cover: Harper's half-
　　　hour series, v. 103)

9111　Cooke, John Esten, 1830-1886.
　　　　　My lady Pokahontas. A true relation of Virginia. Writ
　　　by Anas Todkill, puritan and pilgrim [pseud.] With notes
　　　by John Esten Cooke. Boston, New York, Houghton,
　　　Mifflin and company, 1885.
　　　　　vi, 190 p.　　　18 cm.

9112　Cooke, John Esten, 1830-1886.
　　　　　Out of the foam. A novel. By John Esten Cooke ... New
　　　York, Carleton [etc., etc.] 1871.
　　　　　viii, 9-349 p.　　　18 1/2 cm.
　　　　　First edition.

9113　Cooke, John Esten, 1830-1886.
　　　　　Pretty Mrs. Gaston, and other stories. By John Esten
　　　Cooke ... New York, O. Judd company [c1874]
　　　　　288 p. incl. front.　　　19 cm.
　　　　　CONTENTS.-Pretty Mrs. Gaston.-Annie at the corner.-
　　　The wedding at Duluth.

9114　Cooke, John Esten, 1830-1886.

Professor Pressensee, materialist and inventor: a story, by John Esten Cooke ... New York, Harper & brothers, 1878.
1 p. l. , [7]-133 p. 13 cm. (On cover: Harper's half-hour series, v. 78)

9115 Cooke, John Esten, 1830-1886.
The Virginia Bohemians; a novel, by John Esten Cooke ... New York, Harper & brothers, 1880.
1 p. l. , [7]-233 p. 24 cm. (On cover: Harper's library of American fiction, no. 14)

9116 [Cooke, John Esten] 1830-1886.
The Virginia comedians: or, Old days in the Old Dominion. Ed. from the mss. of C. Effingham, esq. [pseud.] ... New York [etc.] D. Appleton and compnay, 1854.
2 v. 19 1/2 cm.

9117 Cooke, John Esten, 1830-1886.
Wearing of the gray; being personal portraits, scenes and adventures of the war. By John Esten Cooke ... New York, E. B. Treat & co.; Baltimore, J. S. Morrow [etc., etc.] 1867.
xvi, [17]-564, [585]-601 p. front. , plates, 7 port. on 1 pl. 22 cm.
"The lapse of twenty pages after 564 is accounted for by omitting to number the illustrations in their order."
cf. Note, p. 564.

9118 Cooke, John Esten, 1830-1886.
The youth of Jefferson; or, A chronicle of college scrapes at Williamsburg, in Virginia, A. D. 1764 ... New York, Redfield, 1854.
249 p. 20 cm.

9119 Cooke, Mrs. Rose (Terry) 1827-1892.
The deacon's week. By Rose Terry Cooke. Boston, Mass. , J. A. Whipple, Gospel book and tract depository [188-?]
18 p. 12 cm.

9120 Cooke, Mrs. Rose (Terry) 1827-1892.
Huckleberries gathered from New England hills. By Rose

Terry Cooke. Boston and New York, Houghton, Mifflin and company, 1891.
    4 p. 1., 343 p.   18 cm.
    CONTENTS.-Grit.-Mary Ann's mind.-Love.-Old Miss Todd.-An old fashioned thanksgiving.-Hopson's choice.-Clary's trial.-A double thanksgiving.-Home again.-How Cella changed her mind.-A town mouse and a country mouse.

9121 Cooke, Mrs. Rose (Terry) 1827-1892.
    Somebody's neighbors, by Rose Terry Cooke. Boston, J. R. Osgood and company, 1881.
    3 p. 1., 421 p.   20 cm.
    Twelve sketches, reprinted from Harper's magazine, the Atlantic monthly, the Galaxy and Putnam's monthly.

9122 Cooke, Mrs. Rose (Terry) 1827-1892.
    The sphinx's children and other people's, by Rose Terry Cooke ... Boston, Ticknor and company, 1886.
    484 p.   19 1/2 cm.
    Eighteen short stories chiefly reprinted from the Atlantic monthly, Harper's magazine and the Galaxy.

9123 Cooley, Alice (Kingsbury) 1840-
    ... Asaph: an historical novel. By Alice Kingsbury Cooley. New York, United States book company [c1890]
    229 p.   18 1/2 cm. (American authors series, no. 33)

9124 Cooley, Ellen Hodges.
    The boom of a western city, by Ellen Hodges Cooley ... Boston, Lee and Shepard, 1897.
    3 p. 1., 89 p.   19 cm. (The hearthstone series)

9125 Cooley, William Forbes, 1857-
    Emmanuel; the story of the Messiah, by William Forbes Cooley ... New York, Dodd, Mead and company, 1889.
    viii, 546 p.   19 cm.

9126 [Coombs, Mrs. Anne Sheldon]
    As common mortals. A novel. New York, Cassell & co. [1886]
    2 p. 1., vii, [9]-404 p.   19 1/2 cm.

9127 [Cooper, James Fenimore] 1789-1851.
      Afloat and ashore; or, The adventures of Miles Wallingford.
By the author of "The two admirals," "Pilot" [etc.] ...
Philadelphia, The author, 1844.
      4 v. in 2.   17 1/2 cm.
      First edition.

9128 [Cooper, James Fenimore] 1789-1851.
      The bravo: a tale. By the author of "The spy," "The Red
rover," "The water-witch," &c. ... Philadelphia, Carey
& Lea, 1831.
      2 v.   18 cm.
      First edition.

9129 [Cooper, James Fenimore] 1789-1851.
      The chainbearer; or, The Littlepage manuscripts. Ed. by
the author of "Satanstoe," "Spy" ... New York, Burgess,
Stringer & co., 1845.
      2 v.   20 cm.
      First edition.

9130 [Cooper, James Fenimore] 1789-1851.
      The deerslayer; or, The first war-path, a tale. By the
author of "The last of the Mohicans," "The pathfinder" ...
Philadelphia, Lea & Blanchard, 1841.
      2 v.   18 cm.
      First edition.

9131 [Cooper, James Fenimore] 1789-1851.
      The headsman; or, The abbaye des vignerons. A tale.
By the author of the "Bravo," &c. &c. ... Philadelphia,
Carey, Lea & Blanchard, 1833.
      2 v.   18 cm.

9132 [Cooper, James Fenimore] 1789-1851.
      The heidenmauer; or, The Benedictines. A legend of
the Rhine. By the author of "The prairie", "Red Rover",
"Bravo", &c. ... Philadelphia, Carey & Lea, 1832.
      2 v.   18 cm.
      First edition.

9133 [Cooper, James Fenimore] 1789-1851.

Home as found. By the author of Homeward bound,
The pioneers, &c. &c. ... Philadelphia, Lea & Blanchard,
successors to Carey & co., 1838.
2 v.   19 cm.
First edition.
Sequel to Homeward bound.

9134 [Cooper, James Fenimore] 1789-1851.
Homeward bound; or, The chase. A tale of the sea. By
the author of "The pilot," "The spy," etc. ... Philadelphia,
Carey, Lea & Blanchard, 1838.
2 v.   18 cm.
First edition.
Sequel: Home as found.

9135 [Cooper, James Fenimore] 1789-1851.
Jack Tier; or, The Florida reef. By the author of "The
pilot", "Red Rover' ... New York, Burgess, Stringer &
co., 1848.
2 v.   20 cm.
First edition.
Originally published in Graham's magazine under the title
of "Rose Budd".

9136 [Cooper, James Fenimore] 1789-1851.
Lionel Lincoln; or, The leaguer of Boston ... By the
author of the Pioneers, Pilot, &c. ... New York, C. Wiley,
1825, '24.
2 v.   19 cm.
First edition.

9137 [Cooper, James Fenimore] 1789-1851.
Lionel Lincoln; or, The leaguer of Boston ... By the
author of "The spy" ... A new ed. Philadelphia, Lea
& Blanchard, 1847, '43.
2 v.   19 cm.
Covers dated: 1843.
1st edition, 1825.

9138 [Cooper, James Fenimore, 1789-1851.
The monikins; ed. by the author of "The spy" ... Philadelphia, Carey, Lea & Blanchard, 1835.

2 v.   18 cm.
First edition.

9139 Cooper, James Fenimore, 1789-1851.
      Ned Myers; or, A life before the mast. Ed. by J.
      Fenimore Cooper ... Philadelphia, Lea and Blanchard,
      1843.
            3, iv-vii, 9-232 p.   19 1/2 cm.
            First edition.

9140 [Cooper, James Fenimore] 1789-1851.
      The oak openings; or, The bee-hunter. By the author of
      "The pioneers," "Last of the Mohicans" ... New York,
      Burgess, Stringer & co., 1848.
            2 v.   19 1/2 cm.
            First edition.

9141 [Cooper, James Fenimore] 1789-1851.
      The pathfinder; or, The inland sea. By the author of "The
      pioneers," "Last of the Mohicans," "Prairie," &c. ...
      Philadelphia, Lea and Blanchard, 1840.
            2 v.   18 cm.
            First edition.

9142 [Cooper, James Fenimore] 1789-1851.
      The pilot; a tale of the sea. By the author of The pioneers.
      &c. ... New-York, C. Wiley, 1823.
            2 v.   20 cm.
            First edition.

9143 [Cooper, James Fenimore] 1789-1851.
      The pioneers; or, The sources of the Susquehanna; a
      descriptive tale. By the author of "The spy" ... Philadelphia,
      Carey & Lea, 1832.
            2 v.   18 cm.

9144 [Cooper, James Fenimore] 1789-1851.
      The prairie; a tale. By the author of the "Pioneers and
      The last of the Mohicans" ... Philadelphia, Carey & Lea,
      1833.
            2 v.   20 cm.

9145 [Cooper, James Fenimore] 1789-1851.
  Precaution, a novel ... New-York, A. T. Goodrich & co.,
1820.
  2 v. 18 cm.
  First edition.

9146 [Cooper, James Fenimore] 1789-1851.
  Precaution. A novel. By the author of the "Spy,"
"Pioneer," &c. ... A new ed., rev. by the author ...
Philadelphia, Lea & Blanchard, successors to Carey & co.,
1839.
  2 v. 19 cm.

9147 [Cooper, James Fenimore] 1789-1851.
  The Red Rover, a tale. By the author of "The spy," "The
pilot," "The prairie," &c. ... London, H. Colburn, 1828.
  3 v. 20 1/2 cm.

9148 [Cooper, James Fenimore, 1789-1851.
  The redskins; or, Indian and Injin: being the conclusion
of the Littlepage manuscripts. By the author of "The
pathfinder," "Deerslayer" ... etc. New York, Burgess &
Stringer, 1846.
  2 v. 20 cm.
  First eidtion.

9149 [Cooper, James Fenimore] 1789-1851.
  Satanstoe; or, The Littlepage manuscripts. A tale of the
colony. By the author of "Miles Wallingford", "Pathfinder",
&c. ... New York, Burgess, Stringer & co., 1845.
  2 v. 20 cm.
  First edition.
  A description of Westchester County, New York.

9150 [Cooper, James Fenimore] 1789-1851.
  The sea lions; or, The lost sealers. By the author of
"The crater", etc. ... New York, Stringer & Townsend,
1849.
  2 v. 20 cm.
  First edition.

9151 [Cooper, James Fenimore] 1789-1851.

The spy: a tale of the neutral ground ... By the author of
"Precaution" ... Philadelphia, Carey, Lea, & Carey, 1829.
2 v.   17 cm.
Vol. 1: 7th edition: v. 2: 6th edition.

9152 [Cooper, James Fenimore] 1789-1851.
The two admirals. A tale. By the author of "The pilot",
"Red rover" ... Philadelphia, Lea and Blanchard, 1842.
2 v.   19 cm.

9153 [Cooper, James Fenimore] 1789-1851.
The ways of the hour; a tale. By the author of "The spy,"
"The red rover," &c., &c. ... New York, G. P. Putnam,
1850.
vii, 9-512 p.   20 cm. (Added t.-p.: The works of
J. Fenimore Cooper...)

9154 [Cooper, James Fenimore] 1789-1851.
The wept of Wish-ton-wish: a tale; by the author of the
Pioneers, Prairie, &c. &c. ... Philadelphia, Carey,
Lea & Carcy, 1829.
2 v.   18 cm.
First edition.
Published in 1849 under title: The borderers.

9155 [Cooper, James Fenimore] 1789-1851.
The wept of Wish-ton-wish: a tale; by the author of the
Pioneers, Prairie, &c. &c. ... Philadelphia, Carey, Lea
& Carey, 1832.
2 v.   18 cm.
First published, 1829.
Published also under titles: The borderers, and The
Heathcotes.

9156 [Cooper, James Fenimore] 1789-1851.
The Wing-and-wing; or, Le Feu-follet; a tale, by the
author of "The pilot", "Red Rover" ... etc. Philadelphia,
Lea and Blanchard, 1842.
2 v.   19 cm.
First edition.
Published in 1845 under title: The Jack o'lantern.

9157 [Cooper, James Fenimore] 1789-1851.
  Wyandotté, or, The hutted knoll. A tale, by the author of
  "The Pathfinder", "Deerslayer" ... etc. Philadelphia, Lea
  and Blanchard, 1843.
      2 v.   19 cm.
      First edition.

9158 [Cooper, Mrs. Jennie]
  Those orphans; or, The trials of a stepmother. Cleveland,
  O., W. W. Williams, 1883.
      337 p. pl.   22 cm.

9159 Cooper, S   M
  Life in the forest; or, The trials and sufferings of a
  pioneer. By S. M. Cooper. Philadelphia, Perry and Erety,
  1854.
      2 p. l., [vii]-viii. [9]-155 p. front.   15 1/2 cm.

9160 [Cooper, Samuel Williams] 1860-
  The confessions of a society man; ed. by Miss Blanche
  Conscience [pseud.] A novel ... New York and Chicago,
  Bedford, Clarke & co., 1887.
      1 p. l., [7]-266 p. front., plates.   19 cm.

9161 Cooper, Samuel Williams, 1860-
  Three days. A midsummer love-story. By Samuel
  Williams Cooper ... Philadelphia, J. B. Lippincott
  company, 1889.
      155 p. front., 7 pl.   19 1/2 cm.

9162 Copcutt, Francis.
  Leaves from a bachelor's book of life. By Francis
  Copcutt. New York, S. A. Rollo, 1860.
      250 p.   20 cm.
      CONTENTS.-The raven.-Seeking dinner under difficulties.-
  Charlotte May.-The admirality papers.-A day in the Dead-
  letter office.-Fire! Fire!-Edith.

9163 [Coppinger, J   B   ]
  The renegade. A tale of real life. New York, Sherman &
  co., 1855.
      2 p. l., 235 p.   20 1/2 cm.

9164 Corbin, Austin, jr.
      Mneomi; or, The Indian of the Connecticut. By Austin
Corbin, jr. Boston, Gleason's publishing hall, 1847.
      1 p. 1., [5]-50 p.   22 1/2 cm.

9165 Corbin, Mrs. Caroline [Elizabeth] (Fairfield) 1835-
      His marriage vow. By Mrs. Caroline Fairfield Corbin
... Boston, Lee and Shepard, 1874.
      1 p. 1., 5-328 p.   17 1/2 cm.

9166 Corbin, Mrs. Caroline Elizabeth (Fairfield) 1835-
      Our Bible-class, and the good that came of it. By
Caroline E. Fairfield ... New York, Derby & Jackson, 1860.
      viii, 9-352 p.   19 cm.

9167 [Corcoran, D   ]
      Pickings from the portfolio of the reporter of the New
Orleans "Picayune" ... with original designs, by Felix
O. C. Darley. Philadelphia, Carey and Hart, 1846.
      216 p. plates.   19 cm.
      Added t.-p., illustrated.
      Dedication signed: D. Corcoran.

9168 Cornelius, Mrs. Mary Ann (Mann) 1827-1918.
      Uncle Nathan's farm; a novel, by Mrs. M. A. Cornelius.
Chicago, Laird & Lee, 1898.
      1 p. 1., 318 p. front., pl.   19 1/2 cm.

9169 Cornelius, Mrs. Mary Ann (Mann) 1827-1918.
      The white flame [an occult story] by Mary A. Cornelius
... Chicago, Stockham publishing co. [c1900]
      402 p. incl. front.   20 cm.

9170 Cornell, Lillian.
      A country girl. [By] Lillian Cornell. New York, The
Irving company [c1896]
      vi, [7]-145 p.   19 cm.

9171 Cornish, William W   M
      Behind plastered walls. A novel, by Wm. W. M. Cornish.
New York, G. W. Dillingham co., 1896.
      228 p.   19 cm.

9172 Cornwallis, Kinahan, 1839-1917.
 Adrift with a vengeance: a tale of love and adventure, by
 Kinahan Cornwallis. New York, Carleton [etc., etc.] 1870.
 319 p.   18 1/2 cm.

9173 Corwin, Charles Edward, 1868-
 Onesimus: Christ's freedman; a tale of the Pauline Epistles,
 by Charles Edward Corwin ... Chicago, New York, Fleming
 H. Revell company [c1900]
 2 p. 1., 9-11 p., 2 1., 12-332 p. front., plates.
 18 1/2 cm.

9174 Cory, Charles Barney, 1857-1921.
 Montezuma's castle, and other weird tales, by Charles B.
 Cory ... Author's ed. Boston [Press of Rockwell and
 Churchill] 1899.
 233 p. front., 1 illus., 8 pl.   20 cm.
 Title-page wanting.
 CONTENTS. -Montezuma's castle. -The amateur champion-
 ship. -The tragedy of the White Tanks. -Too close for comfort. -
 The strange powder of the Jou Jou priests. -An Aztec mummy. -
 A lesson in chemistry. -An interesting ghost. -The mound of
 eternal silence. -The story of a bad Indian. -A queer coin-
 cidence. -The story of an insane sailor. -The elixir of life. -
 The Voodoo idol. -An Arizona episode. -One touch of nature.

9175 Coryell, Eleanor Hooper.
 Out of the past, by Eleanor Hooper Coryell. New York,
 Street & Smith [c1899]
 1 p. 1., [7]-168 p.   18 1/2 cm.
 A story.

9176 Costello, F[rederick] H[ankerson] 1851-
 Master Ardick, buccaneer. By F. H. Costello. New
 York, D. Appleton and company, 1896.
 vi, 311 p.   18 1/2 cm. (Half-title: Appletons' town
 and country library, no. 204)

9177 Cottage piety exemplified. By the author of "Union to Christ,"
 "Love to God," etc. Philadelphia, J. B. Lippincott & co.,
 1869.
 viii, 9-316 p.   18 cm.

9178 [Coulson, George James Atkinson]
   The Clifton picture; a novel. By the author of "The odd
   trump" ... etc. Philadelphia, J. B. Lippincott & co., 1878.
   312 p.   23 cm.   [The "Odd trump" series of novels]

9179 [Coulson, George James Atkinson]
   Flesh & spirit. A novel. By the author of "The odd trump"
   ... etc. New York, E. J. Hale & son, 1876.
   vi, [7]-245 p.   23 1/2 cm.   [The "Odd trump" series of
   novels]

9180 [Coulson, George James Atkinson]
   The ghost of Redbrook; a novel. By the author of "The
   odd trump" ... etc. Philadelphia, J. B. Lippincott & co.,
   1879.
   1 p. l., 7-313 p.   23 1/2 cm.   [The "Odd trump"
   series of novels]

9181 [Coulson, George James Atkinson]
   Harwood. A novel. By the author of "The odd trump."
   New York, E. J. Hale & son, 1875.
   206 p.   23 1/2 cm.   [The "Odd trump" series of
   novels]

9182 [Coulson, George James Atkinson]
   The Lacy diamonds. A novel. By the author of "The odd
   trump" ... etc. New York, E. J. Hale & son, 1875.
   284 p.   23 1/2 cm.   [The "Odd trump" series of
   novels]

9183 [Coulson, George James Atkinson]
   The odd trump. A novel. New York, E. J. Hale & son,
   1875.
   viii, 9-326 p.   23 1/2 cm.   [The "Odd trump"
   series of novels]

9184 Coulter, James W
   The larger faith; a novel, by James W. Coulter. Chicago,
   C. H. Kerr & company, [c1898]
   4 p. l., [11]-285 p.   20 cm.

9185 Courtney, Mrs. Lydia L   D

Pauline's trial; a novel, by Lydia L. D. Courtney ...
New York, G. W. Carleton & co., 1877.
2 p. 1., [7]-341 p.   19 cm.

9186 [Coverdale, Sir Henry Standish] pseud.
       The fall of the great republic. Boston, Roberts brothers,
       1885.
       226 p.   16 1/2 cm.
       Added t.-p. has title: The fall of the great republic (1886-
       88) By Sir Henry Standish Coverdale... New York, 1895.

9187 Cowan, Frank, 1844-1905.
       An American story-book. Short stories from studies of
       life in southwestern Pennsylvania, pathetic, tragic, humorous,
       and grotesque; by Frank Cowan. Greensburg, Pa., 1881.
       3 p. 1., [9]-390 p.   20 cm.

9188 Cowan, James.
       Daybreak; a romance of an old world, by James Cowan;
       with drawings by Walter C. Greenough. New York, G. H.
       Richmond & co., 1896.
       viii, 399 p. front., plates.   19 1/2 cm.

9189 Cowan, John Franklin, 1854-
       Endeavor doin's down to the Corners. By Rev. J. F.
       Cowan ... Boston, D. Lothrop company, 1893.
       2 p. 1., 387 p. front., plates.   18 1/2 cm.

9190 C[owan], P[amela] H
       Aimée's marriage. By P. H. C. ... Philadelphia,
       W. H. Hirst; New York, J. L. Spicer, 1890.
       1 p. 1., 7-534 p.   19 cm.

9191 [Cowdrey, Robert H   ]
       Foiled. By a lawyer. A story of Chicago. Chicago,
       Clark & Longley, printers, 1885.
       1 p. 1., [v]-viii, 9-337 p.   19 1/2 cm.

9192 [Cowley, Mrs. Winifred Jennings]
       Lorin Mooruck; and other Indian stories, by George
       Truman Kercheval [pseud.] Boston, J. S. Smith & co.,
       1888.

112

viii p., 1 1., 97, 27, 21 p.   18 1/2 cm.
CONTENTS.-Lorin Mooruck.-Three men of Wallowa.-
Samuel, an Arapahoe.

9193 Cox, Charlotte Crisman.
Ione. A sequel to "Vashti." By Charlotte Crisman Cox.
Boston, Eastern publishing company, 1900.
v, 6-225 p.   18 1/2 cm.

9194 Cox, M   H
Emily Mayland; or, The faithful governess. By M. H.
Cox ... Philadelphia, Printed by J. B. Rodgers, 1864.
viii, [9]-288 p.   19 1/2 cm.

9195 Coxey, Willard Douglas.
Tales by the way: a little book of odd stories, by Willard
Douglas Coxey ... Chicago, 1898.
75 p.   20 cm.
CONTENTS.-The village coward.-Col. Edgerly's legacy.-
A circus episode.-An aboriginal coquette.-The Lost Creek
claim.-A masquerade.

9196 [Cozzens, Frederick Swartwout] 1818-1869.
Prismatics, by Richard Haywarde [pseud.] Illustrated
with wood engravings from designs by Elliott, Darley,
Kensett, Hicks, and Rossiter ... New York, London, D.
Appleton & company, 1853.
235 p. illus.   20 cm.
Verse and prose.

9197 Cozzens, Frederick Swartwout, 1818-1869.
The sayings of Dr. Bushwhacker, and other learned men,
by Fred. S. Cozzens ... New York, A Simpson & co.,
1867.
2 p. 1., [3]-7 p., 1 1., 213 p.   19 cm.
Title vignette.

9198 Cozzens, Frederick Swartwout, 1818-1869.
The Sparrowgrass papers; or, Living in the country. By
Frederic S. Cozzens ... New York, Derby & Jackson;
Cincinnati, H. W. Derby, 1856.
xii, [13]-328 p. front.   18 cm.

Added t.-p., engraved.

9199 [Cozzens, Samuel Woodworth] 1834-1878.
     Nobody's husband. Boston, Lee and Shepard; New York,
C. T. Dillingham, 1878.
     1 p. 1., 5-258 p.   17 1/2 cm.

9200 Craddock, Florence Nightingale.
     The soldier's revenge; or, Roland and Wilfred, by Florence
Nightingale Craddock ... New York, London [etc.] The
Abbey press [c1900]
     2 p. 1., [vii]-viii, 9-208 p.   20 1/2 cm.

9201 Craig, B   F
     The rough diamond. By B. F. Craig. [Kansas City, Mo.,
Ramsey, Millet & Hudson, 1880]
     214 p. incl. pl.   19 cm.
     Illustrated t.-p.

9202 Craig, Benjamin Franklin, b. 1814.
     The border ruffian; or, Kansas and Missouri. An historical
western story of the present time, with interesting conversations between Jeff and Abe on the subject of slavery. By
B. F. Craig. Cincinnati, For the author, 1863.
     xi, 13-234 p.   18 cm.

9203 Craigie, Mary E
     John Anderson and I. By Mary E. Craigie. Buffalo,
Moulton, Wenborne and company, 1888.
     2 p. 1., [13]-199 p.   18 cm.

9204 Cram, Ralph Adams, 1863-1942.
     ... Black spirits & white. A book of ghost stories, by
Ralph Adams Cram. Chicago, Stone & Kimball, 1895.
     5 p. 1., 150. [1] p.   16 1/2 cm. (Carnation series)
     CONTENTS.-No. 252 rue M. le Prince.-In Kropfsberg
keep.-The white villa.-Sister Maddelena.-Notre Dame des
eaux.-The dead valley.

9205 [Cram, Ralph Adams] 1863-1942.
     The decadent: being the gospel of inaction: wherein are
set forth in romance form certain reflections touching the

curious characteristics of these ultimate years, and the divers causes thereof. [Boston] Priv. print. for the author, 1893.

    2 p. 1., 41, [1] p. front.   21 1/2 cm.

    Colophon: Here ends the gospel of inaction called the Decadent, which is privately issued for the author by Copeland and Day, of Cornhill, Boston, in an edition limited to one hundred and ten copies on this yellow French handmade paper, and fifteen copies on thick Lalanne paper, which have been printed during October and November, MDCCCXCIII by John Wilson and son, Cambridge, at the University press. The frontispiece and initial letters are designed by Bertram Grosvenor Goodhue and cut upon wood by John Sample, jr.

9206 Crane, Clarence.
    In the next generation, and other stories. By Clarence Crane. (1st ed.) Brooklyn, Franklin printing company, 1896.
    3 p. 1., [13]-40 p. front. (port.)   17 1/2 cm.

9207 Crane, James L
    The two circuits. A story of Illinois life, by J. L. Crane. Chicago, Jansen, McClurg & co., 1877.
    xiii, [4], 18-502 p. front., plates.   19 1/2 cm.

9208 Crane, Mrs. L   H
    The startled sewing society, by Mrs. L. H. Crane ... New York and Chicago, F. H. Revell company [c1891]
    1 p. 1., 25 p.   18 1/2 cm.

9209 Crane, Stephen, 1871-1900.
    Active service; a novel. New York, F. A. Stokes Co. [c1899]
    345 p.   20 cm.

9210 Crane, Stephen, 1871-1900.
    George's mother. New York, E. Arnold, 1896.
    177 p.   18 cm.

9211 Crane, Stephen, 1871-1900.
    The Little Regiment, and other episodes of the American civil war. New York, D. Appleton, 1896.
    196 p.   19 cm.

CONTENTS.-The Little Regiment.-Three miraculous soldiers.-A mystery of heroism.-An Indiana campaign.-A grey sleeve.-The veteran.

9212 Crane, Stephen, 1871-1900.
Maggie, a girl of the streets. New York, D. Appleton, 1896.
vi, 158 p.   19 cm.

9213 Crane, Stephen, 1871-1900.
The monster and other stories. New York, Harper, 1899.
v, 188 p. illus.   20 cm.
CONTENTS.-The monster.-Blue hotel.-His new mittens.

9214 Crane, Stephen, 1871-1900.
The open boat, and other tales of adventure, by Stephen Crane ... New York, Doubleday & McClure Co., 1898.
3 p. 1., 336 p.   17 cm.
CONTENTS.-The open boat.-A man and some other.-One dash-horses.-Flanagan.-The bride comes to Yellow Sky.-The wise men.-Death and the child.-The five white mice.

9215 Crane, Stephen, 1871-1900.
The third violet, by Stephen Crane ... New York, D. Appleton and company, 1897.
2 p. 1., 203 p.   19 cm.

9216 Crane, Stephen, 1871-1900.
Whilomville stories, by Stephen Crane. Illustrated by Peter Newell. New York and London, Harper & brothers, 1900.
vi p., 1 1., 198, [1] p. front. (port.) 33 pl.   19 1/2 cm.
CONTENTS.-The angel child.-Lynx-hunting.-The lover and the tell-tale.-"Showin' off."-Making an orator.-Shame.-The carriage-lamps.-The knife.-The stove.-The trial, execution, and burial of Homer Phelps.-The fight.-The city urchin and the chaste villagers.-A little pilgrimage.

9217 Crane, Stephen, 1871-1900.
Wounds in the rain; war stories, by Stephen Crane ... New York, Frederick A. Stokes company [c1900]

4 p. 1., 347 p.   19 1/2 cm.
     CONTENTS. -The price of the harness. -The lone charge
of William B. Perkins. -The clan of No-name. -God rest ye,
merry gentlemen. -The revenge of the Adolphus.-The
sergeant's private madhouse. -Virtue in war. -Marines
signalling under fire at Guantanamo. -This majestic lie. -
War memories. -The second generation.

9218 [Craven, Braxton] 1822-1882.
     Mary Barker, by Charlie Vernon [pseud.] 2d ed. Raleigh,
N. C., Branson & Farrar, 1865.
     72 p.   19 cm.
     On cover: Mary Barker, a thrilling narrative of early life
in North Carolina.
     Advertising matter: p. [71]-72.

9219 Crawford, Francis Marion, 1854-1909.
     Adam Johnstone's son, by F. Marion Crawford ... New
York, Macmillan and co; London, Macmillan & co., ltd.,
1896.
     viii, 281 p. front., plates.   19 1/2 cm.

9220 Crawford, Francis Marion, 1854-1909.
     A cigarette-maker's romance, by F. Marion Crawford ...
London and New York, Macmillan and co., 1890.
     2 p. 1., 265 p.   19 1/2 cm.

9221 Crawford, Francis Marion, 1854-1909.
     Corleone, a tale of Sicily, by F. Marion Crawford ...
New York, Macmillan and col; London, Macmillan & co.,
ltd., 1896.
     2 v.   18 cm.

9222 Crawford, Francis Marion, 1854-1909.
     Doctor Claudius, a true story by F. Marion Crawford ...
New York, Macmillan and co., 1883.
     3 p. 1., 353 p.   19 cm.

9223 Crawford, Francis Marion, 1854-1909.
     Don Orsino, by F. Marion Crawford ... New York and
London, Macmillan and co., 1892.
     2 p. 1., 448 p.   19 cm.

A sequel to Saint' Ilario.

9224 Crawford, Francis Marion, 1854-1909.
Greifenstein, by F. Marion Crawford ... New York and
London, Macmillan and co. , 1893.
3 p. 1. , 385 p.   19 1/2 cm.

9225 Crawford, Francis Marion, 1854-1909.
In the palace of the king; a love story of old Madrid, by
F. Marion Crawford ... New York, London, The Macmillan
company, 1900.
viii p. , 1 1. , 367 p. front. , plates.   19 1/2 cm.

9226 Crawford, Francis Marion, 1854-1909.
Love in idleness. A Bar Harbour tale, by F. Marion
Crawford ... New York and London, Macmillan and
company, 1894.
2 p. 1. , 230 p.   13 1/2 cm.

9227 Crawford, Francis Marion, 1854-1909.
Marzio's crucifix, by F. Marion Crawford ... London
and New York, Macmillan and co. , 1892.
2 p. 1. , 250 p   19 1/2 cm.

9228 Crawford, Francis Marion, 1854-1909.
Mr. Isaacs, a tale of modern India by F. Marion Crawford
... New York and London, Macmillan and co. , 1892.
2 p. 1. , 320 p. front. (port.)   19 1/2 cm.

9229 Crawford, Francis Marion, 1854-1909.
A Roman singer, by F. Marion Crawford ... Boston,
Houghton, Mifflin and company, 1884.
378 p.   18 1/2 cm.

9230 Crawford, Francis Marion, 1854-1909.
A rose of yesterday, by F. Marion Crawford. New York,
The Macmillan company; London, Macmillan & co. , ltd. ,
1897.
2 p. 1. , 218 p.   19 1/2 cm.

9231 Crawford, Francis Marion, 1854-1909.
Saracinesca, by F. Marion Crawford ... New York,
Macmillan and co. , 1897.

3 p. 1. , 450 p.   19 cm.

9232 Crawford, Francis Marion, 1854-1909.
    A tale of a lonely parish, by F. Marion Crawford ... New
York and London, Macmillan and co. , 1893.
    3 p. 1. , 385 p.   19 1/2 cm.

9233 Crawford, Francis Marion, 1854-1909.
    Taquisara, by F. Marion Crawford ... New York and
London, Macmillan and co. , 1895.
    2 v.   18 cm.

9234 Crawford, Francis Marion, 1854-1909.
    To leeward, by F. Marion Crawford ... Boston,
Houghton, Mifflin and company, 1884.
    411 p.   18 1/2 cm.

9235 Crawford, Francis Marion, 1854-1909.
    Via crucis; a romance of the second crusade, by Francis
Marion Crawford ... illustrated by Louis Loeb. New York,
The Macmillan company; London, Macmillan & co. , ltd. ,
1899.
    v, 396 p.   plates.   20 cm.

9236 Crawford, Francis Marion, 1854-1909.
    With the immortals, by F. Marion Crawford ... New York
and London, Macmillan and co. , 1893.
    3 p. 1. , 312 p.   19 1/2 cm.
    "New edition."

9237 Crawford, Francis Marion, 1854-1909.
    Zoroaster, by F. Marion Crawford ... London and New
York, Macmillan and co. , 1892.
    3 p. 1. , 290 p.   19 1/2 cm.

9238 Crawford, T[heron] C[lark]
    The disappearance syndicate and Senator Stanley's story.
[Also, Napoleon Wolff and his newspaper of the future] By
T. C. Crawford ... New York, C. B. Read, 1894.
    241 p. front. , illus.   19 cm.

9239 Creamer, Hannah Gardner.

Delia's doctors; or, A glance behind the scenes. By
Hannah Gardner Creamer ... New York, Fowler and Wells,
1852.
262 p.   19 cm.

9240 Creamer, Hannah Gardner.
Eleanor; or Life without love. By Hannah Gardner
Creamer ... Boston, J. French, 1850.
202 p.   20 cm.

9241 Crim, Miss Matt.
Elizabeth, Christian scientist; by Matt Crim ... New
York, C. L. Webster & co., 1893.
3 p. 1., 9-350 p.   19 cm.

9242 [Crippen, William G   ] 1820-1863.
Green peas, picked from the patch of Invisible Green,
esq. ... New York, Livermore and Rudd; Cincinnati, Moore,
Wilstach, Keys and Overend [c1856]
311 p. illus.   20 cm.

9243 Crist, Mrs. Maley (Bainbridge)
Patchwork; the poems and prose sketches of Maley
Bainbridge Crist. Atlanta, The Martin & Hoyt company,
1898.
xiii, 15-238 p. front., plates, ports.   19 1/2 cm.

9244 Criswell, R   W
Grandfather Lickshingle, by R. W. Criswell ... New
York, J. W. Lovell company [1884]
1 p. 1., [v]-vii, [11]-208 p. incl. illus., pl.   18 1/2 cm.
(On cover: Lovell's library. v. 7 no. 350)

9245 Criswell, Robert.
"Uncle Tom's cabin" contrasted with Buckingham hall, the
planter's home, or, A fair view of both sides of the slavery
question. By Robert Criswell ... New York, D. Fanshaw.
1852.
152 p. front., illus., plates.   19 1/2 cm.

9246 Crittenden, Edward B   bp.
... The entwined lives of Miss Gabrielle Austin, daughter

of the late Rev. Ellis C. Austin, and of Redmond, the outlaw, leader of the North Carolina "moonshiners." Written by Bishop Crittenden, of North Carolina ... Philadelphia, Barclay & co. [c1879]
    1 p. l., 19-80 p. illus., facsim.   24 cm.

9247 [Crocker, Samuel]
    That Island, by Theodore Oceanic Islet [pseud.] A political romance ... Kansas City, Mo, Press of the Sidney F. Woody printing co., c1892.
    156 p.   17 cm.
    Author's name written in ink on t.-p.

9248 Crofton, Francis Blake, 1841-
    The bewildered querists and other nonsense. By Francis Blake Crofton. New York, G. P. Putnam's sons, 1875.
    127 p.   19 1/2 cm.

9249 Crosby, G[eorge] S
    The mystery; or, Platonic love. By G. S. Crosby ... Philadelphia, J. B. Lippincott & co., 1875.
    564 p, incl. front. plates.   19 cm.

9250 Cross, Mrs. Jane T   H
    Azile [a novel] By Mrs. Jane T. H. Cross ... Nashville, Tenn., Pub. for the author, by A. H. Redford, 1868.
    251 p.   19 cm.

9251 Cross, Mrs. Jane T   H
    Duncan Adair; or, Captured in escaping. A story of one of Morgan's men. By Mrs. Jane T. H. Cross. Macon, Ga., Burke, Boykin & company, 1864.
    51 p.   18 cm.

9252 Crouch, Julia.
    Three successful girls. By Julia Crouch. New York, Hurd and Houghton, 1871.
    vii, 382 p.   18 1/2 cm.

9253 Crowninshield, Mary (Bradford) "Mrs. Schuyler Crowninshield" d. 1913.
    San Isidro, by Mrs. Schuyler Crowninshield. Chicago &

New York, H. S. Stone & company, 1900.
3 p. l. , 312 p. , 1 l.   19 1/2 cm.

9254 Crowninshield, Mary (Bradford) "Mrs. Schuyler Crowninshield,"
d. 1913.
Where the trade-wind blows; West Indian tales, by Mrs.
Schuyler Crowninshield. New York, London, The Macmillan
company, 1898.
v, 308 p.   19 1/2 cm.
CONTENTS. -Candace. -A Christmas surprise. -Paul
Demarisi's mortgage. -Willie Baker's good sense. -Jones's
new fin-keel. -Flandreau. -The value of a banana leaf. -
Anastrasio's revenge. -Corndeau. -Which of three?-
P'lumero the Good. -Paul's orange grove.

9255 Crozier, Robert Haskins.
Deep waters; or, A strange story; by Rev R. H. Crozier
... St. Louis, Farris, Smith & co. [1887]
iv, 5-367 p.   19 1/2 cm.

9256 Crozier, Robert Haskins.
Golden rule; a tale of Texas, by Rev. R. H. Crozier ...
Richmond, Va. , Whittet & Shepperson, printers, 1900.
179 p.   19 cm.

9257 [Cruger, Julie Grinnell (Storrow)] "Mrs. Van Rensselaer Cruger,"
d. 1920.
A diplomat's diary, by Julien Gordon [pseud.] Philadelphia,
J. B. Lippincott company, 1890.
233 p.   19 cm.

9258 [Cruger, Julie Grinnell (Storrow)] "Mrs. Van Rensselaer Cruger,"
d. 1920.
Eat not thy heart, by Julien Gordon [psued.] Chicago &
New York, H. S. Stone & co. , 1897.
2 p. l. , 319 p. , 1 l.   16 1/2 cm.

9259 [Cruger, Julie Grinnell (Storrow)] "Mrs. Van Rensselaer Cruger,"
d. 1920.
His letters, by Julien Gordon [pseud.] New York, Cassell
publishing company [c1892]
2 p. l. , 280 p.   19 cm.

9260 [Cruger, Julie Grinnell (Storrow)] "Mrs. Van Rensselaer
Cruger"] d. 1920.
Marionettes, by Julien Gordon [pseud.] ... New York,
Cassell publishing company [c1892]
1 p. 1. , 320 p.   19 cm.

9261 [Cruger, Julie Grinnell (Storrow) "Mrs. Van Rensselaer
Cruger"] d. 1920.
Poppaea, by Julien Gordon [pseud.] Philadelphia, J. B.
Lippincott company, 1895.
1 p. 1. , 5-320 p.   20 cm.

9262 [Cruger, Julie Grinnell (Storrow) "Mrs. Van Rensselaer
Cruger"] d. 1920.
A Puritan pagan; a novel, by Julien Gordon [pseud.]
... New York, D. Appleton and company, 1891.
367 p.   19 cm.

9263 [Cruger, Julie Grinnell (Storrow)] "Mrs. Van Rensselaer
Cruger," d. 1920.
A successful man, by Julien Gordon [pseud.] ...
Philadelphia, J. B. Lippincott company, 1891.
2 p. 1. , 7-184 p.   18 1/2 cm.

9264 [Cruger, Julie Grinnell (Storrow)] "Mrs. Van Rensselaer
Cruger," d. 1920.
Vampires; Mademoisclle Réséda, by Julien Gordon [pseud.]
... Philadelphia, J. B. Lippincott company, 1891.
299 p.   18 1/2 cm.

9265 [Cruger, Julien Grinnell (Storrow)] "Mrs. Van Rensselaer
Cruger," d. 1920.
A wedding, and other stories, by Julien Gordon [pseud.]
... Philadelphia, J. B. Lippincott company, 1896.
232 p.   20 cm.
CONTENTS. -A wedding. -The first flight. -Morning mists. -
Conquered. -Raking straws. -The moujik.

9266 Cruger, Mary, 1834-
Brotherhood, by Mary Cruger ... Boston, D. Lothrop
company [c1891]
3 p. 1. , 306 p.   19 cm.

9267 Cruger, Mary, 1834–
    The Vanderheyde manor-house, by Mary Cruger ...
New York, Worthington company [c1887]
    1 p. 1., 323 p.   19 cm.

9268 Crumpton, M   Nataline, 1857–1911.
    The silver buckle; a story of the revolutionary days, by
M. Nataline Crumpton; illustrations by Cornelia E. Bedford.
Philadelphia, H. Altemus [c1899]
    3 p. 1., 5–89 p. front., illus.   21 cm.

9269 [Cruse, Mary Anne]
    Cameron hall: a story of the civil war. By M. A. C. ...
Philadelphia, J. B. Lippincott & co., 1867.
    v, 7–543 p.   20 cm.

9270 Cullen, Clarence Louis, d. 1922.
    Taking chances, by Clarence L. Cullen. New York, G. W.
Dillingham company [1900]
    iv, [5]–269 p.   19 cm. [Dillingham's metropolitan
library, no. 66]

9271 Cullen, Clarence Louis, d. 1922.
    Tales of the ex-tanks: a book of hard-luck stories, by
Clarence Louis Cullen ... New York, Grosset & Dunlap,
1900.
    392 p.   18 1/2 cm.
    "The sketches originally appeared in ... the New York
Sun..."

9272 Culter, Mrs. Mary Nantz (McCrae) 1858–
    Four roads to happiness; a story of Hoosier life, by
Mary McCrae Culter. Philadelphia, The Union press
[c1900]
    312 p. front.   19 cm.

9273 Cummings, Arthur.
    The fall of Kilman Kon. By Arthur Cummings. New York,
G. W. Dillingham, 1889.
    iv, 5–348 p.   19 cm.

9274 [Cummins, Maria Susanna] 1827–1866.

El Fureidis. By the author of "The lamplighter" and "Mabel Vaughan". Boston, Ticknor and Fields, 1860.
iv, 379 p.   18 1/2 cm.

9275 Cunningham, Mrs. B   Sim.
For honor's sake. By Mrs. B. Sim Cummingham ...
Philadelphia, J. B. Lippincott & co., 1879.
1 p. 1., 5-281 p.   19 cm.

9276 Cunningham, Mrs. B.   Sim.
In Sancho Panza's pit. By Mrs. B. Sim Cunningham ...
Philadelphia, J. B. Lippincott & co., 1883.
1 p. 1., 5-295 p.   19 cm.

9277 Curran, John Elliott.
Miss Frances Merley. A novel. By John Elliott Curran.
Boston, Cupples and Hurd, 1888.
viii, 406 p.   16 1/2 cm. (Half-title: Collection of
American authors. American Tauchnitz ed. vol. I)

9278 Curran, Mrs. L   P   M
Eunice Quince; a New England romance. By Dane
Conyngham [pseud.] New York, Lovell, Coryell &
company [c1895]
3 p. 1., 5-362 p.   19 1/2 cm.

9279 Currier, Charles Warren, bp., 1857-1918.
Dimitrios and Irene; or, The conquest of Constantinople,
a historical romance, by Charles Warren Currier ...
Baltimore, Gallery & McCann, 1894.
254 p. front., 2 pl.   19 1/2 cm.

9280 Currier, Charles Warren, bp., 1857-1918.
The rose of Alhama; or, The conquest of Granada. An
episode of the Moorish wars in Spain. By Rev. Charles
Warren Currier ... New York, Christian press association
publishing company, 1897.
1 p. 1., 198 p. front., illus., pl.   19 cm.

9281 Currier, Emma C
Hubbub. A story. By Emma C. Currier ... New York,
The Authors' publishing company [c1880]
234 p.   19 cm.

9282 Currier, Sophronia.
Alice Tracy; or, Faint, yet pursuing. A sketch from real
life ... by Mrs. Sophronia Currier. Boston, E. P. Dutton
and company, 1868.
299 p.   18 1/2 cm.

9283 Curry, Erastus S
The No-din' ; romance, history and science of the pre-
historic races of America and other lands ... by Dr. E. S.
Curry. Christy, Mo., The author, 1899.
4 p. 1., 335, ii, v p. front., illus. (incl. double map)
19 cm.

9284 [Curtis, Mrs. Caroline Gardiner (Cary)] 1827-
From Madge to Margaret, by Carroll Winchester [pseud.]
... Boston, Lee and Shepard; New York, C. T. Dillingham,
1880.
1 p. 1., 5-297 p.   17 1/2 cm.

9285 [Curtis, Mrs. Caroline Gardiner (Cary)] 1827-
The love of a lifetime, by the author of "From Madge to
Margaret" ... Boston, Cupples, Upham and company,
1884.
208 p.   19 1/2 cm.
On cover: The love of a lifetime [by] Carroll Winchester
[pseud.]

9286 Curtis, Emma Ghent.
The administratrix, by Emma Ghent Curtis ... New
York, J. B. Alden, 1889.
373 p.   19 1/2 cm.

9287 Curtis, Emma Ghent.
The fate of a fool. By Emma Ghent Curtis. New York,
J. A. Berry & company, 1888.
202 p.   19 1/2 cm.

9288 [Curtis, George Ticknor] 1812-1894.
John Charáxes: a tale of the civil war in America. By
Peter Boylston [pseud.] Philadelphia, J. B. Lippincott
company, 1889.
289 p.   19 1/2 cm.

9289 [Curtis, George William] 1824-1892.
The Potiphar papers. (Reprinted from "Putnam's monthly")
Illustrated by A. Hoppin. New York, G. P. Putnam and
company, 1853.
1 p. l., vii p., 2 l., 251 p. plates.   19 1/2 cm.
First edition.

9290 Curtis, George William, 1824-1892.
Prue and I. By George William Curtis ... New York,
Dix, Edwards & co., 1856.
ix p., 2 l., [3]-214 p.   19 1/2 cm.

9291 Curtis, George William, 1824-1892.
Trumps. A novel. By George William Curtis ...
Illustrated by Augustus Hoppin. New York, Harper &
brothers [c1861]
1 p. l., [v]-vii, [9]-502 p. front., illus.   19 cm.

9292 Curtis, Newton Mallory.
The bride of the northern wilds. A tale of 1743. By
Newton M. Curtis ... Rev., enl. and cor. New York,
Burgess, Stringer & co., [1843]
120 p.   24 1/2 cm.

9293 Curtis, Newton Mallory.
The doom of the tory's guard. A tale. By Newton M.
Curtis ... Troy, N. Y., L. Willard [1843]
95, [1] p.   24 1/2 cm.

9294 Curtis, Newton Mallory.
The foundling of the Mohawk. A tale of the revolution.
By Newton M. Curtis. New York, Williams brothers, 1848.
89, 7 p.   23 1/2 cm.
CONTENTS. -The foundling of the Mohawk. -The adventures
of a night.

9295 Curtis, Newton Mallory.
The hunted chief; or, The female rancher. A tale of the
Mexican war. By Newton M. Curtis ... New York,
Williams brothers, 1847.
86 p.   24 1/2 cm.

9296 Curtis, Newton Mallory.
        The marksmen of Monmouth: a tale of the revolution. By
    Newton M. Curtis ... Troy, L. Willard [1848]
        127 p.   24 1/2 cm.

9297 Curtis, Newton Mallory.
        The patrol of the mountain. A tale of the revolution.
    By Newton M. Curtis... New York, Williams brothers,
    1847.
        112 p.   25 1/2 cm.

9298 Curtis, Newton Mallory.
        The ranger of Ravenstream. A tale of the revolution.
    By Newton M. Curtis ... New York, Boston, Williams
    brothers, 1847.
        118 p.   25 1/2 cm.

9299 [Cushing, Eliza Lanesford (Foster)] b. 1794.
        Saratoga; a tale of the revolution ... Boston, Cummings,
    Hilliard & co., 1824.
        2 v.   20 1/2 cm.

9300 [Cushing, Eliza Lanesford (Foster)] b. 1794.
        Yorktown: an historical romance ... Boston, Wells and
    Lilly, 1826.
        2 v.   18 1/2 cm.
        Published anonymously.

9301 Custead, Elizabeth.
        Rose and Elza. Songs and stories of bygone days in
    Fayette County and elsewhere. By E. C_____. New York,
    Printed by E. O. Jenkins' sons [c1884]
        596 p. front.   19 cm.

9302 Cutler, Mrs. Hannah Maria (Conant) Tracy, 1815-1896.
        Phillipia, a woman's question. By Mrs. H. M. Tracy
    Cutler ... [Dwight, Ill., The C. L. Palmer printing
    house, c1886]
        183 p.   20 cm.

9303 Cutler, Helen R
        Jottings from life; or, Passages from the diary of an

itinerant's wife. By Helen R. Cutler. Cincinnati, Poe &
Hitchcock, 1864.
    282. p.   18 cm.

9304 Cutler, Mary C
    Philip, or, What may have been; a story of the first century,
by Mary C. Cutler. New York, T. Y. Crowell & co. [c1890]
    237 p.   19 cm.

D

9305 Dabney, Owen P
    True story of the lost shackle; or, Seven years with the
Indians. By Owen P. Dabney. [Salem, Or., Capital
printing co., c1897]
    3 p. l., 98 p. front., illus.   20 cm.

9306 Daggett, Mary (Stewart) 1856-1922.
    Mariposilla; a novel, by Mrs. Charles Stewart Daggett.
Chicago and New York, Rand, McNally & company, 1895.
    268 p.   18 1/2 cm.

9307 Daggett, Rollin Mallory, 1831-1901.
    Braxton's bar. A tale of pioneer years in California.
New York, G. W. Carleton, 1882.
    viii, 453 p. illus.   19 cm.

9308 Dahlgren, Mrs. Madeleine (Vinton) 1825-1898.
    Chim: his Wahsington winter, by Madeleine Vinton
Dahlgren. New York, C. L. Webster & co., 1892.
    334 p. incl. front.   19 1/2 cm.

9309 Dahlgren, Mrs. Madeleine (Vinton) 1825-1898.
    Divorced. A novel. By Madeleine Vinton Dahlgren ...
Chicago and New York, Belford, Clarke & co., 1887.
    212 p.   18 1/2 cm.

9310 Dahlgren, Mrs. Madeleine (Vinton) 1825-1898.

129

Lights and shadows of a life; a novel, by Madeleine Vinton
Dahlgren ... Boston, Ticknor and company, 1887.
v p., 1 1., [9]–400 p.   19 1/2 cm.
First appeared as a serial in "Brooklyn magazine",
1885–86.

9311 Dahlgren, Mrs. Madeleine (Vinton) 1825–1898.
The lost name; a novelette, by Madeleine Vinton Dahlgren
... Boston, Ticknor and company, 1886.
1 p. 1., 222 p.   19 1/2 cm.

9312 Dahlgren, Mrs. Madeleine (Vinton) 1825–1898.
The secret directory. A romance of hidden history.
By Madeleine Vinton Dahlgren. Philadelphia, H. L. Kilner
& co. [c1896]
330 p.   19 1/2 cm.

9313 Dahlgren, Mrs. Madeleine (Vinton)1825–1898.
A Washington winter, by Madeleine Vinton Dahlgren ...
Boston, J. R. Osgood and company, 1883.
247 p.   19 cm.

9314 Daintrey, Laura.
Actaeon. By Laura Daintrey ... New York, The
Empire city publishing company [c1892]
4 p. 1., 280 p.   19 1/2 cm.

9315 Daintrey, Laura.
The arrows of love. By Laura Daintrey ... New York,
G. W. Dillingham, 1893.
3 p. 1., 9-150 p.   17 cm.

9316 Daintrey, Laura.
Eros, by Larua Daintrey ... Chicago, New York [etc.]
Belford, Clarke & co. [c1888]
3 p. 1., 255 p.   19 cm.

9317 Dake, Laura M
The flight of the shadow. By Laura M. Dake. Cincinnati,
The Editor publishing co., 1899.
1 p. 1., 128 p.   18 cm.

9318 Dallas, Mrs. Mary (Kyle) 1830-1897.
      Billtry, by Mary Kyle Dallas ... New York, The Merriam
company [c1895]
      133 p. incl. front., illus., plates.   19 1/2 cm.

9319 Daly, James.
      The little blind god on rails. A romaunt of the gold
Northwest, by James Daly ... [Chicago, Rand, McNally
& co., 1888.
      130 p. illus.   26 1/2 cm.
      A trip on the Chicago & Northwestern Railroad

9320 Damon, Sophie M
      Old New-England days. A story of true life, by Sophie
M. Damon. Boston, Cupples and Hurd, 1887.
      1 p. 1., vi, 434 p.   18 cm.

9321 Dana, Francis.
      Leonora of the Yawmish; a novel, by Francis Dana.
New York, Harper & brothers, 1897.
      xii, 310 p.   19 cm.

9322 Dana, Katharine Floyd.
      Our Phil, and other stories, by Katharine Floyd Dana.
With illustrations by E. W. Kemble. Boston and New
York, Houghton, Mifflin and company, 1889.
      viii, 147 p. incl. illus., plates. front.   18 1/2 cm.
      CONTENTS. -Our Phil. -Aunt Rosy's chest. -Marty's
various mercies.

9323 Dana, Olive E
      Under friendly eaves, by Olive E. Dana ... Augusta,
Maine, Burleigh & Flynt, 1894.
      300 p.   19 cm.

9324 Daniel, Charles S
      Ai; a social vision. By Charles S. Daniel. Boston, Arena
publishing co., 1893.
      1 p. 1., 296 p.   19 1/2 cm.

9325 Daniels, Mrs. Cora Linn (Morrison) 1852-
      As it is to be, by Cora Linn Daniels ... 6th thousand.

Boston, Little, Brown and company, 1900.
xiii, 294 p.   18 cm.

9326 Daniels, Mrs. Cora Linn (Morrison) 1852-
        The bronze Buddha; a mystery, by Cora Linn Daniels ...
    Boston, Little, Brown and company, 1899.
        3 p. l., 295 p.   21 cm.

9327 Daniels, Gertrude Potter.
        Halamar, by Gertrude Potter Daniels. Chicago, New
    York, G. M. Hill company, 1900.
        130 p.   17 x 10 cm.

9328 Dark and terrible deeds of George Lathrop, who, after passing
        through the various degrees of crime, was finally convicted
        and hung in New Orleans, June 5, 1848. For the robbery
        and murder of his father, March 8, 1847. New Orleans,
        W. Stuart, 1848.
        31, [1] p. incl. front., illus., pl.   24 1/2 cm.
        Title vignette.

9329 Darling, Mary Greenleaf.
        Gladys; a romance, by Mary Greenleaf Darling ...
    Boston, D. Lothrop company [c1887]
        304 p.   19 cm. (On cover: The round world series)

9330 Darton, Mrs. Alice Weldon (Wasserbach)
        Hexandria ... By Alice Weldon Wasserbach ... Washing-
    ton, D. C., Pathfinder publishing company, 1894.
        85 p., 1 l. front. (port.)   18 cm.
        Short stories and poems.
        CONTENTS.-In changefulness of mood [poems].-The cause
    of it.-The professor's skylarking.-Death's young.-An Easter
    kind.-A quiver of arrows.-Rica's eyes.

9331 Daughters of AEsculapius; stories written by alumnae and
        students of the Woman's medical college of Pennsylvania,
        and ed. by a committee appointed by the Students' associa-
        tion of the college. Philadelphia, G. W. Jacobs & co.,
        1897.
        155 p. front., 5 pl., port.   18 cm.
        CONTENTS.-The genius maker. Dr. E. M. Hiestand-

Moore. -The domestic and professional life of Ann Preston. -
Dr. Rebecca Moore. -A maiden effort. Julia Grice. -Mater
Dolorosa-Mater Felix. Dr. A. M. Fullerton. -One short hour.
B. R. Slaughter. -"The greatest of these is love." Dr. G. A.
Walker. -Reminiscences of medical study in Europe. Dr. K.
C. (Hurd) Mead. -A psycho-physical study. J. E. Hatton. -Dr.
Honora. Dr. H. A. Hewlings. -The house side. Dr. A. M.
Seabrook.

9332 Davenport, Benjamin Rush.
Anglo-Saxons, onward! A romance of the future, by
Benj. Rush Davenport. Cleveland, O. , Hubbell publishing
company [c1898]
279 p.   19 1/2 cm.

9333 Davidson, Mrs. Margaret (Miller) 1787-1844.
Selections from the writings of Mrs. Margaret M.
Davidson, the mother of Lucretia Maria and Margaret M.
Davidson. With a preface, by Miss C. M. Sedgwick.
Philadelphia, Lea & Blanchard, 1843.
1 p. 1. , [ix]-xiv, [15]-272 p.   19 1/2 cm.

9334 D[avieson], S[arah]
The Seldens in Chicago; a domestic tale, by S. D.
New York, Chicago [etc.] Brentano's, 1889.
189 p.   18 1/2 cm.

9335 Davis, Andrew Jackson, 1826-1910.
Tale of a physician; or, The seeds and fruits of crime ...
By Andrew Jackson Davis. Boston, W. White & company,
1869.
325 p.   19 cm.

9336 Davis, Arline E
The romance of Guardamonte, by Arline E. Davis.
New York, J. S. Tait & son [c1896]
2 p. 1. , [7]-136 p.   18 cm.

9337 [Davis, Charles Augustus] 1795-1867.
Letters of J. Downing, major [pseud.] Downingville
militia, Second brigade, to his old friend, Mr. Dwight, of
the New-York Daily advertiser. New York, Harper &
brothers, 1834.

3 p. 1. , [v]-ix, 270 p. , 1 1. , [4] p. front. , plates.
19 1/2 cm.

Added t. -p. , illustrated.

Binder's title (printed label) Davis. Letters of J. Downing.
Not to be confused with "The select letters of Major Jack
Downing" Philadelphia, 1834, written by Seba Smith and
originally published in the Portland Courier 1830-1833, to
which in the Philadelphia, 1834 edition a few of the Davis
letters to the New York Daily advertiser are added by way of
appendix. cf. J. Williamson, Biblio. of ... Maine (1896)
p. 448 whose Philadelphia, 1831 edition is probably a mis-
print for 1834.

9338 Davis, Edith (Smith) 1859-
Whether white or black, a man, by Edith Smith Davis;
illustrations by Bert Cassidy. Chicago, New York [etc] F.
H. Revell company, 1898.
4 p. 1. , 7-198, [1] p. front. , plates.   19 cm.

9339 Davis, Eliza B
Edith; or, The light of home. By Eliza B. Davis ...
Boston, Crosby, Nichols and company, 1856.
2 p. 1. , 282 p.   19 1/2 cm.

9340 Davis, Ella Harding.
Coranna; a novel, by Ella Harding-Davis. St. Louis,
Nixon-Jones printing co. , 1890.
117 p.   20 1/2 cm.

9341 Davis, Ethel.
When love is done; a novel, by Ethel Davis. Boston, Estes
and Lauriat, 1895.
3 p. 1. , 301 p.   19 cm.

9342 Davis, Mrs. Frankie (Parker)
Kentucky folks and some others; [short stories] by Frankie
Parker Davis. Cincinnati, The editor publishing co. , 1900.
7 p. 1. , 232 p. , 2 1. front. (port.)   21 cm.

9343 [Davis, Frederick William] 1858-
Union down; a signal of distress, by Scott Campbell [pseud.]

Boston, Arena publishing company, 1893.
2 p. l., 368 p.   20 cm.

9344 Davis, Garrett Morrow, 1851–
Hugh Darnaby; a story of Kentucky, by Garrett Morrow
Davis. Washington, D. C., Gibson bros., 1900.
253 p.   19 cm.

9345 Davis, Harold McGill.
The City of Endeavor; a religious novel devoted to the
interests of good citizenship in the city of Brooklyn, N. Y.,
by Harold McGill Davis ... Brooklyn, N. Y., Collins &
Day, 1895.
vii, 98 p. front., plan.   18 1/2 cm.

9346 Davis, Harriet Riddle.
In sight of the goddess; a tale of Washington life, by
Harriet Riddle Davis ...
(In Lippincott's monthly magazine. Philadelphia, 1895.
23 1/2 cm. v. 56, p. [577]–672)

9347 [Davis, Lucius Daniel] 1825–1900.
Life in the itinerancy, in its relations to the circuit and
station, and to the minister's home and family. By one "Who,
long devoted to its toils and cares, enjoys it triumphs-its
reserves shares." New York and Auburn, Miller, Orton &
Mulligan, 1856.
viii, [9]–335 p.   19 1/2 cm.

9348 Davis, Lucius Daniel, 1825–1900.
Life in the laity; or, The history of a station. By Rev.
L. D. Davis ... New York, Published for the author by
Carlton & Porter, 1858.
200 p.   16 cm.

9349 Davis, Mrs. Mary Diuguid.
She waited patiently, by Mrs. Mary Diuguid Davis.
Lynchburg, Va., J. P. Bell company, printers, 1900.
270 p.   20 cm.

9350 Davis, Mrs. Mary Evelyn (Moore) 1852–1909.
The queen's garden, by M. E. M. Davis ... Boston and

New York, Houghton, Mifflin and company, 1900.
3 p. 1. , 142 p. , 1 1.   18 1/2 cm.

9351 Davis, Mrs. Rebecca (Harding) 1831-1910.
Doctor Warrick's daughters; a novel, by Rebecca Harding
Davis ... New York, Harper & brothers, 1896.
3 p. 1. , 301 p. front. , 14 pl.   19 cm.

9352 Davis, Mrs. Rebecca (Harding) 1831-1910.
Frances Waldeaux, a novel by Rebecca Harding Davis ...
Illustrated by T. De Thulstrup. New York, Harper &
brothers, 1897.
3 p. 1. , 207 p. front. , 4 pl.   19 cm.

9353 Davis, Mrs. Rebecca (Harding) 1831-1910.
John Andross [a novel] By Rebecca Harding Davis ...
New York, Orange Judd company [c1874]
324 p. incl. front. , 5 pl.   19 cm.

9354 [Davis, Mrs. Rebecca (Harding)] 1831-1910.
Margret Howth; a story of to-day. Boston, Ticknor and
Fields, 1862.
2 p. 1. , [3]-266 p.   18 1/2 cm.

9355 Davis, Mrs. Rebecca (Harding) 1831-1910.
Silhouettes of American life, by Rebecca Harding Davis.
New York, C. Scribner's sons, 1892.
vii, 280 p.   18 1/2 cm.
CONTENTS. -At the station. -Tirar y Soult. -Walhalla. -
The doctor's wife. -Anne. -An ignoble martyr. -Across the
gulf. -A wayside episode. -Mademoiselle Joan. -The end of
the vendetta. -A faded leaf of history. -The Yares of the
Black mountains. -Marcia.

9356 Davis, Richard Harding, 1864-1916.
Cinderella, and other stories, by Richard Harding Davis ...
New York: Charles Scribner's Sons, 1896.
205 p. front.   20 cm.
CONTENTS. -Cinderella. -Miss Delamar's understudy. -The
editor's story. -An assisted emigrant. -The reported who made
himself king.

9357 Davis, Richard Harding, 1864-1916.
Episodes in Van Bibber's life. By Richard Harding Davis,
New York and London, Harper & brothers, 1899.
3 p. 1., 3-98 p. front.   16 x 8 1/2 cm. [Little books
by famous writters]
These stories are taken from his Van Bibber, and others.
CONTENTS.-Her first appearance.-Van Bibber's man-
servant.-The hungry man was fed.-Love me, love my dog.

9358 Davis, Richard Harding, 1864-1916.
The exiles, and other stories, by Richard Harding Davis
... New York, Harper & brothers, 1894.
5 p. 1., [3]-221 p. front. (port.) 16 pl.   19 cm.
CONTENTS.-The exiles.-The writing on the wall.-The
right of way.-His bad angel.-The boy orator of Zepata
City.-The romance in the life of Hefty Burke.-An anonymous
letter.

9359 Davis, Richard Harding, 1864-1916.
The king's jackal. By Richard Harding Davis; with illustrations by C. D. Gibson. New York, C. Scribner's sons,
1898.
3 p. 1., 175 p. front., 8 pl.   19 cm.

9360 Davis, Richard Harding, 1864-1916.
The lion and the unicorn, by Richard Harding Davis;
illustrated by H. C. Christy. New York, C. Scribner's sons,
1899.
5 p. 1., 204 p. front., 5pl.   19 cm.
CONTENTS.-The lion and the unicorn.-On the fever ship.-
The man with one talent.-The vagrant.-The last ride together.

9361 Davis, Richard Harding, 1864-1916.
The Princess Aline, by Richard Harding Davis ...
illustrated by C. D. Gibson. New York, Harper & brothers,
1895.
2 p. 1., 163 p. front., 10 pl.   19 cm.

9362 Davis, Richard Harding, 1864-1916.
Soldiers of fortune, by Richard Harding Davis; with
illustrations by C. D. Gibson. New York, C. Scribner's
sons, 1897.

4 p. 1. , 348 p. front. , 5 pl.   18 1/2 cm.

9363 Davis, Richard Harding, 1864-1916.
    Van Bibber, and others. By Richard Harding Davis ...
New York, Harper & brothers, 1892.
    5 p. 1. , [3]-249 p. front. , 3 pl.   18 1/2 cm.
    CONTENTS. -Her first appearance. -Van Bibber's man-
servant. -The hungry man was fed. -Van Bibber at the races. -
An experiment in economy. -Mr. Travers's first hunt. -Love
me, love my dog. -Eleanore Cuyler. -A recruit at Christmas. -
A patron of art. -Andy M'Gee's chorus girl. -A Leander of
the East River. -How Hefty Burke got even. -Outside the
prison. -An unfinished story.

9364 Davis, Varina Anne Jefferson, 1864-1898.
    A romance of summer seas; a novel. By Varina Anne
Jefferson-Davis ... New York and London, Harper &
brothers, 1898.
    1 p. 1. , 277, [1] p.   19 cm.

9365 Davis, Varina Anne Jefferson, 1864-1898.
    The veiled doctor; a novel, by Varina Anne Jefferson-
Davis, New York, Harper & brothers, 1895.
    1 p. 1. , 220 p.   19 cm.

9366 Davis, William Stearns, 1877-1930.
    A friend of Caesar; a tale of the fall of the Roman republic,
50-47 B. C. , by William Stearns Davis ... New York, The
Macmillan company; London, Macmillan & co. , ltd. , 1900.
    x p. , 1 1. , 501 p.   20 cm.

9367 [Dayton, Amos Cooper] 1813-1865.
    Theodosia Ernest; or, The heroine of faith. Nashville,
Tenn. , Graves, Marks & Rutland; New York, Sheldon,
Blakeman & co. , 1857.
    2 v. fronts. (ports.) diagrs.   19 cm.
    Vol. I without designation of volume number.
    Vol. II has title: Theodosia Ernest ... or, Ten days' travel
in search of the church.

9368 The debtor's prison: a tale of a revolutionary soldier. To which
are added, Remards on imprisonment for debt, by Doctor

Johnson. New-York, Bliss, Wadsworth & co. , 1835.
iv, [5]-174 p. front.   14 1/2 cm.

9369 De Forest, John William, 1826-1906.
The bloody chasm. A novel. By J. W. De Forest ...
New York, D. Appleton and company, 1881.
301 p.   18 cm.
A later ed. has title: The oddest of courtships.

9370 De Forest, John William, 1826-1906.
Honest John Vane. A story. By J. W. De Forest ... New
Haven, Conn. , Richmond & Patten, 1875.
2 p. 1. , [3]-259 p.   18 cm.

9371 De Forest, John William, 1826-1906.
Overland. A novel. By J. W. De Forest ... New York,
Sheldon and company [1872]
209 p. front. (port.)   23 1/2 cm.

9372 De Forest, John William, 1826-1906.
Seacliff; or, The mystery of the Westervelts. By J. W.
De Forest ... Boston, Phillips, Sampson and company,
1859.
vi, [7]-466 p.   19 1/2 cm.

9373 De Forest, John William, 1826-1906.
The Wetherel affair. By J. W. De Forest ... New York,
Sheldon and company, 1873.
iv, [5]-222 p.   23 1/2 cm.

9374 Deland, Mrs. Margaret Wade (Campbell) 1857-1945.
Good for the soul. New York and London, Harper &
brothers, 1899.
86 p. illus.   17 cm.

9375 Deland, Mrs. Margaret Wade (Campbell) 1857-1945.
John Ward, preacher; by Margaret Deland ... Boston
and New York, Houghton, Mifflin and company, 1888.
2 p. 1. , 473 p.   20 cm.

9376 Deland, Mrs. Margaret Wade (Campbell) 1857-1945.
Old Chester tales, by Margaret Deland; with illustrations

by Howard Pyle. New York and London, Harper & brothers, 1899.
    vii, 359, [1] p. front., plates.   19 cm.
    CONTENTS.-The premises of Dorothea.-Good for the soul.-Miss Maria.-The child's mother.-Justice and the judge.-Where the laborers are few.-Sally.-The unexpectedness of Mr. Horace Shields.

9377 Deland, Mrs. Margaret Wade (Campbell) 1857-1945.
    Philip and his wife, by Margaret Deland ... Boston and New York, Houghton, Mifflin and company, 1894.
    2 p. 1., 438 p.   18 1/2 cm.

9378 Deland, Mrs. Margaret Wade (Campbell) 1857-1945.
    The wisdom of fools, by Margaret Deland. Boston and New York, Houghton, Mifflin and company, 1897.
    3 p. 1., 3-248 p., 1 1.   18 1/2 cm.
    CONTENTS.-Where ignorance is bliss, 't is folly to be wise.-The house of Rimmon.-Counting the cost.-The law, or the gospel?

9379 Delaplain, Sophia, pseud.
    A thrilling and exciting account of the sufferings and horrible tortures inflicted on Mortimer Bowers and Miss Sophia Delaplain, by the Spanish authorities, for the supposed participation with Gen. Lopez in the invasion of Cuba ... By Miss Delaplain. Charleston, S. C., E. E. Barclay; M. B. Crosson & co., 1851.
    31, [1] p. incl. front., illus., pl.   23 cm.
    Illustrated covers.

9380 De Leon, Edwin, 1828-1891.
    Askaros Kassis, the Copt. A romance of modern Egypt. By Edwin De Leon ... Philadelphia, J. B. Lippincott & co., 1870.
    xii, 13-462 p.   18 1/2 cm.

9381 De Leon, Thomas Cooper, 1839-1914.
    Crag-nest. A romance of the days of Sheridan's ride. By T. C. DeLeon ... Mobile, Ala., The Gossip printing co., 1897.
    220 p.   20 1/2 cm.

9382 De Leon, Thomas Cooper, 1839-1914.
Cross purposes. A Christmas experience in seven stages.
By T. C. De Leon ... Illustrated by W. B. Myers. Philadelphia, J. B. Lippincott & co., 1871.
117 p. front. 17 cm.

9383 De Leon, Thomas Cooper, 1839-1914.
John Holden, unionist, a romance of the days of destruction
and reconstruction, by T. C. De Leon ... in collaboration
with Erwin Ledyard ... St. Paul, The Price-McGill company
[c1893]
ix, [11]-338 p. front., plates. 20 cm.

9384 De Leon, Thomas Cooper, 1839-1914.
The Puritan's daughter: [sequel to "Creole and Puritan."]
A character romance of two section. By T. C. De Leon ...
Mobile, Ala., The Gossip printing company, 1891.
173 p. 19 cm.

9385 [De Leon, Thomas Cooper] 1839-1914.
The Rock or the Rye; an understudy. After "The quick or
the dead" ... Mobile, Gossip printing company, 1888.
34 p. 17 cm.

9386 [De Lesdernier, Mrs. Emily Pierpont]
Berenice: a novel. Boston, Phillips, Sampson & company,
1856.
332 p. 19 1/2 cm.

9387 De Lesdernier, Mrs. Emily Pierpont.
Fannie St. John; a romantic incident of the American revo-
lution, by Emily Pierpont Dclesdernier ... New York, Hurd
and Houghton, 1874.
vi, [5]-63 p. 20 1/2 cm.
"In writing this book, by main purpose has been to make
known the rare goodness of heart of my grandfather, Captain
Gustavus Fellowes."-Pref.
Includes an account by Michel Guillaume St. Jean de
Crevècoeur of his separation from his children, Fannie and
Louis, of their rescue by Gustavus Fellowes, and his reunion
with them.

9388 Denison, Charles Wheeler, 1809-1881.
    ... The Yankee cruiser: a story of the war of 1812.
Illustrative of scenes in the American navy. By Charles W.
Denison ... Boston, J. E. Farwell & co. , 1848.
    50 p. incl. pl.   25 cm. (American popular tales.
no. 2)

9389 Denison, Mary (Andrews) "Mrs. C. W. Denison," 1826-1911.
    The lover's trials; or, The days before the Revolution...
Philadelphia, T. B. Peterson & brothers [c1865]
    383 p.   20 cm.
Andros rebellion in 1689.

9390 Denison, Mary (Andrews) "Mrs. C. W. Denison,' 1826-1911.
    Raphael Inglesse; or, The Jew of Milan! A thrilling tale
of the victories of virtue, and the punishments of vice.
By Mrs. C. W. Denison... Boston, J. E. Farwell & co. ,
1848.
    112 p. incl. pl.   24 1/2 cm. (On cover: American
popular tales. no. 1)

9391 Denison, Mary (Andrews) "Mrs. C. W. Denison," 1826-1911.
    What not. By Mrs. Mary A. Denison. Illustrated with
engravings from designs by White. Philadelphia, Lippincott,
Grambo & co. , 1855.
    1 p. 1. , xii, 13-384 p. front. , plates.   19 1/2 cm.
    Added t. -p. , illus.
Published in 1856 under title: Orange leaves.

9392 [Derby, George Horatio] 1823-1861.
    Phoenixiana; or, Sketches and burlesques. By John
Phoenix [pseud.]... New York, D. Appleton and company,
1856.
    274 p. front. , illus.   19 1/2 cm.
    "Sundry sketches, recently published in the newspapers
and magazines of California. "-Pref.

9393 Derby, George Horatio, 1823-1861.
    The Squibob papers. By John Phoenix. [Capt. Geo H.
Derby] ... With comic illustrations by the author. New
York, Carleton, 1865.
    247 p. incl. front. , illus. plates.   19 cm.

Imperfect; t.-p. wanting.

9394 Desultoria: the recovered mss. of an eccentric. New York, Baker and Scribner, 1850.
220 p.   19 1/2 cm.

9395 Devereux, George Humphrey, d. 1878.
Sam Shirk: a tale of the woods of Maine. By George H. Devereux. New York, Hurd and Houghton, 1871.
iv, 391 p.   19 cm.

9396 Dexter, Henry Martyn, 1821-1890.
Street thoughts. By Rev Henry M. Dexter... With illustrations by Billings. Boston, Crosby, Nichols, and company, 1859.
3 p. 1., [v]-viii, [9]-216 p. front., plates.   18 1/2 cm.
Added t.-p., illustrated.

9397 The diary of a pawnbroker; or, The three golden balls. New York, H. Long & brothers [c1849]
134 p. incl. front., illus.   24 1/2 cm.

9398 Diaz, Abby (Morton) 1821-1904.
Lucy Maria. By Abby Morton Diaz... Boston, J. R. Osgood and company, 1874.
396 p. incl. front. plates.   18 1/2 cm.

9399 Dickinson, Anna Elizabeth, 1842-1932.
What answer? [A novel] by Anna E. Dickinson. Boston Ticknor and Fields, 1868.
1 p. 1., 301 p.   18 1/2 cm.

9400 Dickson, Harris, 1868-
The black wolf's breed; a story of France in the Old world and the New, happening in the reign of Louis XIV; by Harris Dickson, illustrations by C. M. Relyea. Indianapolis, The Bowen-Merrill company [c1899]
6 p. 1., 288 p. front., plates.   18 1/2 cm.

9401 Dimmick, Francis Marion, 1827-
Anna Clayton; or, The enquirer after truth. By Rev. Francis Marion Dimmick... Philadelphia, Lindsay &

143

Blakiston, 1859.
xii, 13-427 p.   19 1/2 cm.

9402 Disosway, Ella Taylor, 1840-1895.
      South Meadows. A tale of long ago. By E. T. Disosway...
      Philadelphia, Porter and Coates [c1874]
      3 p. 1., [iii]-v, 6-280 p.   19 1/2 cm.

9403 Ditson, G[eorge] Leighton, b. 1812.
      Crimora; or, Love's cross. By G. Leighton Ditson...
      Boston, G. L. Ditson, 1852.
      1 p. 1., [5]-408 p.   18 cm.

9404 Ditson, G[eorge] L[eighton] b. 1812.
      The federati of Italy: a romance of Caucasian captivity,
      by G. L. Ditson... Boston, W. White and company, 1871.
      319 p.   20 cm.

9405 Divoll, Willard.
      The fatal stroke; or, The philosophy of intemperance.
      By Willard Divoll. New York, Baker & Godwin, printers,
      1869.
      4 p. 1 1., [5]-62 p.   18 1/2 cm.

9406 Dixon, Edward H   1808-1880.
      Scenes in the practice of a New York surgeon. By Edward
      H. Dixon... With eight illustrations by Darley... New
      York, DeWitt & Davenport [c1855]
      3 p. 1., [iii]-xvi, [9]-407 p. fronts., plates.   18 1/2 cm.

9407 Dod, Samuel Bayard, 1830-1907.
      A Highland chronicle. By S. Bayard Dod... New York,
      Dodd, Mead & company, 1892.
      v, 290 p.   19 1/2 cm.

9408 Dodd, Mrs. Anna Bowman (Blake) 1855-1929.
      Struthers, and The comedy of the masked musicians. By
      Anna Bowman Dodd... New York, Lovell, Coryell &
      company [c1894]
      vi, 312 p.   19 cm.

9409 [Dodge, Nathaniel Shatswell] 1810-1874.

Sketches of New England, or Memories of the country.
By John Carver, esquire [pseud.] justice of the peace and
quorum. New York, E. French, 1842.
vi p., 1 l., [9]-286 p.   18 1/2 cm.

9410 [Donaldson, James Lowry] 1814-1885.
        Sergeant Atkins. A tale of adventure. Founded on fact.
        By an officer of the United States army... Philadelphia,
        J. B. Lippincott & co., 1871.
        xvi, 17-317 p. front., plates.   19 cm.

9411 [Donaldson, John]
        Jack Datchett, the clerk: an old man's tale... Baltimore,
        H. Colburn, 1846.
        101 p.   19 cm.

9412 [Donnelly, Ignatius] 1831-1901.
        Caesar's column. A story of the twentieth century. By
        Edmund Boisgilbert, M. D. [pseud.]... Chicago, F. J.
        Schulte & company [c1890]
        367 p.   20 1/2 cm.

9413 [Dorr, Benjamin] 1796-1869.
        The history of a pocket prayer book. Written by itself...
        New ed. Philadelphia, R. S. H. George, 1844.
        xvi, [13]-184 p.   15 1/2 cm.
        Advertisement signed: B. Dorr.

9414 Dorsey, Mrs. Anna Hanson (McKenney) 1815-1896.
        ... The Flemmings; or, Truth triumphant. By Mrs.
        Anna H. Dorsey... New York, P. O'Shea, 1870.
        v, [7]-444 p.   19 1/2 cm. (The Notre Dame series
        of Catholic novels)

9415 Dorsey, Mrs. Anna Hanson (McKenney) 1815-1896.
        Nora Brady's vow, and Mona, the vestal. By Mrs.
        Anna H. Dorsey. Philadelphia, J. B. Lipponcott & co.,
        1869.
        viii, 9-324 p.   19 cm.

9416 Dorsey, Mrs. Anna Hanson (McKenney) 1815-1896.
        The oriental pearl; or, The Catholic emigrants. By Mrs.

145

Anna H. Dorsey... Baltimore, J. Murphy [1857]
163 p.   15 x 11 1/2 cm.

9417 Dorsey, Mrs. Anna Hamson (McKenney) 1815-1896.
Tears on the diadem; or, The crown and the cloister. A
tale of the white and red roses. By Mrs. Anna H. Dorsey ...
New York, E. Dunigan, 1846.
223 p. front.   15 1/2 cm.

9418 Dorsey, Mrs. Anna Hanson (McKenney) 1815-1896.
Woodreve Manor; or, Six months in town. A tale of
American life... By Mrs. Anna Hanson Dorsey... Philadelphia, A. Hart, 1852.
2 p. 1. , [13]-334 p.   20 cm.

9419 The double suicide. The true history of the lives of the twin
sisters, Sarah and Maria Williams. Containing an account
of Maria's love, mock marriage, suffering and degradation,
together with Sarah's love and suffering... New-York, G.
C. Holbrook, 1855.
62 p.   23 cm.

9420 Douglas, Amanda Minnie, 1837-1916.
Home Nook; or, The crown of duty. By Amanda M.
Douglas... Boston, Lee and Shepard; New York, Lee,
Shepard and Dillingham, 1874.
1 p. 1. , 5-384 p.   19 cm.

9421 Douglas, Amanda M[innie] 1837-1916.
Lucia: her problem. By Amanda M. Douglas... New
York, Sheldon & company, 1872.
315 p.   18 1/2 cm.

9422 Douglas, Amanda M[innie] 1837-1916.
Osborne of Arrochar. By Amanda M. Douglas... Boston,
Lee and Shepard; New York, C. T. Dillingham, 1890.
iv, 449 p.   19 1/2 cm.

9423 Douglas, Amanda Minnie, 1837-1916.
Stephen Dane. By Amanda M. Douglas... Boston,
Lee and Shepard, 1867.
2 p. 1. , 7-253 p.   19 1/2 cm.

9424 Douglas, Amanda Minnie, 1837-1916.
Sydnie Adriance; or, Trying the world. By Amanda M. Douglas... Boston, Lee and Shepard, 1869.
3 p. l., 9-355 p.   19 cm.

9425 Douglas, Amanda M[innie] 1837-1916.
A woman's inheritance, by Amanda M. Douglas... Boston, Lee and Shepard; New York, C. T. Dillingham, 1886.
345 p.   19 1/2 cm.

9426 [Douglas, Sarah E   ]
Mahaly Sawyer; or, "Putting yourself in her place." By S. E. D. Boston, Cupples and Hurd, 1888.
3 p. l., 328 p.   16 cm.

9427 [Doutney, Mrs. Harriet G   (Storer)] 1822-1907.
An autobiography: being passages from a life now progressing in the city of Boston, an interest in which is not excited simply because founded on fact, but that the incidents therein related are themselves the facts. By R. L. B. [pseud.] ... [Cambridge, Mass.] Sold by subscription only, 1871.
vi, [7]-240 p.   19 cm.
Published in 1873 under titles: "I told you so; or, An autobiography", by Mrs. T. Narcisse Doutney, and "Marrying a moustache; or, An autobiography", by the same.

9428 Downing, Mrs. Frances (Murdaugh) 1835-1894.
Nameless. A novel. By Fanny Murdaugh Downing... Raleigh, N. C., W. B. Smith & co., 1865.
2 p. l., [vii]-viii, [9]-232 p.   19 cm.

9429 Drake, Richard.
Revelations of a slave smuggler: being the autobiography of Capt. Rich'd Drake, an African trader for fity years-from 1807-1857; during which period he was concerned in the transportation of half a million blacks from African coasts to America. With a preface by his executor, Rev. Henry Byrd West... New York, R. M. De Witt [1860]
xi, [9]-100 p. 3 fold. pl. (incl. front., fold. plan) 23 1/2 cm.
Drake is given the forename "Philip" throughout the preface.

9430 Dreiser, Theodore, 1871–
   Sister Carrie, by Theodore Dreiser. New York, Doubleday, Page & co., 1900.
   4 p. 1., 557 p. 20 cm.

9431 [Duane, William] 1808-1882.
   ... Ligan: a collection of tales and essays. By W. D. ...
Philadelphia, Merrihew & Thompson, printers, 1857.
   76 p. 19 cm.
   "Ninety-nine copies printed."
   At head of title: No. 25.

9432 Duffy, Owen.
   Walter Warren; or, The adventurer of the northern wilds.
By Owen Duffy. New York, Stringer & Townsend [c1854]
   105 p. 24 1/2 cm.

9433 Duganne, Augustine Joseph Hickey, 1823-1884.
   The bravo's daughter; or, The Tory of Carolina. A
romance of the American revolution. By Augustine J. H.
Duganne. New-York, E. Winchester, 1850.
   92 p. 24 1/2 cm.

9434 [Duganne, Augustine Joseph Hickey] 1823-1884.
   The knights of the seal; or, The mysteries of the three
cities; a romance of men's hearts and habits... Philadelphia,
Colon and Adriance, 1845.
   1 p. 1., 5-204 p. 21 1/2 cm.

9435 [Dumond], Mrs. Annie [(Hamilton)] Nelles, 1837–
   Ravenia; or, The outcast redeemed. By Annie Nelles...
Topeka, Kan., Commonwealth printing company's press,
1872.
   251 p. front. (port.) 22 1/2 cm.

9436 Dumont, Julia Louise (Corey) 1794-1857.
   Life sketches from common paths: a series of American
tales. By Mrs. Julia L. Dumont... New York, London,
D. Appleton and company, 1856.
   286 p. 20 cm.

9437 Dunbar, Paul Laurence, 1872-1906.

The love of Landry. By Paul Laurence Dunbar... New
York, Dodd, Mead and company [c1900]
3 p. 1., 200 p.   18 1/2 cm.

9438 [Dunne, Finley Peter] 1867-1936.
Mr. Dooley in peace and in war. Boston, Small, Maynard
& company, 1898.
xviii p., 1 1., 260 p.   18 cm.

9439 [Dunne, Finley Peter] 1867-1936.
Mr. Dooley's philosophy, illustrated by William
Nicholson, E. W. Kemble, F. Opper. New York, R. H.
Russell, 1900.
263 p. front., illus., plates.   18 1/2 cm.

9440 [Dunning, Mrs. Annie (Ketchum)]
The step-mother's recompense, or Mrs. Ellerton's trials
and reward. By Nellie Grahame [pseud.]... Philadelphia,
Presbyterian Board of publication [1864]

9441 Dupuy, Eliza Ann, 1814?-1881.
All for love; or, The outlaw's bride. By Miss Eliza A.
Dupuy... Philadelphia, T. B. Peterson & brothers [c1873]
1 p. 1., 19-415 p.   19 cm.

9442 Dupuy, Eliza Ann, 1814?-1881.
The cancelled will. By Miss Eliza A. Dupuy... Philadelphia, T. B. Peterson & brothers [c1872]
1 p. 1., 19-493 p.   19 cm.

9443 Dupuy, Eliza Ann, 1814?-1881.
Celeste, the pirate's daughter... New York, Ely and
Robinson, 1845.
2 v.   20 cm.

9444 Dupuy, Eliza Ann, 1814?-1881.
The clandestine marriage. By Miss Eliza A. Dupuy...
Philadelphia, T. B. Peterson & brothers [c1875]
1 p. 1., 19-454 p.   19 cm.

9445 Dupuy, Eliza Ann, 1814?-1881.
The country neighborhood. By Miss E. A. Dupuy... New

York, Harper & brothers, 1855.
1 p. 1. , [13]-109, [1] p.   23 cm.

9446 Dupuy, Eliza Ann, 1814?-1881.
The dethroned heiress. By Miss Eliza A. Dupuy...
Philadelphia, T. B. Peterson & brothers, [c1873]
1 p. 1. , 19-471 p.   19 cm.

9447 Dupuy, Eliza Ann, 1814?-1881.
The discarded wife; or, Will she succeed. By Miss
Eliza A. Dupuy... Philadelphia, T. B. Peterson &
brothers [c1875]
1 p. 1. , 19-595 p.   19 cm.

9448 Dupuy, E[liza] A[nn] 1814?-1881.
Emma Walton; or, Trials and triumph. By Miss E. A.
Dupuy... Cincinnati, J. A. & U. P. James, 1854.
179 p.   23 1/2 cm.

9449 Dupuy, Eliza Ann, 1814?-1881.
The gipsy's warning. By Miss Eliza A. Dupuy...
Philadelphia, T. B. Peterson & brothers, [c1873]
2 p. 1. , 21-450 p.   19 cm.

9450 Dupuy, Eliza Ann, 1814?-1881.
How he did it... Philadelphia, T. B. Peterson & brothers
[c1871]
456 p.   20 cm.
Also published as: Was he guilty? By Miss Eliza A. Dupuy.
Philadelphia: T. B. Peterson & brothers, 306 Chestnut Street
[cop. 1873]. Information from LC card for copy withdrawn
from circulation.

9451 Durivage, Francis Alexander, 1814-1881.
Edith Vernon: or, Crime and retribution. A tragic story
of New England, founded upon fact. By F. A. Durivage...
Boston, F. Gleason, 1845.
2 p. 1. , [9]-52 p. front.   23 cm.

9452 Durivage, Francis Alexander, 1814-1881.
Life scenes, sketched in light and shadow from the world
around us. By Francis A. Durivage. With illustrations, by

S. W. Rowse... Boston, B. B. Mussey and company, 1853.
4 p. 1., 7-408 p. plates. 18 1/2 cm.
Added t.-p., illustrated.
Some of these skteches were originally published in the
"Boston olive branch," the "Flag of our Union," and other
magazines and papers.

9453 [Durivage, Francis Alexander] 1814-1881.
Stray subjects, arrested and bound over. Being the
fugitive offspring of the "old 'un" and the "young 'un," that
have been "lying round loose," and now "tied up" for fast
keeping. Illustrated by Darley. Philadelphia, Carey and
Hart, 1848.
3 p. 1., [v]-viii p., 1 1., [19]-199 p. front., plates.
19 x 12 cm.

9454 Durivage, Francis Alexander, 1814-1881.
The three brides, Love in a cottage, and other tales, by
Francis A. Durivage. Boston, Sanborn, Carter & Bazin,
1856.
2 p. 1., 7-408 p. 19 1/2 cm.

9455 Dutcher, George M
Disenthralled: a story of my life. By George M. Dutcher
... Hartford, Conn., Columbian book company, 1872.
2 p. 1., [ix]-xv, [17]-276 p. front. (port.) plates.
19 1/2 cm.

E

9456 Earle, Mary Tracy, 1864-
The man who worked for Collister. Boston, Copeland &
Day, 1898.
284 p. 18 cm.

9457 Eastman, Mrs. Mary (Henderson) b. 1818.
Aunt Phillis's cabin; or, Southern life as it is. By Mrs.
Mary H. Eastman. Philadelphia, Lippincott, Grambo &

co., 1852.
>   2 p. 1., 11-280 p. front., plates.   19 cm.
>   Added t.-p., illustrated.

9458 Eastman, Mrs. Mary (H]enderson]) b. 1818.
>   Fashionable life. By Mary H. Eastman. Philadelphia,
>   J. B. Lippincott and co., 1856.
>   x p. 1 1., [13]-394 p.   19 cm.

9459 Eastman, P   O
>   The young captive prince, a tale of allegory and fact. By
>   P. O. Eastman... Sandusky, O., Register steam printing
>   estbalishment [!] 1870.
>   60 p.   22 cm.

9460 Eaton, Arthur Wentworth Hamilton, 1849-1937.
>   Tales of a garrison town, by Arthur Wentworth Eaton and
>   Craven Langstroth Betts. New York and St. Paul, D. D.
>   Merrill company, 1892.
>   250 p. incl. front., plates.   19 cm.
>   CONTENTS.-How Crossaway betrayed his friend.-The fall
>   of the Darcys.-The story of young Gilsby.-An increased
>   allowance.-Simpson of the Slashers.-How Grosvener got his
>   church.-Mrs. Buckingham's revenge.-The Reverend
>   Washington Ham's triumph.-Court-martialled.-Too truthful
>   spirits.-The corporal's trousers.-Touched with the tarbrush.-
>   Whigs and Tories.-A soldier's funeral.

9461 Edgar, Mary C
>   Father Drummond and his orphans: or, The children of
>   Mary. By Mary C. Edgar... Philadelphia, H. & C.
>   McGrath, 1854.
>   178 p.   15 1/2 cm.

9462 Eggleston, Edward, 1837-1902.
>   The circuit rider: a tale of the heroic age. By Edward
>   Eggleston... New York, J. B. Ford & company, 1874.
>   2 p. 1., vii, [1], [9]-332 p. front., illus.   18 1/2 cm.
>   "Originally appeared as a serial in the Christian union."

9463 Eggleston, Edward, 1837-1902.
>   Duffels, short stories, by Edward Eggleston... New York,

D. Appleton and company, 1893.
vi p. , 1 1. , 262 p.   19 1/2 cm.
CONTENTS. -Sister Tabea. -The redemptioner. -A basement
story. -The Gunpowder Plot. -The story of a valentine. -
Huldah, the help. -The new cashier. -Pricilla. -Talking for life.
-Periwinkle. -The Christmas club.

9464 Eggleston, Edward, 1837-1902.
The end of the world. A love story. By Edward Eggleston...
With thirty-two illustrations. New York, O. Judd and company,
[1872]
200 p. incl. front. , illus. , plates.   19 cm.

9465 Eggleston, Edward, 1837-1902.
The faith doctor; a story of New York, by Edward
Eggleston... New York, D. Appleton and company, 1891.
427 p.   19 cm.

9466 Eggleston, Edward, 1837-1902.
The Hoosier schoolmaster. A novel. By Edward Eggleston... New York, Orange Judd and company [c1871]
226 p. incl. front. , illus. , plates.   19 cm.
Originally published as a serial in the Hearth and home.

9467 Eggleston, Edward, 1837-1902.
Roxy, by Edward Eggleston... New York, C. Scribner's
sons, (1878)
viii p. , 1 1. , 432 p. 12 pl. (incl. front.)   19 cm.

9468 Eggleston, George Cary, 1839-1911.
Juggernaut; a veiled record, by George Cary Eggleston
and Dolores Marbourg. New York, Fords, Howard, &
Hulbert, 1891.
2 p. 1. , 343 p.   18 1/2 cm.

9469 Eggleston, George Cary, 1839-1911.
Southern soldier stories, by George Cary Eggleston...
With illustrations by R. F. Zogbaum. New York, The
Macmillan company; London, Macmillan & co. , ltd. , 1898.
xi, 251 p. 6 pl. (incl. front.)   19 cm.

9470 Elder, William 1806-1885.

The enchanted beauty, and other tales, essays, and
sketches. By William Elder... New York, J. C. Derby;
Boston, Phillips, Sampson & co. [etc., etc.] 1855.
   2 p. l., [vii]-viii, [9]-406 p.   18 1/2 cm.

9471 Elemjay, Louise.
   Censoria lictoria; or, What I think of you. From the
notes and minutes of Miss Betsey Trotwood's official tour.
By Louise Elemjay... New York, J. F. Trow, printer,
1855.
   84 p.   19 cm.

9472 Elemjay, Louise.
   Censoria lictoria of facts and folks, from the notes and
minutes of Miss Betsey Trotwood's official tour under the
Frank Pierce dynasty. By Louise Elemjay... 8th ed., rev.
and enl. New York, J. F. Trow, printer, 1859.
   179 p.   19 cm. [With her Rising young men, and other
tales. 4th ed. New York, 1859]

9473 Ellet, Mrs. Elizabeth Fries (Lummis)
   Evenings at Woodlawn... New York, Baker and Scribner,
1849.
   348 p.   12 mo.

9474 [Elliot, Samuel Hayes] 1809-1869.
   Dreams and realities in the life of a pastor and teacher.
By the author of "Rolling ridge"... [etc.] New York, J.
C. Derby; Boston, Phillips, Sampson & co. [etc., etc.]
1856.
   xi, [13]-430 p.   19 1/2 cm.

9475 [Elliot, Samuel Hayes] 1809-1869.
   New England's chattels; or, Life in the northern poor-
house... New-York, H. Dayton, 1858.
   x p., 1 l., [13]-484 p. front. 5 pl.   19 1/2 cm.
   A new and rev. ed. pub. in 1860 with title: A look at home;
or, Life in the poor-house of New England... By S. H. Elliot...

9476 [Elliot, Samuel Hayes] 1809-1869.
   The parish-side. By the ... clerk of the parish of Edge-
field... New York, Mason brothers, 1854.

ix, [11]-258 p. front., plates, plan.   19 cm.

9477 [Elliot, Samuel Hayes] 1809-1869.
         Rolling Ridge; or, The book of four and twenty chapters...
      Boston, Crocker and Brewster, 1838.
         xii, [13]-266 p.   16 cm.

9478 [Elliot, Samuel Hayes] 1809-1869.
         The sequel to Rolling Ridge. By the author of the latter;
      assisted by the worthy Mr. Fory ... Boston, Crocker and
      Brewster, 1844.
         248 p.   16 cm.

9479 [Elliot, Charles Wyllys] 1817-1883.
         Wind and whirlwind; a novel. By Mr. Thom. White
      [pseud.] New York, G. P. Putnam & son, 1868.
         307 p.   19 cm.

9480 Ellsworth, Mrs. Mary Wolcott (Janvrin) 1830-1870.
         Peace; or, The stolen will. An American novel. By
      Mary W. Janvrin... Boston, J. French and company;
      Galesburg, Ill., Hastings and French, 1857.
         407 p.   19 cm.

9481 [Ellsworth, Oliver] of Boston.
         A single gentleman: by Timothy Thistle [pseud.] Designs
      by the author. Illustrations by l. Hyde. Boston, O.
      Ellsworth, 1867.
         x, 11-182 p. incl. front. illus. plates.   17 cm.

9482 English, Thomas Dunn, 1819-1902.
         ... 1844; or, The power of the "S. F." A tale: developing
      the secret action of parties during the presidential campaign
      of 1844. By Thomas Dunn English. New York, Burgess,
      Stringer & co. [etc.] 1847.
         300 p.   19 cm. (Mirror library-new ser.)

9483 English, William B
         Rosina Meadows, the village maid: or, Temptations un-
      veiled; a story of city scenes and every day life. By
      William B. English. Boston, Redding & co.; New York,
      Greeley & McElrath [etc., etc.] 1843.

cover-title, 32 p.   30 cm.

9484   Esperanza; my journey thither and what I found there...
       Cincinnati, V. Nicholson, 1860.
           vi, 7-332 p.   19 1/2 cm.

9485   Estelle Grant; or, The lost wife... New York, Garrett & co.,
       [1855]
           v, [6]-350 p.   18 1/2 cm.

9486   Eugene, Maurice.
           The oak shade; or, Records of a village literary asso-
       ciation. Ed. by Maurice Eugene. Philadelphia, W. P.
       Hazzard, 1855.
           214 p.   19 cm.
           CONTENTS. -Dedication. -Preface. -Hans Dundermann. -
       The wisdom of preserving moderation in our wishes. -The
       sick mother. -The excellencies of lying. -The alchemist. -The
       beauty of a well cultivated heart. -The dream of a loafer. -
       Conclusion.

9487   Eveline Neville; or, "A spirit, yet a woman too." By a lady
       of the South... New York, Burgess, Stringer & co., 1845.
           108 p.   23 cm.

                                  F

9488   Fabens, Joseph Warren, 1821-1875.
           The camel hunt; a narrative of personal adventure. By
       Joseph W. Fabens... Boston and Cambridge, J. Munroe
       and company, 1851.
           v p., 1 1., 219 p.   19 1/2 cm.

9489   [Fabens, Joseph Warren] 1821-1875.
           In the tropics, by a settler in Santo Domingo. With an
       introductory notice by Richard B. Kimball... 2d ed. New
       York, Carleton [etc., etc.] 1863.
           306 p.   18 1/2 cm.

Pub. later under title: Life in Santo Domingo.

9490 Fabens, Joseph Warren, 1821-1875.
        A story of life on the Isthmus. By Joseph W. Fabens...
    New York, G. P. Putnam & co. , 1853.
        viii, [9]-215 p.   19 cm. (On cover: Putnam's popular
    library)
        "Originally composed as a kind of sequel to... 'The
    camel hunt.' "-Pref.

9491 Faber, Christine, pseud.
        Carroll O'Donoghue: a tale of the Irish struggles of 1866,
    and of recent times. [By] Christine Faber [pseud.]...
    New York, P. J. Kennedy [1881]
        vi, 7-501 p.   19 cm.

9492 Fairfield, Sumner Lincoln, 1803-1844.
        The last night of Pompeii; a poem: and Lays and legends.
    By Sumner Lincoln Fairfield. New-York, Printed by
    Elliott and Palmer, 1832.
        vii, [9]-309 p.   21 1/2 cm.
        Contains also "Walter Colebrooke", a prose tale (p. 239-
    300)

9493 The fall of Fort Sumter; or, Love and war in 1860-1861. "By
    the private secretary to_____ , etc." New York, F. A.
    Brady [c1867]
        iv, [5]-167 p. front. , illus.   24 cm.
        Copyrighted by J. B. Newbrough; attributed to him by C.
    A. Searing (Cat. Libbie, 1906, no. 508)

9494 The fanatic, or The perils of Peter Pliant, the poor pedagogue:
    by the author of Winona. Philadelphia, Office of the
    American citizen, 1846.
        1 p. 1. , [5]-73 p.   26 cm.

9495 Farmer, Mrs. P   W
        Louisa Williams; or, The orphan bound-girl. A tale of
    the Queen City; founded on facts. By P. W. F. Cincinnati,
    Printed for the author at the office of the "Cincinnatus,"
    1859
        112 p.   23 cm.

9496　Farnham, Eliza Woodson (Burhans) Mrs. T. J. Farnham,"
1815-1864.
　　　　The ideal attained; being the story of two steadfast souls,
and how they won their happiness and lost it not. By Eliza
W. Farnham... New York, C. M. Plumb & co., 1865.
　　　　510 p.　　　19 1/2 cm.

9497　Farrenc, Edmund.
　　　　Carlotina and the Sanfedesti; or, A night with the Jesuits
at Rome. By Edmund Farrenc... New-York, J. S. Taylor,
1853.
　　　　viii, [9]-432 p.　　　19 cm.

9498　The fatal secret; or, Crime and retribution! Facts most
singular and fearful!! Being a chain of circumstances
recently developed in a very exciting and protracted crim.
con. trial... New York, A. F. Joy; Philadelphia, E. E.
Barclay, 1852.
　　　　1 p. 1., 9-36 p. front., illus.　　　23 cm.

9499　Fawcett, Edgar, 1847-1904.
　　　　The adventures of a widow; a novel, by Edgar Fawcett...
Boston, J. R. Osgood and company, 1884.
　　　　1 p. 1., 7-341 p.　　　19 1/2 cm.

9500　Fawcett, Edgar, 1847-1904.
　　　　An ambitious woman; a novel, by Edgar Fawcett...
Boston, Houghton, Mifflin and company, 1884.
　　　　1 p. 1., 444 p.　　　20 1/2 cm.

9501　Fawcett, Edgar, 1847-1904.
　　　　A mild barbarian; a novel, by Edgar Fawcett... New
York, D. Appleton and company, 1894.
　　　　1 p. 1., 272 p.　　18 1/2 cm.

9502　Fawcett, Edgar, 1847-1904.
　　　　Social silhouettes (being the impressions of Mr. Mark
Manhattan) edited by Edgar Fawcett... Boston, Ticknor
and company, 1885.
　　　　vi, 368 p.　　　19 1/2 cm.

9503　Fawcett, Edgar, 1847-1904.

Tinkling cymbals, a novel, by Edgar Fawcett... Boston, J. R. Osgood and company, 1884.
2 p. 1., 7-332 p.   20 cm.

9504 [Fay, Theodore Sedgwick] 1807-1898.
The Countess Ida. A tale of Berlin. By the author of "Norman Leslie," "Dreams and reveries of a quiet man," &c... New-York, Harper & brothers, 1840.
2 v.   19 cm.

9505 [Fay, Theodore Sedgwick] 1807-1898.
Norman Leslie. A tale of the present times... New-York, Harper & brothers, 1835.
2 v.   18 1/2 cm.
Published anonymously.

9506 [Fay, Theodore Sedgwick] 1807-1898.
Sydney Clifton; or, Vicissitudes in both hemispheres. A tale of the nineteenth century... New-York, Harper & brothers, 1839.
2 v. in 1.   18 cm.

9507 Fidfaddy, Frederick Augustus, pseud.
The adventures of Uncle Sam, in search after his lost honor. By Frederick Augustus Fidfaddy... Middletown [Conn.] Printed by S. Richards, 1816.
142 p.   18 1/2 cm.

9508 Field, Alice Durand.
Palermo, & Christmas story. New York, Putnam's sons, 1885.
212 p.   20 cm.

9509 Field, Charles Kellogg, 1873-
Stanford stories; tales of a young university, by Charles K. Field, Carolus Ager, Will H. Irwin. New York, Doubleday, Page, 1900.
281 p.   20 cm.

9510 Field, Eugene, 1850-1895.
Florence Bardsley's story; the life and death of a remarkable woman, by Eugene Field. Chicago, W. I. Way,

159

1897.
   2 p. 1. , [9]-59, [1] p. incl. 3 pl. , front.   17 1/2 cm.
   A review of a mythical book, ascribed to Whitelaw Reid;
Un aperçu de la vie de Mme la comtesse de la Tour.

9511 Field, Eugene, 1850-1895.
      The holy cross and other tales, by Eugene Field. New
York, C. Scribner's sons, 1896.
      6 p. 1. , 3-293 p.   18 1/2 cm.

9512 Field, Eugene, 1850-1895.
      The house; an episode in the lives of Reuben Baker,
astronomer, and of his wife Alice, by Eugene Field. New
York, C. Scribner's sons, 1896.
      v, 268 p.   18 1/2 cm.

9513 Field, Eugene, 1850-1895.
      Second book of tales... New York, C. Scribner's sons,
1896.
      vii, 314 p.   18 1/2 cm.

9514 Field, Joseph M   1810-1856.
      The drama in Pokerville; The bench and bar of Jurytown,
and other stories. By "Everpoint," (J. M. Field... of the
St. Louis reveille.) With eight illustrations... by F. O. C.
Darley. Philadelphia, Carey and Hart, 1847.
      2 p. 1. , 3-200 p. front. , plates.   19 cm.
      Added t. -p. , illustrated.

9515 Fields, Annie Adams "Mrs. J. T. Fields," 1834-1915.
      Asphodel... Boston, Ticknor and Fields, 1866.
      224 p.   17 cm.

9516 [Fields, James Thomas] 1816-1881, ed.
      Good company for every day in the year... Boston,
Ticknor and Fields, 1866.
      iv, 326 p. front. , plates, ports.   19 1/2 cm.

9517 Fields, William, comp.
      The literary and miscellaneous scrap book: consisting of
tales and anecdotes - biographical, historical, patriotic,
moral, religious, and sentimental pieces in prose and poetry.

Compiled by William Fields, jr. Knoxville, Tenn., W.
Fields, jr., 1837.
600 p.   22 1/2 cm.
2d ed. published in 1851, under title: The scrap book.

9518 [Fisher, Mary Ann] 1839–
A spinster's story, by M. A. F. ... New York, Carleton,
1866.
2 p. 1., [7]–399 p.   18 1/2 cm.

9519 Fitch, Anna M
Bound down, or Life and its possibilities. By Anna M.
Fitch. Philadelphia, J. B. Lippincott & co., 1870.
338 p.   19 cm.

9520 Fitch, [H   P   ]
Through shadow to sunshine. [By] Fitch... Hastings,
Neb., Gazette–Journal company, 1885.
3 p. 1., [5]–193 p.   18 x 14 cm.

9521 Fitch, Thomas.
Better days; or, A millionaire of to-morrow. By
Thomas Fitch and Anna M. Fitch. New ed. rev. ... Chicago,
F. J. Schulte & company [c1892]
373 p.   20 cm. (On cover: The Ariel library, no. 11)

9522 Flagg, William Joseph, 1818–1898.
A good investment. A story of the upper Ohio. By
William Flagg... New York, Harper & brothers, 1872.
1 p. 1., [9]–116 p. front., illus.   23 1/2 cm. (On
cover: Library of select novels, no. 377)

9523 Fleming, Mrs. May Agnes (Early) 1840–1880.
Carried by storm; as published in the New York weekly,
vol. 23 no. 4. A novel. By May Agnes Fleming... New
York, copyright 1879 by G. W. Carleton & co. Publishers,
London, S. Low & co., MDCCCLXXX.
vi, 7–398, [2] p.   18 1/2 cm.

9524 Fleming, Mrs May Agnes (Early) 1840–1880.
The heir of Charlton. A novel. By May Agnes Fleming...
New York, G. W. Carleton & co., 1879.

vi, 7-396 p.   19 cm.

9525 Fleming, Mrs. May Agnes (Early) 1840-1880.
        One night's mystery: a novel... New York, G. W. Carleton
     & co.; London: S. Low & co., 1876.
        443 p.   20 cm.

9526 [Fletcher, Julia Constance]
        Andromeda. A novel. By George Fleming [pseud.]...
     Boston, Roberts brothers, 1885.
        vi, [7]-377 p.   18 cm

9527 Floyd, Mary Faith.
        The Nereid. By Mary Faith Floyd... Macon, Ga.,
     J. W. Burke & company, 1871.
        1 p. 1., [5]-102 p.   25 cm.

9528 [Follen, Eliza Lee (Cabor)] "Mrs. C. T. C. Follen," 1787-1860.
        The skeptic. By the author of "The well-spent hour"...
     Boston and Cambridge, J. Munroe and company, 1835.
        3 p. 1., 143 p.   15 cm. (Added t.-p.: Scenes and
     characters illustrating Christian truth [ed. by H. Ware]
     no. II)

9529 Foote, Mary (Hallock) 1847-1938.
        In exile, and other stories; by Mary Hallock Foote. Boston
     and New York, Houghton, Mifflin and company, 1894.
        2 p. 1., 253 p.   18 1/2 cm.
        CONTENTS.-In exile.-Friend Barton's "concern."-The
     story of the Alcazar.-A cloud on the mountain.-The rapture
     of Hetty.-The watchman.

9530 Forbes, Gerritt Van Husen, 1795-1863.
        Green mountain annals, a tale of truth. By G. V. H. Forbes
     ... New-York, Burnett & Smith, 1832.
        iv, [5]-140 p.   14 cm.
        CONTENTS.-Green mountain annals.-Death's doings.-The
     materialist.-A fragment.

9531 Ford, E   L
        Madelaine Darth [a novel] By E. L. Ford. Chicago,
     Western news company, 1867.

162

cover-title, 71 p.   22 1/2 cm.

9532 Ford, Capt. Edward.
    The Duchess of Baden: a tale of the French revolution.
With a history of the fall of the Marquis Louis de Beau-
harnais, and the flight and perils of his family in France,
Spain, Saint Domingo, and Philadelphia. By Captain
Edward Ford. Philadelphia, Carey & Hart, 1849.
    vii, [17]-110 p.   24 cm.
    Cover-title: Stephanie Beauharnais, the duchess of Baden.
    The narrative does not follow the facts of the life of
Stéphanie de Beauharnais, grand duchess of Baden.

9533 Ford, James Lauren, 1854-1928.
    Bohemia invaded, and other stories; by James L. Ford...
with frontispiece by A. W. B. Lincoln. New York and London,
F. A. Stokes co., 1895.
    4 p. l., 176 p.   front.   16 cm.
    "These stories are reprinted by permission from Puck,
Truth, the New York Herald and other publications."
    CONTENTS. -Bohemia invaded. -Wedded bliss. -High
etiquette in Harlem. -The talent in the napkin. -A dinner in
poverty flat. -The better element. -The squarer. -The joke
that failed. -Dan Briordy's gitaway shadder. -The wardman's
wooing. -The change of the luck. -Mr. Synick's anti-bad-break.
-Freaks and kings.

9534 Ford, James Lauren, 1854-1928.
    Dolly Dillenbeck, a portrayal of certain phases of
metropolitan life and character; by James L. Ford...
illustrated by Francis Day. New York, G. H. Richmond &
co., 1895.
    2 p. l., 392 p. front., 5 pl.   18 cm.

9535 Ford, Paul Leicester, 1865-1902.
    The Honorable Peter Stirling and what people thought of
him... New York, Henry Holt and company, 1894.
    417, [12] p.   20 cm.

9536 Ford, Paul Leicester, 1865-1902.
    Janice Meredith: a story of the American Revolution...
New York, Dodd, Mead and company, 1899.

536 p. front.

9537 Ford, Paul Leicester, 1865-1902.
     The story of an untold love... Boston and New York,
     Houghton, Mifflin and company, 1897.
         348 p., 1 1.

9538 Ford, Paul Leicester, 1865-1902.
     Tattle-tales of Cupid... New York, Dodd, Mead and
     company, 1898.
         264 p.   20 cm.
         CONTENTS.-His version of it.-A warning to lovers.-
     "Sauce for the goose".-The Cortelyou feud.

9539 Ford, Paul Leicester, 1865-1902.
     Wanted - a match maker... New York, Dodd, Mead &
     company, 1900.
         111 p. illus.   20 cm.

9540 Ford, Mrs. Sallie (Rochester) "S. H. Ford," 1828-
     Evangel Wiseman, or, The mother's question. By Sally
     Rochester Ford... St. Louis, Barns & Beynon, 1874.
         507 p.   19 cm.

9541 Fort, G
     We four villagers. A tale of domestic life in Pennsylvania.
     By G. Fort. Philadelphia, J. S. McCalla, 1861.
         iv, [5]-339 p.   18 1/2 cm.

9542 The fortunate discovery: or, The history of Henry Villars. By
     a young lady of the state of New-York. New-York, Printed
     by R. Wilson, for Samuel Cambell, 124, Pearl-street, 1789.
         2 p. 1., 180 p.   16 1/2 cm.

9543 Fosdick, William Whiteman, 1825-1862.
     Malmiztic the Toltec; and the cavaliers of the Cross. By
     W. W. Fosdick. Cincinnati, W. H. Moore & D. Anderson,
     1851.
         xiii, 15-356 p.   19 1/2 cm.

9544 Foster, George G   d. 1850.
     Celio; or, New York above ground and under-ground. By

G. G. Foster... New York, Dewitt & Davenport [c1850]
    144 p.   24 1/2 cm.

9545 Foster, George G   d. 1850.
        Fifteen minutes around New York. By G. G. Foster...
    New York, De Witt & Davenport [c1854]
        v, [7]-111 p.   22 1/2 cm.

9546 [Foster, George G   d.1850]
        New York in slices: by an experienced carver, being the
    original slices published in the N. Y. tribune. Rev., enl.,
    and cor. by the author... New York, W. F. Burgess,
    1849.
        128 p. illus.   23 cm.
        Published anonymously.
        With this is bound: The bastard... A romantic tale...
    from the German of Charles Spindler. New-York, 1845.

9547 Foster, George G   d. 1850.
        New York naked. By George G. Foster... New York, De
    Witt & Davenport [185-]
        1 p. 1., [11]-168 p.   25 cm.

9548 [Foster, Mrs. Hannah (Webster)] 1759-1840.
        The boarding school; or, Lessons of a preceptress to her
    pupils: consisting of information, instruction, and advice, cal-
    culated to improve the manners, and form the character of
    young ladies. To which is added, a collection of letters,
    written by the pupils, to their instructor, their friends, and
    each other. By a lady of Massachusetts; author of The
    coquette... Printed at Boston, by I. Thomas and E. T.
    Andrews. Sold by them, by C. Bingham, and the other book-
    sellers in Boston; by I. Thomas, Worcester; by Thomas,
    Andrews & Penniman, Albany; and by Thomas, Andrews &
    Butler, Baltimore.   June, 1798.
        252 p.   17 cm.

9549 [Foster, Mrs. Hannah (Webster)] 1759-1840.
        The coquette; or, The history of Eliza Wharton; a novel;
    founded on fact. By a lady of Massachusetts. Charlestown,
    Printed by S. Etheridge, for E. and S. Larkin, no. 47,
    Cornhill, Boston. 1802.

261, [1] p.   18 cm.
Second edition. 1st edition, 1797.

9550 [Foster, Mrs. Hannah (Webster)] 1759-1840.
        The coquette; or, The history of Eliza Wharton, a novel:
        founded on fact by a lady of Massachusetts. 30th ed. Boston,
        C. Gaylord, 1840.
            264 p.   14 1/2 cm.
        A reprint of the 30th edition, published in Boston by C.
        Gaylord, in 1833. cf. C. K. Bolton, The Elizabeth
        Whitman mystery, 1912, p. 152.

9551 Fowler, George.
        A flight to the moon; or, The vision of Randalthus. By
        Geo. Fowler... Baltimore: Printed and sold by A.
        Miltenberger, no. 10, North Howard Street, 1813.
            185 p.   18 cm.

9552 Fowler, George.
        The wandering philanthropist: or, Lettres [!] from a
        Chinese. Written during his residence in the United States.
        Discovered and edited by George Fowler... Philadelphia,
        Printed by Bartholomew Graves, No. 40, North Fourth
        street. Published for Geo. Fowler and Barthw. Graves, 1810.
            v, [7]-300 p.   17 1/2 cm.

9553 Fox, John William, 1863-1919.
        Christmas eve on Lonesome, "Hell-fer-sartain," and
        other stories... Illustrated by F. C. Yohn, A. I. Keller,
        W. A. Rogers, and H. C. Ransom. New York, Charles
        Scribner's sons, 1909.
            245 p. illus.,   20 1/2 cm.

9554 Fox, John William, 1863-1919.
        A Cumberland vendetta and other stories... New York,
        Harper & brothers, 1896.
            221 p. illus.   20 cm.
        CONTENTS.-A Mountain Europa.-A Cumberland vendetta.
        -The last Stetson.-Hell fer Sartain.

9555 Fox, John William, 1863-1919.
        The heart of the hills... illustrated by F. C. Yohn.

New York, Charles Scribner's sons, 1913.
396 p. illus. 20 cm.

9556 Fox, John William, 1863-1919.
"Hell fer Sartain" and other stories... New York, Charles
Scribner's sons, 1904.
119 p. 20 1/2 cm.

9557 Fox, John William 1863-1919.
The little shepherd of Kingdom Come... Illustrated by
F. C. Yohn. New York, Charles Scribner's sons, 1909.
404 p. front. 20 cm.

9558 Fox, John William, 1863-1919.
The trail of the lonesome pine... Illustrated by F. C.
Yohn, New York, Grosset & Dunlap, 1908.
422 p. 20 1/2 cm.

9559 Francis, Samuel W[ard] 1835-1886.
A Christmas story, by Dr. Samuel W. Francis. New
York, G. H. Mathews, 1867.
cover-title, 16 p. 21 1/2 cm.
Caption title: Man in his element; or, A new way to keep
house.

9560 [Francis, Samuel Ward] 1835-1886.
Inside out; a curious book. By a singular man... New
York, Miller, Mathews & Clasback, 1862.
4 p. 1., 364 p. 19 cm.

9561 [Francis, Samuel Ward] 1835-1886.
Life and death; a novel. By your humble servant.
New York, Carleton [etc., etc.] 1871.
1 p. 1., 264 p. 18 cm.

9562 Franklin, Josephine.
Rachel: a romance. By Josephine Franklin... Boston,
Thayer & Eldridge, 1860.
300 p. 19 cm.

9563 Fraser, Mrs. C   A
Constance Beverly; a tale of southern life in 1850. By

Mrs. C. A. Fraser. Published in the Sunday Times,
Charleston, S. C. 1879... Charleston, S. C., Sunday Times
publishing house, 1879.
>cover-title, 96 p.   23 1/2 cm.

9564 Fredair, Anna.
>Minor place. By Anna Fredair... New York, E. J. Hale
& sons, 1869.
>281 p.   19 cm.

9565 Frederic, Harold, 1856-1898.
>The deserter, and other stories. A book of the two wars,
by Harold Frederic... Boston, Lothrop publishing company
[c1898]
>v, 401 p. incl. plates. front.   19 1/2 cm.
>CONTENTS. -The deserter. -A day in the wilderness. -How
Dickon came by his name. -Where Avon into Severn flows.

9566 Frederic, Harold, 1856-1898.
>Gloria Mundi, a novel by Harold Frederic. Chicago and
New York, Herbert S. Stone & company, 1898.
>580 p.   18 1/2 cm.

9567 Frederic, Harold, 1856-1898.
>In the sixties, by Harold Frederic, New York, C.
Scribner's sons [c1897]
>xi p., 1 l., 319 p.   19 1/2 cm.
>CONTENTS. -The copperhead. -Marsena. -The war widow. -
The eve of the fourth. -My Aunt Susan.

9568 Frederic, Harold, 1856-1898.
>March hares, by Harold Frederic... New York, D.
Appleton and company, 1896.
>3 p. 1., 281 p.   17 1/2 cm.

9569 Frederic, Harold, 1856-1898.
>The market-place, a novel by Harold Frederic...
Illustrated by Harrison Fisher, New York, Frederic A.
Stokes company [c1899]
>3 p. 1., 401 p. front., plates.   19 cm.

9570 Frederic, Harold, 1856-1898.

Marsena, and other stories of the wartime, by Harold
Frederic. New York, C. Scribner's sons, 1894.
4 p. l., 210 p.   17 1/2 cm.
CONTENTS.-Marsena.-The war widow.-The eve of the
fourth.-My aunt Susan.

9571 Freeman, Mrs. Mary Eleanor (Wilkins) 1852-1930.
The heart's highway: a romance of Virginia in the
seventeenth century... New York, Doubleday, Page & co.,
1900.
308 p. illus.   20 cm.

9572 Freeman, Mrs. Mary Eleanor (Wilkins) 1852-1930.
The Jamesons... New York, Doubleday & McClure
company, Philadelphia, Curtis publishing company, 1899.
177 p. illus.   20 cm.

9573 Freeman, Mrs. Mary Eleanor (Wilkins) 1852-1930.
Jerome, a poorman: a novel... New York and London,
Harper & brothers, 1897.
506 p. illus.   20 cm.

9574 Freeman, Mrs. Mary Eleanor (Wilkins) 1852-1930.
Madelon; a novel, by Mary E. Wilkins... New York,
Harper and brothers, 1896.
2 p. 1., 376 p.   17 cm.

9575 Freeman, Mrs. Mary Eleanor (Wilkins) 1852-1930.
A New England nun, and other stories... New York, Harper
& brothers, 1891.
468 p. front.   20 cm.
Also contains: A village singer-A gala dress-The twelfth
guest-Sister Liddy-Calla-Lilies and Hannah-A wayfaring
couple-A poetess-Christmas Jenny-A pot of gold-The scent
of the roses-A solitary-A gentle ghost-A discovered pearl-
A village Lear-Amanda and love-Up Primrose Hill-A stolen
Christmas-Life everlastin'-An innocent gamester-Louisa-A
church mouse-A kitchen colonel-The revolt of "Mother."

9576 Freeman, Mrs. Mary Eleanor (Wilkins) 1852-1930.
Pembroke: a novel... New York, Harper & brothers, 1894.
330 p. illus.   20 cm.

9577 Freeman, Mrs. Mary Eleanor (Wilkins) 1852-1930.
     The people of our neighborhood, by Mary E. Wilkins...
illustrations by Alice Barber Stephens. Philadelphia, Curtis
publishing company; New York, Doubleday & McClure co.
[c1898]
     viii, 161 p. front. (port.) illus.   15 1/2 cm.
(Ladies Home Journal library of fiction, vol. 3)

9578 Freeman, Mrs. Mary Eleanor (Wilkins) 1852-1930.
     Silence, and other stories, by Mary E. Wilkins... New
York and London, Harper & brothers, 1898.
     3 p. 1. , 279, [1] p. front,, plates.   17 cm.
     CONTENTS. -Silence. -The Buckley Lady. -Evelina's garden.
-A New England prophet. -The little maid at the door. -Lydia
Hersey, of East Bridgewater.

9579 Freeman, Mrs. Theresa J
     Silver lake; or, The belle of Bayou Luie. A tale of the
South. By Theresa J. Freeman. Saint Louis, P. M.
Pinckard, 1867.
     vii, [9]-344 p.   19 cm.
     Binder's title of copy 2: The belle of Bayou Luie.

9580 French, Alice, 1850-1934.
     The captured dream, and other stories... by Octave
Thanet [pseud.] New York and London, Harper & brothers,
MDCCCXCIX.
     128 p.   20 cm.
     CONTENTS. -The captured dream. -His duty. -The stout
Miss Hopkins' bicycle.

9581 French, Alice, 1850-1934.
     The missionary sheriff; being incidents in the life of a
plain man who tried to do his duty, by Octave Thanet
[pseud.] Illustrated by A. B. Frost and Clifford Carleton.
New York, Harper & brothers, 1897.
     3 p. 1. , 248 p. front. , plates.   19 cm.
     CONTENTS. -The missionary sheriff. -The cabinet organ.
-His duty. -The hypnotist. -The next room. -The defeat of
Amos Wickliff.

9582 French, Alice, 1850-1934.

Otto the Knight, and other trans-Mississippi Stories,
by Octave Thanet [pseud.]... Boston and New York,
Houghton, Mifflin and company, 1891.
    3 p. l., 348 p.   18 cm.
    CONTENTS.-Otto the Knight.-The conjured kitchen.-The
first mayor.-Sist' Chaney's black silk.-The loaf of peace.-
The day of the cyclone.-Trust, no. 49.-The plumb idiod.-
The governor's prerogative.-The mortgage on Jeffy.

9583 French, Harry Willard, 1854-
    Ego, a novel: by Harry W. French... Boston, Lee and
Shepard; New York, Charles T. Dillingham, 1880.
    2 p. l., 3-258 p.   18 1/2 cm.

9584 Friend, Julia M
    The Chester family; or, The cruse of the drunkard's
appetite. By Julia M. Friend... Boston, W. White and
company; New-York, The American news company, 1869.
    224 p. front. (port.)   18 1/2 cm.

9585 Frost, John, 1800-1859.
    Border wars of the West. Comprising the frontier wars of
Pennsylvania, Virginia, Kentucky, Ohio, Indiana, Illinois,
Tennessee and Wisconsin, and embracing individual adventures
among the Indians, and exploits of Boone, Kenton... and
other border heroes of the West. By John Frost... Auburn,
[N. Y.] Derby and Miller; Buffalo, Derby, Orton and Milligan;
[etc., etc.] 1853.
    1 p. l., 7-608 p. incl. illus., plates, ports. col. front.
22 1/2 cm.
    Frontispiece includes half-title.

9586 Frothingham, Charles W
    The convent's doom; a tale of Charlestown in 1834. Also
The haunted convent. By Charles W. Frothingham. 5th ed.
Boston, Graves & Weston, 1854.
    32 p.   24 1/2 cm.

9587 Fuller, Anna, 1853-1916.
    A literary courtship under the auspices of Pike's Peak,
by Anna Fuller... New York [etc.] G. P. Putnam's sons,
1893.

3 p. 1., 184 p. illus.   15 1/2 cm.

9588 Fuller, Anna, 1853-1916.
        A Venetian June, by Anna Fuller... Illustrated by
    George Sloane. New York, London, G. P. Putnam's sons,
    1896.
        3 p. 1., 315 p. front., illus.   15 1/2 cm.

9589 Fuller, Edwin Wiley, 1847-1875.
        Sea-gift. A novel. By Edwin W. Fuller... New York,
    E. J. Hale & son, 1873.
        408 p.   18 1/2 cm.

9590 Fuller, Henry Blake, 1857-1929.
        The chatelaine of La Trinité; New York, The Century
    company, 1892.
        176 p.   20 cm.

9591 Fuller, Henry Blake, 1857-1929.
        The last refuge: A Sicilian romance... Boston and New
    York, Houghton, Mifflin and company, The Riverside press,
    Cambridge, 1900.
        284 p.   20 cm.

9592 Fuller, Hulbert, 1865-
        Vivian of Virginia; being the memoirs of our first
    rebellion, by John Vivian, esq., of Middle Plantation,
    Virginia. By Hulbert Fuller; illustrated by Frank T. Merrill.
    Boston, New York [etc.] Lamson, Wolffe and company, 1897.
        vii, 377 p. front., 9 pl.   19 1/2 cm.

9593 [Furman, Garrit] 1782-1848.
        Redfield; a Long-Island tale, of the seventeenth century...
    New York, O. Wilder, & J. M. Campbell, 1825.
        214 p.   19 cm.

9594 [Furniss, Louise E   ]
        An operetta in profile. By Czeika [pseud.] Boston,
    Ticknor and company, 1887.
        265 p.   18 cm.

9595 [Gales, Mrs. Winifred (Marshall)] d. 1822.
Matilda Berkely, or, Family anecdotes; by the author of
The history of Lady Emma Melcombe and her family, &c.
Raleigh, (N. C.) Printed by J. Gales, printer to the state,
1804.
1 p. 1. , [5]-224 p.   18 x 10 1/2 cm.

9596 Gallaher, James, 1792-1853.
The western sketch-book. By James Gallaher. Boston,
Crocker and Brewster; New York, M. W. Dodd [etc. , etc.]
1850.
iv, [5]-408 p.   20 cm.
"The articles... are mostly on religious subjects."-Pref.

9597 [Ganilh, Anthony]
Ambrosio de Letinez; or, The first Texian novel, embracing
a description of the countries bordering on the Rio Bravo,
with incidents of the war of independence. By A. T. Myrthe...
New-York, C. Francis & co. , 1842.
2 v.   19 cm.
Copyright by Anthony Ganilh.
Appeared anonymously under title: Mexico versus Texas...
By a Texian. Philadelphia, W. Siegfried, printer, 1838.

9598 [Ganilh, Anthony]
Mexico versus Texas, a descriptive novel, most of the
characters of which consist of living persons. By a Texian.
Philadelphia, N. Siegfried, printer, 1838.
vii, [9]-348 p.   19 cm.
Published later under title: Ambrosio de Letinez, or, The
first Texian novel... By A. T. Myrthe [pseud.] New York,
1842. 2 v.

9599 Gardener, Helen Hamilton.
An unoffical patriot... Boston, Arena publishing company,
1894.
351 p. front.   cm.

9600 [Gardner]

The life and death of Sam, in Virginia. By a Virginian...
Richmond, A. Morris, 1856.
2 p. 1., vii, 13-308 p.   19 cm.

9601 Cardner, Celia Emmeline, 1844-
Tested; or, Hope's fruition. A story of woman's constancy
... New York, G. W. Carleton & co. [etc., etc.] 1874.
2 p. 1., [7]-430 p.   18 1/2 cm.

9602 Gardner, Mrs. H   C
Glimpses of our lake region in 1863, and other papers.
By Mrs. H. C. Gardner. New York, Nelson & Phillips;
Cincinnati, Hitchcock & Walden [1874]
420 p.   18 cm.

9603 Garland, Hamlin, 1860-1940.
The eagle's heart, by Hamlin Garland... New York,
D. Appleton and company, 1900.
v, 369 p.   19 cm.

9604 Garland, Hamlin, 1860-1940.
Jason Edwards, an average man, by Hamlin Garland...
Boston, Arena Publishing Company, 1892.
2 p. 1., 213 p.   19 1/2 cm.

9605 Garland, Hamlin, 2860-2940.
A little Norsk; or, Ol' pap's Flaxen, by Hamlin Garland...
New York, D. Appleton and company, 1892.
vi, 157 p.   16 1/2 cm.

9606 Garland, Hamlin, 1860-1940.
Main-travelled roads, by Hamlin Garland... New ed.,
with additional stories. New York, London, Harper &
brothers, 1899.
viii, 247 p.   19 1/2 cm.
CONTENTS. -A branch-road. -Up the Coule. -Among the
corn-rows. -The return of a private. -Under the lion's paw. -
Mrs. Ripley's trip. -The creamery man. -A day's pleasure.
-Uncle Ethan Ripley. -God's ravens.

9607 Garland, Hamlin, 1860-1940.
... The spirit of Sweetwater, by Hamlin Garland...

Philadelphia, Curtis publishing company; New York, Doubleday & McClure co. [c1898]
    5 p. l., 33 p., 2 l., 37-63 p., 2 l., 67-100 p. front.
(port.) plates.   15 cm.   (Ladies Home Journal
library of fiction)

9608 Garland, Hamlin, 1860-1940.
        Wayside courtships, by Hamlin Garland... New York,
    D. Appleton and company, 1897.
        vii, 281 p.   19 1/2 cm.

9609 Gay, Mrs. M   M
        Gleanings from real life. By Mrs. M. M. Gay. Buffalo,
    C. E. Felton, printer, 1858.
        1 p. l., [vii]-xii, [13]-291 p.   18 cm.

9610 Gayarré, Charles Étienne Arthur, 1805-1895.
        The school for politics. A dramatic novel. By Charles
    Gayarré. New York, D. Appleton and co., 1854.
        158 p.   18 cm.

9611 Gayler, Charles, 1820-1892.
        Out of the streets, a story of New York life. By Charles
    Gayler. New York, R. M. De Witt [c1869]
        360 p.   18 cm.

9612 Gazer, Giles, pseud.
        Frederick de Algeroy, the hero of Camden plains. A
    revolutionary tale. By Giles Gazer... New York, Collins
    and Hannay [etc.] 1825.
        viii, [9]-235 p.   19 x 11 1/2 cm.

9613 [Gazlay, Allen W   ]
        Races of mankind; with travels in Grubland. By Cephas
    Broaderick [pseud.] Cincinnati, Longley brothers [etc.] 1856.
        viii, 9-310 p. 2 pl.   18 1/2 cm.

9614 Gersoni, Henry, 1844-1897.
        Sketches of Jewish life and history, by Henry Gersoni...
    New York, Hebrew orphan asylum printing establishment,
    1873.
        224 p.   16 1/2 cm.

9615 Gibson, T   Ware.
  The priest of the black cross. A tale of the sea. By Capt.
  T. Ware Gibson... Cincinnati, The "Great West" office,
  1848.
      1 p. 1. , [9]-118 p.   24 cm.

9616 [Gill, William Fearing] 1844-1917, ed.
  Golden treasures of poetry, romance, and art. By
  eminent poets, novelists, and essayists. Boston, W. F. Gill
  and company, 1876.
      7 p. 1. , 13-360 p. front. , illus. , plates.   21 cm.

9617 [Gilman, Mrs. Caroline (Howard)] 1794-1888.
  Recollections of a housekeeper. By Mrs. Clarissa Packard
  ... New-York, Harper & brothers, 1834.
      155 p.   16 cm.

9618 [Gilman, Chandler Robbins] 1802-1865.
  Legends of a log cabin. By a western man... New York,
  G. Dearborn, 1835.
      2 p. 1. , 277 p.   18 1/2 cm.   ·
  CONTENTS. -The log cabin. -The hunter's vow. -The heiress
  of Brandsby. -The log cabin. -The Frenchman's story. -The
  Englishman's story: George Grey, a tale of the English law. -
  The Yankee's story: The sleighride. -The Wyandot's story. -The
  minute men, a tale of '75.

9619 [Gilman, Chandler Robbins] 1802-1865.
  Life on the Lakes: being tales and sketches collected
  during a trip to the pictured rocks of lake Superior. By the
  author of "Legends of a log cabin"... New-York, G. Dearborn, 1836.
      2 v. fronts.   20 cm.

9620 [Gilman, Samuel] 1791-1858.
  Memoirs of a New England village choir. With occasional
  reflections. By a member... 3d ed. Boston, B. H. Greene,
  1846.
      1 p. 1. , 152 p.   17 cm.
  Fictitious names are used, but the scene is supposed to be
  laid in Atkinson, N. H.

9621 [Gilmore, James Roberts] 1822-1903.
        Among the guerrillas. By Edmund Kirke [pseud.]...
New York, Carleton, 1866.
        x, [11]-286 p.   18 cm.

9622 [Gilmore, James Roberts] 1822-1903.
        My Southern friends... By Edmund Kirke [pseud.] New
York, Carleton, 1863.
        308 p.   19 cm.

9623 [Gilmore, James Roberts] 1822-1903.
        On the border. By Edmund Kirke [pseud.]... Boston,
Lee and Shepard, 1867.
        ix, 11-333 p.   19 1/2 cm.

9624 Gladding, Mrs. E   N
        Leaves from an invalid's journal, and poems. By Mrs.
E. N. Gladding. Providence, G. H. Whitney, 1858.
        x, 235 p.   20 cm.

9625 Glasgow, Ellen Anderson Gholson, 1873-1945.
        Phases of an inferior planet [a novel] by Ellen Glasgow...
New York, and London, Harper & brothers, 1898.
        4 p. 1., 3-324 p., 1 1.   19 cm.

9626 Glasgow, Ellen Anderson Gholson, 1873-1945.
        The voice of the people by Ellen Glasgow, New York,
Doubleday, Page, & co., 1900.
        4 p. 1., [3]-444 p.   20 cm.

9627 Glenn, Samuel F
        Gravities and gaieties. By Samuel F. Glenn... Washington,
R. Farnham, 1839.
        2 p. 1., 116 p.   17 1/2 cm.
        Verse and prose.

9628 Godwin, Parke, 1816-1904.
        Vala, a mythological tale, by Parke Godwin. New York,
G. P. Putnam, 1851.
        2 p. 1., 46, [4] p. illus., pl.   28 1/2 cm.
        Illustrated t.-p.
        Written originally for the New York Evening post, but

considerably modified and enlarged. Deals with "the principal incidents in the career of a reigning musical celebrity [i.e. Jenny Lind]" cf. Pref.

9629 [Goodrich, Samuel Criswold] 1793-1860.
A Tale of adventure; or, The Siberian Sable Hunter...
New York, Wiley & Putman, 1843.
170 p.   illus.   12 mo.

9630 Goodwin, Maud (Wilder) 1856-1935.
The head of a hundred: being an account of certain passages in the life of Humphrey Huntoon, esqr., sometyme an officer in the Colony of Virginia. Ed. by Maud Wilder Goodwin...
Boston, Little, Brown company, 1895.
225 p.   18 1/2 cm.

9631 Goss, Charles Frederic, 1852-
The redemption of David Corson, by Charles Frederic Goss. Indianapolis, The Bowen-Merrill company [c1900]
5 p. 1., 418 p.   19 1/2 cm.

9632 Gould, Edward Sherman, 1808-1885.
John Doe and Richard Roe; or, Episodes of life in New York. By Edward S. Gould... New York, Carleton, 1862.
1 p. 1., vi, 9-312 p.   19 cm.

9633 [Gould, Edward Sherman] 1808-1885.
The sleep-rider; or, The old boy in the omnibus. By the man in the claret-colored coat [pseud.] New-York, Winchester [c1843]
1 p. 1., [5]-115, [1] p.   18 1/2 cm.

9634 Gould, John W.   1814-1838.
John W. Gould's private journal of a voyage from New-York to Rio de Janeiro; together with a brief sketch of his life, and his occasional writings, ed. by his brothers.
Printed for private circulation only. New-York, 1838.
207 p.   22 1/2 cm.

9635 Grace, Pierce C
The unknown. A prize tale. By Pierce C. Grace. St. Louis, Chambers and Knapp, 1849.

168 p.   19 cm.

9636 Grainger, Arthur M
      Golden feather; or, The buccaneer of Kings' bridge. A
      war-like romance of the rivers and the bay of New York:
      being a tale of love and glory of the war of 1812-'15. By
      Arthur M. Grainger. New York, F. A. Brady [1860?]
      90 p. incl. plates.   24 1/2 cm.

9637 Grant, Robert, 1852-1940.
      The art of living, by Robert Grant. Illustrated by C.D.
      Gibson, V. West Clinedinst, and W. H. Hyde. New York,
      C. Scribner's sons, 1895.
      xiii, 353 p. incl. illus. plates   20 cm.

9638 Grant, Robert, 1852-1940.
      An average man... Boston, James R. Osgood and
      company, 1884.
      300 p.

9639 Grant, Robert, 1852-1940.
      The bachelor's Christmas, and other stories... New
      York, Charles Scribner's sons, 1895.
      309 p., illus.   20 cm.
      Also contains: An eye for an eye-In fly-time-Richard and
      Robin-The Matrimonial Tontine Benefit Association-By hook
      or crook.

9640 Grant, Robert, 1852-1940.
      The confessions of a frivolous girl: a story of fashionable
      life... Boston, A Williams and Co., New York, Brentano's
      Literary Emporium, 1880.
      220 p.   20 cm.

9641 Grant, Robert, 1852-1940.
      The king's men: a tale of to-morrow... New York, Charles
      Scribner's sons, 1884.
      270 p.   20 cm.
      John Boyle O'Reilly, J. S. of Dale (i.e., Frederic Jesup
      Stimson), and John T. Wheelwright are joint authors.
      England 200 years hence.

9642 Grant, Robert, 1852-1940.
        The knave of hearts; a fairy story of Robert Grant...
      Boston, Ticknor and company, 1886.
        198 p. illus.   19 1/2 cm.

9643 Grant, Robert, 1852-1940.
        The reflections of a married man... New York, Charles
      Scribner's sons, 1892.
        165 p.   20 cm.

9644 Grant, Robert, 1852-1940.
        A romantic young lady... Boston, Ticknor and company,
      1886.
        354 p.   20 cm.
      Of the daughter of a millionaire.

9645 Grant, Robert, 1852-1940.
        Unleavened bread... New York, Charles Scribner's sons,
      1900.
        431 p.   20 cm.

9646 Graves, Mrs. A   J
        Girlhood and womanhood; or, Sketches of my school-
      mates... By Mrs. A. J. Graves... Boston, T. H. Carter &
      co. [etc.] 1844.
        vi p. 1 1., [9]-216 p.   20 cm.

9647 [Gray, Clarence F   ]
        Ancilla DeMontes; or, One summer. With key. By
      The cricket [pseud.] [San Francisco] The author, 1885.
        vii, [9]-135 p.   20 cm.

9648 The great "trunk mystery" of New York city. Murder of the
      beautiful Miss Alice A. Bowlsby, of Paterson, N. J. Her
      body placed in a trunk and labelled for Chicago. Many
      strange incidents made public. Philadelphia, Pa., Barclay
      & co., [1871?]
        1 p. 1., 19-102 p. incl. illus. (plan) plates, fold. front.
      24 cm.

9649 Greeley, Robert F
        Arthur Woodleigh; a romance of the battle field in Mexico.

By Robert F. Greeley. [Also, The bloody nuptials, by R.
F. Greeley, and The female spy, by Samuel Woodworth]
New York, W. B. Smith & co., 1847.
94 p. incl. pl.   24 cm.

9650 Greeley, Robert F
The child of the islands; or, The shipwrecked gold seekers
... New York, Stringer & Townsend, 1850.
87 p.   8 vo.

9651 [Greenc, Asa] 1789-1838.
The perils of Pearl street, including a taste of the dangers
of Wall street, by a late merchant... New York, Betts &
Anstice [etc.] 1834.
232 p.   17 1/2 cm.

9652 [Greene, Asa] 1789-1838.
Travels in America. By George Fibbleton, esq. [pseud.]
ex-barber to His Majesty, the king of Great Britain. New-
York, W. Pearson, P. Hill, and others, 1833.
vi, [7]-216 p.   19 1/2 cm.
"A satire on the Rev. Isaac Fidler's 'Travels in America.' "
-Sabin.

9653 [Greene, Asa] 1789-1838.
A Yankee among the nullifiers: an auto-biography. By
Elnathan Elmwood. esq. [pseud.] New York, W. Stodart,
1833.
152 p.   19 cm.

9654 [Greene, Asa] 1789-1838.
A Yankee among the nullifiers: an auto-biography. By
Elnathan Elmwood, esq. [pseud.] ... 2d ed. New York,
W. Pearson, 1833.
143 p.   15 1/2 x 9 1/2 cm.

9655 Greene, Joseph H
Athaliah: a novel. By Joseph H. Greene, jr. ... New
York, Carleton [etc., etc.] 1869.
1 p. l., [5]-378 p.   18 cm.

9656 Greene, Sarah Pratt (McLean) 1856-1935.

Lastchance Junction, far, far West; a novel by the author of "Cape Cod Folks." Boston, Cupples and Hurd; the Algonquin Press, 1889.
    5 p. 1. , [17]-258 p.   19 1/2 cm.

9657 Greene, Sarah Pratt (McLean), 1856-1935.
    Vesty of the basins: a novel... New York, Harper & brothers, 1892.
    271 p.   20 cm.
    Fishing village on the Maine coast.

9658 Greene, Talbot.
    American nights' entertainments; compiled from pencilings of a United States senator: entitled, A winter in the Federal city ... By Talbot Greene ... Jonesborough, Tenn. , W. A. Sparks & co. , printers, 1860.
    1 p. 1. , [13]-266 p.   19 x 12 1/2 cm.

9659 [Greenough, Henry] 1807-1883.
    Ernest Carroll; or, Artist-life in Italy. A novel ... [Author's ed] Boston, Ticknor and Fields, 1858 [1859]
    iv, [5]-344 p.   18 cm.
    Cover dated 1859.
    Published anonymously.

9660 Greenough, Sarah Dana (Loring) "Mrs. R. S. Greenough," 1827-1885.
    Arabesques: Monarè. Apollyona. Domitia. Ombra. By Mrs. Richard S. Greenough ... Boston, Roberts brothers, 1872.
    4 p. 1. , [3]-213 p. illus.   18 1/2 cm.

9661 Greenough, Sarah Dana (Loring) "Mrs. R. S. Greenough," 1827-1885.
    In extremis. A novelette. By Mrs. Richard S. Greenough ... Boston, Roberts brothers, 1872.
    4 p. 1. , [3]-202 p.   18 1/2 cm.

9662 [Greenough, Sarah Dana (Loring)] "Mrs. R. S. Greenough," 1827-1885.
    Lilian. [A novel] Boston, Ticknor and Fields, 1863.
    1 p. 1. , [5]-312 p.   19 cm.

9663 Greey, Edward, 1835–1888.
      The queen's sailors. A nautical novel. By Edward Greey
... (Sungtie) ... New York, E. Greey & co., 1870.
      3 v. front.   18 1/2 cm.
      Published in 1871 under title: Blue jackets.

9664 [Grey, Jeannie H   ]
      Tactics; or, Cupid in shoulder-straps. A West Point love
story. By Hearton Drille, U. S. A. [pseud.]... New
York, Carleton, 1863.
      3 p. 1., [11]-250 p. illus. (music) pl. (music)   19 cm.

9665 Griest, Ellwood, 1824–1900.
      John and Mary; or, the fugitive slaves, a tale of south-east-
ern Pennsylvania. By Ellwood Griest... Lancaster, Pa.,
Inquirer printing and publishing company, 1873.
      226 p.   20 cm.
      "Written originally for the Lancaster inquirer."

9666 [Griffiths, Julia] ed.
      Autographs for freedom. Boston, J. P. Jewett and
company; Cleveland, O., Jewett, Proctor, and Worthington;
[etc., etc.] 1853.
      viii, 263 p. incl. front. 2 pl.   19 1/2 cm.
      A collection of signed articles, poems, etc., by men and
women prominent in the anti-slavery movement. Most of
the signatures arc in facsimile.
      Preface signed: on behalf of the Rochester ladies' anti-
slavery society, Julia Griffiths, secretary.

9667 [Griswold], Mrs. F[rances Irene] (Burge) Smith, 1826–1900.
      Asleep. By F. Burge Smith... Brooklyn, N. Y., T. B.
Ventres [1871]
      149 p.   19 cm.

9668 [Griswold, Mrs. Frances Irene (Burge) Smith] 1826–1900.
      The bishop and Nannette, by Mrs. F. Burge Smith...
New York, T. Whittaker [1874]
      329 p. front., plates.   19 1/2 cm.

9669 [Griswold, Mrs. Frances Irene (Burge) Smith, 1826–1900.
      Nina, or life's caprices. A story founded on fact. By

F. J. [!] Burge Smith... New York, D. Dana, 1861.
426 p., 1 1. front. 19 cm.
"Introductory account of the Church charity foundation" by
Thomas T. Guion: p. [5]-8.

9670 Griswold, V   M
Hugo Blanc, the artist. A tale of practical and ideal life.
By an artist. New York, Hilton & co.; Philadelphia, J. B.
Lippincott & co., 1867.
vi, [7]-411 p. 19 cm.

9671 Guernsey, Lucy Ellen, 1826-1899.
Lady Betty's governess; or, The Corbet chronicles. By
Lucy Ellen Guernsey... New York, T. Whittaker, 1872.
1 p. 1., 5-369 p. 19 cm.

9672 Gunter, Archibald Clavering, 1847-1907.
Baron Montez of Panama and Paris; a novel, by Archibald
Clavering Gunter... New York, The Home publishing
company, 1893.
266 p. 19 cm.

9673 Gunter, Archibald Clavering, 1847-1907.
Don Balasco of Key West; a novel, by Archibald Clavering
Gunter... New York, The Home publishing co. [c1896]
259 p. 20 1/2 cm.

9674 Guthrie, Mrs. M   J
The silver lining; or, Fair-hope prospect. By Mrs. M. J.
Guthrie. Philadelphia, 1872.
3 p. 1., [9]-203 p. 19 1/2 cm.

9675 Guy, W   H
Abby Forbes: a tale of unparalleled sufferings. Founded on
facts. Written by W. H. Guy, esq. Boston, The author, 1846.
36 p. illus. 20 cm.

9676 Hale, Edward Everett, 1822–1909.
　　　 ... Aunt Caroline's present.　By Edward E. Hale.　Boston,
J. S. Smith & co., [c1895]
　　　 36 p.　　　 14 cm.
　　　 At head of title: "Tell it again."

9677 Hale, Edward Everett, 1822–1909.
　　　 ... Col. Clipsham's calendar.　By Edward E. Hale.
Boston, J. S. Smith & co.　[c1895]
　　　 51 p.　　　 14 cm.
　　　 At head of title: "Tell it again."

9678 Hale, Edward Everett, 1822–1909.
　　　 Crusoe in New York, and other tales, by Edward Everett
Hale...　Boston, Roberts brothers, 1880.
　　　 vi p., 1 1., 259 p.　　　 18 cm.
　　　 CONTENTS. –Crusoe in New York. –Alif-Laila. –A civil
servant. –Nicolette and Aucassin. –The lost place. –The
western Ginevra. –Max Keesler's horse-car. –The modern
Psyche.

9679 Hale, Edward Everett, 1822–1909.
　　　 The fortunes of Rachel, by Edward Everett Hale...　New
York, Funk & Wagnalls, 1884.
　　　 iv, [5]–221 p.　　　 19 cm.　(On cover: Standard library,
no. 115)

9680 Hale, Edward Everett, 1822–1909.
　　　 G. T. T.; or, The wonderful adventures of a Pullman.　By
Edward E. Hale.　Boston, Roberts brothers, 1877.
　　　 x, [5]–221 p.　　　 17 1/2 cm.　(Half-title: Town and
country series)

9681 Hale, Edward Everett, 1822–1909.
　　　 ... Hands off.　By Edward E. Hale.　Boston, J. S. Smith
& co.　[c1895]
　　　 39 p.　　　 14 cm.
　　　 At head of title: "Tell it again."

9682 Hale, Edward Everett, 1822-1909.
>   If Jesus came to Boston... Boston, J. Stilman Smith &
> co. [c1894]
>   45 p.   20 cm.

9683 Hale, Edward Everett, 1822-1909.
>   The Ingham papers: some memorials of the life of Capt.
> Frederic Ingham, U. S. N. , sometime pastor of the First
> Sandemanian church in Naguadavick, and major general by
> brevet in the patriot service in Italy. By Edward E. Hale
> ... Boston, Fields, Osgood, & co. , 1869.
>   2 p. 1. , [vii]-xx, 266 p.   18 1/2 cm.
>   CONTENTS. -Memoir of Captain Frederic Ingham. -The
> good-natured pendulum. -Paul Jones and Denis Duval. -Round
> the world in a hack. -Friends' meeting. -Did he take the prince
> to ride ?-How Mr. Frye would have preached it. -The rag-man
> and the rag-woman. -Dinner speaking. -Good society. -Daily
> bread.

9684 [Hale, Edward Everett] 1822-1909.
>   The man without a country. Boston, Ticknor and Fields,
> 1865.
>   23 p.   17 cm.
>   First separate edition? Appeared first in the Atlantic
> monthly, December, 1863. cf. edition 1898, Author's note,
> p. 5, 13, and 16.

9685 Hale, Edward Everett, 1822-1909.
>   Mr. Tangier's vacations, a novel, by Edward E. Hale...
> Boston, Roberts brothers, 1888.
>   2 p. 1. , [7]-303 p.   18 1/2 cm.

9686 Hale, Edward Everett, 1822-1909.
>   My double & how he undid me, by Edward Everett Hale.
> Boston, New York, Lamson, Wolffe & co. , 1895.
>   50 p. front (port.)   18 1/2 cm.
>   "This edition is limited to 1,000 copies."

9687 Hale, Edward Everett, 1822-1909.
>   My friend the boss. A story of to-day. By Edward E.
> Hale... Boston, J. S. Smith & company, 1888.
>   iv p. , 1 1. , 191 p.   19 cm.

9688 Hale, Edward Everett, 1822-1909.
         The new Harry and Lucy; a story of Boston in the summer of
      1891, by Edward E. Hale and Lucretia P. Hale. Boston,
      Roberts brothers, 1892.
         vi, 321 p. front., plates.   18 cm.

9689 Hale, Edward Everett, 1822-1909.
         One good turn, a story by Edward Everett Hale. Boston,
      Office Lend a Hand [c1893]
         37 p.   16 cm.

9690 Hale, Edward Everett, 1822-1909.
         Our Christmas in a palace, a traveller's story, by Edward
      Everett Hale. New York, Funk & Wagnalls, 1883.
         268 p.   18 1/2 cm. (Standard library, no. 103)
      Advertising matter included in paging.

9691 Hale, Edward Everett, 1822-1909.
         Philip Nolan's friends; a story of the change of western
      empire. By Edward E. Hale... New York, Scribner,
      Armstrong, and company, 1877.
         395 p. front. 4 p.   19 cm.
      "Copyright 1876."

9692 Hale, Edward Everett, 1822-1909.
         ... A safe deposit, By Edward E. Hale, Boston, J. S.
      Smith & co. [c1895]
         43 p.   14 cm.
      At head of title: "Tell it again."

9693 [Hale, Edward Everett] 1822-1909, ed.
         Six of one by half a dozen of the other. An every day
      novel. By Harriet Beecher Stowe, Adeline D. T. Whitney,
      Lucretia P. Hale, Frederic W. Loring, Frederic B. Perkins,
      Edward E. Hale. Boston, Roberts brothers, 1872.
         xv, 245 p.   18 cm.

9694 Hale, Edward Everett, 1822-1909.
         Susan's escort, and others. Illustrated by W. T. Smedley.
      New York, Harper, 1897.
         viii, 416 p. illus.   19 cm.

9695 Hale, Edward Everett, 1822-1909.
　　　　Sybaris and other homes. By Edward E. Hale. Boston,
　　Fields, Osgood, & co., 1869.
　　　　xiv p., 1 1., 206 p.　　　18 1/2 cm.
　　　　CONTENTS.-My visit to Sybaris.-How they lived at
　　Naguadavick.-How they live in Vineland.-How they live in
　　Boston, and how they die there.-Homes for Boston laborers.
　　-Appendix.

9696 Hale, Edward Everett, 1822-1909.
　　　　Sybil Knox; or Home again; a story of to-day, by Edward
　　E. Hale... New York, Cassell publishing company [1892]
　　　　2 p. 1., 321 p.　　　19 1/2 cm.

9697 Hale, Edward Everett, 1822-1909.
　　　　Workingmen's homes. Essays and stories, by Edward E.
　　Hale and others, on the homes of men who work in large
　　towns. Boston, J. R. Osgood and company, 1874.
　　　　2 p. 1., 182 p. front., plan.　　　18 1/2 cm.

9698 [Hale, Lucretia Peabody] 1820-1900.
　　　　Struggle for life. By the author of "Seven stormy
　　Sundays," "The queen of the red chessmen," etc. Boston,
　　Walker, Wise, & co., 1861.
　　　　311 p.　　　19 1/2 cm.

9699 Hale, Robert Beverly, 1869-1895.
　　　　Six stories and some verses, by Robert Beverly Hale,
　　Boston, J. M. Bowles, 1896.
　　　　4 p. 1., 3-188, [3] p. plates.　　　23 1/2 cm.
　　　　Preface signed by his father, Edward E. Hale.

9700 Hale, Mrs. Sarah Josepha (Buell) 1788-1879.
　　　　Northwood; a tale of New England By Mrs. S. J. Hale...
　　Boston, Bowles & Dearborn, 1827.
　　　　2 v.　　　20 cm.

9701 Hale, Mrs. Sarah Josepha (Buell) 1788-1879.
　　　　Northwood; or, Life north and south; showing the true
　　character of both. By Mrs. Sarah Josepha Hale... New
　　York, H. Long & brother [c1852]
　　　　vi, [7]-408 p. front., plates.　　　19 cm.

9702 Hale, Mrs. Sarah Josepha (Buell) 1788-1879.
    Sketches of American character. By Mrs. Sarah J. Hale...
6th stereotype ed. Philadelphia, H. Perkins; Boston, B.
Bradley, 1838.
    287 p. incl. front.   16 1/2 cm.
    CONTENTS.-Walter Wilson.-The soldier of the revolution.
-The wedding and the funeral.-Ann Ellsworth.-The village
schoolmistress.-The belle and the bleu.-The poor scholar.-
The Springs.-Prejudices.-The apparition.-William Forbes.-
A winter in the country.

9703 Hale, Mrs. Sarah Josepha (Buell) 1788-1879.
    Sketches of American character. By Mrs. Sarah J. Hale...
Philadelphia, Perkins & Purves, 1843.
    2 p. 1., [7]-287 p.   15 cm.
    CONTENTS.-Walter Wilson.-The soldier of the revolu-
tion.-The wedding and the funeral.-Ann Ellsworth.-The
village schoolmistress.-The belle and the bleu.-The poor
scholar.-The Springs.-Prejudices.-The apparition.-
William Forbes.-A winter in the country.

9704 Hall, Abraham Oakey, 1826-1898.
    The congressman's Christmas dream, and the lobby
member's happy New Year. A holiday sketch. By A.
Oakley Hall. Illustrations designed by his daughter, Cara
D. Hall, and drawn on wood by H. L. Stephens. New York,
[etc.] Scribner, Welford & co., 1870-71.
    1 p. 1., iv, 64 p.   26 1/2 cm.
    Added t.-p., illustrated.

9705 [Hall, Baynard Rush] 1798-1863.
    The new purchase: or, Seven and a half years in the far
West. By Robert Carleton, esq. [pseud.]... New-York,
D. Appleton & co.; Philadelphia, G. S. Appleton, 1843.
    2 v.   18 1/2 cm.
    An account of pioneer life in Bloomington, Monroe co.,
Ind.; where the author was first principal and then a pro-
fessor in the seminary and college which later developed into
Indiana university.
    Names of persons and places are fictitious.

9706 [Hall, Baynard Rush] 1798-1863,

Something for every body: gleaned in the old purchase,
from fileds often reaped. By Robert Carlton [pseud.]...
New-York, D. Appleton & company; Philadelphia, G. S.
Appleton, 1846.
    1 p. 1. , [5]-223 p.   19 cm. (On cover: Appleton's
literary miscellany, no. 16)

9707 Hall, Charles Winslow, 1843-1916.
    Twice taken: an historical romance of the maritime
British provinces. By Chas. W. Hall. Boston, Lee and
Shepard, 1867.
    1 p. 1. , [5]-242 p.   17 cm.

9708 Hall, James, 1793-1868.
    Legends of the West. By James Hall. New York, T. L.
Magagnos and company, 1854.
    xvi, [17]-435 p. front.   19 cm.
    Added t. -p. , illustrated.

9709 [Hall, Mrs. Louisa Jane (Park)] 1802-1892.
    Alfred [and The better part] By the author of "Sophia
Morton"... Boston, J. Munroe and company, 1836.
    3 p. 1. , 114 p. , 2 p. 1. , 24 p.   15 cm. (Added
t. -p.: Scenes and characters illustrating Christian truth
[ed. by H. Ware] no. VI)

9710 [Hall, Mrs. Louisa Jane (Park)] 1802-1892.
    Joanna of Naples, by the author of "Miriam". Boston,
Hilliard, Gray and company, 1838.
    1 p. 1. , 213 p.   19 1/2 cm.

9711 Hall, Mrs. Louisa Jane (Park) 1802-1892.
    Miriam, and Joanna of Naples, with other pieces in
verse and prose. By Louisa J. Hall. Boston, W. Crosby
and H. P. Nichols, 1850.
    2 p. 1. , 403 p.   19 1/2 cm.

9712 [Hallett, Miss E   V   ]
    Natalie; or, A gem among the sea-weeds. By Ferna
Vale [pseud.] Andover, Printed by W. F. Draper, 1858.
    324 p.   19 1/2 cm.

9713 [Halpine, Charles Graham] 1829-1868.
   Baked meats of the funeral. A collection of essays, poems,
speeches, histories, and banquets. By Private Miles O'Reilly
[pseud.], late of the 47th reg't, New York volunteer infantry,
10th army corps. Collected, rev., and ed., with the requisite
corrections of punctuation, spelling, and grammar. By an
ex-colonel... New York, Carleton, 1866.
   viii, [3]-378 p.   18 cm.
   Title vignette.

9714 Halpine, Charles Graham, 1829-1868.
   The life and adventures, songs, services, and speeches
of Private Miles O'Reilly [pseud.] (47th regiment, New York
volunteers)... With comic illustrations by Mullen. From
the authentic records of the New York Herald. New York,
Carleton, 1864.
   x, [11]-237 p.   illus., 5 pl.   18 cm.

9715 [Halsey, Harlan Page] 1839?-1898.
   Phil Scott; or, The Indian detective, by Judson R. Taylor
[pseud.]... New York, J. S. Ogilvie & company [1882]
   136 p.   18 cm.

9716 Halyard, Harry, pseud.
   The chieftain of Churubusco; or, The spectre of the
cathedral. A romance of the Mexican war. By Harry
Halyard... Boston, F. Gleason, 1848.
   1 p. 1., [7]-100 p. incl. pl.   26 cm.

9717 Halyard, Harry, pseud.
   Geraldine; or, The gipsey of Germantown. A national
and military romance. By Harry Halyard... Boston, F.
Gleason, 1848.
   2 p. 1., [7]-100 p.   26 cm.

9718 Halyard, Harry, pseud.
   The heroine of Tampico; or, Wildfire the wanderer. A
tale of the Mexican war. By Harry Halyard. Boston, F.
Gleason, 1848.
   1 p. 1., [7]-100 p. incl. pl.   26 cm.
   "The belle of Baltimore": p. [91]-100

191

9719 Halyard, Harry, pseud.
　　　　The Mexican spy; or, The bride of Buena Vista. A tale
　　　of the Mexican war. By Harry Halyard... Boston, F.
　　　Gleason, 1848.
　　　　　1 p. 1., [7]-100 p. incl. pl.　　26 cm.

9720 Halyard, Harry, pseud.
　　　　The ocean monarch; or, The ranger of the Gulf. A
　　　Mexican romance. By Harry Halyard... Boston, F.
　　　Gleason, 1848.
　　　　　2 p. 1., [7]-100 p. incl. pl.　　26 cm.
　　　　"The midnight shipwreck': p. [96]-100.

9721 Halyard, Harry, pseud.
　　　　The Peruvian nun; or, The Empress of the ocean. A
　　　maritime romance. By Harry Halyard... Boston, F.
　　　Gleason, 1848.
　　　　　1 p. 1., [7]-100 p. incl. pl.　　25 1/2 cm.

9722 Halyard, Harry, pseud.
　　　　The rover of the reef; or, The nymph of the Nightingale.
　　　A romance of Massachusetts Bay. By Harry Halyard...
　　　Boston, F. Gleason [c1848]
　　　　　2 p. 1., [7]-100 p. incl. plates.　　26 cm.

9723 Hamilton, Mrs. M　　　　J　　　R
　　　　Cachet; or, The secret sorrow. A novel. By Mrs. M.
　　　J. R. Hamilton. New York, G. W. Carleton & co. [etc.,
　　　etc.] 1873.
　　　　　3 p. 1., [9]-351 p.　　18 1/2 cm.

9724 [Hammett, Samuel Adams] 1816-1865.
　　　　The wonderful adventures of Captain Priest; a tale of but
　　　few incidents, and no plot in particular. With other legends;
　　　by the author of "A stray Yankee in Texas." New York,
　　　Redfield, 1855.
　　　　　1 p. 1., viii, [9]-335 p. front.　　18 1/2 cm.

9725 Hammond, Mrs. Adelaide F
　　　　Josephine Eloise, a novel: by Mrs. Adelaide F. Hammond.
　　　Baltimore, Baltimore news company, 1872.
　　　　　93 p.　　24 1/2 cm.

9726 [Hammond, Mrs. Henrietta Hardy] 1854-1883.
      Her waiting heart. By Lou. Capsadell [pseud.]... New
York, The Authors' publishing company, 1875.
      192 p.   19 1/2 cm.

9727 Hammond, Samuel H   1809-1878.
      Country margins and rambles of a journalist. By S. H.
Hammond... and L. W. Mansfield... New York, J. C.
Derby; Boston, Phillips, Sampson & co. [etc., etc.] 1855.
      x p. 1 l., [9]-356 p.   19 cm.
      Sketches of life and travel in the state of New York, first
published in the Albany state register.

9728 Hammond, William Alexander, 1828-1900.
      Robert Severne, his friends and his enemies. A novel.
By William A. Hammond. Philadelphia, J. B. Lippincott &
co., 1867.
      iv, 5-369 p.   19 cm.

9729 Hancock, Sallie J
      Etna Vandemir, a romance of Kentucky and "the great
uprising". By Sallie J. Hancock... New-York, Cutter,
Tower & co., 1863.
      366 p.   19 cm.

9730 Hancock, Sallie J
      The Montanas; or, Under the stars. A romance. By
Sallie J. Hancock... New York, Carleton, 1866.
      2 p. 1., [7]-320 p.   19 cm.

9731 Hankins, Marie Louise.
      Reality; or, A history of human life. [A novel] By Marie
Louise Hankins... New-York and Philadelphia, M. L.
Hankins & co., 1858.
      1 p. 1., 5-92 p.   18 1/2 x 11 1/2 cm.

9732 Hankins, Marie Louise.
      Women of New York. Written and illustrated by Marie
Louise Hankins... New-York, M. L. Hankins & co.,
1861.
      x, 11-354 p. incl. plates. front., plates.   19 cm.

9733 Hanson, Emma (Cole)
      The life and sufferings of Miss Emma Cole, being a
faithful narrative of her life. Written by herself. 2d ed.
Boston, M. Aurelius, 1844.
      36 p. incl. front., illus.   19 cm.

9734 Hapgood, Herbert Jackson, 1870-   ed.
      Echoes from Dartmouth: a collection of poems, stories,
and historical sketches by graduate and undergraduate writers
of Dartmouth college... Ed. by H. J. Hapgood, '96 and
Craven Laycock, '96. Hanover, N. H. [C. M. Stone & co.,
St. Johnsbury, Vt., printers] 1895.
      151 p. plates, ports.   18 cm.

9735 Harbert, Mrs. Elizabeth Morrisson (Boynton) 1845-
      Out of her sphere. [A novel] By Lizzie Boynton Harbert
... Des Moines, Mills & co., 1871.
      4 p. 1., 184 p.   18 1/2 cm.

9736 [Hare, Mrs. R   ]
      Standish: a story of our day... 1st ed. Boston, Loring,
1865.
      3 p. 1., [3]-185 p.   22 1/2 cm.

9737 [Hare, Robert] 1781-1858.
      Standish the Puritan. A tale of the American revolution.
By Eldred Grayson, esq. [pseud.] New York, Harper &
brothers, 1850.
      iv, [5]-320 p.   19 cm.

9738 Harlan, Caleb.
      The fate of Marcel. By Caleb Harlan... Philadelphia,
J. B. Lippincott & co., 1883.
      262 p.   19 1/2 cm.

9739 Harland, Henry, 1861-1905.
      The cardinal's snuff box, by Henry Harland. London &
New York, J. Lane, 1900.
      319 p.   19 cm.

9740 Harland, Henry, 1861-1905.
      Gray roses, by Henry Harland. Boston, Roberts bros.;

London, J. Lane, 1895.
    208 p.   17 1/2 cm.   (On cover: Keynotes series, 10)
    CONTENTS. -The Bohemian girl. -Mercedes. -A broken
looking-glass. -The reward of virtue. -A re-incarnation. -
Flower o' the quince. -When I am king. -A responsibility. -
Castles near Spain.

9741 Harland, Henry, 1861-1905.
    Mademoiselle miss, to which is added; The funeral march
of a marionette. The prodigal father, A sleeveless errand,
A light sovereign. New York, Lovell, Coryell, 1893.
    192 p.   20 cm.

9742 [Harland, Henry] 1861-1905.
    Mrs. Peixada, by Sidney Luska [pseud.] New York,
Cassell & co. , 1886.
    317 p.   18 cm.

9743 [Harrington, John A   ]
    Between the crusts; or, "Ticket 1939." By John
Carboy [pseud.]... New York, Collin & Small, 1875.
    109 p. front. , plates.   24 1/2 cm.

9744 Harris, H   A
    The horse thief; or, The maiden and Negro. A tale of
the prairies. By H. A. Harris. Boston, Gleason's
publishing hall, 1845.
    1 p. 1. , [5]-66 p.   23 1/2 cm.

9745 Harris, Joel Chandler, 1848-1908.
    Balaam and his master, and other sketches and stories,
by Joel Chandler Harris... Boston and New York, Houghton,
Mifflin and company, 1891.
    2 p. 1. , [7]-293 p.   18 cm.
    CONTENTS. -Balaam and his master. -A conscript's
Christmas. -Ananias. -Where's Duncan?-Mom Bi. -The
old Bascom place.

9746 Harris, Joel Chandler, 1848-1908.
    The chronicles of Aunt Minervy Ann, by Joel Chandler
Harris; illustrated by A. B. Frost. New York, C. Scribner's
sons, 1899.

ix, 210 p. front. , plates.   21 cm.

9747 Harris, Joel Chandler, 1848-1908.
     Free Joe, and other Georgian sketches, by Joel Chandler
Harris... New York, C. Scribner's sons, 1887.
     3 p. 1. , 236 p.   19 cm.
     CONTENTS. -Free Joe. -Little Compton. -Aunt Fountain's
prisoner. -Trouble on Lost Mountain. -Azalia.

9748 Harris, Joel Chandler, 1848-1908.
     On the plantation; a story of a Georgia boy's adventures
during the war, by Joel Chandler Harris... With twenty-
three illustrations by E. W. Kemble. New York, D.
Appleton and company, 1892.
     xii, 233 p. front. (port.) illus.   19 1/2 cm.
     Published at London, under title, "A plantation printer."

9749 Harris, Joel Chandler, 1848-1908.
     On the wing of occasions; being the authorized version
of certain curious episodes of the late civil war, including
the hitherto suppressed narrative of the kidnapping of
President Lincoln, by Joel Chandler Harris... New York,
Doubleday, Page & co. , 1900.
     vii, 310 p. front. , plates.   20 1/2 cm.
     CONTENTS. -Why the Confederacy failed. -In the order of
Providence. -The troubles of Martin Coy. -The kidnapping of
President Lincoln. -The whims of Captain McCarthy.

9750 Harris, Joel Chandler, 1848-1908.
     Sister Jane, her friends and acquaintances; a narrative
of certain events and episodes transcribed from the papers
of the late William Wornum, by Joel Chandler Harris.
Boston and New York, Houghton, Mifflin and company, 1896.
     2 p. 1. , 363 p.   20 cm.

9751 Harris, Joel Chandler, 1848-1908.
     Tales of the home folks in peace and war, by Joel
Chandler Harris... Boston and New York, Houghton,
Mifflin and company, 1898.
     4 p. 1. , 417, [1] p. front. , plates.   20 cm.

9752 Harris, Louise S

Linden Hill; or, The vanquished life-dream. By Louise
S. Harris. St. Louis, Southwestern book and publishing
company, 1874.
455 p.   19 cm.

9753 Harris, Miriam (Coles) "Mrs. S. S. Harris," 1834-1925.
Frank Warrington... A novel. By Mrs. Sidney S. Harris.
New York, Carleton, 1863.
478 p.   18 cm.

9754 Harris, Miriam (Coles) "Mrs. S. S. Harris," 1834-1925.
Happy-go-lucky; a novel, by the author of Rutledge.
New York, G. W. Carleton, 1881.
420 p.   19 cm.

9755 [Harris, Miriam (Coles)] "Mrs. S. S. Harris," 1834-1925.
A perfect Adonis... New York, G. W. Carleton & co.;
[etc., etc.] 1875.
1 p. l., [9]-380 p.   19 cm.

9756 [Harris, Miriam (Coles) "Mrs. S. S. Harris"] 1834-1925.
Rutledge. New York, Derby & Jackson, 1860.
504 p.   18 cm.

9757 Harris, Miriam (Coles) "Mrs. S. S. Harris," 1834-1925.
St. Philip's. By the author of "Rutledge"... New York,
Carleton, 1865.
viii, [9]-340 p.   18 1/2 cm.

9758 [Harrison, Constance (Cary) "Mrs. Burton Harrison"] 1843-
1920.
The anglomaniacs. New York, Cassell publishing
company [c1890]
2 p. l., 296 p.   17 1/2 cm.

9759 Harrison, Constance (Cary,"Mrs. Burton Harrison," 1843-
1920.
A bachelor maid, by Mrs. Burton Harrison... With
illustrations by Irving R. Wiles. New York, The Century co.,
1894.
3 p. l., 224 p. incl. 6 pl. front.   19 1/2 cm.

9760 [Harrison, Constance (Cary)] "Mrs. Burton Harrison," 1843-
1920.
    Bar Harbor days, by Mrs. Burton Harrison... with
illustrations by Fenn and Hyde. New York, Harper and
brothers, 1887.
    4 p. 1., 181 [1] p. front. plates.   17 1/2 cm.

9761 Harrison, Constance (Cary) "Mrs. Burton Harrison," 1843-
1920.
    Belhaven tales; Crow's nest; Una and King David, by Mrs.
Burton Harrison... New York, The Century co., 1892.
    5 p. 1., 212 p. front., plates.   19 1/2 cm.
    Belhaven tales are sketches of the social life of Alexandria,
Va., in the early part of the 19th century.

9762 Harrison, Constance (Cary) "Mrs. Burton Harrison," 1843-
1920.
    The Carcellini emerald, with other tales, by Mrs. Burton
Harrison. Chicago and New York, H. S. Stone and company,
1899.
    4 p. 1., 3-314 p. 1 1. front., plates.   19 1/2 cm.
    CONTENTS.-The Carcellini emerald.-An author's reading
and its consequences.-Leander of Betsy's pride.-The three
Misses Benedict at Yale.-A girl of the period.-The stolen
Stradivarius.-Wanted: a chaperon.

9763 Harrison, Constance (Cary) "Mrs. Burton Harrison," 1843-
1920.
    The circle of a century, by Mrs. Burton Harrison. New
York, The Century co., 1899.
    4 p. 1., 225 p.   20 cm.

9764 Harrison, Constance (Cary) "Mrs. Burton Harrison," 1843-
1920.
    An edelweiss of the Sierras; Golden-rod, and other tales.
By Mrs. Burton Harrison. New York, Harper and brothers,
1892.
    3 p. 1., [3]-209 p.   19 cm.
    CONTENTS.-An edelweiss of the Sierras.-Golden-rod: an
idyl of mount Desert.-Under the convent wall.-Cherrycote.-
The shattered violin.-A house built upon the sand.-On a
hill-top.

9765 Harrison, Constance (Cary) "Mrs. Burton Harrison," 1843-
1920.
An errant wooing, by Mrs. Burton Harrison... New
York, The Century co., 1895.
v p., 1 1., 258 p. front., plates.   20 cm.

9766 Harrison, Constance (Cary) "Mrs. Burton Harrison," 1843-
1920.
Flower de Hundred: the story of a Virginia Plantation...
New York, Cassell Publishing Company, 104 & 106 Fourth
Avenue [c1890]
301 p.   20 cm.

9767 Harrison, Constance (Cary) "Mrs. Burton Harrison," 1843-
1920.
Good Americans... New Yor, The Century co., 1898.
220 p. front.   20 cm.

9768 Harrison, Constance (Cary) "Mrs. Burton Harrison," 1843-
1920.
The merry maid of Arcady, His lordship, and other stories,
by Mrs. Burton Harrison... Boston, London, New York,
Lamson, Wolffe and company, 1897.
4 p. 1., 3-348 p. front., plates.   17 cm.
CONTENTS.-The merry maid of Arcady.-Worrosquoyacke.-
Leaves from the diary of Ruth Marchmont, spinster.-Thirteen
at table.-At a winter house-party.-The secret of San Juan.-
"The stranger within thy gate."-His lordship.

9769 Harrison, Constance (Cary) "Mrs. Burton Harrison," 1843-
1920.
Short stories, edited by Constance Cary Harrison. New
York, Harper & brothers, 1893.
4 p. 1., [vii]-ix p., 1 1., 220 p.   15 1/2 cm. (Half-
title: The Distaff series)
CONTENTS.-Introduction [by B. W. Bellamy]-My own
story, by E. D. B. Stoddard.-In honor bound, by C.
Chesebro.-An islander, by M. Crosby.-A speakin' ghost,
by Mrs. A. T. Slosson.-Monsieur Alcibiade, by C. C.
Harrison.

9770 Harrison, Constance (Cary) "Mrs. Burton Harrison," 1843-

1920.

A son of the Old Dominion... Boston, New York, and London, Lamson, Wolffe and company, 1897.
355 p.   20 cm.

9771 Harrison, Constance (Cary) "Mrs. Burton Harrison," 1843-1920.

Sweet bells out of tune... New York, The Century co., 1893.
231 p. illus.   19 cm.

9772 Harrison, Constance (Cary) "Mrs. Burton Harrison," 1843-1920.

A triple entanglement, by Mrs. Burton Harrison...
Philadelphia, J. B. Lippincott company, 1899.
272 p.   front., plates.   19 cm.

9773 Harrison, Constance (Cary) "Mrs. Burton Harrison," 1843-1920.

A Virginia cousin, & Bar Harbor tales, by Mrs. Burton Harrison. Boston and New York, Lamson, Wolffe and co., 1895.
3 p. 1., 3-202 p. front. (port.)   16 1/2 cm.
CONTENTS. -A Virginia cousin. -Out of season. -On Frenchman's Bay.

9774 [Hart, Miss   ]

Letters from the Bahama islands. Written in 1823-4.
Philadelphia, H. C. Carey and I. Lea, 1827.
207 p.   16 1/2 cm.
Published anonymously.
Signed "Adela", "A. D. L.", and "Adela Del Lorraine".
"All that can be. said of this work is, that the manuscript was recommended to the publishers by a gentleman of known literary merit, and that it was written in a fair, but illegible, Italian hand."-Pub. notice.

9775 [Hart, Joseph C   ] d. 1855.

Miriam Coffin; or, The whale-fishermen: a tale... New-York, G. & C. & H. Carvill; Philadelphia, Carey & Hart; [etc., etc.] 1834.
2 v.   19 1/2 cm.

Music ("Serenade by the author of Miriam Coffin... words by Sheridan"): v. 1, p. [180]-187.

9776 Harte, Bret, 1836-1902.
　　　The Argonauts of North Liberty, by Bret Harte. Boston and New York, Houghton, Mifflin and company, 1888.
　　　1 p. l., 206 p.　　15 cm.

9777. Harte, Bret, 1836-1902.
　　　By shore and sedge. Boston, Houghton, Mifflin, 1885.
　　　260 p.　　15 cm.
　　　Copies 1 & 2, blue cloth; copy 3, brown cloth.
　　　CONTENTS. -An apostle of the Tules. -Sarah Walker. -A ship of '49.

9778 Harte, Bret, 1836-1902.
　　　Condensed novels. By Bret Harte. With illustrations by S. Eytinge, jr. Boston, J. R. Osgood and company, 1871.
　　　iv, 212 p.　　front.　　18 1/2 cm.

9779 Harte, Bret, 1836-1902.
　　　Drift from two shores, by Bret Harte. Boston, Houghton, Osgood and company, 1878.
　　　266 p.　　15 1/2 cm.
　　　CONTENTS. -The man on the beach. -Two saints of the foot-hills. -Jinny. -Roger Catron's friends. -Who was my quiet friend?-A ghost of the Sierras. -The hoodlum band (a condensed novel)-The man whose yoke was not easy. -My friend the tramp. -The man from Solano.-The office seeker. -A sleeping-car experience. -Five o'clock in the morning. -With the entrées.

9780 Harte, Bret, 1836-1902.
　　　Flip, and found at Blazing Star by Bret Harte. Boston, New York, Houghton, Mifflin and company, 1882.
　　　3 p. l., 192 p.　　15 cm.

9781 Harte, Bret, 1836-1902.
　　　Frontier stories, by Bret Harte. Boston and New York, Houghton, Mifflin and company, 1887.
　　　2 p. l., 452 p.　　20 1/2 cm.
　　　CONTENTS. -Flip: a California romance. -Found at Blazing

Star. -In the Carquinez woods. -At the Mission of San Carmel. -A blue-grass Penelope. -Left out on Lone Star mountain. -A ship of '49.

9782 Harte, Bret, 1836-1902.
   In a hollow of the hills, by Bret Harte. Boston and New York, Houghton, Mifflin and company, 1895.
   1 p. 1., 210 p.   18 cm.

9783 Harte, Bret, 1836-1902.
   In the Carquinez woods. By Bret Harte. Boston, Houghton, Mifflin and company, 1884.
   241 p.   15 1/2 cm.

9784 Harte, Bret, 1836-1902.
   The luck of Roaring Camp, and other sketches... Boston, Fields, Osgood & co., 1870.
   256 p.   20 cm.

9785 Harte, Bret, 1836-1902.
   Maruja, by Bret Harte. Boston and New York, Houghton, Mifflin and company, 1885.
   1 p. 1., [3]-271 p.   15 cm.

9786 Harte, Bret, 1836-1902.
   A millionaire of rough-and-ready, and Devil's Ford, by Bret Harte. Boston and New York, Houghton, Mifflin and company, 1887.
   299 p.   15 1/2 cm.
   "Devil's Ford": p. 169-299.

9787 Harte, Bret, 1936-1902.
   Mrs. Skaggs's husbands, and other sketches. By Bret Harte. Boston, J. R. Osgood and company, 1873.
   iv, [3]-352 p.   18 1/2 cm.

9788 Harte, Bret, 1836-1902.
   On the frontier, by Bret Harte, Boston, New York, Houghton, Mifflin and company, 1884.
   288 p.   15 1/2 cm.
   CONTENTS. -At the mission of San Carmel. -A blue grass Penelope. -Left out on Lone Star mountain.

9789 Harte, Bret, 1836-1902.
  A Phyllis of the Sierras, and A drift from Redwood Camp,
by Bret Harte. Boston and New York, Houghton, Mifflin
and company, 1888.
  215 p. 15 1/2 cm.
  "Copyright, 1887."

9790 Harte, Bret, 1836-1902.
  A protegée of Jack Hamlin's, and other stories by Bret
Harte. Boston and New York, Houghton, Mifflin and company,
1894.
  2 p. 1., 292 p. 18 cm.
  CONTENTS.-A protegée of Jack Hamlin's.-An ingenue of
the Sierras.-The reformation of James Reddy.-The heir of
the McHulishes.-An episode of West Woodlands.-The home-
coming of Jim Wilkes.

9791 Harte, Bret, 1836-1902.
  Sally Dows, and other stories, by Bret Harte. Boston
and New York, Houghton, Mifflin and company, 1893.
  2 p. 1., 299 p. 18 cm.
  CONTENTS.-Sally Dows.-The conspiracy of Mrs. Bunker.
-The transformation of Buckeye Camp.-Their uncle from
California.

9792 Harte, Bret, 1836-1902.
  Susy, a story of the plains; by Bret Harte. Boston and
New York, Houghton, Mifflin and company, 1893.
  1 p. 1., 264 p. 18 cm.

9793 Harte, Bret, 1836-1902.
  Tales of trail and town. Boston and New York, Houghton,
Mifflin and company, 1898.
  348 p. front. 19 cm. ("Argonaut Edition" of the works
of Bret Harte, v. 14)
  CONTENTS.-The ancestors of Peter Atherly.-Two
Americans.-The judgement of Bolinas Plain.-The strange
experience of Alkali Dick.-A night on the divide.-The
youngest prospector in Calaveras.-A tale of three Truants.

9794 Harte, Bret, 1836-1902.
  Thankful blossom, a romance of the Jerseys, 1779, by

Bret Harte... Boston, J. R. Osgood and company, 1877.
158 p. front., plates   15 1/2 cm.
Title in red and black within red and black line border.
"Copyright, 1876."

9795 Hartmann, Theodore.
Charity Green; or, The varieties of love; by Theodore
Hartmann. New York, J. W. Norton, 1859.
x, [11]-601 p.   19 cm.

9796 The Harvard advocate.
Stories from the Harvard advocate. Being a collection
of stories selected from the Advocate from its founding,
eighteen hundred and sixty-six, to the present day.
Cambridge, Mass., Harvard university, 1896.
1 p. 1., [7]-251 p.   20 1/2 cm.

9797 Hatch, Alice J
Under the cedars; or, What the years brought. By Alice
J. Hatch. Boston, Lee and Shepard; New York, Lee, Shepard
and Dillingham, 1872.
264 p.   19 cm.

9798 [Hathaway, William E   ]
My grandfather's old coat: a political allegory. By
Reisender [pseud.] Cincinnati, R. Clarke & co., print.,
1873.
15 p.   23 cm.

9799 The haunted school-house at Newburyport, Mass. Boston,
Loring [c1873]
21 p. illus.   23 1/2 x 14 cm.
Illustrated t.-p., and cover.

9800 Haven, Mrs. Alice (Bradley) 1827-1863.
The Coopers; or, Getting under way. By Alice B. Haven...
New York, D. Appleton and company, 1858.
336 p.   19 cm.

9801 Haven, Mrs. Alice (Bradley) 1827-1863.
The gossips of Rivertown; with sketches in prose and verse.
By Alice B. Neal. Philadelphia, Hazard and Mitchell, 1850.

v, 7-327 p. front. (port.)   19 cm.

9802 Haven, Mrs. Alice (Bradley) 1827-1863.
      Home stories. By Mrs. Alice B. Haven ("Cousin Alice")
New York, D. Appleton and company, 1869.
      372 p.   17 1/2 cm.
      CONTENTS. -Spring winds. -Carriage friends. -Miss
Bremer's visit to Cooper's Landing. -Only a family party. -
The furnished house. -The ordeal. -Single lessions, five
dollars. -Counsel-the evil and the good.

9803 [Hawes, William Post] 1803-1841?
      Sporting scenes and sundry sketches; being the miscel-
laneous writings of J. Cypress, jr. [pseud.] Ed. by
Frank Forester [pseud.] New York, Gould, Banks & co.,
1842.
      2 v. in 1.   19 cm.
      "Memoir of Wm. P. Hawes. To the memory of Cypress":
vol. I, p. [1]-14.

9804 [Hawkins, Anthony Hope] 1863-1933.
      The Dolly dialogues... by Anthony Hope [pseud.]
New York, George Moore's sons, 1896.
      93 p.   18 cm.
      (Munro's library of popular novels, no. 151)

9805 Hawthorne, Julian, 1846-1934.
      Beatrix Randolph; a story, by Julian Hawthorne. Illus-
trated by Alfred Fredericks. Boston, J. R. Osgood and
company, 1884.
      vii, 280 p. front., 4 pl.   19 1/2 cm.
      "Copyright, 1883"

9806 Hawthorne, Julian, 1846-1934.
      Constance and Calbot's rival; tales by Julian Hawthorne.
New York, D. Appleton and company, 1889.
      227 p.   18 1/2 cm.

9807 Hawthorne, Julian, 1846-1934.
      Dust: a novel by Julian Hawthorne... New York, Fords,
Howard & Hulbert, 1883.
      v, 7-402 p. front. (port.) 3 pl.   18 1/2 cm.

(On cover: Our continent library)
Series title also at head of t.-p.
"Copyright, 1882.

9808 Hawthorne, Julian, 1846-1934.
A fool of nature [a novel] by Julian Hawthorne. New York,
C. Scribner's sons, 1896.
2 p. 1., [vii]-viii p., 1 1., 287 p.   18 cm.
"Written...for the competition of stories instituted by the
New York herald in 1895, and obtained the first prize of
$10,000": 2d prelim. leaf.

9809 Hawthorne, Julian, 1846-1934.
The golden fleece, a romance, by Julian Hawthorne...
Philadelphia, J. B. Lippincott company, 1896.
193 p. incl. front. 3 pl.   16 1/2 cm.   (On cover:
The Lotos Library)

9810 Hawthorne, Julian, 1846-1934.
Idolatry: a romance. By Julian Hawthorne. Boston,
J. R. Osgood and company, 1874.
iv, [5]-372 p.   19 cm.

9811 Hawthorne, Julian, 1846-1934.
Kildhurm's oak, by Julian Hawthorne... New York, A.
L. Burt [c1888]
1 p. 1., [5]-219 p.   19 1/2 cm.

9812 Hawthorne, Julian, 1846-1934.
Love is a spirit; a novel, by Julian Hawthorne. New
York, Harper & brothers, 1896.
1 p. 1., 200 p.   19 cm.

9813 Hawthorne, Julian, 1846-1934.
Love - or a name; a story, by Julian Hawthorne... Boston,
Ticknor and company, 1885.
1 p. 1., [5]-304 p.   19 1/2 cm.

9814 Hawthorne, Julian, 1846-1934.
Prince Saroni's wife, and The pearl-shell necklace, by
Julian Hawthorne... New York, Funk & Wagnalls, 1884.
117 p.   19 cm.

(On cover: Standard library, no. 129)

9815 Hawthorne, Julian, 1846-1934.
    Section 558; or, The fatal letter; from the diary of
Inspector Byrnes, by Julian Hawthorne... New York, Cassell
& company, limited [c1888]
    2 p. 1., 246 p.   17 1/2 cm.

9816 Hawthorne, Julian, 1846-1934.
    Sinfire. By Julian Hawthorne...
    (In Lippincott's monthly magazine. Philadelphia, 1887.
23 1/2 cm. v. 39, p. [1]-83)

9817 Hawthorne, Julian, 1846-1934.
    Six cent Sam's, by Julian Hawthorne; illustrated by John
Henderson Garnsey. St. Paul, The Price-McGill company
[1893]
    3 p. 1., [9]-332, [1] p. incl. front., illus., pl.
19 1/2 cm.
    Also published under title: Mr. Dunton's invention and
other stories.
    CONTENTS. -Mr. Dunton's invention. -Greaves' dis-
appearance. -Raxworthy's treasure. -The John North
mystery. -A model murder. -The Symposium.

9818 Hawthorne, Nathaniel, 1804-1864.
    The Blithedale romance. By Nathaniel Hawthorne.
Boston, Ticknor, Reed, and Fields, 1852.
    viii, [9]-288 p.   19 cm.
    First edition.

9819 [Hawthorne, Nathaniel] 1804-1864.
    Fanshawe, a tale... Boston, Marsh & Capen, 1828.
    141 p.   19 1/2 x 11 1/2 cm.
    "This was Hawthorne's first published work, and was
issued anonymously. Later, all the copies that could be
obtained were destroyed. A dozen years after his death a
copy was found, and the tale reissued by James R.
Osgood & co." cf. N. E. Browne, A bibliography of
Nathaniel Hawthorne, Boston and New York, 1905.

9820 Hawthorne, Nathaniel, 1804-1864.

The gentle boy: a thrice told tale; by Nathaniel Hawthorne: with an original illustration. Boston, Weeks, Jordan & co., 121 Washington street, New York & London; Wiley & Putnam, 1839 [i. e. 1838]
20 p. front.   25 x 32 cm.
Contains dedication to the illustrator, Miss Sophia A. Peabody, and a preface.
Published Dec. 31, 1838; had appeared first in the Token, Boston, 1832, p. 193-240, and secondly in the first series of the "Twice told tales," Boston, 1837.
Brown paper covers, in portfolio.

9821 Hawthorne, Nathaniel, 1804-1864.
The house of the seven gables, a romance. By Nathaniel Hawthorne. Boston, Ticknor, Reed, and Fields, 1851.
vi p., 1 1., [9]-344 p.   17 1/2 cm.
In the first issue of the 1st edition the publishers' advertisements are dated March, 1851, while in this issue they are dated May. There are still others of October. cf. Catheart, Bibl. of Nathaniel Hawthorne, Cleveland, 1905.

9822 Hawthorne, Nathaniel, 1804-1864.
The marble faun; or, The romance of Monte Beni. By Nathaniel Hawthorne... Boston, Ticknor and Fields, 1860.
2 v.   18 1/2 cm.
Preface dated Leamington, December 15, 1859.
Published simultaneously in London, in 3 v., by Smith, Elder, and company, under title: Transformation; or, The romance of Monte Beni.
"The MS. of 'The Marble faun' is in a private collection in England, and, in fact, was never in this country, as the American edition was set up from proof-sheets of the English edition."-Cathcart, Bibliography of Nathaniel Hawthorne, Cleveland, 1905.

9823 Hawthorne, Nathaniel, 1804-1864.
Mosses from an old manse. By Nathaniel Hawthorne... New York, Wiley and Putnam, 1846.
2 v. in 1.   19 cm. (On cover: Wiley and Putnam's library of American books, no. 17-18)
First edition.
This copy has the original paper covers of the first issue,

but lacks the 8 pages of advertisements at the end of part 1.
cf. Cathcart, Bibl. of Nathaniel Hawthorne, Cleveland, 1905.
CONTENTS.-pt. 1. The old manse. The birth-mark. A
select party. Young Goodman Brown. Rappaccini's daughter.
Mrs. Bullfrog. Fireworship. Buds and bird-voices.
Monsieur du Miroir. The hall of fantasy. The celestial
railroad. The procession of life.-pt. 2. The new Adam and
Eve. Egotisme. The Christmas banquet. Drowne's wooden
image. The intelligence office. Roger Malvin's burial. P.'s
correspondence. Earth's holocaust. The old apple dealer.
The aritst of the beautiful. A virtuoso's collection.

9824 Hawthorne, Nathaniel, 1804-1864.
The scarlet letter, a romance. By Nathaniel Hawthore.
[1st ed.] Boston, Ticknor, Reed, and Fields, 1850.
iv, 322 p.   18 1/2 cm.
"The 1st edition has the word reduplicate in line 20 on
p. 21." The 2d edition, 1850, has the word repudiate.

9825 Hawthorne, Nathaniel, 1804-1864.
Septimius Felton; or, The elixir of life. By Nathaniel
Hawthorne. Boston, J. R. Osgood and company, 1872.
2 p. 1., [3]-220 p. · 18 cm.
Preface signed: Una Hawthorne.

9826 Hawthorne, Nathaniel, 1804-1864.
The snow-image, and other Twice-told tales. By Nathaniel
Hawthorne. Boston, Ticknor, Reed, and Fields, 1852.
1 p. 1., [7]-273 p.   18 cm.
Preface dated, Lenox, Nove. 1st, 1851. Published
simultaneously in London and in Boston early in December.
The London issue bears the date 1851, while the Boston
edition is dated 1852.
CONTENTS.-The snow-image.-The great stone face.-Main-
street.-Ethan Brand.-A bell's biography.-Sylph Etherege.-
The Canterbury pilgrims.-Old news.-The man of adamant.-
The devil in manuscript.-John Inglefield's Thanksgiving.-
Old Ticonderoga.-The wives of the dead.-Little Daffydowndilly.
-Major Molineux.

9827 Hawthorne, Nathaniel, 1804-1864.
Twice-told tales. By Nathaniel Hawthorne. Boston,

American stationers co. , 1837.
      334 p.   19 1/2 cm.
      Advertising matter: p. 1-4.
      First edition of the first series.
      The first book with Hawthorne's name on the t.-p. cf. N.
E. Browne. A bibliography of ... Hawthorne.
      CONTENTS -The gray champion.-Sunday at home.-The
wedding knell.-The minister's black veil.-The Maypole of
Merry Mount.-The gentle boy.-Mr. Higginbotham's
catastrophe.-Little Anne's ramble.-Wakefield.-A rill from
the town pump.-The great carbuncle.-The prophetic pictures.
-David Swan.-Sights from a steeple.-The hollow of the three
hills.-The vision of the fountain.-Fancy's show box.-Dr.
Heldegger's experiment.

9828 Hay, John, 1838-1905.
         The bread-winners; a social study. New York, Harper &
      brothers, 1884.
         1 p. l. , [5]-319 p.   17 1/2 cm.

9829 Hazen, Jacob A
         Five years before the mast;, or, Life in the forecastle,
      abroad of a whaler and man-of-war, by Jacob A Hazen, 2d
      ed. ... Philadelphia, W. P. Hazard, 1856.
         3 p. l. , v-xii, 13-444 p. front. , plates.   19 cm.
         Added t.-p. , illustrated.

9830 Hazlett, Helen.
         The colud with a golden border. By Helen Hazlett...
      Philadelphia, T. E. Zell, 1861.
         4 p. l. , [13]-412 p.   20 cm.

9831 Hazlett, Helen.
         Glennair; or, Life in Scotland. By Helen Hazlett...
      Philadelphia, Claston, Remsen & Haffelfinger, 1869.
         2 p. l. , 13-332 p.   19 cm.

9832 Hearn, Lafcadio, 1850-1904.
         Chita: a memory of Last Island, by Lafcadio Hearn...
      New York, Harper & brothers, 1900.
         4 p. l. , [3]-204 p.   19 cm.

9833 Hearn, Lafcadio, 1850-1904.
  Youma: the story of a West-Indian slave... New York,
  Harper & brothers, 1890.
  193 p. front.   20 cm.

9834 The heart of Mabel Ware. A romance. New York, J. C.
  Derby; Cincinnati, H. W. Derby, 1856.
  2 p. l., [vii]-ix, [11]-411 p.   18 1/2 cm.

9835 The heart of the West: an American story. By an Illinoian.
  Time: 1860. Scene: On the Mississippi ... Chicago, Steam
  printing house of Hand & Hart, 1871.
  229, iii p.   22 1/2 cm.

9836 [Heath, James Ewell]
  Edge-hill; or, The family of the Fitzroyals. A novel. By
  a Virginian... Richmond, T. W. White, 1828.
  2 v. in 1.   17 1/2 x 10 1/2 cm.

9837 [Heaven, Mrs. Louise (Palmer)] 1846-
  Aldeane. A novel. By Laura Preston [pseud.]...
  New York, San Francisco, A. Roman & company, 1868.
  403 p.   19 cm.

9838 Helen Leeson; a peep at New-York society... Philadelphia,
  Parry & McMillan, 1855.
  1 p. l., 367 p.   19 cm.

9839 Hentz, Mrs. Caroline Lee (Whiting) 1800-1856.
  Ernest Linwood; a novel, by Caroline Lee Hentz. Twentieth thousand. Boston, J. P. Jewett and company: New
  York, Sheldon, Blakeman and company [etc., etc.] 1856.
  467 p.   20 cm.

9840 [Hentz, Nicholas Marcellus] 1797-1856.
  Tadeuskund, the last king of the Lenape. An historical
  tale. Boston, Cummings, Hilliard & co., 1825.
  276 p.   19 1/2 cm.

9841 [Herbert, Henry William] 1807-1858.
  The brothers. A tale of the Fronde... New York, Harper
  & brothers, 1835.

2 v.   19 cm.
Several of the earlier chapters were originally published
in the American monthly magazine.
A manuscript letter from the author to Col. John Trumbull
inserted in volume one.

9842 Herbert, Henry William, 1807-1858.
The cavaliers of England; or, The times of the revolutions
of 1642 and 1688, by Henry William Herbert... New-York,
Redfield, 1852.
428 p.   18 1/2 cm.
Half-title: Legends of love and chivalry.
CONTENTS.-The brothers in arms.-The rival sisters.
-Jasper St. Aubyn.-Vernon in the vale.

9843 [Herbert, Henry William] 1807-1858.
Cromwell. An historical novel. By the author of "The
borthers"... New York, Harper & brothers, 1838.
2 v. front. (port.)   19 cm.
Published later under title: Oliver Cromwell.

9844 Herbert, Henry William, 1807-1858.
Isabel Graham; or, Charity's reward, by Henry William
Herbert... New York, Williams brothers, 1848.
108 p.   24 cm.

9845 Herbert, Henry William, 1807-1858.
The knights of England, France and Scotland. By
Henry William Herbert... New York, Redfield, 1852.
426 p.   19 cm.
Half-title: Legends of love and chivalry.

9846 Herbert, Henry William, 1807-1858.
Marmaduke Wyvil; or, The maid's revenge. A historical
romance. By Henry William Herbert... New-York, J.
Winchester [c1843]
2 p. 1., 218 p.   22 cm.

9847 Herbert, Henry William, 1807-1858.
Persons and pictures from the histories of France and
England; from the Norman conquest to the fall of the Stuarts.
By Henry William Herbert... New York, Riker, Thorne &

co. , 1854.
440 p.   19 cm.

9848 Herbert, Henry William, 1807-1858.
        Pierre, the partisan; a tale of the Mexican marches. By
     Henry William Herbert... New York, Williams brothers,
     1848.
        99 p.   26 1/2 cm.

9849 Herbert, Henry William, 1807-1858.
        Ruth Whalley; or, The fair Puritan. A romance of the Bay
     province. By Henry William Herbert... Boston, H. L.
     Williams, 1845.
        cover-title, 72 p.   20 1/2 cm.

9850 Herbert, Henry William, 1807-1858.
        Tales of the Spanish seas. By Henry W. Herbert... New
     York, Burgess, Stringer & co. , 1847.
        96 p.   23 1/2 cm.

9851 Herbert, Henry William, 1807-1858.
        Wager of battle; a tale of Saxon slavery in Sherwood
     Forest. By Henry W. Herbert... New York, Mason
     brothers, 1855.
        x, [11]-336 p.   19 cm.

9852 Herbert Wendall: a tale of the revolution... New-York,
     Harper & brothers, 1835.
        2 v.   19 1/2 cm.

9853 The hermit of the Chesapeake; or, Lessons of a lifetime.
     Philadelphia, Barclay & co. [c1869]
        1 p. l. , 5-82 p. plates.   23 1/2 cm.

9854 Herndon, Mary Eliza (Hicks) 1820-
        Louise Elton; or, Things seen and heard. A novel. By
     Mrs. Mary E. Herndon. Philadelphia, Lippincott, Grambo
     & co. , 1853.
        5 p. l. , [13]-407 p.   19 cm.

9855 Herr, A   J
        The maid of the valley; or, The brother's revenge. A

tale of the revolution. By A. J. Herr... New York, W. H. Graham, 1847.

    64 p.   24 cm.

    "The haunted villa": p. 53-64.

9856 Herrington, W   D

    The deserter's daughter. By W. D. Herrington... Raleigh, W. B. Smith & co., 1865.

    27 p.   19 1/2 cm. (Southern field and fireside novelette, no. 3. New series)

9857 Hertford, Joseph.

    Personals; or, Perils of the period. By Joseph Hertford. New York, Printed for the author, 1870.

    vi, [7]-339, viii p.   19 1/2 cm.

9858 [Hewson, John] b. 1768?

    Christ rejected: or, The trial of the eleven disciples of Christ, in a court of law and equity, as charged with stealing the crucified body of Christ out of the sepulchre. Humbly dedicated to the whole nation of the Jews, which are scattered abroad on the face of the earth; and to the deists of modern times. Designed, also, as a help to wavering Christians. An original work. Written by a believer in Christ, under the assumed name of Captain Onesimus... Philadelphia, Printed for the author, by J. Rakestraw, 1832.

    iv, [5]-444, [4] p. illus.   18 cm.

9859 Heywood, Joseph Converse, d. 1900.

    How will it end? A romance. By J. C. Heywood... Philadelphia, J. B. Lippincott & co., 1872.

    vi, 7-301 p.   18 1/2 cm.

9860 Hiatt, James M

    The test of loyalty. By James M. Hiatt. Indianapolis, Merrill and Smith, 1864.

    180 p.   18 1/2 cm.

9861 [Higgins, Alvin S   ]

    The mishaps of Mr. Ezekiel Pelter... Chicago, S. C. Griggs and company, 1875.

    3 p. 1., 11-302 p. incl. front., plates.   19 cm.

Published anonymously.

9862 Higham, Mrs. Mary R
Cloverly. By Mary R. Higham... New York, A. D. F.
Randolph & company [c1875]
256 p.   18 cm.

9863 Hilbourne, Mrs. Charlotte S
Alice Waters; or, The Sandown victory. A temperance
story, for old and young. By Charlotte S. Hilbourne.
Portland [Me.] F. G. Rich, 1867.
22 p.   22 Cm.

9864 Hilbourne, Mrs. Charlotte S
The diamond necklace; or, The island recluse: a tale of
interesting incidents and adventures, connected with the
life of a young nobleman, in pursuit of his birthplace and
parentage. By Mrs. Charlotte Hilborn. Lowell, Mass.,
1852.
31 p.   25 cm.

9865 [Hildreth, Richard] 1807-1865.
The slave; or, Memoirs of Archy Moore... Boston,
John H. Eastburn, printer, 1836.
2 v.   19 cm.

9866 [Hildreth, Richard] 1807-1865.
The white slave; or, Memoirs of a fugitive... Boston,
Tappan and Whittemore; Milwaukie [!] Wis., Rood and
Whittemore, 1852.
408 p. front., plates.   19 1/2 cm.
First published in 1836 under title: The slave; or,
Memoirs of Archy Moore.

9867 Hill, A   F
A tragedy of the mountains; or, The White Rocks. A
thrilling tale of the Alleghenies. By A. F. Hill. Philadelphia, Columbian publishing company, 1890.
1 p. 1., 5-6, vii-x, 11-389, [1] p.   19 1/2 cm.
(On cover: Columbian library, no. 1)
An earlier edition has title: The White Rocks.

9868 Hill, Mrs. Agnes (Leonard) Scanland, 1842-1917.
Heights and depths; by Agnes Leonard Scanland... Chicago,
H. A. Sumner; Boston, Lee & Shepard [etc., etc.] 1871.
271 p.   18 1/2 cm.

9869 [Hill, Mrs. Agnes (Leonard) Scanland] 1842-1917.
Myrtle blossoms, by Molly Myrtle [pseud.]... Chicago,
Ill., Published for the authoress by J. C. W. Bailey, 1863.
304 p.   20 1/2 cm.
Verse and prose.

9870 [Hill, Mrs. Agnes (Leonard) [Scanland] 1842-
Vanquished. A novel. By Agnes Leonard... New York,
G. W. Carleton & co. [etc., etc.] 1867.
2 p. l., [vii]-viii, 9-392 p.   18 1/2 cm.

9871 Hill, Alonzo F
John Smith's funny adventures on a crutch, or The remark-
able peregrinations of a one-legged soldier after the war. By
A. F. Hill... Philadelphia, J. E. Potter and company, 1869.
374 p. front., plates.   19 cm.
Added t.-p., engr.

9872 [Hill, George Canning] 1825-1898.
Cap sheaf, a fresh bundle. By Lewis Myrtle [pseud.]
New York, Redfield, 1853.
313 p.   19 1/2 cm.

9873 [Hill, George Canning] 1825-1898.
Dovecote; or, The heart of the homestead. By the author
of "Cap sheaf". Boston, J. P. Jewett and company; Cleveland, O., Jewett, Proctor, and Worthington [etc., etc.]
1854.
iv, 361 p.   18 1/2 cm.

9874 [Hill, George Canning] 1825-1898.
Homespun; or, Five and twenty years ago. By Thomas
Lackland [pseud.]... New York, Hurd and Houghton, 1867.
viii, [9]-346 p.   17 1/2 cm.
Title vignette.
Verse and prose.

9875 Hilliard, Henry Washington, 1808-1892.
     De Vane: a story of plebeians and patricians. By Hon.
Henry W. Hilliard... New-York, Blelock & company, 1865.
     2 v. in 1.   19 cm.
     Paged continuously.
     Announced by West and Johnston, Richmond, Va. , under
title "De Vere" as in press January 1862, to be published
in February. Probably never issued, however, with
Confederate States imprint.

9876 Hills, Alfred C
     Macpherson, the Confederate philosopher. By Alfred C.
Hills, New York, J. Miller, 1864.
     209 p.   19 1/2 cm.
     Satirical letters on the Southern Confederacy, signed
James B. Macpherson.

9877 Hinckley, Mary.
     The camphene lamp; or, Touch not, taste not, handle
not... By Mary Hinckley... Lowell, J. P. Walker, 1852.
     62 p.   15 cm.

9878 The history of Constantius & Pulchera. Or, Constancy
     rewarded... Printed by T. C. Cushing, Salem [Mass.]
1795.
     54 p.   15 1/2 cm.

9879 A history of the "striped pig"... Boston, Whipple and
     Damrell, 1838.
     72 p.   15.

9880 Hodges, M   C
     The Mestico: or, The war-path and its incidents. A story
of the Creek Indian disturbances of 1836. By M. C. Hodges.
New York, W. H. Graham, 1850.
     1 p. 1. , [5]-204 p.   20 cm.
     On cover: W. C. Hodges.

9881 Hoffman, Mrs. Mary Jane.
     Agnes Hilton; or, Practical views of Catholicity. A tale
of trials and triumphs. By Mary I. Hoffman. New York,
P. O'Shea, 1864.

1 p. 1. , [5]-477 p.   19 cm.

9882 Hoffman, Mrs. Mary [Jane]
        Alice Murray. A tale, by Mary I. Hoffman... New York,
     P. O'Shea [1869]
        1 p. 1. , [5]-490 p.   18 1/2 cm.

9883 Hoffman, Mrs. Mary [Jane]
        The orphan sisters; or, The problem solved. By Mary
     J. Hoffman... New York [etc.] D. & J. Sadlier & co.,
     1875.
        2 p. 1. , [xi]-xii, [13]-352 p.   18 1/2 cm.

9884 [Holbrook Silas Pinckney] 1796-1835.
        Sketches, by a traveller... Boston, Carter and Hendee,
     1830.
        2 p. 1. , 315 p.   20 cm.
        "Originally appeared in the New England galaxy, and
     Boston courier."-Pref.
        CONTENTS.-Letters from a mariner.-Travels of a tin
     pedlar.-Letters from a Boston merchant.-Recollections of
     Japan.-Recollections of China.-The schoolmaster (From
     the Legendary)-The last of the blacklegs.-Selections [poems]

9885 Holgate, Jerome Bonaparte.
        Noachidae; or, Noah, and his descendants. By Jerome B.
     Holgate. Buffalo, Breed, Butler & co., 1860.
        1 p. 1. , [v]-viii, [9]-354 p.   19 1/2 cm.
        Cover-title: Noah and his descendants.

9886 Holland, Josiah Gilbert, 1819-1881.
        Arthur Bonnicastle; an American novel. By J. G. Holland
     ... with twelve full-page illustrations by Mary A. Hallock.
     New York, Scribner, Armstrong & co., 1873.
        401 p. incl. front. plates.   20 cm.

9887 [Holley, Marietta] 1836-1926.
        My opinions and Betsy Bobbet's. Designed as a beacon
     light, to guide women to life, liberty, and the pursuit of
     happiness, but which may be read by members of the sterner
     sect, without injury to themselves or the book. By Josiah
     Allen's wife [pseud.]... Hartford, Conn., American

publishing company [etc., etc.] 1873.
xvi, [17]-432 p. front., illus., plates.   20 1/2 cm.

9888 Holley, Marietta, 1826-1926.
Samantha at Saratoga; or, "Flirtin' with fashion"...
Sold by subscription only, Philadelphia, Hubbard brothers,
1887.
3 p. l., 7-583 p., illus.   20 cm.

9889 Holley, Marietta, 1836-1926.
Sweet Cicely; or, Josiah Allen as a politician... New
York, London, Funk & Wagnalls, 1895.
381 p. illus.   20 cm.

9890 Holman, Jesse Lynch.
The prisoners of Niagara; or, The errors of education.
A new novel, founded on fact. By Jessee [!] L. Holman,
a native of Kentucky... Frankfort, K., Printed by William
Gerard, 1810.
357 p.   21 cm.

9891 Holmes, Mrs. Mary Jane (Hawes) 1828-1907.
Bessie's fortune, a novel... New York, G. W. Carleton
& co., 1886.
453 p.   19 cm.

9892 Holmes, Mrs. Mary Jane (Hawes) 1828-1907.
Chateau d'Or. Norah, and Kitty Craig. By Mrs. Mary
J. Holmes... New York, G. W. Carleton & co., London,
S. Low & co., 1880.
2 p. l., 9-389 p.   19 cm.

9893 Holmes, Mrs. Mary Jane (Hawes) 1828-1907.
Daisy Thornton and Jessie Graham. By Mrs. Mary J.
Holmes... New York, G. W. Carleton & co. [etc., etc.]
1878.
1 p. l., vii-viii, 9-377 p.   19 cm.

9894 Holmes, Mrs. Mary Jane (Hawes) 1828-1907.
Doctor Hathern's daughters: a story of Virginia, in four
parts... New York, G. W. Dillingham, successor to G. W.
Carleton & co., 1895.

471 p.   20 cm.

9895 Holmes, Mrs. Mary Jane (Hawes) 1828-1907.
        Edna Browning; or, The Leighton homestead. A novel.
     New York, G. W. Carleton & co., 1872.
        423 p.   19 cm.

9896 Holmes, Mrs. Mary Jane (Hawes) 1828-1907.
        The homestead on the hillside, and other tales. By Mrs.
     Mary J. Holmes... New York and Auburn, Miller, Orton
     & Mulligan, 1856.
        2 p. 1., [vii]-x, [11]-379 p.   19 1/2 cm.
        CONTENTS. -The homestead on the hillside. -Rice Corner.
     -The Gilberts; or, Rice Corner number two. -The Thanksgiving
     party and its consequences. -The old red house among the
     mountains. -Glen's Creek. -The gable-roofed house at Snowdon.

9897 Holmes, Mrs. Mary Jane (Hawes) 1828-1907.
        Hugh Worthington... A novel. By Mrs. Mary J. Holmes
     ... New York, Carleton, 1865.
        1 p. 1., [vi]-vi, [7]-370 p.   19 cm.

9898 Holmes, Mrs. Mary Jane (Hawes) 1828-1907.
        Madeline, a novel. By Mrs. Mary J. Holmes...
     New York, G. W. Carleton & co. [etc., etc.] 1881.
        1 p. 1., v-vi, 7-374 p.   19 cm.

9899 Holmes, Mrs. Mary Jane (Hawes) 1828-1907.
        Marguerite, a novel... New York, G. W. Dillingham,
     1891.
        473 p.   19 cm.

9900 Holmes, Mrs. Mary Jane (Hawes) 1828-1907.
        Meadow-Brook. By Mrs. Mary J. Holmes... New York,
     Miller, Orton & co., 1857.
        viii, 9-380 p.   19 1/2 cm.

9901 Holmes, Mrs. Mary Jane (Hawes) 1828-1907.
        Millbank; or, Roger Irving's ward. A novel. By Mrs.
     Mary J. Holmes... New York, G. W. Carleton & co.;
     London, S. Low, son & co., 1871.
        viii, [9]-402 p.   19 cm.

9902 Holmes, Mrs. Mary Jane (Hawes) 1828-1907.
 Paul Ralston. A novel. By Mrs. Mary J. Holmes...
New York, G. W. Dillingham co., 1897.
 1 p. 1., v-vi, 7-393 p.   19 cm.

9903 Holmes, Mrs. Mary Jane (Hawes) 1828-1907.
 Queenie Hetherton. A novel. By Mrs. Mary J. Holmes...
New York, G. W. Carleton & co., London, S. Low & co.,
1883.
 1 p. 1., 5-454 p.   19 cm.

9904 Holmes, Mary Jane (Hawes) 1828-1907.
 Tempest and sunshine; or, Life in Kentucky... New York,
G. W. Dillingham, MDCCCXCIV.
 378 p.   20 cm.

9905 Holmes, Oliver Wendell, 1809-1894.
 Elsie Venner; a romance of destiny. By Oliver Wendell
Holmes... Boston, Ticknor and Fields, 1861.
 2 v.   18 cm.
 First edition.
 First published under title "The professor's story" in the
Atlantic monthly January 1860-April 1861, not December
1859 as stated in [publishers'] preface.

9906 Holmes, Oliver Wendell, 1809-1894.
 A mortal antipathy: first opening of the new portfolio...
Boston and New York, Houghton, Mifflin and company, 1885.
 307 p.

9907 [Holt, John Saunders] 1826-1886.
 Abraham Page, esq. A novel... Philadelphia, J. B.
Lippincott & company, 1868.
 354 p.   18 1/2 cm.

9908 Hood, Mrs. Frances Hamilton.
 Maud Mansfield; A novel, By Mrs. Frances Hamilton
Hood... Macon, Ga., J. W. Burke & company, 1876.
 vii, [9]-278,   19 1/2 cm.

9909 [Hooke, Charles Witherle] 1861-
 Automatic Bridget, and other humorous sketches, by

Howard Fielding [pseud.] New York, The Manhattan
therapeutic company [c1889]
32 p. illus. 19 cm.
Advertising matter: p. 32.

9910 [Hooper, George W   ]
Down the river; or, Practical lessons under the code duello.
By an amateur. With twelve full page illustrations by H. L.
Stephens. New York, E. J. Hale & son, 1874.
267, [1] p. front. , plates. 18 1/2 cm.
Appendix: Wilson, J. L. The American code. -Code of
dueling in France from Millingen's "History of dueling."
-Barrington, J. Irish code.

9911 Hooper, Henry.
The lost model. A romance. By Henry Hooper...
Philadelphia, J. B. Lippincott & co. , 1874.
386 p. 19 cm.

9912 Hooper, Lucy, 1816-1841.
Scenes from real life. An American tale. By Lucy Hooper
... New York, J. P. Giffing, 1840.
83 p. 16 cm.

9913 Hope, Cecil.
Seabury castle [a novel] By Cecil Hope. Philadelphia,
J. B. Lippincott & co. , 1869.
96 p. 19 1/2 cm.

9914 Hope's anchor. New York, Everit bros. , printers, 1870.
34 p. 14 1/2 cm.

9915 Hopkins, A[lphonso] A[lva] 1843-
His prison bars; and the way of escape. By A. A.
Hopkins. Rochester, Rural home publishing co.; New
York, Hurd and Houghton [1875]
viii, [9]-256 p. 17 1/2 cm.

9916 Hopkins, Mrs. Margaret Sutton (Briscoe) 1864-
Jimty, and others, by Margaret Sutton Briscoe. Illustrated
by W. T. Smedley and A. B. Frost. New York and London,
Harper & brothers, 1898.

3 p. 1. , 325., [1] p.   8 pl. (incl. front.)   19 cm.
CONTENTS. -Jimty. -The price of peace. -An echo. -The
Christmas mummers. -Concealed weapons. -Annie Tousey's
little game. -Princess I-would-I-wot-not. -It is the custom.
-Salt of the earth. -A goosechase. -An entomological wooing.
-The quarter loaf.

9917 Hopkins, Samuel, 1807-1887.
The youth of the Old Dominion. By Samuel Hopkins.
Boston, J. P. Jewett & co.; New York, Sheldon, Blakeman
& co. [etc., etc.] 1856.
viii, 473 p.   18 1/2 cm.
A romantic sketch of the early history of Virginia,
concluding with Bacon's insurrection.

9918 Hopkinson, Francis, 1737-1791.
The miscellaneous essays and occasional writings of
Francis Hopkinson, esq. Philadelphia, Printed by T. Dobson,
at the stone-house, no. 41, Second street, 1792.
3 v. 2 fold. pl.   20 cm.
CONTENTS. -v. 1. Miscellaneous essays. -v. 2 Orations,
written for, and at the request of young gentlemen of the
university, and delivered by them at public commencements
in the college hall. Essays. -v. 3. Judgments in the
Admiralty of Pennsylvania. Poems.

9919 [Hopkinson, Francis] 1737-1791.
A pretty story written in the year of our Lord 2774.
By Peter Grievous, Esq; A. B. C. D. E. Williamsburg,
Printed by John Pinkney for the benefit of Clementa Rind's
children, 1774.
16 p.   17 cm.

9920 [Horn, Henry J   ] ed.
Strange visitors: a series of original papers, embracing
philosophy, science, government... By the spirits of Irving,
Willis, Thackeray... and others now dwelling in the spirit
world. Dictated through a clairvoyant while in an abnormal
or trance state. New York, Carleton [etc., etc.] 1869.
viii, [9]-249, [1] p.   19 cm.
"Introduction. By the editor", signed: Henry J. Horn.

9921 [Hornblower], Mrs.
"The Julia." By the author of "Vara"... New York,
R. Carter & brothers, 1859.
iv, 9-388 p.   19 cm.

9922 [Hornblower, Mrs.   ]
Nellie of Truro. By the author of "Vara"... New York,
R. Carter & brothers, 1856.
vi, [7]-432 p.   19 cm.
Added t.-p., engraved.

9923 Horton, Mrs. M   B
The wife's messengers [a novel] By Mrs. M. B. Horton.
Philadelphia, J. B. Lippincott & co., 1869.
2 p. l., 7-323 p.   18 cm.

9924 Hosmer, George Washington, 1830-1914.
"As we went marching on"; a story of the war... New
York, Harper & brothers, 1885.
310 p.   18 cm.

9925 Hosmer, James Kendall, 1834-1927.
The thinking bayonet. By James K. Hosmer... Boston,
Walker, Fuller, and company, 1865.
vii, 9-326 p.   17 1/2 cm.

9926 Hosmer, Mrs. Margaret (Kerr) 1830-1897.
Blanche Gilroy. A girl's story. By Mrs. Margaret
Hosmer. Philadelphia, J. B. Lippincott & co., 1871.
2 p. l., 7-330 p.   18 1/2 cm.

9927 Hosmer, Mrs. Margaret (Kerr) 1830-1897.
Ten years of a lifetime [a novel] By Mrs. Margaret
Hosmer... New York, M. Doolady, 1866.
422 p.   19 cm.

9928 Hotchkiss, Chauncey C[rafts] 1852-
In defiance of the king, a romance of the American
revolution: by Chauncey C. Hotchkiss. New York, D.
Appleton and company, 1895.
viii, 334 p.   17 1/2 cm. (Appleton's town and
country library, no. 178)

9929 Hough, Emerson, 1857-1923.
The girl at the halfway house: a story of the plains, by
E. Hough... New York, D. Appleton and company, 1900.
viii, 371 p.   19 1/2 cm.

9930 Housekeeper, M   R   1838-
My husband's crime [a novel] By M. R. Housekeeper...
New York, Harper & brothers, 1868.
1 p. 1. , [9]-115 p. front. , plates.   23 1/2 cm.

9931 Howard, H   R   comp.
The history of Virgil A. Stewart, and his adventure in
capturing and exposing the great "western land pirate" and
his gang, in connexion with the evidence; also of the trials,
confessions, and execution of a number of Murrell's
associates in the state of Mississippi during the summer of
1835, and the execution of five professional gamblers by the
citizens of Vicksburg, on the 6th July, 1835... Comp. by
H. R. Howard. New-York, Harper & brothers, 1836.
1 p. 1. , [v]-vi, [7]-273 p.   18 cm.

9932 [Howard, H.   R   ]
The life and adventures of Joseph T. Hare, the bold robber
and highwayman, with sixteen... engravings. New York, H.
Long and brother, 1847.
107 p. illus.   23 1/2 cm.
On cover: By the author of The life of John A. Murrell.

9933 Howe, Edgar Watson, 1854-1937.
A man story, by E. W. Howe... Boston, Ticknor and
company, 1889.
380 p.   19 1/2 cm.

9934 Howe, Edgar Watson, 1854-1937.
A moonlight boy, by E. W. Howe... Boston, Ticknor and
company, 1886.
342 p. incl. front. (port.)   19 cm.

9935 Howe, Edgar Watson, 1854-1937.
The mystery of the locks, by E. W. Howe... Boston,
J. R. Osgood and company, 1885.
2 p. 1. , 293 p.   20 cm.

9936 Howe, Mary A
          The rival volunteers; or, The black plume rifles. By
      Mary A. Howe. New York, J. Bradburn, 1864.
          377 p.   18 1/2 cm.

9937 [Howe, William Wirt] 1833-1909.
          The Pasha papers. Epistles of Mohammed Pasha, rear
      admiral of the Turkish navy [pseud.] written from New York
      to his friend Abel Ben Hassen. Translated into Anglo-
      American from the original manuscripts. To which are added
      sundry other letters, critical and explanatory... New York,
      C. Scribner; London, S. Low, son & co., 1859.
          xxiii, [25]-312 p.   18 1/2 cm.
      A satire on American society.

9928 Howells, William Dean, 1837-1920.
          Annie Kilburn, a novel, by William D. Howells... New
      York, Harper and brothers, 1889.
          1 p. l., 331 p.   19 1/2 cm.
          "Copyright, 1888."

9939 Howells, William Dean, 1837-1920.
          April hopes... New York, Harper & brothers, 1888.
          484 p.   20 cm.

9940 Howells, William Dean, 1837-1920.
          The coast of Bohemia: a novel... New York, Harper &
      brothers, 1893.
          340 p. illus.   20 cm.

9941 Howells, William Dean, 1837-1920.
          A day's pleasure. By William Dean Howells... Boston,
      James R. Osgood & company, 1876.
          91 p. front. illus.   12 1/2 cm.

9942 Howells, William Dean, 1837-1920.
          Doctor Breen's practice, a novel by William D. Howells...
      Boston, James R. Osgood, 1881.
          2 p. l., [3]-272 p.   19 1/2 cm.

9943 Howells, William Dean, 1837-1920.
          A fearful responsibility and other stories, by William D.

Howells... Boston, James R. Osgood and company, 1881.
3 p. 1., [3]-255 p.   19 1/2 cm.
CONTENTS.-A fearful responsibility.-At the sign of the
savage.-Tonelli's marriage.

9944 Howells, William Dean, 1837-1920.
A foregone conclusion. By W. D. Howells... Boston,
J. R. Osgood and company, 1875.
1 p. 1., 265 p.   19 cm.

9945 Howells, William Dean, 1837-1920.
A hazard of new fortunes; a novel, by William D.
Howells... New York, Harper and brothers, 1890 (c1889)
2 v.   19 cm.

9946 Howells, William Dean, 1837-1920.
The lady of the Aroostook... Boston; Houghton, Osgood
and company, 1879.
326 p.   20 cm.

9947 Howells, William Dean, 1837-1920.
The landlord at Lion's Head, Novel... New York, Harper
& brothers, 1897.
461 p.   20 cm.

9948 Howells, William Dean, 1837-1920.
A modern instance, a novel, by William D. Howells...
Boston, J. R. Osgood and company, 1882 [c1881]
514 p.   19 1/2 cm.

9949 Howells, William Dean, 1837-1920.
An open-eyed conspiracy: an idyl of Saratoga... New
York and London, Harper & brothers, 1897.
181 p.   20 cm.

9950 Howells, William Dean, 1837-1920.
A parting and a meeting, story by W. D. Howells...
New York, Harper & brothers, 1896.
2 p. 1., 98 p., 1 1.   front., 2 pl.   15 cm.
(On cover: Harper's little novels)

9951 Howells, William Dean, 1837-1920.

The quality of mercy: a novel... New York, Harper &
brothers, 1892.
474 p.   20 cm.

9952 Howells, William Dean, 1837-1920.
Ragged lady, a novel... New York and London, Harper
& brothers, 1899.
357 p., illus.   20 cm.

9953 Howells, William Dean, 1837-1920.
The story of a play; a novel, by William D. Howells...
New York and London, Harper & brothers, 1898.
1 p. 1., 321 p.   19 cm.

9954 Howells, William Dean, 1837-1920.
Their silver wedding journey. New York and London,
Harper & brothers, 1899.
2 v. illus.   20 cm.

9955 Howells, William Dean, 1837-1920.
A traveler from Altruria. New York, Harper & brothers
Publishers, 1894.
318 p.   20 cm.

9956 Howells, William Dean, 1837-1920.
The undiscovered country... Boston, Houghton, Mifflin
and company, 1880.
419 p.   20 cm.

9957 Howells, William Dean, 1837-1920.
A woman's reason, a novel, by William D. Howells...
Boston, J. R. Osgood and company, 1883.
2 p. 1., 466 p.   19 1/2 cm.

9958 Howells, William Dean, 1837-1920.
The world of chance, a novel, by William D. Howells...
New York, Harper & brothers, 1893.
1 p. 1., 375 p.   19 cm.

9959 Hoyt, Jehiel Keeler, 1820-1895.
The romance of the table. In three parts. I. Breakfast.
II. Dinner, III. Tea, by J. K. Hoyt... New Brunswick, N. J.

Times publishing co., 1872.
445 p.   22 cm.

9960 Hubbard, Elbert, 1856–1915.
Time and chance; a romance and a history; being the story
of the life of a man, by Elbert Hubbard... East Aurora, N.Y.
The Roycrofters, 1899.
2 v. fronts., port.   20 1/2 cm.

9961 [Huet, M   M   ]
Eva May, the foundling; or, The secret dungeon. A
romance of New York. By the author of "Seven brothers of
Wyoming"... New York, Garrett & co., 1853.
105 p.   23 1/2 cm.

9962 Huet, M   M
Davis, the pirate: or, The true history of the freebooters
of the Pacific. A companion to "Morgan, the buccaneer".
By M. M. Huett... New York, H. Long & brother [c1853]
iv, [5]-104 p.   25 1/2 cm.

9963 Huet, M   M
Morgan, the buccaneer: or, The true history of the freebooters of the Antilles. By M. M. Huett... New York,
H. Long & brother [1853]
iv, [5]-112 p.   24 1/2 cm.

9964 Huet, M   M
Silver and pewter: a tale of high life and low life in
New York. By M. M. Huet... New York, H. Long &
brother; Cincinnati, O., H. B. Pearson & co. [c1852]
106 p.   24 cm.

9965 Hughes, Margie S
Annetta; or, The story of a life. By Margie S. Hughes.
Cincinnati, Hitchcock and Walden; New York, Nelson and
Phillips, 1873.
282 p. front., plates.   17 1/2 cm.

9966 [Hughes, Mrs. Reginald]
Oxley. By Lyndon [pseud.]... New York, Scribner,
Armstrong & company, 1873.

2 p. 1., [vii]-viii, [5]-441 p.   18 1/2 cm.

9967 [Hughs, Mrs. Mary (Robson)]
Julia Ormond; or, The new settlement. By the authoress
of "The two schools." New York, E. Dunigan, 1846.
220 p. front.   15 cm. (Half-title: Dunigan's home
library, no. VII)

9968 Hughs, Mrs. Mary (Robson)
The two schools: a moral tale. By Mrs. Hughs. Baltimore,
F. Lucas, jr. [1835]
247 p. pl.   19 cm.

9969 [Hume, John Ferguson] 1830-
Five hundred majority; or, The days of Tammany. By
Willys Niles [pseud.] New York, G. P. Putnam & sons,
1872.
v, [7]-200 p.   23 1/2 cm.

9970 Hume, Mrs. R   S
Woman's wrongs: a history of Mary and Fidelia. By
Mrs. R. S. Hume. Portland, Printed by B. Thurston and
company, 1872.
vi, [7]-223 p.   19 cm.

9971 Hungerford, James.
The old plantation, and what I gathered there in an autumn
month. By James Hungerford... New York, Harper &
brothers, 1859.
xii, [13]-369 p.   20 cm.

9972 Hunt, Jedediah, b. 1815.
An adventure on a frozen lake: a tale of the Canadian
rebellion of 1837-8. By J. Hunt, jr. Cincinnati, Printed
at the Ben Franklin book and job office, 1853.
46 p.   20 cm.
Running title: My adventure on a frozen lake.

9973 Hunt, Thomas Poage, 1794-1876.
The wedding days of former times. By Thomas P. Hunt...
Philadelphia, Griffith & Simon; New York, Saxton & Miles,
1845.

87 p.   front. , plates.   15 1/2 cm.

9974 [Huntington, Jedediah Vincent] 1815-1862.
     Alban. A tale of the new world. By the author of "Lady
Alice." New York, The author, 1852.
     viii, [9]-496 p.   19 cm.
     Sequel: The forest.

9975 Huntington, Jedediah Vincent, 1815-1862.
     The forest, by J. V. Huntington... New York, Redfield,
1852.
     384 p.   19 cm.
     Sequel to "Alban".

9976 [Hyde, Thomas Alexander]
     Won by a bicycle; or, A race for a wife. By Luke
Double, B. A. [pseud.] Boston, Mass., Greater Boston
publishing co. , 1895.
     2 p. 1. , [7]-191 p.   19 cm.

I

9977 Ilsley, Charles Parker, 1807-1887.
     Forest and shore; or, Legends of the Pine-tree state. By
Charles P. Ilsley. 4th thousand. Boston, J. P. Jewett and
company; Cleveland, O. , Jewett, Proctor, and Worthington;
[etc. , etc.] 1856.
     vi p. , 1 l. , 9-126 p.   19 1/2 cm.
     CONTENTS. -The wrecker's daughter. -The scout. -The
light-keeper. -The settlers. -The liberty pole. -The storm at
sea. -The Canadian captive.

9978 Incidents of the revolution. Tales illustrating the events of the
American revolution... Bath [N. Y.] R. L. Underhill &
co. , 1841.
     239 p.   front. , pl.   18 cm.

9979 [Ingraham, Joseph Holt] 1809-1860.

Captain Kyd; or, The wizard of the sea. A romance.
By the author of "The Southwest," "Lafitte," "Burton," &c.
... New York, Harper & brothers, 1839.
2 v.   19 cm.

9980 Ingraham, Joseph Holt, 1809, 1860.
Grace Weldon; or, Frederica, the bonnet-girl. A tale
of Boston and its bay ... Boston, H. L. Williams, 1845.
108 p.   20 cm.

9981 Ingraham, Joseph Holt, 1809-1860.
Henry Howard; or, Two noes make one yes. By J. H.
Ingraham... Boston, H. L. Williams, 1845.
32 p.   23 cm.
"Trout fishing; or, Who is the captain?": p. [15]-32.

9982 [Ingraham, Joseph Holt] 1809-1860.
Montezuma, the serf; or, The revolt of the Mexitili; a
tale of the last days of the Aztec dynasty. By the author of
'Lafitte,' 'Kyd,' 'Burton,' 'The quadroone, etc.' Boston,
H. L. Williams, 1845.
2 v. in 1.   23 1/2 cm.
Issued in 5 parts. Part 1 without name of author; on
covers of pts. 2-5: J. H. Ingraham, Esq., author.

9983 Ingraham, Joseph Holt, 1809-1860.
Paul Perril, the merchant's son; or, The adventures of a
New-England boy launched upon life. By Professor J. H.
Ingraham... Boston, Williams & brothers [1847]
2 v. in 1.   24 1/2 cm.

9984 Ingraham, Joseph Holt, 1809-1860.
The pillar of fire; or, Israel in bondage. By Rev. J. H.
Ingraham... New York, Pudney & Russell, 1859.
600 p. front.   20 cm.
Bibliography: p. 599-600.

9985 Ingraham, Joseph Holt, 1809-1860.
Ringold Griffitt; or, The raftsman of the Susquehannah. A
tale of Pennsylvania. By Prof. J. H. Ingraham. Boston,
F. Gleason, 1847.
1 p. 1., [7]-100 p.   25 cm.

9986 Ingraham, Joseph Holt, 1809-1860.
      Scarlet Feather; or, The young chief of the Abenaquies.
A romance of the wilderness of Maine. By J. H. Ingraham
... Boston, F. Gleason, 1845.
      1 p. 1., [5]-66 p. illus.   21 1/2 cm.

9987 [Ingraham, Joseph Holt] 1809-1860.
      The South-west. By a Yankee... New-York, Harper &
brothers, 1835.
      2 v.   18 x 10 1/2 cm.

9988 Ingraham, Joseph Holt, 1809-1860.
      The surf skiff; or, The heroine of the Kennebec. By J.
H. Ingraham... New York and Boston, Williams brothers,
1847.
      1 p. 1., [5]-98 p.   25 cm.
      "Captain Velasco; and the young lieutenant. Or, Our
private buccaneering adventure": p. [86]-98.

9989 Ingraham, Joseph Holt, 1809-1860.
      The throne of David; from the consecration of the shepherd
of Bethlehem, to the rebellion of Prince Absalom... in a
series of letters addressed by an Assyrian ambassador...
to his lord and king on the throne of Nineveh... By the
Rev. J. H. Ingraham... Philadelphia, G. G. Evans, 1860.
      2 p. 1., [7]-603 p. front., plates.   19 cm.
      Appendix: p. 597-603.

9990 An interesting love story, found in a rebel camp ground. Written
by a southern soldier, drafted into the rebel army, whose
sympathies were with the North. New York, 1863.
      12 p.   18 cm.

9991 The Irish emigrant. An historical tale founded on fact, by an
Hibernian [pseud.]... Winchester, Va., J. T. Sharrocks,
1817.
      2 v.   14 cm.

9992 [Irving, Thomas J   ]
      In the rapids. A romance. By Gerald Hart [pseud.]
Philadelphia, J. B. Lippincott & co., 1871.
      319 p.   18 cm.

9993 [Irving, Washington] 1783-1859.
  The Alhambra: a series of tales and sketches of the Moors
  and Spaniards. By the author of The sketch book... [1st ed.]
  Philadelphia, Carey & Lea, 1832.
    2 v.   19 cm.

9994 Irving, Washington, 1783-1859.
  The beauties of Washington Irving... Philadelphia, Carey,
  Lea & Blanchard, 1835.
    viii, [9]-270 p.   16 cm.

9995 [Irving, Washington] 1783-1859.
  A book of the Hudson. Collected from the various works
  of Diedrich Knickerbocker. Edited by Geoffrey Crayon
  [pseud.] New York, G. P. Putnam, 1849.
    viii, [11]-215 p.   15 1/2 cm.
  CONTENTS. -Communipaw. -Guests from Gibbet island.
  -Peter Stuyvesant's voyage up the Hudson. -The chronicle of
  Bearn island. -The legend of Sleepy Hollow. -Dolph Heyliger.
  -Rip Van Winkle. -Wolfert Webber, or Golden dreams.
  Published in 1912, with an additional tale, under the
  title: Stories of the Hudson.

9996 [Irving, Washington] 1783-1859.
  Bracebridge Hall; or, The humourists. A medley, by
  Geoffrey Crayon, gent. [pseud.]... New York, Printed
  by C. S. Van Winkle, 1822.
    2 v.   22 1/2 cm.
  Only 1000 copies of this 1st American edition were printed.
  Irving had made great alterations and additions as the work
  was printing, so that the 1st English edition differed considerable from the 1st American. The two editions were
  published within two days of each other, the American
  appearing on the 21st, and the English on the 23d of May.
  cf. Life and letters of Washington Irving, ed. by P. M.
  Irving, London, 1862, v. 2, p. 56 and 58.

9997 [Irving, Washington] 1783-1859.
  A chronicle of the conquest of Granada. By Fray Antonio
  Agapida [pseud.]... Philadelphia, Carey, Lea & Carey,
  1829.
    2 v.   24 cm.

First American edition.

9998   [Irving, Washington] 1783-1859.
        The devil and Tom Walker: together with Deacon Grubb
        and the Old Nick. Woodstock, Vt., Printed and published
        by R. & A. Colton, 1830.
        32 p.   24 mo.

9999   [Irving, Washington] 1783-1859.
        A history of New York, from the beginning of the world to
        the end of the Dutch dynasty. Containing, among many
        surprising and curious matters, the unutterable ponderings
        of Walter the Doubter, the disastrous projects of William
        the Testy, and the chivalric achievements of Peter the
        Headstrong. The three Dutch governors of New Amsterdam...
        4th American ed. By Diedrich Knickerbocker... New York,
        Printed by C. S. Van Winkle, 1824.
        2 v. in 1.   18 cm.

10000   [Irving, Washington] 1783-1859.
        A history of New York from the beginning of the world
        to the end of the Dutch dynasty... by Diedrich Knicker-
        bocker [pseud.]... With illustrations by Felix O. C.
        Darley, engraved by eminent artists. New York, G. P.
        Putnam, 1850.
        xvi, [13]-454 p. front., illus., plates (1 fold.)
        22 1/2 cm.
        Added t.-p., engr.

10001   [Irving, Washington] 1783-1859.
        The sketch book of Geoffrey Crayon, gent^{n} [pseud.]...
        The author's rev. ed. ... New York, G. P. Putnam, 1849.
        xii, [9]-465 p.   19 1/2 cm. (Added t.-p.: The works
        of Washington Irving. New ed., rev. vol. II)

10002   [Irving, Washington, 1783-1859.
        Tales of a traveller, by Geoffrey Crayon, gent. [pseud.]...
        New ed. Philadelphia, Carey, Lea & Blanchard, 1837.
        2 v.   18 1/2 cm.

10003 [Jackson, Frederick]
          The Effinghams; or, Home as I found it... New York,
     S. Colman, 1841.
          2 v.   18 1/2 cm.

10004 [Jackson, Frederick]
          A week in Wall street. By one who knows. New York,
     For the booksellers,1841.
          xp., 1 1., 152 p.   18 1/2 cm.

10005 Jackson, Helen Maria (Fiske) Hunt, 1831-1885.
          Ramona. A story. By Helen Jackson (H.H.)... Boston,
     Roberts brothers, 1884.
          1 p. 1., 490 p.   19 cm.

10006 Jackson, Helen Maria (Fiske) Hunt, 1831-1885.
          Saxe Holm's [pseud.] stories. First series. New York,
     Scribner, Armstrong & co., 1874.
          350 p.   20 cm.
          CONTENTS.-Draxy Miller's Dowry.-The Elder's Wife.
     -Whose wife was she?-The One-legged dancers.-How one
     woman kept her husband.-Ester Wynn's love-letters.

10007 Jackson, Mary E
          The spy of Osawatomie; or, The mysterious companions
     of Old John Brown... St. Louis, Mo., W. S. Bryan, 1881.
          439 p. illus.   20 cm.

10008 [Jacobs, Harriet (Brent), 1818-1896.
          Incidents in the life of a slave girl. Written by herself...
     Edited by L. Maria Child. Boston, Pub. for the author,
     1861.
          1 p. 1., 5-306 p.   19 1/2 cm.
          Preface signed: Linda Brent.
          By Mrs. Harriet Jacobs. cf. Cushing, Initials and
     pseudonyms.

10009 James, George Payne Rainsford, 1801?-1860.
          Adrian; or, The clouds of the mind. A romance. By

G. P. R. James... and Maunsell B. Field... New York,
D. Appleton & company, 1852.
    301 p.   11 1/2 cm.
    Added t.-p., illus.

10010 James, Henry, 1843-1916.
    Confidence... Boston, Houghton, Mifflin and company,
1880.
    347 p.   20 cm.

10011 James, Henry, 1834-1916.
    The diary of a man of fifty, and a bundle of letters, by
Henry James... New York, Harper & brothers, 1880.
    2 p. 1., [9]-135 p.   12 1/2 cm. (On cover: Harper's
half-house series. no. 13-51)

10012 James, Henry, 1843-1916.
    Embarrassments... New York, The Macmillan company,
London, Macmillan & co., ltd., 1896.
    320 p.   20 cm.
    CONTENTS.-The figure in the carpet.-Glasses.-The
next time.-The way it came.

10013 James, Henry, 1843-1916.
    The other house [a novel] by Henry James... New York,
London, The MacMillan company, 1896.
    3 p. 1., 3-388 p.   20 cm.

10014 James, Henry, 1843-1916.
    A passionate pilgrim, and other tales. By Henry James,
jr. Boston, J. R. Osgood and company, 1875.
    496 p.   19 cm.
    CONTENTS.-A passionate pilgrim.-The last of the
Valerii.-Eugene Pickering.-The madonna of the future.
-The romance of certain old clothes.-Madame de Mauves.

10015 James, Henry, 1843-1916.
    The siege of London, The Pension Beaurepas, and The
point of view... Boston, James R. Osgood and company,
1883.
    294 p.   20 cm.

10016 James, Henry, 1843-1916.
     The soft side, by Henry James... New York, The
Macmillan company; London, Macmillan & co., Ltd., 1900.
     v, 326 p.   20 cm.
     CONTENTS.-The great good place.-'Europe'.-Paste.
-The real right thing.-The great condition.-The tree of
knowledge.-The abasement of the Norhtmores.-The given
case.-John Delavory.-The third person.-Maud Evelyn.-
Miss. Gunton of Poughkeepsie.

10017 James, Henry, 1843-1916.
     The spoils of Poynton, by Henry James. Boston and
New York, Houghton, Mifflin and company, 1897.
     1 p. 1., 323 p.   19 1/2 cm.
     Originally appeared in the Atlantic monthly from April to
Oct. 1896 under the title: The Old things.

10018 James, Henry, 1843-1916.
     The tragic muse, a novel, by Henry James... Boston
and New York, Houghton, Mifflin and company, 1890.
     2 v.   18 1/2 cm.
     Paged continuously.

10019 James, Henry, 1843-1916.
     What Maisie knew... Chicago & New York: Herbert
Stone & co., 1897.
     470 p.   20 cm.

10020 James, Henry, 1843-1916.
     The wheel of time; Collaboration; Owen Wingrave, by
Henry James, New York, Harper & brothers, 1893.
     3 p. 1., [3]-220 p.   18 cm.

10021 [James, Samuel Humphreys] 1857-
     A prince of good fellows; a picture from life, written by
the author of "A woman of New Orleans", and ed. by N.
Warrington Crabtrie [pseud.] New York, The American
news co. [c1890]
     208 p.   19 1/2 cm.

10022 [Jamison, Mrs. Cecilia Viets (Dakin)] 1844-1909.
     A crown from the spear. By the author of "Woven of many

threads"... Boston, J. R. Osgood and company, 1872.
vi, 172 p.   23 1/2 cm.

10023 [Jamison, Mrs. Cecilia Viets (Dakin)] 1844-1909.
Ropes of sand: and other stories. By the author of "Woven
of many threads"... Boston, J. R. Osgood and company,
1873.
176 p.   23 1/2 cm.

10024 Jamison, Mrs. Cecilia Viets (Dakin) 1844-1909.
Something to do. A novel. Boston, J. R. Osgood and
company, 1871.
1 p. 1., 150 p.   23 cm.

10025 Janvier, Thomas Allibone, 1849-1913.
Color studies, and a Mexican campaign, by Thomas A.
Janvier... New York, Charles Scribner's sons, 1891.
391 p.   17 cm.

10026 Janvier, Thomas Allibone, 1849-1913.
In the Sargasso Sea, a novel. New York, Harper, 1898.
293 p.

10027 Janvier, Thomas Allibone, 1849-1913.
The uncle of an angel, and other stories... New York,
Harper and brothers, 1891.
287 p., illus.   20 cm.

10028 Jarves, James Jackson, 1818-1888.
Kiana: a tradition of Hawaii. By James J. Jarves...
Boston and Cambridge, J. Munroe and company, 1857.
277 p.   19 cm.

10029 Jarves, James Jackson, 1820-1888.
Why and what am I? The confessions of an inquirer. In
three parts. Part 1. Heart-experience; or, the education of
the emotions. By James Jackson Jarves... Boston,
Phillips, Sampson and company, 1857.
viii, [9], 320 p.   20 cm.

10030 Jarvis, Mary Elizabeth (Woodson), 1842-1924.
The way it all ended: a novel. Richmond, Va. [Printed

by Chas. H. Wynne] 1859.
  1 p. 1. , [xi]-xii, [13]-375 p.   19 cm.
  "Author's edition.

10031 Jay, Charles W
       My new home in northern Michigan, and other tales. By
       Charles W. Jay. Trenton, N. J. , Printed by W. S. & E. W.
       Sharp, 1874.
         2 p. 1. , [9]-180 p.   20 cm.

10032 Jenkins, Mrs. Daphne Smith (Giles) b. 1812.
       East and West [a temperance story] By Daphne S. Giles...
       New York, Printed by R. Craighead, 1853.
         4 p. 1. , [7]-246 p.   14 cm.

10033 [Jenks, William] 1778-1866.
       Memoir of the northern kingdom, written A. D. 1872,
       by the late Rev. Williamson Jahnsenykes, LL. D. [pseud.]
       in six letters to his son... Quebeck, A. D. 1901. [Boston,
       1808]
         vi p. 1 1. , [9]-48 p.   23 cm.
       It purports to be an account of the breaking up of the Union
       by the secession of the southern states, which had adopted a
       monarchical form of government, under the protection of
       France; while the north-eastern states had become annexed
       to Canada, under the control of an English prince, and a
       republic, called the "Illinois" had been established in the
       West.

10034 Jewett, Sarah Orne, 1849-1909.
       A country doctor, by Sarah Orne Jewett. Boston and New
       York, Houghton, Mifflin and company, 1884.
         2 p. 1. , 351 p.   18 cm.

10035 Jewett, Sarah Orne, 1849-1909.
       The country of the pointed firs, by Sarah Orne Jewett,
       Boston and New York, Houghton, Mifflin and company, 1896.
         3 p. 1. , 213 p.   18 cm.

10036 Jewett, Sarah Orne, 1849-1909.
       Deephaven, By Sarah O. Jewett. Boston and New York,
       Houghton Mifflin Co. , 1877.

254 p.   15 1/2 cm.

10037 Jewett, Sarah Orne, 1849-1909.
      The king of Folly Island and other people, by Sarah Orne
Jewett. Boston and New York, Houghton, Mifflin and company,
1888.
      4 p. l. , 339 p.   18 cm.
      CONTENTS.-The king of Folly Island.-The courting of
Sister Wisby.-The landscape chamber.-Law Lane.-Miss
Peck's promotion.-Miss Tempy's watchers.-A village shop.
-Mère Pochett.

10038 Jewett, Sarah Orne, 1849-1909.
      The life of Nancy... Boston and New York, Houghton,
Mifflin and company, 1895.
      322 p.   20 cm.
      Also contains: Fame's little day-A war debt-The Hiltons'
holiday-The only rose-A second spring-Little French Mary-
The guests of Mrs. Timms-A neighbor's landmark-All my
sad captains.

10039 Jewett, Sarah Orne, 1849-1909.
      A marsh island, by Sarah Orne Jewett. Boston and New
York, Houghton, Mifflin and company, 1885.
      292 p.   18 cm.

10040 Jewett, Sarah Orne, 1849-1909.
      The mate of the daylight, and friends ashore, by Sarah
Orne Jewett. Boston, Houghton, Mifflin and company,
1884.
      3 p. l. , 254 p.   16 cm.
      CONTENTS.-The mate of the daylight.-Friends ashore.-
A landless farmer.-A new parishoner.-An only son.-Miss
Debby's neighbors.-Tom's husband.-The confession of a
house-breaker.-A little traveler.

10041 Jewett, Sarah Orne, 1849-1909.
      A native of Winby, and other tales, by Sarah Orne Jewett.
Boston and New York, Houghton, Mifflin and company, 1893.
      3 p. l. , 309 p.   18 cm.
      CONTENTS.-A native of Winby.-Decoration day.-Jim's
little woman.-The failure of David Berry.-The passing of

Sister Barsett.-Miss Esther's quest.-The flight of Betsey Lane.-Between Mass and Vespers.-A little captive maid.

10042 Jewett, Sarah Orne, 1849-1909.
　　　　The queen's twin, and other stories, by Sarah Orne Jewett. Boston and New York, Houghton, Mifflin and company, 1899.
　　　　　　3 p. 1., 232 p., 1 1.　　18 cm.
　　　　CONTENTS.-The queen's twin.-A Dunnet shepherdress. -Where's Nora?-Bold works at the bridge.-Martha's lady. -The coon Dog.-Aunt Cynthia Dallett.-The night before Thanksgiving.

10043 Jewett, Sarah Orne, 1849-1909.
　　　　Strangers and wayfarers... Boston and New York, Houghton, Mifflin and company, 1890.
　　　　　　279 p.　　20 cm.
　　　　CONTENTS.-A winter courtship-The mistress of Sydenham Plantation-The town poor-The quest of Mr. Teaby-The luck of the Bogans-Fair day-Going to Shrewsbury.-The taking of the Captain Ball-By the morning boat-In dark New England days-The White Rose Road.

10044 Jewett, Mrs. Susan W
　　　　From fourteen to fourscore. By Mrs. S. W. Jewett. New York, Hurd and Houghton, 1871.
　　　　　　iv, 416 p.　　19 cm.

10045 Johnson, Virginia Wales, 1849-1916.
　　　　The Calderwood secret. A novel. By Virginia W. Johnson ... New York, Harper & brothers, 1875.
　　　　　　2 p. 1., [9]-136 p.　　23 1/2 cm. (On cover: Library of select novels, no. 448)

10046 Johnson, Virginia Wales, 1849-1916.
　　　　The cricket's friends. Tales told by the cricket, teapot, and saucepan. Boston, Nichols and Noyes, 1868.
　　　　　　219 p.　　18 cm.
　　　　CONTENTS.-The travelled spider.-The ambitious wasp. -The disappointed caterpillar.-The four silver peaches.-Gone maying.-Grandpapa mouse and his family.-The enchanted babyhouse.-The Story of an umbrella.-The godmother's gifts.

10047 [Johnson, Virginia Wales] 1849-1916.
      Joseph, the Jew. The story of an old house... New York,
Harper & brothers, 1874.
      2 p. 1., [9]-131 p.   23 1/2 cm. (On cover: Library of
select novels, no. 402)

10048 Johnson, Virginia Wales, 1849-1916.
      A sack of gold. A novel. By Virginia W. Johnson...
New York, Harper & brothers, 1874.
      1 p. 1., [7]-121 p.   23 1/2 cm. (On cover: Library
of select novels, no. 419)

10049 Johnson, Virginia Wales, 1849-1916.
      Travels of an American owl. A satire. By Virginia W.
Johnson. With sixteen silhouette illustrations by Augustus
Hoppin, engraved by Jasper Green. Philadelphia, Claxton,
Remsen & Haffelfinger, 1871.
      2 p. 1., ix-xii, 13-179 p. front., illus., plates.
20 cm.

10050 [Johnson, Virginia Wales] 1849-1916.
      What the world made them. By the author of "Travels of
an American owl." New York, G. P. Putnam & sons, 1871.
      284 p.   18 1/2 cm.

10051 [Johnston, Algernon Sidney] 1801-1853.
      Memoirs of a nullifier, written by himself. By a native of
the South. Columbia, S. C., Telescope Off., 1832.
      110 p.   20 cm.
      Written by Algernon S. Johnston according to R. M. Hughes:
General Johnston, New York, 1893, p. 10, and E. E. Hume:
Peter Johnston, Junior, Virginia soldier and jurist. Attributed
also to Thomas Cooper, but according to Malone, without
justification. cf. Dumas Malone. The public life of Thomas
Cooper; Sabin, and Halkett & Laing.

10052 Johnston, Annie Fellows
      In the desert of waiting, the legend of Camelback mountain
... Boston, L. C. Page & company [1904]
      36 p. illus.   18 1/2 cm.

10053 [Johnston, James Wesley] 1850-

Dwellers in Gotham; a romance of New York, by Annan Dale [pseud.] New York, Eaton & Mains; Cincinnati, Curts & Jennings, 1898.

vi, 392 p.   19 1/2 cm.

10054 Johnston, Mrs. Maria Isabella, 1835-

The siege of Vicksburg. By Maria I. Johnston. Boston, Pratt brothers, 1869.

4 p. l. , [13]-330 p.   19 1/2 cm.

A novel.

10055 [Jolliffe, John] 1804-1868.

Belle Scott; or, Liberty overthrown! A tale for the crisis ... Columbus, D. Anderson; Cincinnati, G. S. Blanchard, 1856.

1 p. l. , 7-426 p.   18 1/2 cm.

Published anonymously.

10056 [Jolliffe, John] 1804-1868.

Chattanooga... Cincinnati, Wrightson & company, printers, 1858

400 p.   18 1/2 cm.

10057 Jones, Buehring H   b. 1823, comp.

The sunny land; or, Prison prose and poetry, containing the production of the ablest writers in the South, and prison lays of distinguished Confederate officers, by Col. Buehring H. Jones... Ed. , with preface, biographies, sketches, and stories, by J. A. Houston... Baltimore [Innes & co. , printers] 1868.

viii, 540 p. , 1 l.   20 cm.

10058 Jones, Erasmus W   1817-

The captive youths of Judah. By Erasmus W. Jones. New York, J. C. Derby & co. , 1856.

3 p. l. , ix-xii, [13]-465 p.   19 cm.

Imperfect; t. -p. wanting.

10059 Jones, J   Elizabeth.

The young abolitionists; or, Conversations on slavery. By J. Elizabeth Jones. Boston, Pub. at the Anti-slavery office, 1848.

131 p.   16 cm.

10060 Jones, James Athearn, 1791-1854.
        Haverhill; or, Memoirs of an officer in the army of Wolfe.
By James A. Jones... New-York, J. & J. Harper, 1831.
        2 v.   21 cm.

10061 [Jones, James Athearn] 1791-1854.
        The refugee. A romance. By Captain Matthew Murga-
troyd [pseud.] of the Ninth continentals in the revolutionary
war... New-York, Wilder & Campbell, 1825.
        2 v.   20 cm.

10062 Jones, John Beauchamp, 1810-1866.
        Freaks of fortune; or, The history and adventures of Ned
Lorn. By J. B. Jones... Philadelphia, T. B. Peterson
[c1854]
        401 p. incl. front., pl.   20 cm.

10063 Jones, John Beauchamp, 1810-1866.
        The Spanglers and Tingles; or, The rival belles. A
tale, unveiling some of the mysteries of society and politics
as they exist at the present time in the United States. By
J. B. Jones... Philadelphia, A. Hart, 1852.
        3, [15]-270 p.   19 1/2 cm. (On cover: Library of
humorous American works)
        Republished in 1878 under title: The rival belles.

10064 Jones, John Beauchamp, 1810-1866.
        Wild western scenes; a narrative of adventures in the west-
ern wilderness, forty years ago; wherein the conduct of
Daniel Boone, the great American pioneer, is particularly
described... By J. B. Jones. New York, S. Coleman;
Baltimore, N. Hickman, 1841.
        247, [1] p. illus.   22 1/2 cm.
        First edition.

10065 [Jones, John Beauchamp] 1810-1866.
        The Winkles; or, The merry monomaniacs. An American
picture with portraits of the natives. By the author of "Wild
western scenes," etc. New York [etc.] D. Appleton and
company, 1855.

xii, 424 p.   20 cm.
Imperfect; p. iii–viii wanting; p. 37–38 mutilated.

10066 Jones, John Richter, 1803–1863.
        The Quaker soldier; or, The British in Philadelphia. An
       historical novel... Philadelphia, T. B. Peterson and brothers
       [c1858]
         1 p. 1., xxi–xxix, 31–569 p. front.   19 cm.
         Published anonymously.

10067 [Jones, Joseph Stevens] 1811–1877.
        Life of Jefferson S. Batkins, member from Cranberry
       Centre. Written by himself, assisted by the author of the
       "Silver spoon"... Boston, Loring [c1871]
         496 p. front.   20 cm.

10068 [Jones, Justin]
        Big Dick, the king of the negroes; or, Virtue and vice
       contrasted. A romance of high & low life in Boston. By
       Harry Hazel [pseud.]... Boston, "Star spangled banner"
       office, 1846.
         2 p. 1., [9]–100 p.   26 cm.

10069 [Jones, Justin]
        ... The light dragoon; or, The rancheros of the poisoned
       lance. A tale of the battle fields of Mexico. By Harry Hazel
       [pseud.]... Boston, 'Star spangled banner' office, 1848.
         2 p. 1., [9]–100 p. incl. illus., plates.   26 cm.
         At head of title: A mexican military romance.

10070 [Jones, Justin]
        The nun of St. Ursula; or, The burning of the convent. A
       romance of Mount Benedict. By Harry Hazel [pseud.]...
       Boston, F. Gleason, 1845.
         2 p. 1., [9]–64 p. pl.   21 cm.

10071 [Jones, Justin]
        Sylvia Seabury; or, Yankees in Japan: the romantic
       adventures of a sailor-boy. By Harry Hazel [pseud.]...
       New York, H. Long & brother; Cincinnati, H. B. Pearson
       & co. [c1850]
         112 p. incl. plates   24 1/2 cm.

Added to. -p. , illus.

10072 Jones, Pascal.
My uncle Hobson and I; or, Slashes at life with a free
broadaxe. By Pascal Jones. New-York, D. Appleton & co.;
Philadelphia, G. S. Appleton, 1845.
268 p.   19 1/2 cm.

10073 Jordan, Kate "Mrs. F. M. Vermilye."
A circle in the sand, by Kate Jordan (Mrs. F. M.
Vermilye)... Boston, New York and London, Lamson,
Wolffe and company, 1898.
3 p. l., 303 p.   21 cm.

10074 [Judah, Samuel Benjamin Herbert] b. 1799.
The buccaneers; a romance of our own country in its
ancient day; illustrated with divers marvellous histories,
and antique and facetious episodes; gathered from the most
authentic chronicles & affirmed records extant from the
settlement of the Nieuw Nederlandts, until the times of the
famous Richard Kid: carefully collated from the laborious
researches, and minute investigations, of that excellent anti-
quary and sublime philosopher, yclept Teretius Phlogobombos
lpseud.]... Boston, Munroe & Francis; New-York, C. S.
Francis, 1827.
2 v.   20 1/2 cm.
Vol. 2 is 2d edition.
Vol. 1 is imperfect: p. xix and xxiv were suppressed;
in this copy p. xix-xx is a cancel, only p. xxi-xxiv being
wanting.

10075 [Judd Sylvester] 1813-1853.
Margaret. A tale of the real and ideal, blight and bloom;
including sketches of a place not before described, called
Mons Christi... Boston, Jordan and Wiley, 1845.
2 p. l., [3]-460 p.   20 1/2 cm.
Published anonymously.

10076 [Judd, Sylvester] 1813-1853.
Margaret: a tale of the real and the ideal, blight and
bloom; including sketches of a place not before described,
called Mons Christi... Rev. ed.... By the author of

"Philo"... Boston, Phillips, Sampson, and company, 1851.
2 v.   19 cm.

10077 [Judd, Sylvester] 1813-1853.
       Richard Edney and the governor's family. A rus-urban
       tale... of morals, sentiment, and life... containing, also,
       hints on being good and doing good. By the author of
       "Margaret"... Boston, Phillips, Sampson & company,
       1850.
       1 p. 1., [v]-vi, [7]-468 p.   19 cm.

10078 [Judson, Edward Zane Carroll] 1822-1886.
       Cruisings, afloat and ashore, from the private log of
       Ned Buntline [pseud.] Sketches of land and sea, humorous
       and pathetic; tragical and comical... [2d ed.] New York,
       R. Craighead, printer, 1848.
       102 p. illus.   23 1/2 cm.

10079 Judson, Edward Zane Carroll, 1822-1886.
       The king of the sea: a tale of the fearless and free. By
       Ned Buntline. Boston, Flag of Our Union Office, 1847.
       2 p. 1., [9]-100 p. incl. pl.   26 cm.
       At head of title: 100 dollar tale.

10080 [Judson, Edward Zane Carroll] 1822-1886.
       The mysteries and miseries of New York: a story of real
       life, by Ned Buntline [pseud.]... New York, Berford & co.,
       1848.
       5 v. in 1. illus.   22 cm.

10081 [Judson, Edward Zane Carroll] 1822-1886.
       Stella Delorme; or, The Comanche's dream. A wild and
       fanciful story of savage chivalry, by Ned Buntline [pseud.]
       New York, F. A. Brady [c1860]
       71 p. incl. 1 illus., plates.   22 cm.

10082 [Judson, Mrs. Emily (Chubbuck)] 1817-1854.
       Alderbrook: a collection of Fanny Forester's village
       sketches, poems, etc., by Miss Emily Chubbuck... Boston,
       W. D. Ticknor & company, 1847.
       2 v. front. (port.)   20 1/2 cm.

10083 [Judson, Mrs. Emily (Chubbuck)] 1817-1854.
      The great secret; or, How to be happy. By the author of
"Charles Linn". New York, Dayton & Newman, 1842.
      iv, [5]-311 p.   15 cm.

10084 [Judson, Mrs. Emily (Chubbuck)] 1817-1854.
      Trippings in author-land, by Fanny Forester [pseud.]
New-York, Paine and Burgess, 1846.
      vi, [13]-281 p.   19 cm.

10085 Justina; or, The will. A domestic story... New-York,
C. Wiley, 1823.
      2 v.   19 1/2 cm.

K

10086 Kate Marstone; or, Happy hearts make happy homes. A
      fireside story... New York, Carleton, 1866.
      303 p.   18 1/2 cm.

10087 Keeler, Ralph, 1840-1873.
      Gloverson and his silent partners. By Ralph Keeler.
Boston, Lee and Shepard, 1869.
      viii, [9]-372 p.   19 cm.

10088 Kellogg, Sarah Winter.
      The Livelies, and other short stories. By Sarah Winter
Kellogg. [Reprint from Lippincott's magazine] Philadelphia,
J. B. Lippincott & co., 1875.
      90 p. front.   23 cm.
      CONTENTS.-The Livelies.-Deshler & Deshler.-When I
was a boarder.-Her chance.-Mrs. Twitchell's inventions.

10089 [Kelly, John L   ]
      Fact and fiction! Disappointed love: a story drawn from
incidents in the lives of Miss Clara C. Cochran and Miss
Catherine B. Cotton, who committed suicide, by drowning,
in the canal at Manchester, N. H., August 14, 1853.

Manchester, N. H., Daily and weekly mirror steam printing
works, 1853.
32 p.   23 cm.

10090 Kelly, Jonathan Falconbridge, 1818-1854.
The homors of Falconbridge: a collection of humorous and
every day scenes. By Jonathan F. Kelley [!] Philadelphia,
T. B. Peterson and brothers [c1856]
2 p. l., 21-436 p.   19 cm.

10091 Kelso, Isaac.
Light, more light; or, Danger in the dark... By Isaac
Kelso. Cincinnati, E. Hampson, 1855.
vii, [9]-300 p. front.   19 1/2 cm.

10092 Kelso, Isaac.
The stars and bars; or, The reign of terror in Missouri.
By Isaac Kelso... Boston, A. Williams & co., 1864.
vi, 7-324 p.   19 1/2 cm.

10093 Kendall, Edmund Hale.
The twin sisters; a narrative of facts. By Edmund Hale
Kendall, esq. Lawrence City [Mass.] 1848.
32 p. illus.   17 cm.

10094 [Kennedy, John Pendleton] 1795-1870.
Horse Shoe Robinson; a tale of the Tory ascendency. By
the author of 'Swallow barn'... Philadelphia, Carey, Lea
& Blanchard, 1835.
2 v.   19 cm.
Author's pseudonym, "Mary Littleton", at end of preface.

10095 [Kennedy, John Pendleton] 1795-1870.
Quodlibet: containing some annals thereof... edited by
Solomon Secondthoughts [pseud.] From original mss. indited
by him, and now made public at the request and under the
patronage of the great New light democratic central committee
of Quodlibet. Philadelphia, Lea & Blanchard, 1840.
xxiv, [25]-350 (i.e. 250) p.   19 1/2 cm.
Page 250 incorrectly numbered 350.

10096 [Kennedy, John Pendleton] 1795-1870.

Rob of the Bowl: a legend of St. Inigoe's. By the author of "Swallow barn"... Philadelphia, Lea & Blanchard, 1838.
2 v.   19 cm.

10097 [Kennedy, John Pendleton] 1795-1870.
Swallow barn; or, A sojourn in the Old Dominion...
Philadelphia, Carey & Lea, 1832.
2 v.   20 1/2 cm.
Preface signed: Mark Littleton [pseud.]

10098 Ketchum, Mrs. Annie (Chambers) 1824-1904.
Nelly Bracken, a tale of forty years ago. By Annie
Chambers Bradford. Philadelphia, Lippincott, Grambo &
co., 1855.
1 p. 1., v-[vi], 7-377 p.   19 1/2 cm.

10099 [Kettell, Samuel] 1800-1855.
Daw's doings; or, History of the late war in the Plantations.
By Sampson Short-and-Fat... Boston, W. White & H. P.
Lewis, 1842.
68 p. front., plates.   16 1/2 cm.

10100 [Kettell, Samuel] 1800-1855.
Quozziana; or, Letters from Great Goslington, Mass.,
giving an account of the Quoz dinner, and other matters.
By Sampson Short-and-Fat [pseud.]... Boston, W. White
& H. P. Lewis, 1842.
68 p.   17 cm.

10101 [Kettell, Samuel] 1800-1855.
Yankee notions. A medley. By Timo. Titterwell, esq.
[pseud.]... 2d ed. with illustrations by D. C. Johnston.
Boston, Otis, Broaders and company, 1838.
xvi, [17]-251, [1] p. front., plates.   17 cm.

10102 [Keyes, F   ]
Evan Dale... Boston, A. Williams & co., 1864.
iv, 387 p.   20 1/2 cm.

10103 [Kilbourn, Diana Treat]
The lone dove: a legend of revolutionary times. By a lady.
Philadelphia, G. S. Appleton; New York, D. Appleton & co.,

1850.
    1 p. 1. , [7]-281 p.   19 cm.

10104 Kimball, Richard Burleigh, 1816-1892.
        Romance of student life abroad. By Richard B. Kimball
   ... New York, G. P. Putnam & co. , 1853.
        2 p. 1. , [xi]-xv, [17]-261 p.   19 cm.

10105 Kimball, Richard Burleigh, 1816-1892.
        Saint Leger; or, The threads of life. By Richard B.
   Kimball... 3d ed. New York, G. P. Putnam, 1850.
        384 p.   18 1/2 cm.

10106 Kimball, Richard Burleigh, 1816-1892.
        To-day: a romance. By Richard B. Kimball... New York,
   Carleton [etc. , etc.] 1870.
        viii p. , 1 1. , [11]-480 p.   19 cm.

10107 Kimball, Richard Burleigh, 1816-1892.
        Under-currents of Wall-street. A romance of business.
   By Richard B. Kimball... New York, G. P. Putnam, 1862.
        2 p. 1. , [7]-428 p.   18 1/2 cm.
        Published anonymously in 1884 under title: Fettered yet
   free.

10108 Kimball, Richard Burleigh, 1816-1892.
        Was he successful? A novel. By Richard B. Kimball...
   New York, Carleton [etc. , etc.] 1864.
        407 p. front. (port.)   18 cm.

10109 King, Charles, 1844-1933.
        An army wife... New York, F. Tennyson Neely, 1896.
        278 p. , illus.   20 cm.

10110 King, Charles, 1844-1933.
        Between the lines: a story of the war... New York, Harper
   & brothers, 1889.
        312. , illus.   20 cm.

10111 King, Charles, 1844-1933.
        Cadet days, a story of West Point, by Captain Charles
   King... New York, Harper and brothers, 1894.

vi, 293 p.   19 cm.

10112 King, Charles, 1844-1933.
        Campaigning with Crook, and stories of army life... New
    York, Harper & brothers, 1890.
        295 p., illus.   20 cm.
        "Campaigning with Crook" is a factual account, first
    published in 1880; the other contents are fiction.

10113 King, Charles, 1844-1933.
        Captain Blake... Philadelphia, J. B. Lippincott company,
    1891.
        495 p. illus.   20 cm.

10114 King, Charles, 1844-1933.
        Captain Close, and Sergeant Croesus: two novels...
    Philadelphia, J. B. Lippincott company, 1895.
        245 p.   20 cm.

10115 King, Charles, 1844-1933.
        Captain Dreams, and other stories... Philadelphia, J. B.
    Lippincott company, 1895.
        210 p.   20 cm.
        Also contains: The ebb-tide, by Lieutenant A. H. Sydenham. -
    White lilies, by Alice King Hamilton. -A strange wound, by
    Lieutenant W. H. Hamilton. -The story of Alcatraz, by
    Lieutenant A. H. Sydenham. -The other fellow, by R. Monckton
    Dene. -Buttons, by Captain J. G. Leefe.

10116 King, Charles, 1844-1933 ed.
        The colonel's Christmas dinner. Ed. by Capt. Charles
    King... Philadelphia, L. R. Hamersly & co., 1890.
        182, [2] p.   20 cm.
        CONTENTS. -Introduction, by Capt. C. King. -The adjutant's
    story, by Capt. C. King. -The senior lieutenant's story, by
    Lieut. T. H. Wilson. -The senior captain's story, by Capt. E.
    Field. -The captain's story, by Capt. H. Romeyn. -The colonel's
    daughter's story, by C. F. Little. -A major's story, by Capt.
    W. C. Bartlett. -The quartermaster's story, by E. L. Keys.
    -The major's story, by Maj. W. H. Powell. -A guest's story,
    by A. K. Livingston. -The colonel's story, by Col. H. W.
    Closson.

10117 King, Charles, 1844-1933.
   The Colonel's daughter; or, Winning his spurs...
  Philadelphia, J. B. Lippincott & co. , 1883.
   440 p. 20 cm.

10118 King, Charles, 1844-1933.
   The deserter, and from the ranks: two novels... Philadelphia, J. B. Lippincott company, 1887.
   324 p. 20 cm.

10119 King, Charles, 1844-1933.
   Foes in ambush. By Capt. Charles King... Philadelphia,
  J. B. Lippincott company, 1893.
   1 p. 1. , 5-263 p. 19 cm.

10120 King, Charles, 1844-1933.
   A garrison tangle, by Charles King. New York, F. T.
  Neely, 1896.
   280 p. 20 cm.

10121 King, Charles, 1844-1933.
   The general's double: a story of the Army of the Potomac...
  Philadelphia, J. B. Lippincott company, 1898.
   446 p. illus. 20 cm.

10122 King, Charles, 1844-1933, ed.
   An initial experience, and other stories. Ed. by Capt.
  Charles King. Philadelphia, J. B. Lippincott company, 1894.
   1 p. 1. , 254 p. 19 cm.
   CONTENTS. -An initial experience. By Captain Charles
  King. -In the "Never never country." By R. Monckton-Dene.
  -The siren of Three-mile bend. By R. Monckton-Dene. -
  The lost pine mine. By Alvin Sydenham. -Private Jones of
  the Eighth. By R. Monckton-Dene. -Jack Hilton's love-affair.
  By T. H. Farnham. -Wauna, the witch-maiden. By Alvin
  Sydenham. -Conyngham Foxe and the charity ball. By Alvin
  Sydenham. -The soldier's aid society. By C. F. Little. -A
  pitiful surrender. By J. P. Wisser. -The story of a recruit.
  By D. Robinson. -Chronicles of Carter barracks. By H. W.
  Closson.

10123 King, Charles, 1844-1933.

Laramie, or The queen of bedlam, a story of the Sioux
War of 1876... Philadelphia, J. B. Lippincott company,
1889.

10124 King, Charles, 1844-1933.
Marion's faith, by the author of "The Colonel's daughter."
Capt. Charles King... Philadelphia, J. B. Lippincott
company, 1887.
vii, 5-446 p.   19 cm.

10125 King, Charles, 1844-1933.
... Rancho del Muerto, by Capt. Chas. King, and other
stories of adventure... New York and London, Outing
publishing company [1894]
3 p. l., [11]-190 p. illus.   18 1/2 cm. (Outing
library. v. 1, no. 3)
CONTENTS.-Rancho del Muerto. C. King.-A mighty
hunter before the Lord. V. Dabney.-A Cohutta Valley
shooting match. W. H. Harben.-Moeran's moose. E. W.
Sandys.-The mystery of a Christmas hunt. T. Torrance.-
Herne the hunter. W. P. Brown.-Uncle Duke's "b'ar"
story. Lillian Gilfillan.-A cigarette from Carcinto. E.
French.

10126 King, Charles, 1844-1933.
Ray's recruit, by Captain Charles King... Philadelphia,
J. B. Lippincott, company, 1898.
2 p. l., 7-249 p. front, 3 pl.   17 cm.

10127 King, Charles, 1844-1933.
The story of Fort Frayne, by Captain Charles King...
adapted from the drama of the same name of which, in
collaboration with Evelyn Greenleaf Suther and Emma V.
Sheridan Fry he is the author. Chicago, New York, F.
Tennyson Neely [1895]
310 p. front. (port.)   19 1/2 cm.

10128 King, Charles, 1844-1933.
A trooper Galahad. Philadelphia, Lippincott, 1899
(c. 1898)
257 p. front.   19 cm.

10129 King, Charles, 1844-1933.
       Trumpeter Fred; a story of the plains... New York,
       Chicago, F. Tennyson Neely, 1896.
       201 p., illus.   20 cm.

10130 King, Charles, 1844-1933.
       Under fire... Philadelphia, J. B. Lippincott Company,
       1895.
       511 p., illus.   20 cm.

10131 King, Charles, 1844-1933.
       A war-time wooing, a story... New York, Harper &
       brothers, 1888.
       195 p., illus.   20 cm.

10132 King, Charles, 1844-1933.
       Waring's peril... Philadelphia, J. B. Lippincott company,
       1894.
       230 p.   20 cm.

10133 King, Edward, 1848-1896.
       Kentucky's love; or, Roughing it around Paris. By
       Edward King... Boston, New York, Lee and Shepard, 1873.
       287 p.   18 cm.

10134 King, Elisha Sterling.
       The wild rose of Cherokee; or, Nancy Ward, "The
       Pocahontas of the west." A story of the early exploration,
       occupancy, and settlement of the state of Tennessee. A
       romance, founded on and interwoven with history...
       Nashville, Tenn., University press, 1895.
       119 p.   20 cm.

10135 King, Grace Elizabeth, 1852-1932.
       Monsieur Matte, by Grace King. New York, A. C.
       Armstrong and son, 1888.
       4 p. 1., [11]-327 p.   18 1/2 cm.
       CONTENTS. -Monsieur Motte. -On the plantation. -The
       drama of an evening. -Marriage of Marie Modeste.

10136 Kingsbury, John H
       Kingsbury sketches. A truthful and succinct account of

the doings and misdoings of the inhabitants of Pine Grove; their private trials and public tribulations. By John H. Kingsbury. New York, G. W. Carleton & co., 1875.
xii, [13]-296 p. incl. front. plates.   19 cm.

10137 Kingsley, Mrs. Florence (Morse), 1859-1937.
Stephen, a soldier of the cross, by Florence Morse Kingsley... Philadelphia, H. Altemus, 1896.
2 p. l., 3-369 p. front. (port.)   19 1/2 cm.

10138 Kingsley, Mrs. Florence (Morse), 1859-1937.
Titus, a comrade of the cross... Chicago, David C. Cook publishing company, 1895.
280 p. illus.   20 cm.

10139 Kinkead, Eleanor Talbot, "Mrs. Thompson Short."
Florida Alexander, a Kentucky girl... Chicago, A. C. McClurg and company, 1898.
276 p.   19 cm.

10140 Kinkead, Eleanor Talbot, "Mrs. Thompson Short."
Young Greer of Kentucky. A novel... Chicago and New York, Rand, McNally & company, 1895.
332 p.   19 cm.

10141 Kinzie, Juliette Augusta (Magill) "Mrs. John H. Kinzie," 1806-1870.
Wau-bun, the "early day" in the North-west. By Mrs. John H. Kinzie... New York, Derby & Jackson; Cincinnati, H. W. Derby & co., 1856.
xii, 13-498 p. front., plates.   22 1/2 cm.
Narrative of travel in Wisconsin and Illinois; life at Fort Winnebago (Portage) Wisconsin, 1830-1833; Chicago in 1831; Chicago massacre of 1812.

10142 [Kip, Leonard] 1826-1906.
Ænone: a tale of slave life in Rome. New York, J. Bradburn, 1866.
308 p.   18 1/2 cm.

10143 Kip, Leonard, 1826-1906.
The dead marquise; a romance, by Leonard Kip... New

257

York, G. P. Putnam's sons, 1873.
viii, 356 p.   19 cm.

10144 Kip, Leonard, 1826-1906.
... Hannibal's man. By Leonard Kip. Albany, The Argus
company, printers, 1873.
46 p.   18 1/2 cm.
At head of t.-p.: The Argus Christmas story.

10145 [Kip, Leonard] 1826-1906.
The volcano diggings; a tale of California law. By a
member of the bar... New York, J. S. Redfield, 1851.
131 p.   19 cm.

10146 Kipling, Rudyard, 1865-1936.
The naulahka; a story of West and East [by] Rudyard
Kipling and Wolcott Balestier. New York and London,
Macmillan and co. , 1892.
vi, 379 p.   19 1/2 cm.

10147 Kirkland, Mrs. Caroline Matilda (Stansbury) 1801-1864.
The evening book: or, Fireside talk on morals and man-
ners, with sketches of western life. By Mrs. Kirkland...
New York, C. Scribner, 1852.
4 p. l. , [vii]-xi, [13]-312 p. 6 pl. (incl.front.)   22 cm.
Added t.-p. , engraved.

10148 [Kirkland, Mrs. Caroline Matilda (Stansbury)] 1801-1864.
Forest life. By the author of "A new home"... New York,
C. S. Francis & co.; Boston, J. H. Francis, 1844.
2 v.   18 1/2 x 11 cm.

10149 [Kirkland, Mrs. Caroline Matilda (Stansbury)] 1801-1864.
A new home-who'll follow? or, Glimpses of western life.
By Mrs. Mary Clavers [pseud.]... New York, C. S. Francis;
Boston, J. H. Francis, 1839.
vi, [7]-317 p.   20 cm.

10150 Kirkland, Mrs. Caroline Matilda (Stansbury) 1801-1864.
Western clearings. By Mrs. C. M. Kirkland... New
York, Wiley and Putnam, 1845.

3 p. 1., [v]-viii, 238 p.   18 1/2 cm. (Half-title:
Wiley and Putnam's library of American books)
    CONTENTS. -The land-fever. -Ball at Thram's Huddle. -A
forest fete. -Love vs. aristocracy. -Harvest musings. -The
bee-tree. -Idle people. -Chances and changes. -Ambuscades.
-Old thoughts on the New Year. -The schoolmaster's progress. -Half-lengths from life. -An embroidered fact. -Bitter
fruits from chance-sown seeds.

10151 [Knapp, Samuel Lorenzo] 1783-1838.
    Extracts from a journal of travels in North America,
consisting of an account of Boston and its vicinity. By
Ali Bey, &c. [pseud.] Translated from the original
manuscript... Boston: Printed by Thomas Badger, June,
1818.
    124 p.   19 cm.

10152 [Knapp, Samuel Lorenzo] 1783-1838.
    Extracts from the journal of Marshal Soult [pseud.]
addressed to a friend: how obtained, and by whom translated is not a subject of enquiry... Newburyport, W. B.
Allen & co., 1817.
    143 p.   19 cm.

10153 Knapp, Samuel Lorenzo, 1783-1838.
    Tales of the garden of Kosciusko. By Samuel L. Knapp...
New York, Printed by West & Trow, 1834.

10154 The Knickerbocker gallery: a testimonial to the editor of the
    Knickerbocker magazine [i.e. Lewis Gaylord Clark] from
    its contributors. With forty-eight portraits on steel...
    engraved expressly for this work. New-York, S. Hueston,
    1855.
    1 p. 1., [ix]-xiv, 15-505 p.   49 port. (incl. front.)
23 1/2 cm.
    Added t.-p., engraved with vignette.

10155 [Knight, Mrs. S   G   ]
    Man's wrongs; or, Woman's foibles. By Kate Manton
[pseud.] Boston, Crosby & Damrell, 1870.
    272 p.   18 1/2 cm.

10156 Knorr, James.
      The two roads; or, The right and the wrong. By James
Knorr. Philadelphia, Lippincott, Grambo & co., 1854.
xi, 25-372 p.   19 cm.
Temperance stories, poems and sketches.

10157 Knox, Adeline (Trafton) 1845-
      An American girl abroad. By Adeline Trafton. Illustrated
by Miss L. B. Humphrey. Boston, Lee & Shepard, 1872.
245 p. front., pl.   17 1/2 cm.

L

10158 Labree, Lawrence.
      Rebels and tories; or, The blood of the Mohawk! A tale
of the American revolution... By Lawrence Labree. New
York. Dewitt & Davenport [c1851]
202 p.   24 cm.

10159 Lamas, Maria.
      The glass; or, The trials of Helen More, a thrilling
temperance tale, ed. by Maria Lamas... Philadelphia,
M. E. Harmstead, 1849.
32 p.   23 cm.

10160 Lamb, Mrs. Martha Joanna Reade (Nash) 1829-1893.
      Spicy. A novel. By Mrs. Martha J. Lamb... New York,
D. Appleton and company, 1873.
vi, [7]-178 p. front., plates.   24 cm.

10161 Landis, Simon Mohler.
      An entirely new feature of a thrilling novel! Entitled, The
social war of the year 1900; or, The conspirators and lovers!
By S. M. Landis... Philadelphia, Pa., Landis publishing
society, 1872.
419 p.   18 1/2 cm.
Pages 403-416, advertising matter.

10162 [Landon, Melville De Lancey] 1838-1910.
   Saratoga in 1901. By Eli Perkins [pseud.] Fun, love,
society & satire. Illustrated with 200 photo-etchings by
Arthur Lumley. New York, Sheldon & company, 1872.
   vii, 249, [1] p. illus.   20 1/2 cm.
   Illustrated t.-p.
   "Many of the letters in this volume appeared in the New
York commercial advertiser."-p. iii.

10163 Langford, Mrs. Laura (Carter) Holloway, 1848- comp.
   The woman's story, as told by twenty American women;
with portraits and sketches of the authors, by Laura C.
Holloway... New York, J. B. Alden, 1889.
   xi, 541 p. ports.   19 1/2 cm.
   Paging irregular; several portraits included in paging.
   CONTENTS.-Stowe, H. B. Uncle Lot.-Spofford, H. P.
Old Madame.-Davis, R. H. Tirar y Soult.-Proctor, E. D.
Tom Foster's wife.-Holley, M. Fourth of July in Jonesville.
-Perry, N. Dorothy.-Wilson, A. E. The trial of Beryl.-
Moulton, L. C. "Nan."-Thaxter, C. A memorable murder.
-Lippincott, S. J. A cup of cold water.-Woolson, A. G. An
evening's adventure.-Holmes, M. J. Adam Floyd.-Sangster,
M. E. My borrowing neighbor.-Miller, O. T. The girls'
sketching camp.-Champney, E. W. A crisis.-Dorr, J. C.
R. Meg.-[Terhune, M. V.] A Confederate idyl. By Marion
Harland [pseud.]-Alcott, L. M. Transcendental wild oats.
-Wilcox, E. W. Dave's wife.-Cooke, R. T. The deacon's week.

10164 Lanier, Sidney, 1842-1881.
   Tiger-lilies. A novel. By Sidney Lanier... New York,
Hurd and Houghton, 1867.
   v, 252 p.   18 cm.

10165 Lanza, Clara (Hammond)
   Horce Everett: a novel... New York, G. W. Dillingham
co., 1897.
   275 p.   20 cm.

10166 Lasselle, Mrs. Nancy Polk.
   Annie Grayson; or, Life in Washington. By Mrs. N. P.
Lasselle. Washington, H. Lasselle, 1853.
   viii, [5]-345 p.   18 1/2 cm.

10167 Latimer, Mrs. Elizabeth (Wormeley) 1822-1904.
        Amabel; a family history. By Elizabeth Wormeley...
New York, G. P. Putnam, co. , 1853.
        xii p. , 1 1. , [15]-466 p.   19 cm.

10168 Latimer, Mrs. Elizabeth (Wormeley) 1822-1904.
        Our cousin Veronica; or, Scenes and adventures over the
Blue Ridge. By Mary Elizabeth Wormeley... New York,
Bunce & brother, 1855.
        3 p. 1. , [9]-437 p.   18 1/2 cm.

10169 [Lawrence, Mrs. Margaret Oliver (Woods)] 1813-1901.
        Esperance. By Meta Lander [pseud.]... New York,
Sheldon and company, 1865.
        336 p.   19 1/2 cm.

10170 [Lawrence, Mrs. Margaret Oliver (Woods), 1813-1901.
        Marion Graham; or, "Higher than happiness." By Meta
Lander [pseud.]... Boston, Crosby, Nichols, Lee and
company, 1861.
        506 p.   18 1/2 cm.

10171 Lawson, Mrs. J   W
        Brockley Moor. A novel. By J. W. L. New York,
D. Appleton and company, 1874.
        307 p.   20 cm.

10172 [Lawson, James] 1799-1880.
        Tales and sketches, by a Cosmopolite [pseud.] ... New-
York, E. Bliss, 1830.
        4 p. 1. , [5]-256 p.   20 cm.
        CONTENTS. -Introduction. -The Clyde. -The tent. -Flora
McDonald. -The dapper gentleman's story. -Dramatic sketch.
-On revisiting an exiles grave. -The bridal eve. -A legend of
Kent. -The spendthrift.

10173 ... Leandro; or, The sign of the cross. A Catholic tale.
Philadelphia, P. F. Cunningham, 1870.
        vi, 7-318 p.   18 1/2 cm. ("Messenger" series.
[v. 1])
        Reprinted from the Messenger of the sacred heart.
Attributed by the American catalogue to J. S.

10174 Leaves from the diary of a celebrated burglar and pickpocket. Being a compliation of the events and occurrences of the most exciting, interesting and extraordinary character in the life of a thief. Written by himself. Detailing incidents, hair-breath [!] excapes, and remarkable adventures. New York, G. W. Matsell & co., 1865.
    iv, [5]-174 p.   illus., pl.   24 cm.

10175 [Leavitt, John McDowell] 1824-
    The American cardinal. A novel. New York, Dodd & Mead, 1871.
    1 p. 1., vii-xi, 13-315 p.   18 1/2 cm.
    Published anonymously.

10176 Le Cato, Nathaniel James Walter, 1835-
    Mahalinda; or, The two cousins... N. J. W. Le Cato. Locust Mount, Va., Printed for the author by J. A. Gray, New York, 1858.
    271 p.   19 cm.
    Dedication and preface signed: Nat.

10177 Lee, Day Kellogg, 1816-1869.
    Merrimack; or, Life at the loom; a tale, by Day Kellogg Lee... New-York, Redfield, 1854.
    iv p., 1 1., [7]-353 p.   18 cm.

10178 Lee, Mrs. Eliza (Buckminster) 1794-1864.
    Florence, the parish orphan; and A sketch of the village in the last century. By Eliza Buckminster Lee... Boston, Ticknor and Fields, 1852.
    2 p. 1., 176 p.   18 cm.

10179 Lee, Mrs. Eliza (Buckminster) 1794-1864.
    Naomi; or, Boston, two hundred years ago. By Eliza Buckminster Lee... Boston, W. Crosby & H. P. Nichols, 1848.
    vii, 448 p.   17 1/2 cm.

10180 Lee, Mrs. Eliza (Buckminster) 1794-1864.
    Naomi; or, Boston two hundred years ago. By Eliza Buckminster Lee... 2d ed. Boston, W. Crosby and H. P. Nichols, 1848.

iv, 324 p.   20 cm.

10181 Lee, Mrs. Eliza (Buckminster) 1794-1864.
           Parthenia; or, The last days of Paganism. By Eliza
       Buckminster Lee... Boston, Ticknor and Fields, 1858.
           x, 420 p.   18 1/2 cm.

10182 Lee, Mrs. Eliza (Buckminster) 1794-1864.
           Sketches of a New-England village, in the last century.
       Boston, J. Munroe & company, 1838.
           2 p. l., [3]-110 p.   16 1/2 cm.

10183 [Lee, Mrs. Hannah Farnham (Sawyer)] 1780-1865.
           The backslider. By***... Boston and Cambridge, 1835.
           3 p. l., 144 p.   15 cm. (Added t.-p.: Scenes and
       characters illustrating Christian truth [ed. by H. Ware] no.
       v.)

10184 [Lee, Mrs. Hannah Farnham (Sawyer)] 1780-1865.
           The contrast: or, Modes of education. [A novel] By the
       author of 'Three experiments of living', 'Elinor Fulton',
       and 'Rich enough'... Boston. Whipple and Damrell;
       New York, Scofield & Voorhies, 1837.
           116 p.   15 cm.

10185 [Lee, Mrs. Hannah Farnham (Sawyer)] 1780-1865.
           Elinor Fulton. By the author of 'Three experiments of
       living'... 9th ed. Boston, Whipple & Damrell; New York,
       S. Colman, 1837.
           viii, [9]-144 p.   15 1/2 cm. (On cover: Stories
       from real life. no. 2)
           Sequel to "Three experiments of living."

10186 [Lee, Mrs. Hannah Farnham (Sawyer)] 1780-1865.
           Historical sketches of the old painters. By the author
       of "Three experiments of living"... Boston, Hilliard, Gray,
       and co., 1838.
           4 p. l., 296 p.   18 cm.

10187 [Lee, Mrs. Hannah Farnham (Sawyer)] 1780-1865.
           Rosanna: or, Scenes in Boston. A story. By the author
       of "Three experiments of living", "The contrast, or, Modes

of education", etc. ... Cambridge, J. Owen, 1839.
134 p.   17 cm.
"Written and sold for the benefit of the infant school in
Broad street, Boston."

10188 [Lee, Mrs. Hannah Farnham (Sawyer)] 1780-1865.
Tales, by the author of "Three experiments of living,"
"Luther," "Cranmer," "Old painters," & c. ... Boston,
Hilliard, Gray and company, 1842.
vi p., 1 l., 337 p.   18 cm.
CONTENTS.-The true and the false.-Emigration, or the
township in Maine.-Patronage and friendship.-A sketch of
fashionable life.

10189 [Lee, Mrs. Hannah Farnham (Sawyer)] 1780-1865.
Three experiments of living: Living within the means.
Living up to the means. Living beyond the means...
Boston, W. S. Damrell, and B. H. Greene, 1837.
x p., 1 l., [13]-143 p.   15 1/2 cm. (On cover:
Stories from real life. no. 1)
Sequel: Elinor Fulton.

10190 Leland, Anna.
Home. By Anna Leland... New York, J. C. Derby;
Boston, Phillips, Sampson & co. [etc., etc.] 1856.
xii, [13]-352 p.   18 1/2 cm.

10191 Leland, Henry Perry, 1828-1868.
Americans in Rome. By Henry P. Leland. New York,
C. T. Evans, 1863.
311 p.   19 cm.

10192 Leonhardt, Josephus, pseud.
The confessions of a minister. Being leaves from the
diary of the Rev. Josephus Leonhardt, D. D. ... Philadelphia, H. Peterson & co., 1874.
136 p.   18 cm.

10193 Leonhart, Rudolph.
Dolores: a tale of Maine and Italy. By Rudolph Leonhart...
Pittsburgh, Pa., E. Luft, job printer, 1870.
432 p.   19 1/2 cm.

10194 Leslie, Eliza, 1787-1858.
       Althea Vernon; or, The embroidered handkerchief. To
       which is added, Henrietta Harrison; or, The blue cotton
       umbrella. By Miss Leslie... Philadelphia, Lea & Blanchard,
       1838.
           1 p. 1. , [9]-276 p.   18 1/2 x 10 1/2 cm.

10195 Leslie, Eliza, 1787-1858.
       The Dennings and their beaux; and, Alina Derlay, &c. &c.
       By Miss Leslie... Philadelphia, A. Hart, 1851.
           111 p.   23 cm.
           CONTENTS.-The Dennings and their beaux.-Alina Derlay.
       -Eliza Farnham.-Nothing morally wrong.

10196 Leslie, Eliza, 1787-1858.
       The maid of Canal street; and The Bioxhams [also, Barclay
       Compton] By Miss Leslie... Philadelphia, A. Hart, 1851.
           2 p. 1. , [9]-115 p.   24 cm.

10197 Leslie, Eliza, 1787-1858.
       Pencil sketches; or Outlines of character and manners. By
       Miss Leslie... Philadelphia, Carey, Lea & Blanchard,
       1833-1837.
           3 v.   19 x 11 cm.
           CONTENTS.-1st ser. The escorted lady. A pic-nic at
       the sea-shore. The Miss Vanlears. Country lodgings.
       Sociable visiting. Frank Finlay. The travelling tin-man.
       Mrs. Washington Potts. Uncle Philip. The revolutionary
       officer. Poland and liberty. The duchess and Sancho. The
       clean face. Lady Jane Grey.-2d ser. The Wilson House.
       The album. The reading parties. The set of china. Laura
       Lovel. John W. Robertson. The ladies' ball.-3rd ser. The
       red box. Constance Allerton. The officers. The serenades.
       The old farm house. That gentleman. Chase Loring. Alphonsine.

10198 [Levison, William H   ] 1822-1857.
       Black diamonds; or, Humor, satire, and sentiment, treated
       scientifically by Professor Julius Ceasar Hannibal [pseud.]
       In a series of burlesque lectures, darkly colored. Originally
       published in "The New York picayune." New York, A. Ranney;
       Chicago, R. Blanchard [etc. , etc.] 1855.
           3 p. 1. , [v]-viii, [13]-364 p. front. , plates.   18 cm.

10199 Lewis, Harriet Newell (O'Brien)
Lady Kildare: a novel... New York, Robert Bonner's sons
[c1889]
402 p. front.   20 cm.

10200 [Lewis, Martha Lewis (Beckwith) Ewell] 1841-1902.
Blue ribbons, by the author of "Harvest of years," "Lovette"
... &c. New Haven, Conn., The Protective publishing company, 1882.
387 p.   19 cm.

10201 Libbey, Laura Jean.
The flirtations of a beauty; or, A summer's romance at
Newport... New York, Norman L. Munro, 1890.
234 p. illus.   20 cm.

10202 Libbey, Laura Jean.
A forbidden marriage; or, Love with a handsome spendthrift. A novel... New York, The American News company,
1888.
212 p. front.   20 cm.

10203 Libbey, Laura Jean.
Little Rosebud's lovers; or, A cruel revenge. New York,
George Munro's sons, 1888.
253 p.   18 cm.

10204 Life and adventures of Charles Anderson Chester, the notorious
leader of the Philadelphia "killers", who was murdered,
while engaged in the destruction of the California house,
on election night, October 11, 1849... Philadelphia, Printed
for the publishers, 1850.
2 p. 1., 11-36 p. front., illus.   21 1/2 cm.

10205 Life in town; or, The Boston spy. Being a series of sketches
illustrative of whims and women in the 'Athens of America.'
By an Athenian... Boston, Redding and company; New York,
Burgess & Stringer [etc., etc.] 1844.
24 p. front.   27 cm.
On cover: In twelve monthly numbers, each complete in
itself... No. 1. Sewing circles.

10206　The life of General M. D. Stanley, an American militia
　　　　general: the celebrated roué, swindler, pickpocket, and
　　　　murderer. Who was executed at Vienna, Austria, Septem-
　　　　ber 17, 1853. Comprising details of bold deeds, daring
　　　　adventures and thrilling scenes in the career of a villain.
　　　　Baltimore [etc.] A. R. Orton, 1855.
　　　　　　1 p. 1., 23-50 p.　front. (port.) illus.　　　8 o.

10207　Lights and shadows of domestic life, and other stories.　By
　　　　the author of Rose and her lamb - The two new scholars,
　　　　etc., etc.　Boston, Ticknor, Reed and Fields, 1850.
　　　　　　2 p. 1., 267 p.　　　18 cm.
　　　　　　CONTENTS. -Lights and shadows of domestic life. -The
　　　　secret of happiness. -Laura Seymour. -The intimate friends.
　　　　-Shadows and realities. -Sketches of character; or, Who is
　　　　free?

10208　Linden, Clarence.
　　　　　　Our general. By Col. C. Linden... Philadelphia. Barclay
　　　　& co., [187-?]
　　　　　　1 p. 1., 19-20, iv, 21-201 p.　front., plates.　24 1/2 cm.
　　　　　　On cover: A work of absorbing interest, whose characters
　　　　are real personages.

10209　Lindo, F
　　　　　　Revenge; or, The robber of Guatemala.　By F. Lindo
　　　　... Cincinnati, Robinson & Jones, 1848.
　　　　　　104 p.　　　24 cm.

10210　[Linn, John Blair] 1777-1804.
　　　　　　Miscellaneous works, prose and poetical.　By a young
　　　　gentleman of New-York... New-York-Printed by Thomas
　　　　Greenleaf.　1795.
　　　　　　6 p. 1., [7]-353, [1] p.　　　17 cm.

10211　Lippard, George, 1822-1854.
　　　　　　'Bel of Prairie Eden.　A romance of Mexico.　By George
　　　　Lippard... Boston, Hotchkiss & co., 1848.
　　　　　　1 p. 1., [7]-88 p.　　　26 cm.

10212　Lippard, George, 1822-1854.
　　　　　　Blanche of Brandywine; or, September the eleventh, 1777.

A romance, combining the poetry, legend, and history of the battle of Brandywine. By George Lippard... Philadelphia, G. B. Zieber & co. , 1846.
viii,9-351 p.   23 1/2 cm.

10213 Lippard, George, 1822-1854.
Legends of Mexico, by George Lippard... [1st ser. The battles of Taylor] Philadelphia, T. B. Peterson, 1847.
1 p. l. , 11-136 p.   23 1/2 cm.

10214 Lippard, George, 1822-1854.
The Nazarene; or, The last of the Washingtons, a revelation of Philadelphia, New York, and Washington, in the year 1844. By George Lippard... [Book 1st] Philadelphia, G. Lippard and co. , 1846.
vii, 9-240 p.   22 1/2 cm.
Running title: Paul Mount-Laurel.

10215 Lippard, George, 1822-1854.
Original revolutionary chronicle. The battle-day of Germantown. By George Lippard... Philadelphia, A. H. Diller, 1843.
2 p. l. , 34 p.   front.   23 cm.

10216 Lippard, George, 1822-1854.
Paul Ardenheim, the monk of Wissahikon. By George Lippard... Philadelphia, T. B. Peterson [1848]
536 p. front. , illus.   23 1/2 cm.

10217 Lippard, George, 1822-1854.
The Quaker City; or, The monks of Monk-Hall. A romance of Philadelphia life, mystery, and crime. By George Lippard ... [16th ed.] Philadelphia, Pub. by the author, 1846.
2 v. fronts.   22 1/2 cm.
Paged continuously.

10218 Lippard, George, 1822-1854.
The Rose of Wissahikon; or, The fourth of July, 1776. A romance, embracing the secret history of the Declaration of independence. By George Lippard... Philadelphia, G. B. Zieber & co. , 1847.
70 p.   16 1/2 cm.

10219 Lippard, George, 1822-1854.
          Washington and his generals; or, Legends of the revolution.
       By George Lippard... With a biographical sketch of the
       author, by Rev. C. Chauncey Burr. Philadelphia, G. B.
       Zieber and co., 1847.
          iv, xxvii, 25-538 p.   23 1/2 cm.
          A second series issued, New York, 1850, under title:
       Washington and his men. A later edition of the first series
       published (Philadelphia, 1876) with title: Legends of the
       American revolution.

10220 Lippard, George, 1822-1854.
          Washington and his men: a new series of legends of the
       revolution. By George Lippard... New York, Stringer &
       Townsend, 1850.
          ix, [11]-184 p. inc. plates, ports.   26 cm.
          The first series appeared, Philadelphia, 1847, under title:
       Washington and his generals.

10221 [Lippincott, Mrs. Sara Jane (Clarke)] 1823-1904.
          A forest tragedy, and other tales. By Grace Greenwood
       [pseud.]... Boston, Ticknor and Fields, 1856.
          4 p. 1., 343 p.   18 cm.
          CONTENTS. -A forest tragedy. -The minister's choice. -St.
       Pierre, the soldier. -Alice's tryst. -The child-seer.

10222 [Lippincott, Mrs. Sara Jane (Clarke)] 1823-1904.
          Greenwood leaves: a collection of sketches and letters.
       By Grace Greenwood [pseud.] Second series. Boston,
       Ticknor, Reed, and Fields, 1852.
          vii, 382 p. front. (port.)   20 cm.

10223 Little, George, b. 1791?
          The American cruiser; a tale of the last war. By Capt.
       Geo. Little... Illustrations by Billings. Boston, W. J.
       Reynolds and company, and Waite, Peirce, and co., 1847.
          390 p. incl. front., plates.   19 1/2 cm.

10224 Lloyd, John Uri, 1849-1936.
          Etidorhpa; or, The end of earth. The strange history of a
       mysterious being and the account of a remarkable journey as
       communicated in manuscript to Llewellyn Drury who promised

to print the same, but finally evaded the responsibility which
was assumed by John Uri Lloyd. With many illustrations
by J. Augustus Knapp. Eighth edition. Cincinnati, The
Robert Clarke company, 1897.
    386 p. illus.   24 1/2 cm.
    At end of this copy is a group of eleven numbered pages
containing clippings (from Cincinnati Times-Star ?) relating
to Lloyd, mainly dealing with Stringtown on the pike, and
also containing pictures of Lloyd.

10225 Lloyd, John Uri, 1849-1936.
    The right side of the car, by the author of Etidorhpa (John
Uri Lloyd) Boston, Richard G. Badger & company, M DCCC
XCVII.
    3 1., 21-59 p. illus.   18 1/2 cm.
    "A story of the Northern Pacific Railway," p. 25.

10226 Locke, David Ross, 1833-1888.
    Nasby in exile; or, Six months of travel in England, Ireland,
Scotland, France, Germany, Switzerland and Belgium, with
many things not of travel. By David R. Locke (Petroleum V.
Nasby)... Toledo and Boston, Locke publishing company,
1882.
    xv, [16]-672 p. incl. front. illus.   23 cm.

10227 [Locke, David Ross] 1833-1888.
    The Nasby papers. Letters and sermons containing the
views on the topics of the day, of Petroleum V. Nasby [pseud.]
... Indianapolis, C. O. Perrine & co., 1864.
    64 p.   19 1/2 cm.

10228 Locke, David Ross, 1833-1888.
    ... Nashby on inflation. A new comic book by Petroleum
V. Nasby. (D. R. Locke)... Philadelphia, Barclay & co.
[1876]
    1 p. 1., 19-78 p., 1 1., incl. illus., plates.   23 1/2 cm.

10229 Locke, David Ross, 1833-1888.
    A paper city, by D. R. Locke, (Petroleum V. Nasby)...
Boston, Lee and Shepard; New York, C. T. Dillingham,
1879.
    431 p.   20 cm.

10230 [Locke, David Ross] 1833-1888.
"Swingin round the cirkle." By Petroleum V. Nasby [pseud.] ... His ideas of man, politics, and things, as set forth in his letters to the public press, during the year 1866. Illustrated by Thomas Nast. Boston, Lee and Shepard, 1867.
299 p. front., plates.   19 cm.

10231 [Locke, Richard Adams] 1800-1871.
A complete account of the late discoveries in the moon. From a supplement to the Edinburgh journal... [New York? 1835?]
11 p.   24 cm.
Published anonymously.
Caption title.
A hoax.

10232 [Lockwood, Ralph Ingersoll] 1798-1855.
The insurgents: an historical novel... Philadelphia, Carey, Lea & Blanchard, 1835.
2 v.   19 cm.
Published anonymously.

10233 [Lockwood, Ralph Ingersoll] 1798-1855.
Rosine Laval: a novel. By Mr. Smith [pseud.]... Phila- delphia, Carey, Lea & Blanchard, 1833.
v, 300 p.   19 1/2 cm.

10234 Lofland, John, 1798-1849.
The poetical and prose writings of Dr. John Lofland, the Milford bard, consisting of sketches in poetry and prose... With a portrait of the author and a sketch of his life. Collected and arranged by J. N. M'Jilton, A. M. Baltimore, J. Murphy & co.; Wilmington [Del.] J. T. Heald, 1853.
x, 30, [25]-587 p. front. (port.)   23 cm.

10235 Logan, Mrs. Olive (Logan) Sikes, 1839-1909.
... The good Mr. Bagglethorpe. By Olive Logan... New- York, The American news company, 1869.
27 p.   23 cm.
At head of title: Olive Logan's new story.

10236 Logan, Mrs. Olive (Logan) Sikes, 1839-1909.

Olive Logan's Christmas story, Somebody's stocking...
New York, The American news company [c1867]
16 p.   23 1/2 cm.

10237 Logan, Mrs. Olive (Logan) Sikes, 1839-1909.
They met by chance: a society novel. By Olive Logan,
(Mrs. Wirt Sikes,)... New York, Adams, Victor & co.
[c1873]
1 p. l., [7]-320 p.   19 cm.

10238 Long, John Luther, 1861-1921.
Madame Butterfly. Purple eyes. A gentleman of Japan
and a lady. Kito. Glory ... New York, The Century co.,
1898.
224 p. front.   20 cm.

10239 Long, John Luther, 1861-1927.
Miss Cherry-Blossom of Tokyo, by John Luther Long.
Philadelphia, J. B. Lippincott company, 1895.
vii, 5-364 p.   19 cm.

10240 Longfellow, Henry Wadsworth, 1807-1882.
Hyperion, a romance. By Henry Wadsworth Longfellow
... 2d ed. Cambridge [Mass.] J. Owen, 1845.
2 p. l., 370 p.   18 1/2 cm.

10241 Longfellow, Henry Wadsworth, 1807-1882.
Outre-mer, a pilgrimage beyond the sea. By Henry
Wadsworth Longfellow... 2d ed. Boston, W. D. Ticknor &
co., 1846.
1 p. l., [v]-vi, [7]-374 p.   19 cm.

10242 [Longstreet, Augustus Baldwin] 1790-1870.
Georgia scenes, characters, incidents, &c., in the first
half entury of the republic. By a native Georgian. Augusta,
Ga., Printed at the S. R. sentinel office, 1835.
iv, [5]-235 p.   19 cm.
A series of newspaper sketches of humble life in the South.

10243 Loth, Moritz.
"The forgiving kiss;" or, Our destiny. A novel. By Moritz
Loth... New York, G. W. Carleton & co. [etc., etc.] 1874.

vi p. , 1 1. , [9]-364 p.   18 1/2 cm.

10244 Loth, Moritz.
       Our prospects; a tale of real life. By Moritz Loth...
       Cincinnati, R. Clarke & co. , printers, 1870.
       vi, 5-377 p.   22 1/2 cm.

10245 The lottery ticket: an American tale. To which is added, The
       destructive consequences of dissipation and luxury.
       Hartford, D. F. Robinson & co. , 1827.
       105 p.   14 1/2 cm.

10246 Loud, Jeremy.
       Gabriel Vane: his fortune and his friends. By Jeremy Loud
       ... New York, Derby & Jackson; Cincinnati, H. W. Derby &
       co. , 1856.
       x, [11]-423 p.   18 1/2 cm.

10247 Lowell, Robert Traill Spence, 1816-1891.
       Antony Brade. By Robert Lowell... Boston, Roberts
       brothers, 1874.
       viii, 415, [1] p.   18 cm.

10248 Lucretia and her father. A narrative founded on fact. By a
       clergyman of New England. Approved by the board of
       managers. 2d ed. Hartford, D. F. Robinson & co. , 1828.
       96 p. front.   14 cm.

10249 [Ludlow, Fitz Hugh] 1836-1870.
       The hasheesh eater: being passages from the life of a
       Pythagorean... New York, Harper & brothers, 1857.
       xiv, [15]-371 p.   19 1/2 cm.

10250 Ludlow, Fitz Hugh, 1836-1870.
       Little brother; and other genre-pictures. By Fitz Hugh
       Ludlow... Boston, Lee and Shepard, 1867.
       293 p.   19 1/2 cm.
       Published also under title: "Augustus Jones, jr."
       CONTENTS. -Little brother. -Fleeing to Tarshish. -Little
       Briggs and I. -A brace of boys.

10251 Luff, Lorry, pseud.

Antonita, the female contrabandista. A Mexican tale of
land and water. By Lorry Luff. New York, Williams brothers,
1848.
95 p.   25 cm.

10252 Luff, Lorry, pseud.
The Texan captain and the female smuggler. A Mexican
tale of land and water. By Lorry Luff. New-York, W. F.
Burgess, 1850.
96 p.   23 cm.

10253 [Lukens, Henry Clay] 1838-
Jets and flashes, by Erratic Enrique [pseud.]... Illustrated by René Bache... New York, J. W. Lovell company
[c1883]
200 p. illus.   18 1/2 cm.   (On cover: Lovell's
library, no. 131)
Preface signed: H. C. L.
"Skimmed from various originalities recently contributed
to the periodical humorous press of America."-p. [3]

10254 Lummus, Aaron.
The life and adventures of Dr. Caleb; who migrated from
Eghpt, and afterwards practised physic in the land of Canaan
and elsewhere: an allegory; designed principally to amuse and
edify young people. By Aaron Lummus, evangelii praedicator
... Boston; Printed for the author by Lincoln & Edmands, 1822.
iv, [5]-230 p., 1 l.,   13 1/2 x 7 1/2 cm.

10255 [Lunt, George] 1803-1885.
Eastford; or, Household sketches. By Wesley Brooke
[pseud.]... Boston, Crocker & Brewster, 1855.
viii, [9]-328 p.   20 cm.

M

10256 M   ,S   H
Miranda Elliot; or, The voice of the spirit. By S. H.

M. Philadelphia, Lippincott, Grambo & co., 1855.
2 p. 1., 9-308 p.   18 1/2 cm.

10257 Mabie, Hamilton Wright, 1845-1916.
My study fire... New York, Dodd, Mead & co., 1899.
288 p.   20 cm.

10258 [McAlpine, Emily Eliza Jours]
Doings in Maryland; or, Matilda Douglas... Philadelphia,
J. B. Lippincott & co., 1871.
xi, 13-316 p.   19 cm.

10259 [McAndrew, William A   ]
Silhouette, a tale of Minnetonka. Being an account of
a peculiar case by Howard Bronson, M. D.; ed. with notes
by W. J. D. Ann Arbor, Mich., The Register publishing
company, 1891.
24, [2] p. illus.   24 cm.

10260 McCabe, John Collins, 1810-1875.
Scraps, by John Collins M'Cabe... Richmond, Printed
by J. C. Walker, 1835.
vi, [7]-192 p.   18 1/2 cm.
Prose and verse.

10261 McClellan, Harriet (Hare).
St. John's wooing: a story... New York, Harper & brothers,
1895.
175 p. illus.   20 cm.

10262 McClelland, Mary Greenway, 1838-1895.
... Princess, by M. G. McClelland... New York, J. W.
Lovell [1886]
2 p. 1., 207 p.   17 cm. (American authors' series
no. 17)

10263 McConnel, John Ludlum, 1826-1862.
The Glenns; a family history. By J. L. M'Connel... New
York, C. Scribner, 1851.
ix, [11]-280 p.   18 1/2 cm.

10264 [McConnel, John Ludlum] 1826-1862.

Grahame; or, Youth and manhood. A romance. By the author of "Talbot and Vernon"... New York, Baker and Scribner, 1850.
>385 p. 18 1/2 cm.

10265 McConnel, John Ludlum, 1826–1862.
>Western characters; or, Types of border life in the western states, by J. L. McConnel... With illustrations by Darley. New York, Redfield, 1853.
>>378 p. front., plates. 18 cm.
>>Added t.-p., engr.

10266 McCook, Henry Christopher.
>The Latimers, A tale of the western insurrection of 1794. Philadelphia, George W. Jacobs & co., 1897.
>>593 p. front. 20 cm.

10267 [McCormick, M   R   ]
>The duke's chase; or, The diamond ring vs. the gold ring. By Forest Warbler [pseud.] Cincinnati, R. Clarke & co., printers, 1871.
>>2 p. l., 9–271 p. 20 cm.
>>Running title: The duke's wonderful escape.
>>"End of vol. 1" on last page; no more published?

10268 [McDonnell, William]
>Exeter Hall. A theological romance. New York, The American news company, 1869.
>>186 p. 24 cm.

10269 McDougall, Mrs. Frances Harriet (Whipple) Greene, 1805–1878.
>The mechanic [a story] By Frances Harriet Whipple... Providence, Burnett & King; Boston, Little & Brown [etc., etc.] 1842.
>>2 p. l., [ix]-x p., 1 l., [13]-219 p. 18 1/2 cm.

10270 [McDougall, Mrs. Frances Harriet (Whipple) Greene] 1805–1878.
>Shahmah in pursuit of freedom; or, The branded hand. Tr. from the original Showiah, and ed. by an American citizen. New York, Thatcher & Hutchinson, 1858.
>>xxviii, 20–599 p. front. (port.) 19 1/2 cm.

10271 McElgun, John.
        Annie Reilly; or, The fortunes of an Irish girl in New York.
A tale founded on fact. By John McElgun. New York, J. A.
McGee, 1873.
        viii p., 2 l., [9]-245 p.   front.   18 cm.

10272 [McElhinney, Mrs. Jane]
        Only a woman's heart [a novel] By Ada Clare [pseud.]
New York, M. Doolady, 1866.
        1 p. 1., [5]-336 p.   19 cm.

10273 M'Gaw, James Franklin, 1823-1872.
        Philip Seymour, or, Pioneer life in Richland county, Ohio.
Founded on facts. By Rev. James F. M'Gaw... Mansfield
[O.] R. Brickerhoff, 1858 [i.e. 1908]
        279 p.   illus.   20 1/2 cm.
On cover: Last edition 1908.

10274 MacGowan, Alice, 1858-
        Return; a story of the Sea Islands in 1739, by Alice
MacGowan and Grace MacGowan Cooke... illustrated by
C. D. Williams. Boston, L. C. Page & company, inc.,
1905.
        3 p. 1., v-vi p., 2 l., 11-544 p.   front. 5 pl.
19 1/2 cm.

10275 MacGregor, Annie Lyndsay.
        The professor's wife; or, It might have been. By Annie L.
MacGregor... Philadelphia, J. B. Lippincott & co., 1870.
        305 p.   19 cm.

10276 [McHenry, James] 1785-1845.
        The Hearts of steel. An Irish historical tale of the last
century. By the author of "The wilderness", "O'Halloran"
... Philadelphia, A. R. Poole, 1825.
        2 v.   18 cm.

10277 [McHenry, James] 1785-1845.
        Meredith; or, The mystery of the Meschianza. A tale of
the American revolution. By the author of "The betrothed of
Wyoming"... Philadelphia, Sold by the principal booksellers,
and in New York, Boston, Baltimore, and Washington, 1831.

260 p.   18 1/2 cm.
Copyright by Henry H. Porter.

10278 McIntosh, Maria Jane, 1803-1878.
      Evenings at Donaldson manor; or, The Christmas guest.
By Maria J. McIntosh... New York, D. Appleton & company;
Philadelphia, G. S. Appleton, 1851.
      286 p. front., 9 pl.   22 cm.

10279 McIntosh, Maria Jane, 1803-1878.
      The lofty and the lowly; or, Good in all and none all-good.
By M. J. McIntosh... New York, D. Appleton & company,
1853.
      2 v.   19 cm.

10280 McIntosh, Maria Jane, 1803-1878.
      Two lives; or, To seem and to be. By Maria J. McIntosh
... New-York, D. Appleton & co.; Philadelphia, G. S.
Appleton, 1846.
      2 p. l., 318 p.   18 cm.

10281 [McIntosh, Maria Jane] 1803-1878.
      Woman an enigma; or, Life and its revealings. By the
author of "Conquest and self-conquest." &c. ... New-York,
Harper & brothers, 1843.
      1 p. l., [5]-238 p.   16 cm.

10282 Mack, Thomas C
      The priest's turf-cutting day. A historical romance. By
T. C. M. New York, Printed for the author, 1841.
      82 p.   17 1/2 cm.

10283 McKay, Frederic Edward, ed.
      Vignettes: real and ideal; stories by American authors.
ed. by Frederic Edward McKay. Boston, De Wolfe, Fiske
& co. [c1890]
      288 p.   19 1/2 cm.
      CONTENTS.-A light man. W. C. Fitch.-The untold word.
F. C. de Sumichrast.-An artistic necessity. Mabel L. Fuller.
-Madame Clerc. E. I. Stevenson.-A choice. Emma V.
Sheridan.-A difference in clay. J. C. Bull.-A night with
William of Wykeham. O. F. Adams.-Safe in purgatory.

Jane G. Austin._A quarter past six. Matthew White, jr.-An
inherited debt. W. M. Graydon.-The vigil of Fenton Barlowe.
J. J. à Becket.-The face of Abel. W. D. Moffat.-The return.
Algernon Tassin.-At Suk Wady Barada. Clinton Scollard.-An
interrupted finesse. F. E. McKay.

10284 McKeen, Phebe Fuller.
      Theodora: a home story. By Phebe F. McKeen... New
York, A. D. F. Randolph & company, [c1875]
      1 p. 1., v-vi, 480 p.   19 1/2 cm.

10285 McKeever, Harriet Burn, 1807-1886.
      Maude and Miriam; or, The fair crusader. By Harriet B.
McKeever... Philadelphia, Claxton, Remsen & Haffelfinger,
1871.
      2 p. 1., vii-xii, 13-337 p.   19 cm.

10286 McKeever, Harriet Burn, 1807-1886.
      Twice crowned. A story of the days of Queen Mary. By
Harriet B. McKeever... Philadelphia, Claxton, Remsen &
Haffelfinger, 1873.
      xi, 13-360 p.   19 1/2 cm.

10287 McKeever, Harriet Burn, 1807-1886.
      Westbrook parsonage. By Harriet B. M'Keever...
Philadelphia, Claxton, Remsen & Haffelfinger, 1870.
      3 p. 1., v-viii, 9-359 p. front.   19 cm.
      Added t.-p., illustrated.

10288 McKeever, Harriet Burn, 1807-1886.
      Woodcliff. By Harriet McKeever... Philadelphia,
Lindsay & Blakiston, 1865.
      1 p. 1., v-vi, 13-464 p.   19 cm.

10289 Mackenzie, Mrs. Adelheid.
      Aureola; or, The black sheep. A story of German social
life. By Mrs. Adelheid Shelton-Mackenzie... Philadelphia,
Claxton, Remsen & Haffelfinger, 1871.
      2 p. 1., ix-xi, 13-263 p.   19 1/2 cm.

10290 Mackenzie, Mrs. Adelheid.
      Married against reason. By Adelheid Shelton-Mackenzie.

Boston, Loring [c1869]
97 p.   22 1/2 cm.

10291 Mackenzie, Robert Shelton, 1809-1880.
     Bits of blarney, by R. Shelton Mackenzie... New York,
     Redfield [1855]
     vi p. 1 1. , [9]-426 p.   18 cm.
     CONTENTS. -Legends. -Irish stories. -Eccentric characters.
     -Irish publicists.

10292 Mackenzie, Robert Shelton, 1809-1880.
     Tressilian and his friends. By Dr. R. Shelton Mackenzie
     ... Philadelphia, J. B. Lippincott & co. , 1859.
     372 p.   18 cm.

10293 McKnight, Charles, 1826-1881.
     Old Fort Duquesne; or, Captain Jack, the scout. An
     historical novel with copious notes. By Charles McKnight...
     Pittsburgh, Peoples monthly publishing co. , 1873.
     501 p.   front. , 6 pl.   18 1/2 cm.

10294 [McLain, Mary Webster]
     Lifting the veil... New York, C. Scribner & co. , 1870.
     200 p.   17 1/2 cm.

10295 Maclellan, Rufus Charles.
     The story reader's garland; a cluster of tales. By Rufus
     Charles Maclellan. Baltimore, Printed by J. D. Toy, 1849.
     82, [1] p.   19 cm.

10296 MacLeod, Xavier Donald, 1821-1865.
     Pynnshurst; his wanderings and ways of thinking. By Donald
     MacLeod... New York, C. Scribner, 1852.
     2 p. 1. , iii p. , 1 1. , [7]-431 p.   19 1/2 cm.

10297 McSherry, James, 1819-1869.
     Père Jean; or, the Jesuit missionary: a tale of the North
     American Indians. By James McSherry, esq. Baltimore,
     J. Murphy; Dublin, R. Grace & sons [etc. , etc.] 1847.
     1 p. 1. , 256 p. front. , pl.   11 1/2 cm.   (Half-title:
     Murphy's cabinet library, no. ix)
     Published in 1860 under title: Father Laval.

281

10298 ... Maga stories. New York, G. P. Putnam & son, 1867.
325 p.   17 cm. (Putnam's railway classics)
Reprinted from Putnam's monthly.
CONTENTS. – Found and lost. – My three conversations with
Miss Chester. – Mrs. Macsimum's bill. – The feast of the
cranberries. – Tolliwotte's ghost. – Professor Phantillo. – The
Mormon's wife. – The rich merchant of Cairo. – The legend of
Goodman Poverty. – The double veil. – My husband's mother.
– The old woman who dried up and blew away. The ambassador
in spite of himself. – Elegant Tom Dillar. – A toss–up for a
husband. – Uncle Bernard's story. – How I came to be married.

10299 Magill, Mary Tucker, 1830–1899.
The Holcombes. A story of Virginia home–life. By Mary
Tucker Magill... Philadelphia, J. B. Lippincott & co.,
1871.
viii, 9–290 p.   19 1/2 cm.

10300 Magill, Mary Tucker, 1830–1899.
Women; or, Chronicles of the late war. By Mary Tucker
Magill... Baltimore, Turnbull brothers, 1871.
xvii, 393 p.   18 1/2 cm.

10301 Magruder, Julia.
A heaven–kissing hill... Chicago and New York, Herbert S.
Stone and company, 1899.
159 p. front.   20 cm.

10302 Magruder, Julia.
A magnificent plebeian... New York, Harper & brothers,
1888.
228 p.   20 cm.

10303 Magruder, Julia.
A manifest destiny... New York and London, Harper &
brothers, 1900.
225 p. illus.   20 cm.

10304 Magruder, Julia.
Miss Ayr of Virginia, & other stories... Chicago, Herbert
S. Stone & co., 1896.
395 p.   20 cm.

Also contains: A new thing under the sun. -The thirst and the draught -A bartered birthright. -His heart's desire. -The masked singer. -The story of an old soul. -Once more.

10305 Magruder, Julia.
The Princess Sonia... New York, The Century co. , 1895.
225 p.   illus.   20 cm.

10306 Magruder, Julia.
A realized ideal... Chicago & New York, Herbert S. Stone & company, 1898.
135 p.   20 cm.

10307 Magruder, Julia.
Struan... Boston, Richard G. Badger & co. , 1899.
330 p.   20 cm.

10308 Magruder, Julia.
The violet... New York, London, and Bombay, Longmans, Green and co. , 1896.
210 p.   illus.   20 cm.

10309 [Major, Charles] 1856-1913.
When knighthood was in flower; or, The love story of Charles Brandon and Mary Tudor, the king's sister, and happening in the reign of his august majesty, King Henry VIII... by Edwin Caskoden [pseud.] Indianapolis and Kansas City, The Bowen-Merrill company, 1898.
249 p.   illus.   20 cm.

10310 [Mallory, Daniel]
Short stories and reminiscences of the last fity years. By an old traveller... New York, D. Mallory; Philadelphia, Carey & Hart [etc. , etc.] 1842.
2 v.   15 1/2 cm.
Vol. 1: 3d ed.
CONTENTS. -I. The pest house. The maniac. Recollections of New York. Caroline Nichols. Visit to the vineyard. Eccentric characters. John Randolph. A new way to pay debts of honour, &c. A visit to the wounded English officers. Burning of Havre de Grace. A night in Fort McHenry. General Washington's marquee. A visit to Mount Vernon. A young

American in England. Scenes of a soldier. Mr. B_____.
The mistake. Mr. Curran, &c.- II. A visit to Cincinnati.
The jewels. Yellow fever, and deer hunt. The English lady.
A visit to St. Louis. La Fay, the pickpocket. A visit to
Louisville. General Harrison. Mr. H_____. Incidents of
a voyage. Wilcox, the counterfeiter. A visit to New-Orleans
and the battle ground. Curious incidents. An attempt to
murder. The pirate. The dangerous ford. Catfish catching
squirrels. The tame seal, &c. The stork. Mr. Smith. Jaco.
Waterloo. Turn the sausages.

10311 Mancur, John H
... Christine. A tale of the revolution. By John H. Mancur
... New York, W. H. Colyer, 1843.
cover-title. [13]-60 p.   23 1/2 cm. [Tales of the
revolution, no. 1]

10312 Mancur, John H
The Palais Royal. An historical romance. By John H.
Mancur... New-York, W. H. Colyer, 1845.
252 p.   18 cm.

10313 Mandell, D   J
The adventures of Search for Life, a Bunyanic narrative,
as detailed by himself. By D. J. Mandell... Portland [Me.]
S. H. Colesworthy, 1838.
iv, [5]-88 p.   16 cm.

10314 [Maingault, Gabriel] 1809-1888.
Saint Cecilia. A modern tale from real life. Part first.
Adversity... Philadelphia, J. B. Lippincott & co., 1871.
372 p.   18 cm.
Published anonymously.

10315 [Mansfield, Lewis William]
Up-country letters: ed. by Prof. B_____, National
observatory... New York, D. Appleton and company, 1852.
1 p. 1., 331 p. front.   19 cm.
Added t.-p., illustrated.
Letters signed Z. P. [i. e. Zachary P'undison, psued.]

10316 Manvill, Mrs. P   D

Lucinda; or, The mountain mourner: being recent facts, in
a series of letters from Mrs. Manvill of the state of New York,
to her sister in Pennsylvania. 5th ed. Ithaca, Mack, Andrus,
& Woodruff, 1836.
xiii, [1], [15]-172 p. 12 1/2 cm.
Letters XIV, XXX and XXXI from Mrs. Manvill are signed
P. D. Manvill. Letter XIII from Mr. Manvill is signed A. M.
Said to be founded on facts. cf. The recommendations
(p. [iii]-xiii)

10317 [Markoe, Peter] 1752?-1792.
The Algerine spy in Pennsylvania: or, Letters written by
a native of Algiers on the affairs of the United States in
America, from the close of the year 1783 to the meeting of
the convention... Philadelphia: Printed and sold by Prichard
& Hall, in Market between Front and Second streets. 1787.
x, [11]-129 p. 15 1/2 cm.
Translator's letter to the publisher, in which the letters
are ascribed to "Mehemet," is signed S. T. P.
The letters in the first 66 pages purport to be written
from Gibraltar and Lisbon; such of the others as were written
by Mehemct, from Philadelphia.

10318 Marsh, Jenny.
Toiling and hoping: the story of a little hunchback. By
Jenny Marsh... New York, Derby and Jackson, 1856.
398 p. 19 cm.

10319 Martell, Martha.
Second love. By Martha Martell. New-York, G. P.
Putnam, 1851.
viii, [13]-356 p. 18 cm.

10320 Mason, Charles Welsh.
Rape of the gamp. A novel. By C. Welsh Mason...
New York, Harper & brothers, 1875.
1 p. l., [9]-152 p. front., illus. 23 1/2 cm.

10321 Massett, Stephen C 1820-1898.
"Drifting about"; or, What "Jeems Pipes, of Pipesville,"
saw-and-did. An autobiography by Stephen C. Massett. With
many comic illustrations by Mullen. New-York, Carleton, 1863.

viii, [11]-371 p. front. , illus.   18 1/2 cm.

10322 [Mathews, Cornelius] 1817-1889.
        Behemoth: a legend of the mound-builders. New York,
      J. & H. G. Langley; Boston, Weeks, Jordan & co. , 1839.
      vi p. , 1 1. , 192 p.   17 1/2 cm.

10323 Mathews, Cornelius, 1817-1889.
        Big Abel, and the little Manhattan: by Cornelius Mathews.
      New York, Wiley and Putnam, 1845.
        4 p. 1. , 93 p.   19 cm.   (On cover: Wiley and
      Putnam's library of American books, no. 5)

10324 [Mathews, Cornelius] 1817-1889.
        Chanticleer: a Thanksgiving story of the Peabody family.
      2d ed. Boston, B. B. Mussey & co.; New York, J. S.
      Redfield, 1850.
        155 p.   19 1/2 cm.

10325 [Mathews, Cornelius] 1817-1889.
        The motley book: a series of tales and sketches. By the
      late Ben Smith [pseud.] With illustrations by Dick and
      others. New ed. New York, J. & H. G. Langley; Boston,
      Weeks, Jordan & co. [etc. , etc.] 1838.
        2 p. 1. , [3]-190 p. front. , plates.   23 cm.

10326 Mathews, Cornelius, 1817-1889.
        The various writings of Cornelius Mathews... New York,
      Harper & brothers, 1863 [i. e. 1843]
        viii, [11]-370 p.   23 cm.
        CONTENTS. -The motley book. -Behemoth. -The politicians.
      -Poems on man in the republic. -Wakondah. -Puffer Hopkins. -
      Miscellanies. -Selections from Arcturus. -International
      copyright.

10327 Matthews, James Brander, 1852-1929.
        A confident to-morrow: a novel of New York... New York
      and London, Harper & brothers, 1900.
        300 p.   illus.   20 cm.

10328 Matthews, James Brander, 1852-1929.
        His father's son: a novel of New York... New York, Harper

& brothers, 1896.
248 p. illus. 20 cm.

10329 Matthews, James Brander, 1852-1929.
The last meeting: a story... New York, Charles Scribner's sons, 1885.
268 p. illus. 20 cm.

10330 [Mattson, Morris] 1809?-1885.
Paul Ulric; or, The adventures of an enthusiast... New York, Harper & brothers, 1835.
2 v. 19 1/2 cm.

10331 Maturin, Edward, 1812-1881.
Montezuma; the last of the Aztees. A romance. By Edward Maturin... New York, Paine & Burgess, 1845.
2 v. 19 1/2 x 12 cm.

10332 Mauren, Frank.
Isadore Merton; or, The reverses of fortune. A story of real life. By Frank Mauren. Boston, F. Gleason, at the Flag of our union office, 1847
2 p. 1., [7]-50 p. 23 cm.

10333 Maxwell, Mrs. Ellen (Blackmar) 1853?-1938.
The bishop's conversion, by Ellen Blackmar Maxwell; with an introduction by James M. Thoburn... New York, Hunt & Eaton; Cincinnati, Cranston & Curts, 1892.
384 p. front., plates. 19 cm.

10334 Maxwell, Maria.
Ernest Grey; or, The sins of society. A soty of New York life. By Maria Maxwell. With six fine illustrations, by M'Lenan. New York, T. W. Strong, 1855.
vii, [9]-335 p. front., plates. 18 1/2 cm.
Added t.-p., illus.

10335 Mayo, Sarah Carter (Edgarton) 1819-1848.
Selections from the writings of Mrs. Sarah C. Edgarton Mayo; with a memoir, by her husband... Boston, A. Tompkins, 1849.
viii, [9]-432 p. front. (port.) 20 cm.

"Memoir": p. 9-125.

10336 Mayo, William Starbuck, 1812-1895.
The Berber; or, The mountaineer of the Atlas. A tale of
Morocco. By William Starbuck Mayo... New-York, G. P.
Putnam [etc. , etc.] 1850.
454 p.   19 cm.

10337 Mayo, William Starbuck, 1812-1895.
Kaloolah; or, Journeyings to the Djébel Kumri: an auto-
biography of Jonathan Romer. Edited by W. S. Mayo, M. D.
New-York, G. P. Putnam; London, D. Bogue, 1849.
3 p. l. , [v]-xi, [3]-514 p. front.   19 cm.
Added t.p. , illustrated.
A novel.

10338 Mayo, William Starbuck, 1812-1895.
Romance dust from the historic placer. By William
Starbuck Mayo... New-York, G. P. Putnam [etc. , etc.]
1851.
278 p.   19 1/2 cm.
Re-issued under title: Flood and field.
CONTENTS. -Preface. -Don Sebastian; from the chronicles
of Portugal. -The captain's story. -Washington's first battle,
or Braddock's defeat. -A legend of the Cape de Verdes. -A
real pirate. -The astonishing adventure of James Botello. -
Dragut, the corsair. -The pious constancy of Inez de Mencia
Mont-Roy. -Appendix.

10339 [Meaney, Mary L   ]
The confessors of Connaught; or, The tenants of a lord
bishop. A tale of our own times. By M. L. M. ... Philadelphia, P. F. Cunningham, 1865.
viii, 7-319 p.   17 cm.

10340 [Meaney, Mary L   ]
Grace Morton; or, The inheritance. A Catholic tale. By
M. L. M. ... Philadelphia, P. F. Cunningham, 1864.
324 p.   17 1/2 cm.

10341 Meline, Mary Miller, d. 1898.
Charteris. A romance. By Mary M. Meline... Phila-

288

delphia, J. B. Lippincott & co., 1874.
260 p.   19 1/2 cm.

10342 Meline, Mary Miller, d. 1898.
       In six months; or, The two friends. By Mary M. Meline
       ... Baltimore, Kelly, Piet and company, 1874.
       3 p. l., 299 p.   17 1/2 cm.

10343 Melville, Herman, 1819-1891.
       The confidence-man: his masquerade. By Herman
       Melville... New York, Dix, Edwards & co., 1857.
       vi, 394 p.   19 cm.

10344 Melville, Herman, 1819-1891.
       Mardi: and a voyage thither. By Herman Melville...
       New York, Harper & brothers, 1849.
       2 v.   19 1/2 cm.

10345 Melville, Herman, 1819-1891.
       Omoo: a narrative of adventures in the South Seas. By
       Herman Melville... 5th ed. [Pt. 1] New York, Harper &
       brothers [etc., etc.] 1847.
       xv, [17]-196 p. incl. front. (map)   18 1/2 cm.
       Sequel to "Typee."

10346 Melville, Herman, 1819-1891.
       The piazza tales. By Herman Melville... New York, Dix
       & Edwards [etc., etc.] 1856.
       2 p. l., 431 p.   18 1/2 cm.
       CONTENTS.-The piazza.-Bartleby.-Benito Cereno.-The
       lightning-rod man.-The Encantadas; or, Enchanted islands.
       -The bell-tower.

10347 Melville, Herman, 1819-1891.
       Pierre; or, The ambiguities. By Herman Melville. New
       York, Harper & brothers, 1852.
       viii, 495 p.   18 1/2 cm.

10348 Melville, Herman, 1819-1891.
       Redburn: his first voyage. Being the sailor-boy con-
       fessions and reminiscences of the son-of-a-gentleman, in
       the merchant service. By Herman Melville... New York,

Harper & brothers, 1850.
xi, [13]-390 p.   19 1/2 cm.

10349 Melville, Herman, 1819-1891.
White-jacket; or, The world in a man-of-war. By Herman
Melville ... New York, Harper & brothers; London, R.
Bentley, 1850.
vii, [9]-465 p.   19 1/2 cm.
First edition.

10350 Miles, George Henry, 1824-1871.
The governess; or, The effects of good example. An
original tale. Being a leaf from every-day life. By George
H. Miles. Baltimore, Hedian & O'Brien [c1851]
256 p.   15 cm.

10351 Miles, George Henry, 1824-1871.
The truce of God, a tale of the eleventh century. By
George H. Miles. Baltimore, J. Murphy & co.; New
York, Catholic publication society, 1871.
3 p. 1., 9-384 p.   16 cm.

10352 Miller, Joaquin, 1841-1913.
First fam'lies of the Sierras. By Joaquin Miller...
Chicago, Jansen, McClurg & co., 1876.
2 p. 1., iii-iv, 5-258 p.   18 1/2 cm.
Prose sketches.
Published later in a revised form, under title: The
Danities in the Sierras.

10353 Miller, Joaquin, 1841-1913.
'49, the gold-seeker of the Sierras, by Joaquin Miller...
New York [etc.] Funk & Wagnalls, 1884.
viii, [9]-148 p.   19 cm.
Revised and enlarged edition of the story, which was
originally published in Bret Harte's Overland Monthly.

10354 Miller, Joaquin, 1841-1913.
The one fair woman. By Joaquin Miller... London,
Chapman and Hall; New York, G. W. Carleton & co., 1876.
3 v. in 1.   19 cm.
Paged continuously.

10355 Miller, Joaquin, 1841-1913.
   Unwritten history: life amongst the Modocs, by Joaquin
   Miller... Hartford, American publishing company, 1874.
   xvi, 17-445 p. incl. front. (port.) 23 pl.   22 1/2 cm.

10356 Miller, Stephen Franks, 1810-1867.
   Wilkins Wylder; or, The successful man. [Also, Mind and
   matter: a story of domestic life] By Stephen F. Miller...
   Philadelphia, J. B. Lippincott & co., 1860.
   420 p.   20 cm.

10357 [Minor, Mrs. Kate Pleasants] comp.
   From Dixie. Original articles contributed by southern
   writers for publication as a souvenir of the Memorial bazaar
   for the benefit of the monument to the private soldiers and
   sailors of the Confederacy and the establishment of the
   Museum for confederate relics, with heretofore unpublished
   poems by some who have "crossed over the river". Richmond, West, Johnston & co., 1893.
   167 p.   19 cm.
   Preface signed: Kate Pleasants Minor

10358 Mitchel, Frederic Augustus, 1839-1921.
   Sweet revenge, a romance of the Civil War; by F. A.
   Mitchel... New York, Harper & brothers, 1897.
   2 p. 1., 248 p.   19 cm.

10359 [Mitchell, Donald Grant] 1822-1908.
   Doctor Johns: being a narrative of certain events in the life
   of an orthodox minister of Connecticut. By the author of "My
   farm of Edgewood." New York, C. Scribner and company,
   1866.
   2 v.   18 1/2 cm.
   First edition.

10360 [Mitchell, Donald Grant] 1822-1908.
   Dream life; a fable of the seasons. By Ik. Marvel [pseud.]
   ... New York, C. Scribner, 1851.
   1 p. 1., vii, [11]-286 p. front.   19 1/2 cm.
   First edition.

10361 [Mitchell, Donald Grant] 1822-1908.

The lorgnette; or, Studies of the town. By an opera goer
... 2d ed., set off with Mr. Darley's designs. New York,
Printed for Stringer and Townsend [c1850]
    2 v. fronts., illus., plates. 19 1/2 cm.
    Preface signed: John Timon.
    Published also under title "The opera-goer".

10362 [Mitchell, Donald Grant] 1822-1908.
    Reveries of a bachelor; or, A book of the heart. By
Ik. Marvel [pseud.]... New York, Baker & Scribner, 1850.
    xi p., 1 1., [15]-298 p. front. 18 1/2 cm.
    Added t.-p., engr.
    First edition.
    Front. and vignette by Darley.

10363 [Mitchell, Donald Grant] 1822-1908.
    Seven stories, with basement and attic. By the author of
"My farm of Edgewood". New York, C. Scribner, 1864.
    viii, 314 p. 19 cm.
    First edition.

10364 Mitchell, John Ames, 1845-1918.
    The last American: A fragment from the journal of Khan-
Li, Prince of Dimph-Yoo-Chur and admiral in the Persian
Navy. Edited by J. A. Mitchell. New York, Frederick A.
Stokes & brother, 1899.
    78 p. illus. 20 cm.

10365 Mitchell, Silas Weir, 1829-1914.
    The adventures of François, foundling, thief, juggler, and
fencing-master during the French Revolution... New York,
The Century co., 1898.
    321 p., illus. 20 cm.

10366 Mitchell, Silas Weir, 1829-1914.
    Characteristics... New York, The Century, 1892.
    307 p. 20 cm.
    Dr. North and his friends (1900) is a sequel.

10367 Mitchell, Silas Weir, 1829-1914.
    Dr. North and his friends... New York, The Century co.,
1900.

499 p.   20 cm.
A sequel to Characteristics (1892)

10368 Mitchell, Silas Weir, 1829-1914.
       Philip Vernon, a tale in prose and verse; by S. Weir
       Mitchell... New York, The Century co. , 1895.
       55 p.   19 1/2 cm.

10369 Modêt, Helen.
       Light [a novel] By Helen Modêt. New York, D. Appleton
       and company, 1863.
       339 p.   20 1/2 cm.

10370 "Monk," pseud.
       Going and son: a novel. By "Monk." New York, American
       news company, 1869.
       167 p.   24 cm.

10371 Montague, Charles Howard, 1858-1889.
       Written in red; or, The conspiracy in the North case.
       (A story of Boston). By Chas. Howard Montague and C. W.
       Dyar. New York, Cassell publishing company [c1890]
       1 p. 1. , iv, 335 p.   19 cm.

10372 Moody, Edwin F
       Bob Rutherford and his wife: an historical romance...
       Louisville, Ky. , Printed for the author by John P. Morton &
       company, 1888.
       212 p.   20 cm.
       During the Texas Revolution.

10373 Moore, Emily H
       A lost life. A novel. By Emily H. Moore. ["Mignonette."]
       New York, G. W. Carleton & co. [etc. , etc.] 1871.
       3 p. 1. , [ix]-x, [11]-300 p.   18 cm.

10374 [Moore, Mrs. H   J   ]
       The golden legacy: a story of life's phases. By a lady
       ... New York, D. Appleton and company, 1857.
       vii, 382 p.   19 cm.

10375 Moore, Mrs. H   J

Wild Nell, the White Mountain girl. By Mrs. H. J.
Moore... New York, Sheldon & company; Philadelphia, J.
B. Lippincott & company [etc., etc.] 1860.
x, [11]-293 p. front. (port.) plates. 19 cm.

10376 Moore, Horatio Newton, 1814-1859.
Fitzgerald and Hopkins; or, Scenes and adventures in
theatrical life. By H. N. Moore... Philadelphia, S. G.
Sherman, 1847.
1 p. l., 166 p. front., 5 pl. 21 cm.
Added t.-p., engr.

10377 Moos, Herman M   1836-1894.
Hannah; or, A glimpse of paradise. A tale... By H. M.
Moos... Cincinnati, Literary eclectic publishing house
[c1868]
351 p. front., plates. 23 cm. (On cover: Library
of select novels)

10378 Moran, Jeannie Wormley (Blackburn) 1842-
Miss Washington, of Virginia. A semi-centennial
love-story. By Jeannie Blackburn. Richmond, Va., The
author, 1889.
vi p., 1 l., [9]-77 p. 19 cm.

10379 Morford, Henry, 1823-1881.
The coward. A novel of society and the field in 1863.
By Henry Morford... Philadelphia, T. B. Peterson &
brothers [c1864]
2 p. l., 21-520 p. 18 1/2 cm.

10380 Morford, Henry, 1823-1881.
The days of shoddy, A novel of the great rebellion in 1861.
By Henry Morford... Philadelphia, T. B. Peterson &
brothers [c1863]
3 p. l., 23-478 p. front. (port.) 18 cm.

10381 Morford, Henry, 1823-1881.
Turned from the door. A Christmas story for 1869-70. By
Henry Morford... New York, The American news company,
1869.
80 p. 23 1/2 cm.

On cover: "The governor's" Christmas story.

10382 Morford, Henry, 1823-1881.
Utterly wrecked; a novel of American coast life. By
Henry Morford... New York, The American news company,
[c1866]
182 p.   24 cm.

10383 Morgan, Nathan Denison, 1818-
George Cardwell; or, A month in a country parish. By
N. D. Morgan... New York, Dana and company, 1856.
62 p.   19 cm.
"Bibliographical catalogue of works on life insurance,
etc.": p. 59-62.

10384 Morganiana, or The wonderful life and terrible death of Morgan.
Written by himself. Illustrated with gritholaphic plates, by
Hassan Straightshanks, Turkey. First American ed., tr.
from the original Arabic manuscript. By Baron Munchausen,
jr. ... Boston, Printed and published by the proprietors,
1828.
92 p.   plates.   22 cm.
p. 34-35 numbered 36 and 33; p. 38-39 numbered 40 and 37.

10385 Morris, George Pope, 1802-1864.
The little Frenchman and his water lots, with other sketches
of the times. By George P. Morris... With etchings by
Johnson. Philadelphia, Lea & Blanchard, 1839.
155 p.   illus.   21 cm.
Lettered on cover: Hits at the times.
CONTENTS. -The little Frenchman and his water lots. -The
monopoly and the people's line. -Letters from the Springs. -A
letter and a poem. -Leaves from an editor's portfolio. -Mr.
Beverley Lee; or, The days of the shin-plasters.

10386 [Morris, James W   ]
... K. N. Pepper, and other condiments; put up for
general use, by Jacques Maurice [pseud.]... New York,
Rudd & Carleton, 1859.
xii, [13]-258 p.   19 1/2 cm.

10387 Morris, Robert, 1818-1888.

Life in the Triangle, or, Freemasonry at the present time. By Rob. Morris... Louisville, Printed by J. F. Brennan & co., 1854.
284 p.   12 cm.

10388 Mortimer, Charlotte B   b. 1807.
Marrying by lot. A tale of the primitive Moravians. By Charlotte B. Mortimer... New York, G. P. Putnam & son, 1868.
xi [1]-405 p.   19 cm.

10389 Mortimer, Charlotte B   b. 1807.
Morton Montagu; or, A young Christian's choice. A narrative founded on facts in the early history of a deceased Moravian missionary clergyman. By C. B. Mortimer. New-York, Philadelphia, D. Appleton & company, 1850.
1 p. 1., [5]-255 p.   19 cm.

10390 [Motley, John Lothrop] 1814-1877.
Merry Mount; a romance of the Massachusetts colony... [1st ed.] Boston and Cambridge, J. Munroe and company, 1849.
2 v. in 1.   20 cm.

10391 [Motley, John Lothrop] 1814-1877.
Morton's Hope; or, The memoirs of a provincial... [1st ed.] New York, Harper & brothers, 1839.
2 v.   18 cm.

10392 Moulton, Mrs. Louise (Chandler)1835-1908.
More bed-time stories, by Louise Chandler Moulton... With illustrations by Addie Ledyard. Boston, Roberts brothers, 1875.
238 p.   front.   18 1/2 cm.

10393 Moulton, Mrs. Louise (Chandler) 1835-1908.
My third book. A collection of tales. By Louise Chandler Moulton... New York, Harper & brothers, 1859
434 p.   19 1/2 cm.

10394 Moulton, Mrs. Louise (Chandler) 1835-1908.

Some women's hearts. By Louise Chandler Moulton...
Boston, Roberts brothers, 1874.
    4 p. 1., 364 p.   18 cm.
    CONTENTS. -Fleeing from fate. -Brains. -Twelve years of
my life. -Little Gibraltar. -Household gods. -The judge's wife.
-A letter, and what came of it. -Out of Nazareth.

10395 Mountford, William, 1816-1885.
    Thorpe, a quiet English town, and human life therein. By
William Mountford. Boston, Ticknor, Reed, and Fields,
1852.
    390 p.   18 cm.

10396 Murdoch, David.
    The Dutch dominie of the Catskills; or, The times of the
"Bloody Brandt." By Rev. David Murdoch, D. D. New
York, Derby & Jackson, 1861.
    xvi, 17-471 p.   19 cm.

10397 Murphy, Mrs. Rosalie (Miller)
    Destiny; or, Life as it is. By Rosalie Miller Murphy.
New York, M. Doolady, 1867.
    336 p.   19 cm.

10398 Murray, William Henry Harrison, 1840-1904.
    Adventures in the wilderness; or, Camp-life in the Adiron-
dacks. By William H. H. Murray... Boston, Fields, Osgood
& co., 1869.
    vi, [7]-236 p. front., plates.   18 cm.

10399 Murray, William Henry Harrison, 1840-1904.
    Deacons. By W. H. H. Murray... Boston, H. L. Shep-
ard and company, 1875.
    82 p. incl. front., illus., plates.   19 1/2 cm.

10400 Murray, William Henry Harrison, 1840-1904.
    Holiday tales. Christmas in the Adirondacks. By W. H. H.
Murray. [Springfield, Mass., Springfield printing and binding
company] c1897.
    113 p. incl. front. (port.) illus., plates.   24 x 19 1/2 cm.
    CONTENTS. -How John Norton the trapper kept his
Christmas. -John Norton's vagabond.

10401 [Myers, Peter Hamilton] 1812-1878.
       The first of the Knickerbockers: a tale of 1673... New
   York, G. P. Putnam [etc., etc.] 1848.
       vi, [9]-221 p.   20 cm.   (On cover: Putnam's choice
   library)
       Published anonymously.

10402 The mysteries of Nashua; or, Revenge punished and constancy
   rewarded... Nashua, C. T. Gill, 1844.
       40 p. incl. front. illus.   22 1/2 cm.

                              N

10403 Nack, James, 1809-1879.
       Earl Rupert, and other tales and poems, by James Nack.
   With a memoir of the author, by P. M. Wetmore. New
   York, G. Adlard, 1839.
       xx, 220 p.   19 1/2 cm.

10404 Nahant, or "The floure of souvenance." Philadelphia, H. C.
   Carey and I. Lea, 1827.
       31 p.   20 1/2 cm.

10405 Narrative and confessions of Lucretia P. Cannon, who was
   tried, convicted, and sentenced to be hung at Georgetown,
   Delaware, with two of her accomplices. Containing an
   account of some of the most horrible and shocking murders
   and daring robberies ever committed by one of the female sex.
   New York, Printed for the publishers, 1841.
       24 p. incl. front.   22 1/2 cm.

10406 [Neal, John] 1793-1876.
       Authorship, a tale. By a New Englander over-sea. Boston,
   Gray and Bowen, 1830.
       iv, 267 p.   18 1/2 cm.

10407 Neal, John, 1793-1876.
       The Down-easters, &c. &c. &c. By John Neal... New

York, Harper & brothers, 1833.
2 v   20 1/2 cm.

10408 [Neal, John] 1793-1876.
Keep cool, a novel. Written in hot weather. By somebody,
M. D. C. &c. &c. &c. Author of sundry works of great
merit... never published, or read, from his-story. Reviewed
by - himself - "Esquire"... In 2 vols. ... Baltimore, J.
Cushing, 1817.
2 v.   18 1/2 cm.

10409 [Neal, John] 1793-1876.
Logan, a family history... Philadelphia, H. C. Carey &
I. Lea, 1822.
2 v.   19 cm.
Published anonymously.

10410 Neal, John, 1793-1876.
Rachel Dyer: a North American story. By John Neal.
Portland [Me.] Shirley and Hyde, 1828.
xx, [21]-276 p.   19 cm.

10411 [Neal, John] 1793-1876.
Randolph, a novel... By the author of Logan - and Seventy-
six. [Baltimore?] 1823.
2 v.   20 cm.

10412 [Neal, John] 1793-1876.
Seventy-six. By the author of Logan... Baltimore, J.
Robinson; Federick, Md., J. Robinson & co., 1823.
2 v.   18 1/2 cm.

10413 Neal, John, 1793-1876.
True womanhood: a tale: by John Neal... Boston, Ticknor
and Fields, 1859.
iv, [5]-487 p.   20 cm.

10414 Neal, Joseph Clay, 1807-1847.
Charcoal sketches; or, Scenes in a metropolis. By Joseph
C. Neal. With illustrations by David C. Johnston. 6th ed.
Philadelphia, E. L. Carey and A. Hart, 1841.
2 p. 1., 3-222 p. 3 pl.   17 1/2 cm.

Added t.-p., engraved.

10415 [Nelson, Augusta R   ]
The prize essay, and The mitherless bairn, originally
published in the Missouri republican. By Roswytha [pseud.]
St. Louis, G. Knapp & co., 1857.
cover-title, 104 p.   25 cm.

10416 Newell, Charles Martin, 1821-
... The isle of Palms; adventures while wrecking for gold,
encounter with a mad whale, battle with a devil-fish and
capture of a mermaid, by C. M. Newell... Boston, De
Wolfe, Fiske & co., 1888.
vi, [2], 460 p. front., 6 pl.   19 1/2 cm.   (The
Fleetwing series. [v. 2])

10417 [Newell, Robert Henry] 1836-1901.
Avery Glibun; or, Between two fires. A romance. By
Orpheus C. Kerr [pseud.] New York, G. W. Carleton & co.
[etc., etc.] 1867.
3 p. l., [ix]-x, 11-301 p.   24 cm.

10418 [Newell, Robert Henry] 1836-1901.
Smoked glass. By Orpheus C. Kerr [pseud.]... With
illustrative anachronisms by Thomas Worth. New York,
G. W. Carleton [etc., etc.] 1868.
1 p. l., v-viii, 9-277 p. front., plates.   19 cm.

10419 Newell, Robert Henry, 1836-1901.
The walking doll; or, the Asters and disasters of society,
by R. H. Newell. New York, H. B. Felt & company, 1872.
371 p.   19 cm.

10420 [Newhall, James Robinson] 1809-1893.
Liñ; or, Jewels of the Third plantation... By Obadiah
Oldpath [pseud.] Lynn [Mass.] T. Herbert and J. M. Munroe,
1862.
viii, 9-400 p.   19 1/2 cm.

10421 Nichols, George Ward, 1837-1885.
The sanctuary: a story of the civil war. By George Ward
Nichols... New York, Harper & brothers, 1866.

300

3 p. 1., [ix]-x p., 1 1., [13]-286 p. incl. front., 5 pl.
18 1/2 cm.

10422 [Nichols, Mary Sargeant Gove] 1810-1884.
Mary Lyndon; or, Revelations of a life. An autobiography.
New York, Stringer and Townsend, 1855.
388 p.   19 1/2 cm.

10423 Nicholson, Joseph J
The Blemmertons; or, Dottings by the wayside. By the
Reverend Joseph J. Nicholson... New York, Dana and
company [etc., etc.] 1856.
423 p.   19 cm.

10424 [Nickerson, Susan D   ]
Bread-winners. By a lady of Boston. Boston, Nichols
and Hall, 1871.
vi, 7-295 p.   16 1/2 cm.

10425 Noble, Annette Lucile, 1844-
Love and shawl-straps, by Annette L. Noble... with the
collaboration of Pearl Clement Coann. New York [etc.]
G. P. Putnam's sons, 1894.
2 p. 1., 291 p.   18 cm.

10426 Nolan, Alice.
The Byrnes of Glengoulah. A true tale. By Alice Nolan.
New York, P. O'Shea, 1870.
viii, 362 p.   19 cm.

10427 Nordhoff, Charles, 1830-1901.
Cape Cod and all along shore; stories. By Charles Nord-
hoff... New York, Harper & brothers, 1868.
4 p. 1., [13]-235 p.   19 1/2 cm.
Previously published in Harper's magazine and Atlantic
monthly.
CONTENTS. -Captain Tom: a resurrection. -What is best?-
A struggle for life. -Elkanah Brewster's temptation. -One pair
of blue eyes. -Mehetable Roger's cranberry swamp. -Maud
Elbert's love match.

10428 Norris, Frank, 1870-1902.

301

McTeague; a story of San Francisco, by Frank Norris...
New Yor, Doubleday & McClure co., 1899.
3 p. l., 442 p.   20 1/2 cm.

10429 Norris, Mary Harriott, 1848-1919.
       Lakewood; a story of to-day, by Mary Harriott Norris,
       illustrated by Louise L. Heustis, New York and London,
       F. A. Stokes company [c1895]
       2 p. l., 331 p. front., plates   20 cm. (West End
       series)

10430 Norton, John Nicholas, 1820-1881.
       Full proof of the ministry; a sequel to The boy who was
       trained up to be a clergyman, by John N. Norton... New
       York, Redfield, 1855.
       245 p.   19 1/2 cm.

10431 Norton, John Nicholas, 1820-1881.
       Rockford parish; or, The fortunes of Mr. Mason's suc-
       cessors. By John N. Norton... New York, Dana and
       company [etc., etc.] 1856.
       216 p.   19 cm.

10432 Norvel Hastings: or, The frigate in the offing. A nautical
       tale of the war of 1812. By a distinguished novelist...
       Philadelphia, A. Hart, late Carey and Hart, 1850.
       1 p. l., 9-143 p.   20 cm.

10433 Notes of hospital life from November, 1861, to August, 1863...
       Philadelphia, J. B. Lippincott & co., 1864.
       xiv, 16-210 p.   19 cm.
       Introduction by Bishop Potter.

10434 Nott, Henry Junius, 1797-1837.
       Novellettes of a traveller; or, Odds and ends from the
       knapsack of Thomas Singularity, journeyman printer. Ed. by
       Henry Junius Nott... New-York, Harper & brothers, 1834.
       2 v.   19 1/2 cm.
       CONTENTS.-v. 1. Biographical sketch of Thomas Singularity.
       The Andalusian rope-dancer. The solitary.-v. 2. Cock Robin.
       The shipwreck. The counterfeiters. The French officer.

10435 Nourse, James Duncan, 1817-1854.
Levenworth. A story of the Mississippi and the prairies.
By J. D. Nourse... Louisville, G. W. Noble, 1848.
143 p.   23 cm.

10436 Nye, Edgar Wilson, 1850-1896.
A guest at the Ludlow, and other stories, by Edgar Wilson
Nye [Bill Nye] with illustrations by Louis Braunhold. In-
dianapolis and Kansas City, The Bowen-Merrill company, 1897.
7 p. l., 272 p. front., plates.   19 cm.
"An article on the writings of James Whitcomb Riley by
'Chelifer' ": p. [263]-272.

10437 Nye, Edgar Wilson, 1850-1896.
Remarks by Bill Nye (Edgar W. Nye)... With over one
hundred and fifty illustrations, by J. H. Smith. Chicago,
A. E. Davis & company, 1887.
ix, [1], 11-504 p. incl. front., illus.   22 1/2 cm.

O

10438 O'Brien, Dillon.
The Dalys of Dalystown. By Dillon O'Brien... Saint
Paul, Pioneer printing company, 1866.
518 p.   20 cm.
Error in paging: p. 257-266 omitted.

10439 O'Brien, Dillon.
Dead broke, a western tale. By Dillon O'Brien... Saint
Paul, Pioneer company print, 1873.
2 p. l., [3]-193 p.   18 1/2 cm.

10440 O'Flarrity, Paddy, pseud.
The life of Paddy O'Flarrity, who, from a shoe black, has,
by perseverance and good conduct, arrived to a member of
Congress... Written by himself. [Washington, D. C.] 1834.
xii, 56 p.   17 1/2 cm.
Cover;title: A spur to youth; or Davy Crockett beaten.

10441 [Ogden, Mrs. C   A   ]
      Into the light; or, The Jewess. By C. A. O. ... Boston,
      Loring, 1868.
        2 p. 1. , 3-322 p.   19 1/2 cm.

10442 [Ogden, Robert N   ] 1839-
      Who did it? A novel. Philadelphia, Claxton, Remsen,
      and Haffelfinger; New Orleans, J. A. Gresham, 1870.
        87 p.   23 1/2 cm.

10443 Old Fort Duquesne, a tale of the early toils, struggles and
      adventures of the first settlers at the forks of the Ohio, 1754
      ... Pittsburgh, Cook's literary depot, 1844.
        79 p.   23 1/2 cm.
        Cover has imprint: Philadelphia, R. G. Bedford; New York,
      M. Y. Beagh [etc. , etc.] 1844.

10444 Old Friends. A remembrance of beloved companions, and
      years bygone... New York, Bliss, Wadsworth and co. , 1835.
        327 p.   19 cm.

10445 Old Honesty; or, The guests of the Beehalt Tavern. A tale of
      the early days of Kentucky. New York, Beadle and Adams
      [1867]
        100 p.   16 1/2 cm.

10446 The old Pine farm: or, The southern side. Comprising loose
      sketches from the experience of a southern country minister,
      S. C. Nashville, Southwestern publishing house; New York,
      Sheldon & company [etc. , etc.] 1860.
        vi, 7-202 p.   front. , plates.   19 1/2 cm.

10447 Oliphant, Margaret Oliphant (Wilson) 1828-1897.
      The second son; a novel, by M. O. W. Oliphant and T. B.
      Aldrich. Boston and New York, Houghton, Mifflin and
      company, 1888.
        vi, 524 p.   20 cm.

10448 One of those coincidences and ten other stories, by Julian
      Hawthorne [and others] New York, Funk & Wagnalls, 1899.
        315 p. illus. , plates.   19 cm.
        CONTENTS. -One of those coincidences, by J. Hawthorne.

-Francisco, by W. L. Beard.-The taper, by L. Tolstoy.-
How Viardeau obeyed the black abbé, by C. G. D. Roberts.
-John Merrill's experiment in palmistry, by F. M. Kingsley.
-The strange case of Esther Atkins, by Mrs. L. E. L.
Hardenbrook.-Jacob City, by A. S. Clarke.-Selma the
soprano, by M. Wagnalls.-At the end of his rope, by F. M.
Kingsley -The Easter of La Mercedes, by M. C. Francis.
-Romance of a tin roof and a fire-escape, by M. L. Avary.

10449 Oran, the outcast; or, A season in New-York... New York,
Peabody & co., 1833.
2 v. in 1.   18 1/2 cm.

10450 Orton, Jason Rockwood, 1806-1867.
Camp fires of the red men; or, A hundred years ago. By
J. R. Orton... Illustrated by Walcutt. New-York, J. C.
Derby; Boston, Phillips, Sampson & co. [etc., etc.] 1855.
viii, [9]-401 p. front., pl.   18 1/2 cm.

10451 [Osborn, Laughton] 1809-1878.
Confessions of a poet... Philadelphia, Carey, Lea &
Blanchard, 1835.
2 v.   19 cm.

10452 [Osborn, Laughton] 1809-1878.
Sixty years of the life of Jeremy Levis... New York,
G. & C. & H. Carvill, 1831.
2 v.   19 cm.

10453 [Osborn, Laughton] 1809-1878.
Travels by sea and land of Alethitheras [pseud.] New
York, Moorhead, Simpson & Bond, 1868.
viii p., 1 1., 381 p.   19 1/2 cm.

10454 [Osborne, Mrs. D   C   ]
Under golden skies; or, In the new Eldorado; a story of
southern life, by a southern author... Raleigh, N. C.,
Edwards & Broughton, printers, 1898.
485 p.   20 1/2 cm.

10455 [Osborne, Elise]
Life and its aims: in two parts. Part first - Ideal life.
Part second - Actual life. Philadelphia, Lippincott,
Grambo & co. , 1854.
2 p. 1. , 9-362 p.   19 cm.
Published in 1869 under title: Life's lottery; or, Life
and its aims.

10456 Otis, Eliza Henderson (Bordman) "Mrs. Harrison Gray Otis,"
1796-1873.
The Barclays of Boston. By Mrs. Harrison Gray Otis...
Boston, Ticknor, Reed, and Fields, 1854.
2 p. 1. , 419 p.   20 1/2 cm.

10457 Our "first families," a novel of Philadelphia good society.
By a descendant of the "Pens"... Boston, J. French and
company, 1857.
2 p. 1. , 7-xii, 13-404 p.   19 1/2 cm.

10458 Owen, George Washington, d. 1916.
The Leech club; or, The mysteries of the Catskills. By
George W. Owen. Boston, Lee & Shepard; New York,
Lee, Shepard & Dillingham, 1874.
298 p.   19 cm.

10459 Owen, Robert Dale, 1801-1877.
... Beyond the breakers. A story of the present day.
By Robert Dale Owen... Philadelphia, J. B. Lippincott
& co. , 1870.
2 p. 1. , 9-274 p.   front. , plates.   22 cm.
At head of title: Village life in the West.

P

10460 Page, Thomas Nelson, 1853-1922.
Elsket, and other stories, by Thomas Nelson Page. New
York, C. Scribner's sons, 1891.
vii, 208 p.   18 1/2 cm.

CONTENTS. -Elsket. -"George Washington's" last duel. -P'laski's tunament. -"Run to seed."-"A soldier of the empire."

10461 Page, Thomas Nelson, 1853-1922.
Marse Chan; a tale of old Virginia, by Thomas Nelson Page: illustrated by W. T. Smedley. New York, C. Scribner's sons, 1892.
4 p. 1., 53 p. incl. front., illus., 4 pl.   21 1/2 cm.

10462 Page, Thomas Nelson, 1853 1922.
Meh Lady: a story of the war... New York, Charles Scribner's sons, 1893.
70 p.   illus.   20 cm.

10463 Page, Thomas Nelson, 1853-1922.
The old gentleman of the black stock, by Thomas Nelson Page. New York, C. Scribner's sons, 1897.
3 p. 1., 137 p.   16 1/2 x 10 cm.   [The ivory series]

10464 Page, Thomas Nelson, 1853-1922.
On Newfound river, by Thomas Nelson Page... New York, C. Scribner's sons, 1891.
3 p. 1., 240 p.   19 cm.

10465 Page, Thomas Nelson, 1853-1922.
Pastime stories, by Thomas Nelson Page... Illustrated by A. B. Frost. New York, Harper & brothers, 1894.
x, 220 p.   illus. 21 pl.   18 cm.
CONTENTS. -Old Sue. -How Jinny eased her mind. -Isrul's bargain. -The true story of the surrender of the Marquis Cornwallis. -When little Mordecal was at the bar. -Charlie Whittler's Christmas party. -How Relius "bossed the ranch." -The prosecution of Mrs. Dullet. -One from four. -The danger of being too thorough. -Uncle Jack's views of geography. -Billington's valentine. -She had on her geranium leaves. -A story of Charles Harris. -He would have gotten a lawyer. -How Andrew carried the precinct. -"Rasmus."-Her sympathetic editor. -He knew what was due to the court. -Her great-grandmother's ghost. -Rachel's lovers. -John's wedding suit. -When the colonel was a duellist.

10466 Page, Thomas Nelson, 1853-1922.
   Polly; a Christmas recollection, by Thomas Nelson Page;
illustrated by A. Castaigne. New York, C. Scribner's sons,
1894.
   3 p. 1. , 49 p. front. , plates. 21 1/2 cm.

10467 Page, Thomas Nelson, 1853-1922.
   Red Rock; a chronicle of reconstruction, by Thomas
Nelson Page... New York, C. Scribner's sons, 1898.
   xv. 584 p. 11 pl. (incl. front.) 19 cm.

10468 Paine, Susanna.
   Roses and thorns; or, Recollections of an artist; a tale
of truth for the grave and the gay. By Susanna Paine.
Providence, B. T. Albro, printer, 1854.
   204 p. 19 1/2 cm.

10469 Paine, Susanna.
   Wait and see... By Susanna Paine. Boston, Printed
by J. Wilson and son, 1860.
   2 p. 1. , ix p. 1 1. , [13]-400 p. 20 cm.

10470 [Palfrey, Sara Hammond] 1823-1914.
   Agnes Westworth. By E. Foxton [pseud.] Philadelphia,
J. B. Lippincott & co. , 1869.
   2 p. 1. , 3-316 p. 18 cm.

10471 Palfrey, Sara Hammond, 1823-1914.
   Herman, or, Young knighthood, by E. Foxton [pseud.]
Boston, Lee and Shepard, 1866.
   2 v. 19 cm.

10472 [Palmer, John Williamson] 1825-1906.
   ... After his kind, by John Coventry [pseud.]... New
York, H. Holt and company, 1886.
   3 p. 1. , 324 p. 17 cm. (Leisure hour series, no.
184)

10473 Parker, Henry Webster, 1822-1903.
   Poems, by H. W. Parker. Auburn, J. M. Alden, 1850.
   238 p. 18 1/2 cm.
   CONTENTS. -Creations. -Imitations. -Prose-poems.

10474 Parker, Jane (Marsh) 1836-1913.
      Barley Wood; or, Building on the rock. By Mrs. J. M.
Parker... New York, D. Dana, jr., 1860.
      320 p.   17 1/2 cm.

10475 Parkman, Francis, 1823-1893.
      Vassall Morton. A novel. By Francis Parkman... Boston,
Phillips, Sampson and company, 1856.
      414 p.   19 1/2 cm.

10476 [Parton, Mrs. Sara Payson (Willis)] 1811-1872.
      ... Fern leaves from Fanny's port-folio. With original
designs by Fred M. Coffin. Auburn, Derby and Miller;
Buffalo, Derby, Orton and Mulligan [etc., etc.] 1853.
      1 p. 1., vi. [7]-400 p. 7 pl.   20 cm.
      Added t.-p., engraved.
      At head of title: Fiftieth thousand.
      Preface signed: Fanny Fern [pseud.]

10477 [Parton, Mrs. Sara Payson (Willis)] 1811-1872.
      Fresh leaves. By Fanny Fern [pseud.] New York, Mason
brothers, 1857.
      viii, [9]-336 p.   14 1/2 cm.

10478 [Parton, Mrs. Sara Payson (Willis)] 1811-1872.
      Rose Clark. By Fanny Fern [pseud.] New York, Mason
brothers, 1856.
      xiv, [15]-417 p.   18 1/2 cm.

10479 [Parton, Mrs. Sara Payson (Willis)] 1811-1872.
      Ruth Hall: a domestic tale of the present time. By Fanny
Fern [pseud.] New York, Mason brothers, 1855.
      xiv, [15]-400 p.   18 cm.

10480 [Paulding, James Kirke] 1778-1860.
      The book of Saint Nicholas. Translated from the original
Dutch of Dominie Nicholas AEgidius Oudenarde [pseud.] New-
York, Harper & brothers, 1836.
      xii, [13]-237 p.   19 1/2 cm.   (On cover: Pauldings'
works, v. 14)
      CONTENTS. -The legend of Saint Nicholas. -The little Dutch
sentinel of the Manhadoes. -Cobus Yerks. -A strange bird in

Niew-Amsterdam-Claas Schlaschenschlinger.-The revenge of
Saint Nicholas.-The origin of the bakers' dozen.-The ghost.
-The nymph of the mountain.-The ride of Saint Nicholas on
Newyear's eve.

10481 [Paulding, James Kirke] 1778-1860.
       Chronicles of the city of Gotham, from the papers of a
       retired common councilman. Containing: The azure hose.
       The politician. The dumb girl. Ed. by the author of "The
       backwoodsman" [etc.]... New York, G. & C. & H. Carvill,
       1830.
       ix, [11]-270 p.   18 cm.

10482 [Paulding, James Kirke] 1778-1860.
       The diverting history of John Bull and Brother Jonathan.
       By Hector Bull-us [pseud.] New ed. New-York, Harper &
       brothers, 1835.
       1 p. 1., 5-193 p.   19 1/2 cm.   (On cover: Paulding's
       works. [No.] IX)
       CONTENTS.-The diverting history of John Bull and
       Brother Jonathan.-The history of Uncle Sam and his boys.

10483 [Paulding, James Kirke] 1778-1860.
       ... The Dutchman's fireside. A tale. By the author of
       "Letters from the South" [etc.]... New York, J. & J.
       Harper, 1831.
       2 v.   18 cm.   (Harper's stereotype ed.)

10484 [Paulding, James Kirke] 1778-1860.
       The Dutchman's fireside. A tale. By the author of "Letters
       from the South" [etc.]... 5th ed. ... New-York, Harper &
       brothers, 1837.
       2 v. in 1.   17 1/2 cm.

10485 [Paulding, James Kirke] 1778-1860.
       John Bull in America; or, The new Munchausen. New
       York, C. Wiley, 1825.
       xvii, 226 p.   18 cm.

10486 [Paulding, James Kirke] 1778-1860.
       Koningsmarke, the long Finne, a story of the New world...
       New-York, C. Wiley, 1823.

2 v.   19 1/2 cm.

10487 [Paulding, James Kirke] 1778-1860.
           The merry tales of the three wise men of Gotham. By the
           author of "The Dutchman's fireside," "Westward Ho!"...
           New-York, Harper & brothers, 1839.
           236 p.   18 1/2 cm.
           CONTENTS.-The man machine.-The perfection of reason.
           -The perfection of science.

10488 [Paulding, James Kirke] 1778-1860.
           The new mirror for travellers; and guide to the springs.
           By an amateur... New-York, G. & C. Carvill, 1828.
           292 p.   18 cm.

10489 [Paulding, James Kirke] 1778-1860.
           The old Continental; or, The price of liberty. By the author
           of "The Dutchman's fireside," &c., &c. ... New-York,
           Paine and Burgess, 1846.
           2 v. in 1.   19 cm.

10490 Paulding, James Kirke, 1778-1860.
           The Puritan and his daughter. By J. K. Paulding...
           New York, Baker and Scribner, 1849.
           2 v. in 1.   18 cm.

10491 [Paulding, James Kirke] 1778-1860.
           A sketch of old England, by a New-England man... New-
           York, C. Wiley, 1822.
           2 v. in 1.   19 cm.

10492 [Paulding, James Kirke] 1778-1860.
           Tales of the good woman. By a doubtful gentleman. New
           ed. ... New-York, Harper & brothers, 1836.
           2 v.   19 1/2 cm.   (On cover: Paulding's works. X-XI)
           CONTENTS.-v. 1. Memoir of the unknown author. The
           Yankee roue. The drunkard. Dyspepsy.-v. 2. The cradle of
           the new world. The politician. The dumb girl.

10493 [Payson, George] 1824-1893.
           The new age of gold; or, The life and adventures of Robert
           Dexter Romaine [pseud.] Written by himself. Boston,

Phillips, Sampson and company, 1856.
xii, [13]-403 p.   19 cm.

10494   Payson, George, 1824-1893.
        Totemwell. By George Payson... New York, Riker,
        Thorne & co. , 1854.
            2 p. l. , [9]-519 p.   18 cm.

10495   Peacocke, James S
        The Creole orphans; or, Lights and shadows of southern
        life. A tale of Louisiana, by James S. Peacocke... New
        York, Derby & Jackson: Cincinnati, H. W. Derby, 1856.
            365 p.   19 cm.
        Published in 1890 under title: Two white slaves.

10496   [Pearson, Emily Clemens]
        Cousin Franck's household; or, Scenes in the Old Dominion,
        by Pocahontas [pseud.] 2d ed. Boston, Upham, Ford and
        Olmstead; New York, L. Colby & co. [etc. , etc.] 1853.
            vii, 259 p.   front. , plates.   19 cm.
        Published in 1863 under title: Ruth's sacrifice.

10497   Pearson, Emily Clemens.
        Gutenberg, and the art of printing. By Emily C. Pearson
        ... Boston, Noyes, Holmes and company, 1871.
            2 p. l. , [iii]-vi, 292 p. front. , illus. , plates.   19 cm.

10498   [Peck Ellen]
        Ecce femina. New York, Schuyler & Gracie, 1874.
            46 p.   23 cm.
        Published anonymously.

10499   [Peck, Ellen]
        Ecce femina; or, The woman Zoe. By Cuyler Pine
        [pseud.] New York, G. W. Carleton & co. [etc. , etc.] 1875.
            2 p. l. , [7]-133 p.   18 1/2 cm.

10500   [Peck, Ellen]
        Renshawe. A novel. By the author of "Mary Brandegee."
        Ed. by Cuyler Pine [pseud.] New York, G. W. Carleton &
        co. [etc. , etc.] 1867.
            3 p. l. , [9]-384 p.   18 cm.

10501 [Peck, George Washington] 1817-1859.
Aurifodina; or, Adventures in the gold region. By Cantell
A. Bigly [pseud.] New-York, Baker and Scribner, 1849.
103 p.   17 1/2 cm.

10502 Peck, George Wilbur, 1840-1916.
The grocery man and Peck's bad boy: being a continuation
of Peck's bad boy and his Pa... Chicago and New York,
Belford, Clarke & co., 1883.
240 p.   illus.   20 cm.   ′

10503 [Peirce, Isaac]
The Narraganset chief; or, The adventures of a wanderer.
Written by himself... New York, J. K. Porter, 1832.
viii, [9]-195, [1] p.   18 1/2 cm.
"Advertisement" signed: I. P.

10504 Perce, Elbert, 1831-1869.
Gulliver Joi: his three voyages; being an account of his
marvelous adventures in Kailoo, Hydrogenia and Ejario.
Ed. by Elbert Perce. New York, C. Scribner, 1851.
3 p. 1., [v]-x p., 1 1., [13]-272 p.   front.   16 1/2 cm.
Added t.-p., engr.

10505 Perce, Elbert, 1831-1869.
The last of his name. By Elbert Perce... New York,
Riker, Thorne & co., 1854.
vi p., 1 1., [9]-309 p.   18 1/2 cm.

10506 Perkins, Frederic Beecher, 1828-1899.
Scrope; or, The lost library. A novel of New York and
Hartford. By Frederic B. Perkins... Boston, Roberts
brothers, 1874.
4, [7]-278 p.   23 1/2 cm.

10507 [Perkins, Geroge]
Before the dawn; a story of Paris and the Jacquerie, by
George Dulac [pseud.] New York & London, G. P. Putnam's
sons, 1888.
1 p. 1., 307 p.   19 1/2 cm.

10508 [Perrie, George W   ]

Buckskin Mose; or, Life from the lakes to the Pacific, as
actor, circus-rider, detective, ranger, gold-digger, Indian
scout, and guide. Written by himself... Ed. , and with
illustrations, by C. G. Rosenberg. New York, H. L.
Hinton, 1873.
  1 p. l. , [5]-285 p.   plates.   19 1/2 cm.

10509 [Peterson, Charles Jacobs] 1819-1887.
    The cabin and parlor; or, Slaves and masters. By J.
    Thornton Randolph [pseud.]... With... illustrations. From
    original designs by Stephens, engraved by Beeler. Philadelphia,
    T. B. Peterson [c1852]
      324 p.   front. , plates.   19 1/2 cm.

10510 Peterson, Charles Jacobs, 1819-1887.
    Grace Dudley; or, Arnold at Saratoga. An historical novel.
    By Charles J. Peterson... Philadelphia, T. B. Peterson
    [c1849]
      1 p. l. , 7-111 p.   illus.   24 1/2 cm.

10511 Peterson, Charles Jacobs, 1819-1887.
    Kate Aylesford. A story of the refugees. By Charles J.
    Peterson... Philadelphia, T. B. Peterson; Boston,
    Phillips, Sampson & co. [etc. , etc. , c1855]
      1 p. l. , 21-356 p.   18 1/2 cm.

10512 Peterson, Charles Jacobs, 1819-1887.
    The old stone mansion. By Charles J. Peterson...
    Philadelphia, T. B. Peterson and brothers [c1859]
      1 p. l. , 21-367 p.   front. 18 1/2 cm.

10513 Peterson, Henry, 1818-1891.
    Pemberton; or, One hundred years ago. By Henry
    Peterson... Philadelphia, J. B. Lippincott & co. , 1873.
      v. 7-393 p. front. , illus.   19 cm.

10514 Phelps, Mrs. Almira (Hart) Lincoln, 1793-1884.
    Ida Norman; or, Trials and their uses. By Mrs. Lincoln
    Phelps... Baltimore, Cushing & brother, 1848.
      viii, [13]-272 p.   19 1/2 cm.

10515 [Phelps, Mrs. Elizabeth (Stuart)] 1815-1852.

A peep at "number five;" or, A chapter in the life of a city
pastor. By H. Trusta [pseud.]... Boston, Phillips, Sampson,
and company, 1852.
    296 p. incl. front.   16 cm.
    "Tenth thousand."

10516 [Phelps, Mrs. Elizabeth (Stuart)] 1815-1852.
    The tell-tale; or, Home secrets told by old travellers. By
H. Trusta [pseud.]... Boston, Phillips, Sampson and company,
1853.
    262 p. 4 pl. (incl. front)   18 cm.

10517 Phillips, George Searle, 1815-1889.
    The gypsies of the Danes' dike. A story of hedge-side life
in England, in the year 1855. By George S. Phillips. (January Searle.) Boston, Ticknor and Fields, 1864.
    xii, 416 p.   20 cm.

10518 Phillips, Waldorf Henry, d. 1915.
    The world to blame. A novel. By Waldorf H. Phillips...
Philadelphia, Claxton, Remsen & Haffelfinger, 1874.
    3 p. 1., xi-xii, 13-190 p.   18 cm.

10519 Phillips, William Barnet.
    The diamond cross; a tale of American society. By William
Barnet Phillips. New York, Hilton & company; Philadelphia,
J. B. Lippincott & co. [etc., etc.] 1866.
    353 p.   18 1/2 cm.

10520 Piatt, Louise (Kirby) 1826-1864.
    Bell Smith abroad. Illustrated by Healy, Walcutt, and
Overarche. New-York, J. C. Derby [etc., etc.] 1855.
    1 p. 1., viii, [9]-326 p. front., illus., plates.   18 cm.
    Added t.-p., engraved.
    "Letters to the Home journal." cf. Appleton.

10521 Pickard, Kate E   R
    The kidnapped and the ransomed. Being the personal re-
collections of Peter Still and his wife "Vina," after forty
years of slavery. By Mrs. Kate E. R. Pickard. With an
introduction, by Rev. Samuel J. May; and an appendix, by
William H. Furness, D. D. Syracuse, W. T. Hamilton; New

York [etc.] Miller, Orton and Mulligan, 1856.
  xxiii (i.e. xxi), 25-409 p. 3 pl. (incl. front.) 19 cm.
  Pages ix-x omitted in paging.
  Added t.-p., engraved.
  "Appendix. Seth Concklin [by William H. Furness]":
p. 377-409.

10522 Pierson, Mrs. Emily Catharine.
  Jamie Parker, the fugitive. By Mrs. Emily Catharine
Pierson... Hartford, Brockett, Fuller and co., 1851.
  vii, [2], 10-192 p.   17 1/2 cm.

10523 [Pike, Mrs. Frances West (Atherton)] b. 1819.
  Every day. By the author of "Katherine Morris" ...
Boston, Noyes, Holmes, and company, 1871.
  v, 282 p.   19 1/2 cm.

10524 [Pike, Mrs. Frances West (Atherton)] b. 1819.
  Here and hereafter; or, The two altars. By Anna Athern
  [pseud.]... Boston, Crosby, Nichols, and company [etc.,
  etc.] 1858.
  iv, 376 p.   19 1/2 cm.

10525 [Pike, Mrs. Mary Hayden (Green)] 1825-
  Agnes. A novel. By the author of "Ida May." Boston,
Phillips, Sampson & company, 1858.
  1 p. 1., [5]-509, [1] p.   19 cm.

10526 Pinkerton, Allan, 1819-1884.
  Bank-robbers and the detectives. By Allan Pinkerton...
New York, G. W. Carleton & co. [etc., ect.] 1883.
  1 p. 1., v-x, 11-339 p. front., plates.   19 cm.

10527 Pinkerton, Allan, 1819-1884.
  The burglar's fate and the detectives... New York,
G. W. Carleton & co., 1884.
  344 p.   illus.   19 cm.

10528 Pinkerton, Allan, 1819-1884.
  Claude Melnotte as a detective, and other stories. By
Allan Pinkerton... 15th thousand. Chicago, W. B. Keen,
Cooke & co., 1875.

6 p. 1., [9]-282 p.   front., plates, facsims,   19 1/2 cm.
CONTENTS.-Claude Melnotte as a detective.-L'envoi; sequel.
-The two sisters: or, The avenger.-The Frenchman and the
bills of exchange.

10529 Pinkerton, Allan, 1819-1884.
     The expressman and the detective. By Allan Pinkerton.
Chicago, W. B. Keen, Cooke & co., 1874.
     278 p. front., plates.   19 cm. (Half-title: Allan
Pinkerton's detective stories)

10530 Pinkerton, Allan, 1819-1884.
     The spiritualists and the detectives. By Allan Pinkerton...
New York, G. W. Carleton & co., London, S. Low & co.,
1878.
     xii, [13]-354 p. plates.   19 cm. (Half-title: Allan
Pinkerton's detective stories, vol. V)

10531 [Pise, Charles Constantine] 1802-1866.
     Father Rowland, a North American tale... 2d ed., enl.
Baltimore, F. Lucas, jr. [c1831]
     iv, [5]-195 p.   15 cm.
     Published anonymously.

10532 Pitrat, John Claudius.
     Paul and Julia; or, The political mysteries, hypocrisy, and
cruelty of the leaders of the church of Rome. By John Claudius
Pitrat... Boston, E. W. Hinks and company, 1855.
     319 p. front., illus.   19 cm.

10533 [Poe, Edgar Allan] 1809-1849.
     The narrative of Arthur Gordon Pym [pseud.] of Nantucket.
Comprising the details of a mutiny and atrocious butchery on
board the American brig Grampus, on her way to the South
seas... With an account of the recapture of the vessel by the
survivors; their shipwreck and subsequent horrible sufferings
from famine... [1st ed.] New-York, Harper & brothers,
1838.
     1 p. 1., [v]-vii, [9]-201 p.   19 cm.

10534 Pomeroy, Marcus Mills, 1833-1896.
     Brick-dust: a remedy for the blues, and a something for

317

people to tale about. By M. M. Pomeroy "Brick" Pomeroy
... New York, G. W. Carleton & co. [etc. , etc.] 1871.
xi, [13]-255 p. incl. front. 5 pl.   19 cm.

10535 Pomeroy, Marcus Mills, 1833-1896.
Gold-dust for the beautifying of lives and homes. By M. M.
Pomeroy ["Brick" Pomeroy] ... New York, G. W. Carleton
[etc. , etc.] 1871.
xi, 13-275 p. incl. front. 5 pl.   19 cm.

10536 [Pomeroy, Marcus Mills] 1833-1896.
Nonsense; or, Hits and criticisms on the follies of the day.
By "Brick" Pomeroy [pseud.]... With illustrations by J. H.
Howard. New York, G. W. Carleton & co. [etc. , etc.] 1868.
3 p. 1. , [9]-274 p. 6 pl.   19 cm.

10537 Pomeroy, Marcus Mills, 1833-1896.
Our Saturday nights, by Mark M. Pomeroy... With thirty
illustrations by H. L. Stephens. New York, Carleton
[etc. , etc.] 1870.
2 p. 1. , [vii]-xvi, 17-271 p. illus.   19 cm.
On back of cover: By "Brick" Pomeroy.

10538 [Pomeroy, Marcus Mills] 1833-1896.
Sense; or, Saturday-night musings and thoughtful papers.
By "Brick" Pomeroy [pseud.]... With illustrations by J. H.
Howard. New York, G. W. Carleton & co. [etc. , etc.] 1868.
2 p. 1. , [7]-273 p. 6 pl.   19 cm.

10539 Pool, Maria Louise, 1841-1898.
Against human nature, a novel, by Maria Louise Pool...
New York, Harper & brothers, 1895.
2 p. 1. , 361 p.   19 cm.

10540 Pool, Maria Louise, 1841- 1898.
Dally, by Maria Louise Pool... New York, Harper &
brothers, 1891.
iv, 280 p.   19 cm.

10541 Pool, Maria Louise, 1841-1898.
A golden sorrow. Chicago, H. S. Stone, 1898.
441 p.   20 cm.

10542 Pool, Maria Louise, 1841-1898.
       In a dike shanty, by Maria Louise Pool. Chicago, Stone
& Kimball, 1896.
       4 p. 1 , 7-231 p. , 1 1.   17 1/2 cm.

10543 Pool, Maria Louise, 1841-1898.
       In Buncombe County, by Maria Louise Pool. Chicago,
H. S. Stone & company, 1896.
       1 p. 1. , 295 p. 1 1.   18 cm.

10544 Pool, Maria Louise, 1841-1898.
       In the first person, a novel, by Maria Louise Pool...
New York, Harper & brothers, 1896.
       2 p. 1. , 315 p.   19 cm.
       Sequel: The Meloon Farm.

10545 Pool, Maria Louise, 1841-1898.
       Sand 'n' bushes, by Maria Louise Pool. Chicago & New
York, H. S. Stone & company, 1899.
       3 p. 1. , 364 p.   19 1/2 cm.

10546 Poor, Agnes Blake, d. 1922.
       Boston neighbors in town and out, by Agnes Blake Poor.
New York and London, G. P. Putnam's sons, 1898.
       iii, 321 p.   front.   18 cm.
       CONTENTS.-Our Tolstoi Club.-A little fool.-Why I
married Eleanor.-The story of a wall-flower.-Poor Mr.
Ponsonby.-Modern Vengeance.-Three cups of tea.-The
tramp's wedding.

10547 A poor fellow. By the author of "Which: the right, or the left?"
   ... New York, Dick & Fitzgerald, 1858.
       480 p.   18 1/2 cm.

10548 Porter, Miss C   B   ed.
       The silver cup of sparkling drops, from many fountains
for the friends of temperance. Ed. by Miss C. B. Porter...
Buffalo, Derby and co. , 1852.
       3 p. 1. , [v]-vi, [7]-312 p.   19 cm.
       Added t.-p. , engraved.

10549 Porter, Calvin.

Leslie Wilmot: or, Witchcraft. By Calvin Porter. Boston, F. Gleason, 1848.
1 p. 1. , [5]-50 p.   23 cm.
p. [47]-50: "Shopping with a country cousin. A sketch of city life."

10550 Porter, Linn Boyd, 1851-1916.
Caring for no man; a novel, by Linn Boyd Porter. Boston, W. F. Gill & company, 1875.
173 p.   24 cm.

10551 [Porter, Linn Boyd] 1851-1916.
Young Miss Giddy. By Albert Ross [pseud.]... New York, G. W. Dillingham, 1893.
1 p. 1. , v-viii. 9-343 p.   19 cm.

10552 Porter, Mrs. Lydia Ann (Emerson) 1816-1898.
Married for both worlds. By Mrs. A. E. Porter... Boston, Lee and Shepard; New York, Lee, Shepard and Dillingham, 1871.
3 p. 1. , 9-281 p.   17 cm.

10553 Porter, Mrs. Lydia Ann (Emerson) 1816-1898.
My hero; or, Contrasted lives. By Mrs. A. E. Porter... Boston, D. Lothrop & co.; Dover, N. H., G. T. Day & co., 1872.
332 p.   front., plates.   17 1/2 cm.

10554 Porter, Rose, 1845-1906.
Foundations; or, Castles in the air. By Rose Porter... New York, A. D. F. Randolph & co. [c1871]
194 p.   18 cm.

10555 Porter, Rose, 1845-1906.
Summer drift-wood for the winter fire. By Rose Porter. New York, A. D. F. Randolph & co., 1870.
173 p.   18 cm.
Sequel: The winter fire.

10556 Porter, Rose, 1845-1906.
Uplands and lowlands; or, Three chapters in a life. By Rose Porter... New York, A. D. F. Randolph & company

[c1872]
     3 p. 1. , 5-303 p.   18 cm.

10557 Porter, Rose, 1845-1906.
     The winter fire. A sequel to "Summer drift-wood". By
Rose Porter... New York, A. D. F. Randolph & company
[c1874]
     1 p. 1. , 5-231 p.   18 cm.

10558 Potwin, Mrs. H   K
     Ruby Duke. By Mrs. H. K. Potwin. Boston, Lee and
Shepard; New York, Lee, Shepard, and Dillingham, 1872.
     iv, [5]-421 p.   18 cm.

10559 [Pratt, Mrs. Ella (Farman)] 1843-1907.
     A white hand. A story of noblesse oblige. By Ella
Farman... Boston, D. Lothrop & co.; Dover, N. H. , G. T.
Day & co. , 1875.
     251 p. incl. front.   18 1/2 cm.

10560 Pray, Isaac Clarke, 1813-1869.
     Prose and verse, from the port folio of an editor, by
Isaac C. Pray, jr. ... Boston, Russell, Shattuck and co.,
1836.
     186, [2] p.   19 cm.
     Prose includes "Sketches of American poets" (p. 25-40)
and "English bards: Samuel Taylor Coleridge, William
Wordsworth, Robert Southey" (p. 54-64)

10561 Prentiss, Mrs. Elizabeth (Payson) 1818-1878.
     Aunt Jane's hero. By E. Prentiss... New York, A. D.
F. Randolph & co. [1871]
     292 p.   19 1/2 cm.

10562 [Prentiss, Mrs. Elizabeth (Payson)] 1818-1878.
     Fred, and Maria, and me. By the author of "The flower
of the family". Illustrated by W. Magrath. New York, C.
Scribner & company, 1868.
     3 p. 1. , [3]-71 p. front. , plates.   17 cm.

10563 Prentiss, Mrs. Elizabeth (Payson) 1818-1878.
     Pemaquid; a story of old times in New England. By Mrs.

Elizabeth Prentiss... New York, Anson D. F. Randolph
and company [c1877]
  370 p. incl. front. , plates.   19 cm.

10564 Prentiss, Mrs. Elizabeth (Payson) 1818-1878.
      Stepping heavenward. By E. Prentiss... New York, A. D.
   F. Randolph & co. , 1870.
      426 p.   19 1/2 cm.

10565 Preston, Harriet Waters, 1843-1911.
      Aspendale. By Harriet W. Preston... Boston, Roberts
   brothers, 1871.
      1 p. 1. , [5]-219 p.   17 cm.

10566 Preston, Harriet Waters, 1843-1911.
      Love in the nineteenth century. A fragment. By Harriet
   W. Preston... Boston, Roberts brothers, 1873.
      2 p. 1. , 153 p.   18 cm.

10567 [Price, William] 1794?-1868.
      Clement Falconer; or, The memoirs of a young Whig...
   Baltimore, N. Hickman, 1838.
      2 v.   19 1/2 cm.

10568 Priest, Josiah, 1788-1851.
      The robber; or, A narrative of Pye and the highwayman:
   being a detailed and particular account of an attempted
   robbery of the inn of John Pye, between the cities of Albany
   and Troy, N. Y. in 1808... Together with a history of the
   Old men of the mountain, or, The gold hunters of Joes hills.
   Now first published. By Josiah Priest... Albany, Printed
   by Stone and Munsell, 1836.
      32 p.   illus.   24 cm.

10569 Priest, Josiah, 1788-1851.
      Stories of early settlers in the wilderness: embracing
   the life of Mrs. Priest... with various and interesting accounts
   of others: the first raftsmen of the Susquehannah: a short account of Brant, the British Indian chief: and of the massacre
   of Wyoming. Embellished with a large... engraving. By
   Josiah Priest... Albany, Printed by J. Munsell, 1837.
      40 p.   fold. pl.   24 1/2 cm.

10570 Priest, Josiah, 1788-1851.
      Stories of the revolution. With an account of the lost child
of the Delaware; Wheaton and the panther, &c. ... By Josiah
Priest. Now first published. Albany, Printed by Hoffman
and White, 1836.
      32 p.   fold. pl.   22 1/2 cm.
      Another edition of same year contains one more article.
      CONTENTS. -The captive boys of Rensselaerville. -The
feats and intrepidity of Colonel Harper. -The escape of
Cowley and Sawyer from the Indians. -The escape of the
British Indians when Burgoyne was taken. -The escape of
McKean's scouting party in Otsego county. -The story of the
Hessian woman in the camp of Burgoyne. -The five prisoners
of Brandt at the massacre of Cherry valley. -The wonderful
preservation of Mrs. Moore, when a prisoner among the
Indians. -The lost child of the Delaware. -Wheaton and the
panther. -La Fayette and the Indian girl of Illinois. -The
contest between three Indians and one white man.

10571 Prime, William Cowper, 1825-1905.
      I go a-fishing, by W. C. Prime. New York, Harper &
brothers, 1873.
      365 p.   21 cm.

10572 [Prime, William Cowper] 1825-1905.
      Later years. By the author of "The old house by the river,"
and "The Owl Creek letters." New York, Harper & brothers,
1854.
      xiv p., 1 1., [17]-353 p.   18 1/2 cm.

10573 [Prime, William Cowper] 1825-1905.
      The old house by the river. By the author of The Owl
Creek letters. New York, Harper & brothers, 1853.
      318 p.   19 cm.

10574 [Prince, George] b. 1817.
      Rambles in Chili, and life among the Araucanian Indians,
in 1836. By "Will the Rover." Thomaston [Me.] D. J.
Starrett, 1851.
      2 p. 1., 9-88 p   23 cm.

10575 Prince, Mrs. Helen Choate (Pratt) 1857-

The story of Christine Rochefort, by Helen Choate Prince
... Boston and New York, Houghton, Mifflin and company,
1895.
313 p.   19 cm.

10576 The princess of the moon. A Confederate fairy story. Written
by a lady of Warrenton, Va. Warrenton, Va. [Baltimore,
Md., Printed at the Sun book and job office, 1869]
72 p.   front.   15 cm.

10577 Pugh, Mrs. Eliza Lofton (Phillips) 1841–
In a crucible: a novel. By Mrs. Eliza Lofton Pugh...
Philadelphia, Claxton, Remsen & Haffelfinger; New Orleans,
J. A. Gresham, 1872.
x, 5–389 p.   18 1/2 cm.

10578 Pugh, Mrs. Eliza Lofton (Phillips) 1841–
Not a hero. A novel. By Mrs. Eliza Lofton Pugh. New-
York, Blelock & co., 1867.
131 p.   23 cm.

10579 [Pullen, Charles Henry]
Miss Columbia's public school; or, Will it blow over! By
a cosmopolitan. With 72 illustrations by Thomas Nast...
New York, F. B. Felt & co., 1871.
1 p. l., [7]–82 p.   illus. pl.   19 cm.
Title vignette.

10580 Puritan, Job, pseud.
Household tales. By Job Puritan... Boston, J. Munroe
and company, 1861.
3 p. l., 5–6 [9]–367 p.   19 1/2 cm.
CONTENTS. –The old windmill. –The trial of genius. –The
profane swearer. –Love a victor. –Dora Norton. –The forest
bride. –A will and a way. –Married for a dinner. –Stella Lea.
–The betrayed. –The skipper's daughter. –The Sabbath
breakers.

10581 [Putnam, Mrs. Mary Traill Spence (Lowell)] 1810–1898.
Fifteen days. An extract from Edward Colvil's journal...
Boston, Ticknor and Fields, 1866.
2 p. l., 299 [1] p.   18 cm.

324

Edward Colvil, pseud. of the author.

10582 [Putnam, Mrs. Mary Traill Spence (Lowell)] 1810–1898.
Recond of an obscure man... Boston, Ticknor and Fields,
1861.
1 p. 1., 216 p.　　18 cm.

Q

10583 [Quincy, Edmund] 1808–1877.
Wensley: a story without a moral. Boston, Ticknor and
Fields, 1854.
1 p. 1., 302 p.　　19 cm.

R

10584 [Ram, Stopford James]
Greatness in little things; or, Way-side violets. By
Ruth Vernon [pseud.]... New York, Dayton & Wentworth
[etc.] Cincinnati, H. M. Rulison, 1854.
2 p. 1., 11–322 p. front.　　19 1/2 cm.
Published in 1859 under title: The bride of love.

10585 [Ram, Stopford James]
Unseen hand. By Ruth Vernon [pseud.] Cincinnati, J. R.
Hawley, 1863.
1 p. 1., vii–x, 11–321 p. incl. plates.　　20 cm.

10586 Ramon, the rover of Cuba, the personal narrative of that
celebrated pirate. Tr. from the original Spanish. Boston,
Richardson, Lord and Holbrook, 1829.
xii [13]–162 p.　　18 cm.

10587 [Randolph, Paschal Beverly] b. 1825.

Dealings with the dead; the human soul, its migrations and its transmigrations. Penned by the Rosicrucian... Utica, N. Y., M. J. Randolph, 1861-'62.
    2 p. l., [3]-268 p.   18 1/2 cm.
    Preface signed: G. D. S.

10588 [Rankin, Fannie W   ]
    True to him ever; a novel. By F. W. R. New York, T. W. Carleton & co., 1874.
    2 p. l., [7]-290 p.   18 1/2 cm.

10589 [Ransom, James Birchett]
    Osceola; or, Fact and fiction: a tale of the Seminole war. By a Southerner... New-York, Printed by Harper & brothers, 1838.
    150 p. front. (port.)   19 cm.

10590 Raybold, George A
    The fatal feud; or, Passion and piety. A moral tale. By Rev. George A. Raybold... New-York, Lane & Scott, 1850.
    156 p.   15 1/2 cm.

10591 [Raymond, Rossiter Worthington] 1840-1918.
    Brave hearts. An American novel. By Robertson Gray [pseud.] Illustrated by Darley, Beard, Stephens, and Kendrick. New York, J. B. Ford and company, 1873.
    iv, 284 p.   front., plates.   19 cm.

10592 Rayner, Emma, d. 1926.
    Visiting the sin; a tale of mountain life in Kentucky and Tennessee, by Emma Rayner. Boston, Small, Maynard & company, 1900.
    vi. 448 p.   20 cm.

10593 Read, Opie Percival, 1852-1939.
    Bolanyo; a novel, by Opie Read... Chicago, Way & Williams, 1897.
    3 p. l., 309 p. front.   17 1/2 cm.
    Title within ornamental border.

10594 Read, Opie Percival, 1852-1939.

The colossus, a story, by Opie Read... Chicago, F. J. Schultz & company, 1893.
254 p.   19 1/2 cm.

10595 Read, Opie Percival, 1852-1939.
In the Alamo, by Opie Read... Chicago and New York, Rand, McNally, and company [c1900]
2 p. l., 367 p. front.   20 cm.
A novel.

10596 Read, Opie Percival, 1852-1939.
The Jucklins; a novel, by Opie Read... Chicago, Laird & Lee [1896]
2 p. l., [9]-291 p. front., pl.   20 cm.

10597 Read, Opie Percival, 1852-1939.
Judge Elbridge, by Opie Read... Chicago and New York, Rand, McNally & co., 1899.
205 p. front., plates.   19 cm.

10598 Read, Opie Percival, 1852-1939.
Up Terrapin River. By Opie P. Read. Chicago and New York, Rand, McNally & company, 1889.
226 p. incl. front.   19 cm.
CONTENTS. -Up Terrapin River. -Behind a bugler. -In the Cumberland Mountains. -A commercial rip-snorter. -His friend Flanders. -Hendricks knew it. -Wearing out the carpet. -A bridegroom. -Dave Summers. -The Captain's romance. -Old Tildy.

10599 Read, Thomas Buchanan, 1822-1872.
Paul Redding: a tale of the Brandywine. By T. B. Read. 2d ed. New York, Philadelphia, E. Ferrett & co., 1845.
136 p.   19 1/2 cm.

10600 Realities of life: sketches designed for the improvement of the head and heart. By a philanthropist. New Haven, S. Babcock, 1839.
3 p. l., [9]-197 p.   18 cm.

10601 Recollections of the United States army. A series of thrilling tales and sketches. By an American soldier. Boston, J.

Munroe and company, 1845.
xi, [1] 167 p. incl. front. , plates.   16 1/2 cm.

10602 [Reed, Isaac George, jr.]
Erring, yet noble. A tale of and for women... New-York,
J. Bradburn, 1865.
vi, [7]-569 p.   19 cm.

10603 Reeder, Louise.
Currer Lyle; or, The stage in romance, and the stage in
reality: by Louise Reeder. New-York, E. D. Long, 1856.
vii, [9]-361 p.   19 cm.

10604 Rees, James, 1802-1885.
Mysteries of city life; or, Stray leaves from the world's
book, being a series of tales, sketches, incidents, and scenes,
founded upon the notes of a home missionary. By James
Rees... Philadelphia, J. W. Moore, 1849.
8, [13]-408 p.   18 1/2 cm.

10605 [Reeves, Marian Calhoun Legare]
Wearithorne; or, In the light of to-day. By "Fadette"
[pseud.]... Philadelphia, J. B. Lippincott & co. , 1872.
214 p.   19 cm.

10606 Reflections and tales. By a lady of Philadelphia. Philadelphia,
The authoress, 1830.
108 p.   14 1/2 cm.

10607 Remick, Martha.
Agnes Stanhope: a tale of English life. By Miss Martha
Remick... Boston, J. M. Usher, 1862.
2 p. 1. , [vii]-viii, [9]-444 p.   18 1/2 cm.

10608 Remington, Frederic, 1861-1909.
Men with the bark on, by Frederic Remington; illustrated
by the author. New York and London, Harper & brothers,
1900.
6 p. 1. , 3-208, [1] p. front. , plates.   19 cm.
CONTENTS.-The war dreams.-The bowels of a battle-ship.
-The honor of the troop.-A sketch by MacNei.-The story of
the dry leaves.-A failure of justice.-Sorrows of Don Tomas

Pidal, reconcentrado.-When a document is official.-The
white forest.-They bore a hand.-The trouble brothers: Bill
and the wolf.-With the fifth corps.

10609 Retrenchment; or, Ways and means. Family sketches in the
nineteenth century... Boston, Whipple & Damrell, 1841.
106 p.   16 cm.

10610 Reynolds, Elhanan Winchester, 1827-1867.
The new doctrine: or, Teachings and tendencies. By
E. Winchester Reynolds... Fredonia, N. Y., Printed at
the Censor office, 1848.
iv, [5]-144 p.   21 1/2 cm.

10611 [Reynolds, Elhanan Winchester] 1827-1867.
The Tangletown letters: being the reminiscences, observations, and opinions of Timotheus Trap, esq. Including a
report of the great mammothic reform convention. Ed. by
the author of "Records of the Bubbleton parish"... Buffalo,
Wanzer, McKim & co., 1856.
300 p.   front., plates.   19 cm.

10612 Reynolds, William D
Miss Martha Brownlow; or, The heroine of Tennessee. A
truthful and graphic account of the many perils and priva-
tions endured by Miss Martha Brownlow... daughter of the
celebrated Parson Brownlow, during her residence with her
father in Knoxville. By Major W. D. Reynolds... Philadelphia, Barclay & co., [c1863]
1 p. l., 21-49 [1] p.   illus.   24 cm.
First published under title: The Rebel fiend.

10613 Rich, Benjamin E.
Mr. Durant of Salt Lake City, "That Mormon"... Salt
Lake City, George Q. Cannon & sons co., printers, 1893.
320 p.   front. (port.)   18 cm.
"Quotations from the sermons of President Brigham
Young": p. 285-320.

10614 [Richards, Mrs. A   M   ]
Memories of a grandmother. By a lady of Massachusetts
... Boston, Gould and Lincoln; New York, Sheldon, Lamport

& Blakeman, 1854.
    141 p.   18 1/2 cm.
    "Editor's preface" signed: G. K.

10615 Richards, C   French.
    John Guilderstring's sin. A novel. By C. French
    Richards... New York, Carleton, 1864.
    1 p. 1. , [v]-vi, [7]-244 p.   19 cm.

10616 Richards, Mrs. Maria (Tolman) 1821-
    Life in Israel; or, Portraitures of Hebrew character. By
    Maria T. Richards... New York, Sheldon, Blakeman and
    company; Chicago, S. C. Griggs and company, 1857.
    xi, 13-389 p.   19 1/2 cm.

10617 Riddle, Albert Gallatin, 1816-1902.
    Alice Brand. A romance of the capital. By A. G.
    Riddle... New York, D. Appleton and company, 1875.
    384 p.   19 1/2 cm.

10618 [Riddle, Albert Gallatin] 1816-1902.
    Bart Ridgeley; a story of northern Ohio. Boston, Nichols
    and Hall, 1873.
    iv, [5]-374 p.   18 1/2 cm.

10619 Riddle, Albert Gallatin, 1816-1902.
    The portrait; a romance of the Cuyahoga Valley. By
    A. G. Riddle... Boston, Nichols & Hall; Cleveland, Cobb,
    Andrews & co. , 1874.
    iv, 5-378 p.   18 cm.

10620 Riley, Henry Hiram, 1813-1888.
    Puddleford, and its people. By H. H. Riley... New York,
    S. Hueston, 1854.
    xii, [9]-269 p.   front. , plates.   19 1/2 cm.

10621 Riley, Henry Hiram, 1813-1888.
    The Puddleford papers; or, Humors of the West. By H. H.
    Riley... New York, Derby & Jackson; Cincinnati, H. W.
    Derby & co. , 1857.
    xiii, [9]-353 p.   front. , plates.   18 1/2 cm.

10622 Ritchie, Mrs. Anna Cora (Ogden) Mowatt, 1819-1870.
Fairy fingers. A novel. By Anna Cora Ritchie... New York, Carleton, 1865.
1 p. 1. , v-vi, 7-460 p.   18 cm.

10623 Ritchie, Mrs. Anna Cora (Ogden) Mowatt, 1819-1870.
Mimic life; or, Before and behind the curtain. A series of narratives, by Anna Cora Ritchie (formerly Mrs. Mowatt) ... Boston, Ticknor and Fields, 1856.
xiv p. , 1 1. , [9]-408 p.   front.   17 1/2 cm.

10624 Ritchie, Mrs. Anna Cora (Ogden) Mowatt, 1819-1870.
The mute singer. A novel. By Anna Cora Ritchie (Mowatt)... New York, Carleton, 1866.
1 p. 1. , [v]-vi, [7]-360 p.   18 1/2 cm.

10625 Ritchie, Mrs. Anna Cora (Ogden) Mowatt, 1819-1870.
Twin roses. A narrative. By Anna Cora Ritchie... Boston, Ticknor and Fields, 1857.
x, 273 p.   18 1/2 cm.

10626 Rives, Judith Page (Walker) "Mrs. W. C. Rives," 1802-1882.
Home and the world. New York, D. Appleton, 1857.
408 p.   20 cm.

10627 [Rives, Judith Page (Walker)] "Mrs. W. C. Rives," 1802-1882.
Tales and souvenirs of a residence in Europe. By a lady of Virginia. Philadelphia, Lea & Blanchard, 1842.
vii, [9]-301 p.   20 cm.

10628 Robb, John S
Kaam; or, Daylight. The Arapahoe half-breed, a tale of the Rocky mountains... Boston, "Star spangled banner" office, 1847.
212 p.   illus. ,   22 cm.

10629 Robb, John S
Streaks of squatter life, and far-West scenes. A series of humorous sketches descriptive of incidents and character in the wild West. To which are added other miscellaneous pieces. By "Solitaire," (John S. Robb, of St. Louis, Mo.) ... Philadelphia, Carey and Hart, 1847.

2 p. 1., iii-x, 11-187 p.   front., plates.   19 1/2 cm.
(On cover: Carey & Hart's library of humorous American
works)
Added t.-p., illustrated.
Published later under title: Western scenes.

10630 [Roberts, Maggie]
Home scenes during the rebellion. By Eiggam Strebor
[anagr.] New York, J. F. Trow & son, printers, 1875.
xi, 204 p.   front., plates.   21 1/2 cm.

10631 Robinson, Benjamin.
Dolores: a tale of disappointment and distress. Compiled,
arranged and edited from the journal, letters, and other mss.
of Roland Vernon, esq.: and from contributions by and conversations with the Vernon family, of Rushbrook, in Carolina.
By Benjamin Robinson... New York, E. J. Hale & sons,
1868.
180 p.   22 1/2 cm.

10632 Robinson, John Hovey, 1825-
The Boston conspiracy; or, The royal police. A tale of
1773-1775. By J. H. Robinson. Boston, Dow & Jackson,
1847.
1 p. 1., [7]-110 p.   20 cm.

10633 Robinson, Mrs. John Hovey.
Evelyn, the child of the revolution. A romance of real
life. By Mrs. J. H. Robinson, of Boston. Boston,
Hotchkiss & company, 1850.
104 p.   25 cm.
Cover-title: Evelyn: the child of the revolution. A tale
of Boston and vicinity.

10634 Robinson, Martha Harrison.
Helen Erskine. By Mrs. M. Harrison Robinson. Philadelphia, J. B. Lippincott & co., 1870.
255 p.   19 cm.

10635 Robinson, Mrs. Mary Dummett (Nauman) 1839-1920.
Clyde Wardleigh's promise. By Mary D. Nauman...
Philadelphia, Claxton, Remsen & Haffelfinger, 1873.

2 p. 1., xi-xii, 13-300 p.   19 cm.

10636   Robinson, Mrs. Mary Dummett (Nauman) 1839-1920.
        Sidney Elliott: a novel. By M. D. Nauman... Philadelphia,
        Claxton, Remsen & Haffelfinger, 1869.
        xi, 13-235 p.   19 cm.

10637   Robinson, Mrs. Mary Dummett (Nauman) 1839-1920.
        Twisted threads. By M. D. Nauman... Philadelphia,
        Claxton, Remsen & Haffelfinger, 1870.
        2 p. 1., vii-xii, 13-202 p.   19 1/2 cm.

10638   Robinson, Solon, 1803-1880.
        Hot corn: life scenes in New York illustrated. Including
        the story of little Katy, Madalina, the rag-picker's daughter,
        wild Maggie, &c. With original designs, engraved by N. Orr.
        By Solon Robinson... New York, De Witt and Davenport,
        1854.
        3 p. 1., v-xii, [13]-408 p.   plates.   18 1/2 cm.
        Added t.-p., engr.

10639   Robinson, Solon, 1803-1880.
        Me-won-i-toc. A tale of frontier life and Indian character;
        exhibiting traditions, superstitions, and character of a race
        that is passing away. A romance of the frontier. By Solon
        Robinson... New York, New York news company, 1867.
        133 p.   25 cm.

10640   [Robinson, Mrs. Thérèsa Albertine Louise (von Jacob)] 1797-
        1870.
        Heloise; or, The unrevealed secret. A tale. By Talvi
        [pseud.]... New York, D. Appleton & company; Philadelphia,
        G. S. Appleton, 1850.
        1 p. 1., [vii]-viii, [9]-264 p.   18 1/2 cm.

10641   [Robinson, Mrs. Thérèsa Albertine Louise (von Jacob)] 1797-
        1870.
        Life's discipline: a tale of the annals of Hungary. By
        Talvi [pseud.] ... New York, D. Appleton & co.; Phila-
        delphia, G. S. Appleton, 1851.
        171 p.   18 1/2 cm.

10642 Roddan, John T
John O'Brien; or, The orphan of Boston. A tale of real
life. By Rev. John T. Roddan. Boston, P. Donahoe, 1856.
1 p. 1., 264 p.   19 1/2 cm.

10643 Roe, Edward Payson, 1838-1888.
Barriers burned away. By the Rev. Edward P. Roe...
New York, Dodd & Mead, 1872.
1 p. 1., [v]-x, [7]-488 p.   illus.   18 1/2 cm.

10644 Roe, Edward Payson, 1838-1888.
A day of fate. By Rev. E. P. Roe... New York, Dodd,
Mead & company [c1880]
viii p., 1 1., [11]-450 p.   19 cm.

10645 Roe, Edward Payson, 1838-1888.
A face illumined. New York, Dodd, Mead and Company
[n.p. 1878]
658 p.   19 cm.

10646 Roe, Edward Payson, 1838-1888.
From jest to earnest. By Rev. E. P. Roe... New York,
Dodd, Mead & company, [1875 ?]
2 p. 1., [7]-548 p.   19 cm.

10647 Roe, Edward Payson, 1838-1888.
He fell in love with his wife, by Edward P. Roe... New
York, Dodd, Mead, and company [c1886]
iv, 333 p.   19 1/2 cm.

10648 Roe, Edward Payson, 1838-1888.
His sombre rivals. By Edward P. Roe... New York,
Dodd, Mead & company [c1883]
viii, [9]-487 p.   19 cm.

10649 Roe, Edward Payson, 1838-1888.
"Miss Lou," by Edward P. Roe... New York, Dodd,
Mead and company, 1888.
vi, 368 p.   19 cm.

10650 Roe, Edward Payson, 1838-1888.
Near to nature's heart. By Rev. E. P. Roe... New York,

334

Dodd, Mead & company, 1876.
1 p. 1., [7]-536 p.   19 cm.

10651 Roe, Edward Payson, 1838-1888.
Opening a chestnut burr. By Rev. E. P. Roe... New
York, Dodd & Mead [1874]
2 p. 1., [7]-561 p.   19 1/2 cm.

10652 Roe, Edward Payson, 1838-1888.
An original belle, by Edward P. Roe... New York, Dodd,
Mead & company [c1885]
x, 533 p.   19 1/2 cm.

10653 Roe, Edward Payson, 1838-1888.
Taken alive, and other stories; with an autobiography, by
Edward P. Roe... New York, Dodd, Mead, and company
[c1889]
vi p., 7-375 p. front. (port.)   20 cm.
CONTENTS.-"A native author called Roe".-Taken alive.
-Found yet lost.-Queen of spades.-An unexpected result.-A
Christmas-eve suit.-Three Thanksgiving kisses.- Susie
Rolliffe's Christmas.-Jeff's treasure.-Caught on the ebb-tide.
Christmas eve in war times.-A brave little Quakeress.

10654 Roe, Edward Payson, 1838-1888.
An unexpected result, and other stories, New York,
Dodd, Mead [1883]
134 p.   18 cm.
CONTENTS.-An unexpected result.-Christmas Eve in
war times.-Three Thanksgiving kisses.

10655 Roe, Edward Payson, 1838-1888.
What can she do? By Rev. E. P. Roe... New York, Dodd
& Mead [c1873]
xii, 509 p.   19 cm.

10656 Roe, Edward Payson, 1838-1888.
A young girl's wooing. New York, Dodd, Mead [1884]
482 p.   19 cm.

10657 Roe, Edward Reynolds.
The gray and the blue; a story founded on incidents

connected with the war for the Union. By E. R. Roe.
Chicago, Rand, McNally [1884]
292 p.   20 cm.

10658 [Roe, Mary Abigail]
Free, yet forging their own chains. By C. M. Cornwall
[pseud.] New York, Dodd, Mead & company [c1876]
1 p. 1. , [5]-378 p.   19 1/2 cm.

10659 [Rogers, Rev. George]
Adventures of Elder Triptolemus Tub; comprising important and startling disclosures concerning hell; its magnitude,
morals, employments, climate &c. , all very satisfactorily
authenticated. To which is added, The old man of the hillside. Boston, A. Tompkins, 1846.
vi, [7]-197 p. incl. front. , illus. , pl.   16 cm.
Publisher's lettering: Adventures of Elder Tub. G.
Rodgers.

10660 Rogers, Lebbeus Harding, 1847-
... The kite trust (a romance of wealth) by Lebbeus Harding
Rogers. [3d ed.] New York, Kite trust publishing company
[c1900]
vi, 475 p.   front. (port.)   19 1/2 cm.

10661 Rohlfs, Mrs. Anna Katharine (Green) 1846-1935.
Agatha Webb, by Anna Katharine Green... New York and
London, G. P. Putnam's sons, 1899.
vi p. , 1 1. , 360 p.   18 cm.

10662 Rohlfs, Mrs. Anna Katharine (Green) 1846-1935.
Behind closed doors, by A. K. G. (Mrs. Charles) Rohlfs
... New York & London, G. P. Putnam's sons. The
Knickerbocker Press, 1888.
v, 523 p.   19 cm.

10663 Rohlfs, Mrs. Anna Katharine (Green) 1846-1935.
The circular study, by Anna Katharine Green Rohlfs...
New York, McClure, Phillips & co. , 1900.
2 p. 1. , 289 p. diagr.   19 cm.

10664 Rohlfs, Mrs. Anna Katharine (Green) 1846-1935.

Cynthia Wakeham's money... New York and London, G.
P. Putnam's sons [1892]
    iv, 336 p.   front.   19 1/2 cm.

10665 Rohlfs, Mrs. Anna Katharine (Green) 1846-1935.
       Doctor Izard, by A. K. G. (Mrs. Charles) Rohlfs...
New York [etc.] G. P. Putnam's sons, 1895.
       v, 268 p.   front.   17 1/2 cm.

10666 Rohlfs, Mrs. Anna Katharine (Green) 1846-1935.
       Marked "personal," by Anna K. G. (Mrs. Charles)
Rohlfs... New York and London, G. P. Putnam's sons,
1893.
       vi, 415 p.   17 cm.

10667 Rohlfs, Mrs. Anna Katharine (Green) 1846-1935.
       Miss Hurd; an enigma, by Anna Katharine Green (Mrs.
Charles Rohlfs) ... New York [etc.] G. P. Putnam's
sons, 1894.
       v, 357 p.   17 1/2 cm.

10668 Rohlfs, Mrs. Anna Katharine (Green) 1846-1935.
       The old stone house and other stories, by Anna Katharine
Green... New York [etc.] G. P. Putnam's sons, 1891.
       2 p. 1., 202 p.   17 1/2 cm.
       CONTENTS.-The old stone house.-A memorable night.-The
black cross.-A mysterious case.-Shall he wed her?

10669 Rollins, Mrs. Clara Harriot (Sherwood) 1874-
       A Burne-Jones head and other sketches, by Clara Sherwood
Rollins. New York, Lovell, Coryell & company, 1894.
       164 p.   front.   19 1/2 cm.
       CONTENTS.-A Burne-Jones head.-Kismet.-Human
sunshine.-Aunt Charlotte.-A chance shot.-A case in point.

10670 The Romantic historian; a series of lights and shadows,
       elucidating American annals... Philadelphia, Hogan &
Thompson, 1834.
       2 p. 1., 315 p.   14 cm.
       CONTENTS.-A midnight tramp in the Jerseys.-The sister
of charity. L. H. Medina.-The Martys [!]-a tale of the
revolution. H. A. L.-The battle of Lexington. J. F.-The

deserter. -The Moravian Indians. -A midnight scene during the revolution. -The victims of revenge. M. A. B. -A tale of St. Domingo. B. B. -Wacousta (an extract)-Croghan. M. K. R. -The Italian bride. E. C. S.

10671 Roosevelt, Robert Barnwell, 1829-1906.
Five acres too much. A truthful elucidation of the attractions of the country, and a careful consideration of the question of profit and loss as involved in amateur farming, with much valuable adivce and instruction to those about pur- chasing large or small places in the rural districts. By Robert B. Roosevelt... New York, Harper & brothers, 1869. xvii, [19]-296 p.   illus.   19 cm.

10672 Roosevelt, Robert Barnwell, 1829-1906.
Progressive petticoats; or, Dressed to death. An auto- biography of a married man. By Robert B. Roosevelt. New York, G. W. Carleton & co [etc. , etc.] 1874. 3 p. 1. , [9]-316 p.   19 cm.

10673 Rosewood, Emma.
Alford and Selina; or, The mystery disclosed, and the reputed orphan restored to a father's embrace. A tale of real life... by Miss Emma Rosewood... Boston, Dow & Jackson, 1845. 30 p.   25 cm.

10674 Ross, Clinton, 1861-1920.
The puppet, by Clinton Ross. New York, Stone & Kimball, 1896. 183 p. , 1 1.   16 1/2 cm.

10675 A Round table of the representative American Catholic novel- ists, at which is served a feast of excellent stories, by Eleanor C. Donnelly... [and others] With portraits, bio- graphical sketches, and bibliography. New York, Cincinnati [etc.] Benziger brothers, 1897. 353 p.   illus. (ports.)   19 1/2 cm.
CONTENTS. -A lost prima donna, by Eleanor C. Donnelly. -The mad penitent of Todi, by Anna H. Dorsey. -Speculum justitae, by Ella L. Dorsey. -How Perseus became a star, by M. F. Egan. -My strange friend, by F. J. Finn. -Gillman

Ogley, by W. Lecky.-In the Quebrada, by Christian Reid. -Shan Dempsey's story, by Mary A. Sadlier.-Mistress Rosamond Trevor, by Anna T Sadlier.-The Baron of Cherubusco, by J. T. Smith.-Joe of Lahaina, by C. W. Stoddard.

10676 Rowson, Mrs. Susanna (Haswell) 1762-1824.
Charlotte Temple. A tale of truth. By Mrs. Rowson... 5th American ed. Harrisburgh, Pennsyl. , Printed for Mathew Carey of Philadelphia, by John Wyeth, 1802.
2 v. in 1.   17 1/2 cm.
Paged continuously.

10677 Rowson, Mrs. Susanna (Haswell) 1762-1824.
Charlotte's daughter: or, The three orphans. A sequel to Charlotte Temple. By Susannah Rowson... To which is prefixed, a memoir of the author. Boston, Richardson & Lord, 1828.
184 p.   18 cm.

10678 Rowson, Mrs. Susanna (Haswell) 1762-1824.
The inquisitor; or, Invisible rambler. In three volumes. By Mrs. Rowson... 2d American ed. ... Philadelphia: Printed for Mathew Carey, Bookseller, South Market Street, near Fourth, 1794.
3 v. in 1.   18 1/2 cm.
Paged continuously.

10679 Rowson, Mrs. Susanna (Haswell) 1762-1824.
Mentoria; or, The young lady's friend... By Mrs. Rowson... Philadelphia: Printed for Robert Campbell, by Samuel Harrison Smith, 1794.
2 v in 1.   17 cm.
Letters of advice to young ladies, interspersed with moral tales, the longest being: Marian and Lydia (including the story of Dorcas) Includes also: Essay on female education; Urganda and Fatima; The incendiary.

10680 Rowson, Mrs. Susanna (Haswell) 1762-1824.
Rebecca; or, The fille de chambre. A novel. By Mrs. Rowson... 2d American ed. , cor. and rev. by the author... Boston, Published by R. P. & C. Williams, J. Belcher,

printer, 1814.
    vi, [7]-249 p.   18 1/2 cm.

10681 [Ruddy, Mrs. Ella (Giles)] 1851-
    Bachelor Ben. By Ella A. Giles... Madison, Wis.,
Atwood & Culver; Chicago, Jansen, McClurg & company,
1875.
    308 p.   20 cm.

10682 Runkel, William M
    Wontus; or, The corps of observation. By Col. William
M. Runkel... Philadelphia, J. B. Lippincott & co., 1874.
    303 p.   front., plates.   19 cm.

10683 Rush, Mrs. Caroline E
    Robert Morton, or The step-mother: a book founded on
fact. Containing Edmund and Ione, Letters from the South,
&c. &c. By Caroline E. Rush. Philadelphia, Crissy &
Markley, 1850.
    vi p., 1 l., 191, [1] p.   front.   19 1/2 cm.

10684 [Rush Rebecca]
    Kelroy, a novel. By a lady of Pennsylvania. Philadelphia:
Published by Bradford and Inskeep, and Inskeep and Bradford,
New York. Jane Aitken, printer, 1812.
    1 p. l., 301 p.   18 1/2 x 11 cm.

10685 [Russell, Charles Wells] 1818-1867.
    Roebuck: a novel. New York, M. Doolady, 1866.
    329 p.   19 1/2 cm.

10686 Ryals, John Vincent.
    Yankee doodle Dixie; or, Love the light of life. An
historical romance, illustrative of life and love in an old
Virginia country home, and also an explanatory account of the
passions, prejudices and opinions which culminated in the
civil war. By J. V. Ryals... Richmond, Va., E. Waddey
co., 1890.
    vii, [1], [9]-532 p.   19 1/2 cm.

10687 Ryan, Mrs. Marah Ellis Martin, 1866-1934.
    A flower of France; a story of old Louisiana. By Marah

340

Ellis Ryan... Chicago, Rand, McNally & company, 1894.
327 p.   20 cm.

10688 Ryan, Mrs. Marah Ellis Martin, 1866-1934.
A pagan of the Alleghanies, by Marah Ellis Ryan...
Chicago and New York, Rand, McNally & company, 1891.
297 p.   20 1/2 cm.   (On cover: Rialto series, no. 38)

10689 Ryan, Mrs. Marah Ellis (Martin) 1866-1934.
Told in the hills; a novel... Chicago and New York, Rand,
McNally & co. , 1891.
362 p.   front.   24 cm.

S

10690 Sabin, Elijah Robinson, 1776-1818.
The life and reflections of Charles Observator: in which
are displayed, the real characters of human life. By Rev.
Elijah R. Sabin... Boston, Printed by Rowe & Hooper,
1816.
271 p.   18 cm.

10691 [Sage, Robert F   ]
Charette: a tale "of lovers' sorrows and their tangled sin"
... New York, G. W. Carleton & co. [etc. , etc.] 1875.
2 p. l. , [7]-327 p.   19 cm.
Published anonymously.

10692 St. Clair, Frank.
Six days in the metropolis; or, Phases of life in town. By
Frank St. Clair... Boston, Redding & company, 1854.
96 p.   23 cm.

10693 St. Clair, Henry, comp.
Tales of terror; or, The mysteries of magic: a selection
of wonderful and supernatural stories, translated from the
Chinese, Turkish, and German. Compiled by Henry St.
Clair... Philadelphia, J. Harding, 1848.

2 v. in 1. front.   18 1/2 cm.
Appeared later, with additions, under title: Evening tales for the winter.
Title vignette.
CONTENTS.-v. 1. The magic dice. The gored huntsman. The Nikkur Holl. Der Freischutz. The story of Judar. The boarwolf. The cavern of death. The mysterious bell. The dervise of Alfouran. Hassan Assar, caliph of Bagdat.-v. 2. The astrologer of the nineteenth century. The Flying Dutchman. The tiger's cave. Peter Rugg, the missing man. The haunted forest. The lonely man of the ocean. The Hungarian horse dealer. The wreckers of St. Agnes.

10694 St. Clar, Robert.
The metropolites; or, Know thy neighbor. A novel. By Robert St. Clar... New York, American news company [c1864]
1 p. 1. , [5]-575 p.   18 1/2 cm.

10695 St. George De Lisle; or, The serpent's sting: a tale of woman's devotion & self-sacrifice... A true and thrilling narrative of crime in high life, in the city of New York. Philadelphia, Barclay & co. [c1858]
1 p. 1. , 9-34. , 1 1. incl. plates. front.   25 cm.

10696 Sanborn, Mary Farley (Sanborn)
It came to pass, by Mary Farley Sanborn. Boston, Lee and Shepard, 1892.
339 p.   18 cm.

10697 Sands, Robert Charles, 1799-1832.
The writings of Robert C. Sands, in prose and verse. With a memoir of the author... New-York, Harper & brothers, 1834.
2 v. front. (port.)   24 cm.
Memoir by Verplanck. cf. Duyckinck, Cyclopaedia of American literature.

10698 [Sargent, Charles Lenox]
The life of Alexander Smith, captain of the island of Pitcairn; one of the mutineers on board His Majesty's ship Bounty; commanded by Lieut. Wm. Bligh. Written by Smith

himself, on the above island, and bringing the accounts from
Pitcairn, down to the year 1815. Boston, Printed by S. T.
Goss, 1819.
    1 p. 1., iii, [9]-240 p.   19 cm.
    "Smith was a Gloucester man, as represented in the story;
but his career, as related by Mr. Sargent, is believed to be
wholly fictitious." - J. J. Babson, History of the town of
Gloucester, 1860, p. 163. (cf. also Sabin, Bibl. amer.,
v. 20, p. 149)
    Smith was afterwards known as John Adams. cf. p. 228.

10699 Sargent, Epes, 1813-1880.
    Peculiar; a tale of the great transition, by Epes Sargent.
[7th ed.] New York, Carleton, 1864.
    iv, 500 p.   18 1/2 cm.

10700 [Sargent, Lucius Manlius] 1786-1867.
    ... As a medicine. Founded on fact. Boston, Whipple
& Damrell; New York, Scofield & Voorhies, 1839.
    155 p.   14 cm.   (On cover: Temperance tales,
v. 6, no. 18)

10701 Sargent, Lucius Manlius, 1786-1867.
    Diary of the Rev. Solomon Spittle... (anon.) Boston,
William White, 1847.
    54 p.   17 cm.

10702 [Sargent, Lucius Manlius] 1786-1867.
    ... Margaret's bridal. Founded on fact. 1st thousand.
Boston, Whipple & Damrell; New York, Scofield and Voorhies [etc., etc.] 1839.
    4, [7]-86 p.   14 cm.   (On cover: Temperance tales,
v. 7, no. 20)

10703 [Sargent, Lucius Manlius] 1786-1867.
    ... My mother's gold ring. Founded on fact. 3d ed.
Boston, Ford and Damrell, 1833.
    iv, [5]-24 p.   14 1/2 cm. [Temperance tales,
v. 1, no. 1]

10704 [Sargent, Lucius Manlius] 1786-1867.
    ... The stage-coach. Founded on fact. 4th ed. Boston,

Whipple & Damrell; New York, Scofield & Voorhies, 1838.
288 p.   15 cm.
At head of title: Number sixteen.
Published anonymously. Appeared also in his "Temperance tales".

10705 Sauzade, John S   1828-
Garret van Horn; or, The beggar on horseback. By
John S. Sauzade. New York, Carleton, 1863.
iv, [5]-376 p.   18 1/2 cm.

10706 Sauzade, John S   1828-
Mark Gildersleeve. A novel. By John S. Sauzade.
New York, G. W. Carleton & co. [etc., etc.] 1873.
1 p. l., [5]-379 p.   18 1/2 cm.

10707 Savage, Timothy.
The Amazonian republic, recently discovered in the
interior of Peru [fictitious description] By ex-Midshipman
Timothy Savage... New York, S. Colman, 1842.
177 p.   17 1/2 cm.

10708 [Savage, Mrs. William T   ]
Miramichi. 2d ed. Boston, Loring, 1865.
v, [7]-232 p.   18 1/2 cm.
Published later under title: Adèle Dubois.

10709 [Savile, Frank Mackenzie]
John Ship, mariner; or, By dint of valor, by Knarf Elivas
[anagram] New York, F. A. Stokes company [c1898]
2 p. l., 304 p.   19 cm.

10710 Sawyer, Mrs. Caroline Mehetabel (Fisher) 1812-1894.
The merchant's widow, and other tales. By Mrs. Caroline
M. Sawyer. New York, P. Price, 1841.
192 p.   15 1/2 cm.
CONTENTS.-The merchant's widow.-The unequal marriage.
-The lonely burial.-The valley of peace.

10711 Saymore, Sarah Emery.
Hearts unveiled; or, "I know you would like him." By
Sarah Emery Saymore. New-York, D. Appleton & company,

344

1852.
>   300 p.   19 cm.

10712 Scenes at Washington; a story of the last generation. By a
>   citizen of Baltimore. New York, Harper & brothers, 1848.
>   197 p.   19 cm.

10713 [Schaefer, Konrad]
>   Agnes Goodmaid. A mystery explained. On the waves of
>   ether sphere. [By] Grete Fischer [pseud.] Chicago, Ill.,
>   1899.
>   4 p. l., 450 p.   front., plates.   20 cm.

10714 Schnap, Julius, pseud.
>   Old times and new; or, A few raps over the knuckles of
>   the present age. By Julius Schnap and Hans van Garretson,
>   the orange blossoms of New Amsterdam... New York,
>   Printed for the publishers, 1846.
>   viii, 93 p.   19 1/2 cm.

10715 Schoolcraft, Mary (Howard) "Mrs. H. R. Schoolcraft."
>   The black gauntlet: a tale of plantation life in South
>   Carolina. By Mrs. Henry R. Schoolcraft... Philadelphia,
>   J. B. Lippincott & co., 1860.
>   x, 11-569 p.   18 1/2 cm.

10716 Schuyler, Montgomery, 1814-1896.
>   The pioneer church; or, The story of a new parish in the
>   West. By the Rev. M. Schuyler... New York, Hurd and
>   Houghton; Boston, E. P. Dutton and company, 1867.
>   vii, 211 p.   front., pl.   18 cm.

10717 Sealsfield, Charles, 1793-1864.
>   The cabin book; or, Sketches of life in Texas. By
>   Seatsfield [!]... New York, J. Winchester, 1844.
>   155 p.
>   Printed in double columns.
>   Issued in 3 pts.
>   Author born Karl Anton Postl.

10718 [Sealsfield, Charles] 1793-1864.
>   Life in the New world; or, Sketches of American society.

By Seatsfield [!] Tr. from the German by Gustavus C.
Hebbe, L. L. D. , and James Mackay, M. A. New York,
J. Winchester [1844]
    349 p.   23 cm.
    Translation of Lebensbilder aus der westlichen Hemi-
sphäre, first published under title, Lebensbilder aus beiden
Hemisphären.

10719 [Sealsfield, Charles] 1893-1864.
    North and South; or, Scenes and adventures in Mexico,
by Seatsfield [!]... Tr. from the German, by J. T. H.
New-York, J. Winchester [1844]
    iv, [5]-118 p.   23 cm.

10720 Seawell, Molly Elliot, 1860-1916.
    The house of Egremont; a novel, by Molly Elliot Seawell;
illustrated by C. M. Relyea. New York, C. Scribner's sons,
1900.
    vi p. , 1 1. , 515 p. front. , 5 pl.   19 1/2 cm.

10721 Seawell, Molly Elliot, 1860-1916.
    The sprightly romance of Marsac, by Molly Elliot Seawell
... illustrated by Gustave Verbeek. New York, C. Scribner's
sons, 1896.
    xii p. , 1 1. , 194 p. incl. front. , illus.   17 1/2 cm.
    The $3000 prize novelette of the New York herald
competition in 1805.

10722 [Sedgwick, Catharine Maria] 1789-1867.
    The boy of Mount Rhigi... By the author of "Redwood,"
"Poor rich man," "Home," etc. , etc. Boston, C. H. Peirce,
1848.
    3 p. 1. , [5]-252 p. front.   17 1/2 cm.
    Added t. -p. , engraved, with vignette.

10723 [Sedgwick, Catharine Maria] 1789-1867.
    Clarence; or, A tale of our own times. By the author of
"Hope Leslie", &c. &c. ... Philadelphia, Carey & Lea,
1830.
    2 v.   20 1/2 cm.

10724 [Sedgwick, Catharine Maria] 1789-1867.

Hope Leslie: or, Early times in the Massachusetts. By the author of "The Linwoods," "Poor rich man"... New York, Harper & brothers, 1842.
    2 v.   18 cm.

10725 [Sedgwick, Catherine Maria] 1789-1867.
    The Linwoods; or, "Sixty years since" in America. By the author of "Hope Leslie," "Redwood," &c. ... New-York, Harper & brothers, 1835.
    2 v.   18 1/2 x 10 1/2 cm.

10726 [Sedgwick, Catharine Maria] 1789-1867.
    Live and let live; or, Domestic service illustrated. By the author of "Hope Leslie", "The Linwoods"... New York, Harper & brothers, 1837.
    viii, [9]-216 p.   16 cm.

10727 [Sedgwick, Catharine Maria] 1789-1867.
    A New-England tale; or, Sketches of New-England character and manners. New York, E. Bliss & E. White, 1822.
    viii, [5]-277 p.   19 1/2 cm.

10728 [Sedgwick, Catharine Maria] 1789-1867.
    The poor rich man, and the rich poor man. By the author of "Hope Leslie," "The Linwoods," &c. ... New York, Harper & brothers, 1836.
    2 p. 1., [3]-186 p.   16 cm.

10729 [Sedgwick, Catharine Maria] 1789-1867.
    Redwood; a tale... New York, E. Bliss and E. White, 1824.
    2 v.   19 x 11 cm.

10730 Sedgwick, Catharine Maria, 1789-1867.
    Tales and sketches by Miss Sedgwick... Philadelphia, Carey, Lea, and Blanchard, 1835.
    3 p. 1., [9]-285 p.   19 x 11 cm.
    CONTENTS. -A reminiscence of federalism.-The Catholic Iroquois.-The country cousin.-Old maids.-The chivalric sailor.-Mary Dyre.-Cacoethes scribendi.-The eldest sister.-St. Catharine's eve.-Romance in real life.-The canary family.

10731 Sedley, Henry, 1835-1899.
        Marian Rooke; or, The quest for fortune. A tale of the
younger world. By Henry Sedley... London, S. Low, son
& Marston, 1865.
        3 v.   19 cm.

10732 [Seemüller, Mrs. Anne Moncure (Crane)] 1838-1872.
        Emily Chester. A novel... Boston, Ticknor and Fields,
1864.
        2 p. l. , 367 p.   19 cm.

10733 Seemüller, Mrs Anne Moncure (Crane) 1838-1872.
        Opportunity. A novel. By Anne Moncure Crane... Boston,
Ticknor and Fields, 1867.
        2 p. l. , [7]-336 p.   19 1/2 cm.

10734 Seemüller, Mrs. Anne Moncure (Crane) 1838-1872.
        Reginald Archer. A novel. By Anne M. Crane Seemuller
... Boston, J. R. Osgood & company, 1871.
        2 p. l. , 7-386 p.   19 cm.

10735 Seldon, William N. , pseud.
        The extraordinary and all-absorbing journal of Wm. N.
Seldon, one of a party of three men who belonged to the
exploring expedition of Sir John Franklin, and who left
the ship Terror, frozen up in ice, in the Arctic ocean, on the
10th day of June, 1850... together with an account of the discovery of a new and beautiful country, inhabited by a strange
race of people... Detroit, Mich. , E. E. Barclay, A. R.
Orton & co. , 1851.
        1 p. l. , 9-36 p. incl. illus. , pl. front.   23 cm.
        Plate printed on both sides.
        "Biography of Sir John Franklin": p. 9-10.

10736 Senter, A   E
        The diddler. By A. E. Senter... New York, M. Doolady,
1868.
        2 p. l. , [ix]-xii, [13]-96, 34, 21, 40 p. front. , illus.
19 cm.
        CONTENTS. -The diddler. -Hodgepodge. -Items from Joe
Miller. -Raising the wind; a farce, by James Kenney.

10737 The Septameron... Philadelphia, D. McKay, 1888.
   171 p. 18 1/2 cm.
   CONTENTS.-Williams, F. H. Boscosel.-Morris, H. S.
  A symphony.-Cooper, S. W. Hazard.-Lüders, C. H. The
  lost elixir.-Cooper, C. C., jr. Parthenope's love.-Schel-
  ling, F. E. Villa Vielle's one mystery.-Fox, W. H. An
  old town tale.

10738 Seton, William, 1835-
   Nat Gregory; or, The old maid's secret. A novel. By
  W. Seton, jr. New-York, Hilton & company, 1867.
   144 p. 23 1/2 cm. (On cover: Library of standrad
  novels)

10739 The seven brothers of Wyoming; or, The brigands of the
  revolution. New York, H. Long & brother [c1850]
   iv., [5]-114 p. 22 cm.

10740 Shadow, Ben, pseud.
   Echoes of a belle; or, A voice from the past. By Ben
  Shadow... New York, G. P. Putnam & co., 1853.
   vi p., 1 l., [9]-196 p. 19 cm.

10741 [Sharon, Thomas]
   Viola; or, Life in the Northwest. By a western man. This
  book illustrates the peculiar habits and customs of the people,
  political life, government transactions, monopolies, and nearly
  every form of fraud, deception, and intrigue, with incidents
  of the Minnesota massacre; by historical sketches, anecdotes,
  and burlesques, all written in an original and interesting style.
  Chicago, R. R. McCabe & co., printers, 1874.
   422 p. front., pl. 19 cm.

10742 [Shaw, Henry Wheeler] 1818-1885.
   Everybody's friend; or, Josh Billing's encyclopedia and
  proverbial philosophy of wit and humor. Profusely illustrated by Thomas Nast and other artists... Hartford,
  Conn., American publishing company, 1874.
   xxxii, 33-617 p. incl. front. (port.) illus. 15 pl.
  23 cm.

10743 [Shaw, Henry Wheeler] 1818-1885.

... Josh Billings, hiz sayings. With comic illustrations.
New York, Carleton, 1866.
    3 p. l., [ix]-xii, [13]-232 p. front., plates.   18 cm.

10744 [Shecut, John Linnaeus Edward Whitridge] 1770-1836.
    Ish-noo-ju-lut-sche; or, The eagle of the Mohawks. A
tale of the seventeenth century... New-York, P. Price,
1841.
    2 v.   16 cm.

10745 [Shecut, John Linnaeus Edward Whitridge] 1770-1836.
    The scout; or, The fast of Saint Nicholas. A tale of the
seventeenth century. By the author of The eagle of the
Mohawks. New-York, C. L. Stickney, 1844.
    viii, [9]-312 p.   15 1/2 cm.

10746 Shelton, Frederick William, 1814-1881.
    Crystalline; or, The heiress of Fall Down castle. A
romance. By F. W. Shelton... New York, C. Scribner,
1854.
    2 p. l., 11-202 p. front., plates.   19 cm.
    Clarence, a domestic story: p. [169]-202.

10747 Shelton, Frederick William, 1814-1881.
    Peeps from a belfry. By Rev. F. W. Shelton... New
York, Dana and company [etc., etc.] 1856.
    2 p. l., [3]-304 p.   19 cm.
    Added t.-p., engr.; title vignette.
    CONTENTS.-The seven sleepers.-Father Boyle.-The
lost tomb-stone.-Golden-mouthed Taylor.-A burial among
the mountains.-St. Peter's at Rosendale.-The square pew.
-The model parish.-The child's funeral.-The two neighbors.
-The heart of adamant.

10748 Shelton, Frederick William, 1814-1881.
    The rector of St. Bardolph's; or, Superannuated. By F. W.
Shelton... New York, C. Scribner, 1853.
    xvii, [11]-344 p.   front.   18 1/2 cm.

10749 Shelton, Frederick William, 1814-1881.
    Salander and the dragon: a romance of the Hartz prison.
By Frederic William Shelton... New-York, S. Hueston,

G. P. Putnam, 1850.
2 p. 1., [9]-184 p. incl. plates.   front.   16 1/2 cm.

10750 Shepard, Isaac Fitzgerald, 1816-1889.
Scenes and songs of social life. A miscellany. By Isaac
Fitzgerald Shepard... Boston, Saxton & Kelt; New York,
Saxton & Miles, 1846.
vi p., 1 1., [9]-336 p. front.   18 cm.
Added t.-p., engraved.

10751 [Shepherd, Daniel]
Saratoga. A story of 1787. New York, W. P. Fetridge &
co.; Boston, Williams & co., 1856.
viii, [9]-400 p.   19 1/2 cm.
Published anonymously.

10752 Sheppard, Francis Henry, 1846-
Love afloat. A story of the American navy. By F. H.
Sheppard, U. S. N. ... New York, Sheldon & company,
[c1875]
2 p. 1., [3]-483 p.   19 cm.

10753 Sherwood, John D   1818-1891.
The comic history of the United States, from a period
prior to the discovery of America to times long subsequent
to the present. By John D. Sherwood... With original
illustrations by Harry Scratchly. Boston, Fields, Osgood,
& co., 1870.
549 p. incl. front., illus.   19 1/2 cm.

10754 Shillaber, Benjamin Penhallow, 1814-1890.
Knitting-work: a web of many textures, wrought by Ruth
Partington (B. P. Shilaber)... Boston, Brown, Taggard
& Chase; New York, Sheldon & company [etc., etc.] 1859.
viii, [9]-408 p. front., 7 pl.   20 cm.

10755 Shillaber, Benjamin Penhallow, 1814-1890.
Partingtonian patchwork. Blifkins the martyr: the domestic trials of a model husband. The modern syntax: Dr.
Spooner's experiences in search of the delectable. Partington
papers: Strippings of the warm milk of human kindness. New
and old dips from an unambitious inkstand. Humorous,

eccentric, rhythmical. By B. P. Shillaber... Boston, Lee and Shepard; New York, Lee, Shepard and Dillingham, 1873.
360 p. plates. 19 cm.

10756 Shipman, Louis Evan, 1869-1933.
Urban dialogues, by Louis Evan Shipman. New York, Stone & Kimball, 1896.
xi, 115 p., 1 1. front., plates. 18 cm.

10757 Short story masterpieces, by the best American authors...
illustrations by J. G. Wilmot. Chicago, Daily story pub. co., 1900.
825 p. incl. pl. 16 cm.

10758 [Shubrick, Mrs. Harriet Cordelia (Wethered)]
Violet; or, The times we live in. Philadelphia, J. B. Lippincott & co., 1858.
247 p. 19 1/2 cm.

10759 Sigourney, Mrs. Lydia Howard (Huntley) 1791-1865.
Lucy Howard's journal. By Mrs. L. H. Sigourney...
New York, Harper & brothers, 1858.
343 p. 18 1/2 cm.

10760 Sigourney, Mrs. Lydia Howard (Huntley) 1791-1865.
Myrtis, with other etchings and sketchings. By Mrs. L. H. Sigourney. New York, Harper & brothers [c1846]
vi p., 2 1., [3]-292 p. front. 18 cm.
CONTENTS.-Myrtis.-Bertha.-Lady Arabella Johnson.-Mary Rice.-Fall of the Pequod.-The Yankee.-A legend of Pennsylvania.-The lady of Mount Vernon.-A tale of Poland. -The alms-house.-The plough and the sword.-The reverse. -The lost children.

10761 [Sigourney, Mrs. Lydia Howard (Huntley) 1791-1865.
Sketch of Connecticut, forty years since... Hartford, O. D. Cooke & sons, 1824.
1 p. 1., 278 p. 19 cm.
"A descriptive prose work... tracing primitive habits and traditions, with some intermingling of fiction. The scene is among the wild and beautiful regions of my native place [Norwich]; and the object of its construction was to embalm

the memory and virtues of an ancient lady, my first and most beloved benefactress" [Mrs. Jerusha Lathrop] - Sigourney, Letters of life, 1866, p. 328-329.

10762 Sigourney, Mrs. Lydia Howard (Huntley) 1791-1865.
  Sketches, by Mrs. Sigourney. Philadelphia, Key & Biddle, 1834.
   2 p. 1., [9]-216 p. front., port. 17 cm.
   CONTENTS. -The father. -Legend of Oxford. -The family portraits. -Oriana. -The intemperate. -The patriarch.

10763 Sigourney, Mrs. Lydia Howard (Huntley) 1791-1865.
  Water-drops. By Mrs. L. H. Sigourney... New York and Pittsburgh, R. Carter, 1848.
   v, [2], [9]-275 p. 17 1/2 cm.
   Verse and prose.

10764 Sikes, Wirt i.e. William Wirt, 1836-1883.
  One poor girl: the story of thousands. By Wirt Sikes... Philadelphia, J. B. Lippincott & co., 1869.
   1 p. 1., vi, [7]-255 p. 18 1/2 cm.

10765 Simms, Jeptha Root, 1807-1883.
  The American spy, or Freedom's early sacrifice: a tale of the revolution, founded upon fact. By J. R. Simms... Albany, Printed by J. Munsell, 1846.
   63 p. 23 cm.

10766 [Simms, William Gilmore] 1806-1870.
  Beauchampe; or, The Kentucky tragedy. A tale of passion. By the author of "Richard Hurdis," "Border beagles," etc. ... Philadelphia, Lea and Blanchard, 1842.
   2 v. 19 1/2 cm.
   A sequel to Charlemont.

10767 [Simms, William Gilmore] 1806-1870.
  The book of my lady. A melange. By a bachelor knight... Boston, Allen & Ticknor, 1833.
   3 p. 1., [11]-334 p. 18 cm.
   Many of the tales in this collection had previously seen the light in magazines and were subsequently republished in various forms.

10768 [Simms, William Gilmore] 1806-1870.
Border beagles; a tale of Mississippi. By the author of
"Richard Hurdis"... Philadelphia, Carey and Hart, 1840.
2 v.   19 1/2 cm.
First edition.

10769 [Simms, William Gilmore] 1806-1870.
Carl Werner, an imaginative story; with other tales of
imagination. By the author of "The Yemassee", "Guy
Rivers", "Mellichampe", &c. ... [1st ed.] New-York,
G. Adlard, 1838.
2 v.   18 1/2 x 11 cm.
CONTENTS.-v. 1. Carl Werner. Ipsistos. The star
brethren. Onea and Anyta.-v. 2. Conrad Weickhoff.
Logoochie. Jocassee. The Cherokee embassage.

10770 [Simms, William Gilmore] 1806-1870.
Castle Dismal: or, The bachelor's Christmas. A domestic
legend. By the author of "Guy Rivers"... &c. New York,
Burgess, Stringer & co., 1844.
vi, [7]-192 p.   19 cm.
Brown paper cover, dated 1845, gives the author's name:
W. G. Simms.

10771 [Simms, William Gilmore] 1806-1870.
The damsel of Darien. By the author of "The Yemassee"
... Philadelphia, Lea and Blanchard, 1839.
2 v.   20 cm.
1st edition.

10772 [Simms, William Gilmore] 1806-1870.
Guy Rivers: a tale of Georgia. By the author of "Martin
Faber"... [1st ed.] New York, Harper & brothers, 1834.
2 v.   20 x 11 1/2 cm.

10773 Simms, William Gilmore, 1806-1870.
Helen Halsey: or, The Swamp state of Conelachita. A
tale of the borders. By W. Gilmore Simms... New York,
Burgess, Stringer & co., 1845.
216 p.   19 cm.
Republished in 1869 under title: The island bride.

10774 [Simms, William Gilmore] 1806-1870.
       Katharine Walton: or, The rebel of Dorchester. An historical romance of the revolution in Carolina. By the author of "Richard Hurdis"... [1st ed.] Philadelphia, A. Hart, 1851.
       2 p. 1., [9]-186 p.   23 1/2 cm.
       Sequel to Mellichampe.

10775 [Simms, William Gilmore] 1806-1870.
       The kinsmen; or, The Black Riders of Congaree. A tale. By the author of "The partisan"... [1st ed.]... Philadelphia, Lea and Blanchard, 1841.
       2 v.   18 x 10 cm.
       Published later under title: The scout.

10776 Simms, William Gilmore, 1806-1870.
       Marie de Berniere: a tale of the Crescent city, etc. etc. etc. By W. Gilmore Simms... [1st ed.] Philadelphia, Lippincott, Grambo, and co., 1853.
       2 p. 1., [13]-422 p.   18 1/2 cm.
       The first story published later under title: The ghost of my husband.
       CONTENTS.-Marie de Berniere.-The maroon.-Maize in milk.

10777 [Simms, William Gilmore] 1806-1870.
       Martin Faber; the story of a criminal... [1st ed.] New York, J. & J. Harper, 1833.
       2 p. 1., 189 p.   17 cm.

10778 [Simms, William Gilmore] 1806-1870.
       Mellichampe. A legend of the Santee. By the author of "The Yemassee"... [1st ed.] New-York, Harper & brothers, 1836.
       2 v.   19 1/2 x 11 cm.
       Sequel to The partisan.
       Sequel: Katharine Walton.

10779 [Simms, William Gilmore] 1806-1870.
       The partisan: a tale of the revolution. By the author "The Yemassee"... [1st ed.] New York, Harper & brothers, 1835.

2 v.   18 x 11 cm.
Sequel: Mellichampe.

10780 [Simms, William Gilmore] 1806-1870.
         Pelayo: a story of the Goth. By the author of "Mellichampe,"
"The Yemassee," "Guy Rivers"... [1st ed.] New York,
Harper & brothers, 1838.
         2 v.   19 1/2 x 11 cm.

10781 Simms, William Gilmore, 1806-1870.
         Southward ho! a spell of sunshine, by W. Gilmore Simms...
New York, Redfield, 1854.
         472 p.   18 1/2 cm.

10782 [Simms, William Gilmore] 1806-1870.
         The sword and the distaff; or "Fair, fat and forty," a story
of the South, at the close of the revolution. By the author of
"The partisan..." 3rd ed. Charleston, Walker, Richards
& co., 1852.
         iv, 591 p.   17 1/2 cm.
         Published later under title: Woodcraft.

10783 [Simms, William Gilmore] 1806-1870.
         The wigwam and the cabin. By the author of "The
Yemassee"... 1st [and 2d] series. [1st ed.] New York,
Wiley and Putnam, 1845.
         2 v.   19 x 12 cm.   (On cover: Wiley and Putnam's
library of American books, no. 4, 12)
         Published later, under title: Life in America.
         CONTENTS.-1st ser. Grayling. The two camps. The
last wager. The arm-chair of Tustenuggee. The snake of
the cabin. Oakatibbe. Jocassee.-2d ser. The giant's
coffin. Sergeant Barnacle. Those old lunes. The lazy
crow. Caloya. Lucas de Ayllon.

10784 [Simms, William Gilmore] 1806-1870.
         The Yemassee. A romance of Carolina. By the author
of "Guy Rivers," "Martin Faber," &c. ... [1st ed.] New
York, Harper & brothers, 1835.
         2 v.   19 1/2 x 11 1/2 cm.

10785 The sisters of Orleans: a tale of race and social conflict.

356

New York, G. P. Putnam & sons, 1871.
2 p. 1., [7]-341 p.   19 cm.

10786 Six hundred dollars a year. A wife's effort at low living, under
       high prices. Boston, Ticknor and Fields, 1867.
       vii, 183 p.   16 cm.

10787 Sketch, Walter.
       The down-trodden; or, Black blood and white. By Walter
       Sketch. Being in part related to the author by "Nelse", a
       fugitive slave. New York, J. Miller, jr., 1853.
       89 p.   25 cm.

10788 [Sleeper, John Sherburne] 1794-1878.
       Mark Rowland. A tale of the sea. By Hawser Martingale
       [pseud.]... Boston, Loring, 1867.
       206 p.   18 cm.

10789 [Sleeper, John Sherburne] 1794-1878.
       Salt water bubbles; or, Life on the wave. By Hawser
       Martingale [pseud.] With original illustrations by Kilburn
       & Mallory... Boston, W. J. Reynolds & co., 1854.
       xii, 408 p. front., illus.   19 cm.
       Added t.-p., illustrated.

10790 Slosson, Annie (Trumbull) 1838-1926.
       Seven dreamers, by Annie Trumbull Slosson... New York,
       Harper & brothers, 1891.
       2 p. 1., 281 p. front.   19 cm.
       CONTENTS. - Introductory.-How Faith came and went.-
       Botany Bay.-Aunt Randy.-Fishin' Jimmy.-Butterneggs.
       -Deacon Pheby's selfish nature.-A speakin' ghost.

10791 Sly, Costard, pseud.
       Sayings and doings at the Tremont House. In the year
       1832. Extracted from the note book of Costard Sly... and
       ed. by Dr. Zachary Philemon Vangrifter [pseud.]... Boston,
       Allen and Ticknor, 1833.
       2 v.   21 cm.
       Published in London, 1834 under title: Sayings and doings
       in America.

10792 [Small, George G   ]
      Farming for fun; or, Back-yard grangers. By Bricktop
      [pseud.] New York, Collin & Small, 1874.
      59 p.   illus.   24 cm.

10793 [Small, George G   ]
      Fred Douglass and his mule; a story of the war. By
      Bricktop [pseud.] New York, Collin & Small, 1873.
      95 p.   illus.   22 1/2 cm.

10794 [Small, George G   ]
      Joining the grangers; or, Trying to be a Patron of
      husbandry. By Bricktop [pseud.] New York, Collin &
      Small, 1873.
      64 p.   illus.   24 cm.

10795 [Small, George G   ]
      The Knights of Pythias shown up. By Bricktop [pseud.]
      New York, Collin & Small, 1873.
      67 p.   illus.   24 1/2 cm.

10796 [Small, George G   ]
      My mother-in-law. By Bricktop [pseud.] Illustrated by
      Hopkins. New York, Collin & Small, 1875.
      79 p.   illus.   25 cm.   (On cover: Laughing series,
      no. 2)

10797 [Small, George G   ]
      Parson Beecher and his horse. A humorous adventure, by
      Bricktop [pseud.] New York, Winchell & Small, 1871.
      96 p.   illus.   19 cm.

10798 [Small, George G   ]
      The trip of the Porgie; or, Tacking up the Hudson. The
      sentiment and humor of events en route, by Bricktop (pseud.]
      New York, Collin & Small, 1874.
      124 p.   illus.   24 1/2 cm.   (On cover: Laughing
      series, no. 1)

10799 Smart, Charles, 1841-1905.
      Driven from the path. A novel. Ed. by Dr. Charles

Smart... New York, D. Appleton and company, 1873.
467 p.   18 cm.
Preface signed: Polywarp Oldfellow, M. D.

10800 [Smith, C   Hatch]
George Melville. An American novel... New York,
W. R. C. Clark & co., 1858.
viii, 9-386 p. front.   19 cm.

10801 Smith, Denis E
Leaves from a physician's journal. By D. E. Smith...
New York, New York publishing company, 1867.
836 p.   19 cm.

10802 [Smith, Elizabeth Oakes (Prince)] 1806-1893.
The newsboy. 7th thousand. New York, J. C. Derby;
Boston, Phillips, Sampson & co. [etc., etc.] 1854.
2 p. l., [iii]-iv, [5]-527 p. front.   18 1/2 cm.
Added t.-p., illustrated.

10803 Smith, Mrs. Elizabeth Oakes (Prince) 1806-1893.
Riches without wings, or, The Cleveland family. By Mrs.
Seba Smith... Boston, New York, G. W. Light, 1838.
2 p. l., [9]-162 p.   16 cm.

10804 Smith, Mrs. Elizabeth Oakes (Prince) 1806-1893.
The salamander; found amongst the papers of the late
Ernest Helfenstein [pseud.]... Edited by E. Oakes Smith.
2d ed. New-York [etc.] G. P. Putnam, 1849.
149 p. front., plates.   20 cm.

10805 [Smith, Fannie N   ]
Brazen gates: a true history of the blossoms which grew in
the garden at Cragenfels. Comp. by Christabel Goldsmith
[pseud.] and preface by the author of "Widow Goldsmith's
daughter"... New York, G. W. Carleton & co. [etc., etc.]
1872.
2 p. l., [vii]-x, [11]-248 p. front., plates.   18 1/2 cm.

10806 [Smith, Fannie N   ]
Shiftless folks. An undiluted love story. By Christabel
Goldsmith [pseud.]... New York, G. W. Carleton & co.

[etc. , etc.] 1875.
2 p. l. , [7]-454 p.   18 1/2 cm.

10807 Smith, Francis Hopkinson, 1838-1915.
Colonel Carter of Cartersville, by F. Hopkinson Smith;
with illustrations by E. W. Kemble and the author. Boston
and New York, Houghton, Mifflin and company, 1891.
vi, 208 p.   front. , illus.   18 1/2 cm.

10808 Smith, Francis Hopkinson, 1838-1915.
The other fellow, by F. Hopkinson Smith. Boston and
New York, Houghton, Mifflin and company, 1899.
4 p. l. , 218 p. , 1 l. front. , plates.   19 cm.
CONTENTS. -Dick Sands, convict. -A Kentucky Cinderella.
-A water-logged town. -The boy in the cloth cap. -Between
showers in Dort. -One of Bob's tramps. -According to the law.
-"Never had no sleep. "-The man with the empty sleeve. -
"Tincter ov iron. "-"Five meals for a dollar. "

10809 Smith, Francis Hopkinson, 1838-1915.
Tom Grogan, by F. Hopkinson Smith; with illustrations by
Charles S. Reinhart. Boston and New York, Houghton,
Mifflin and company, 1896.
3 p. l. , 246, [1] p. incl. plates. front.   19 cm.

10810 Smith, John Hyatt, 1824-1886.
Gilead; or, The vision of All souls' hospital. An allegory.
By J. Hyatt Smith... New York, C. Scribner; Buffalo, Breed,
Butler & co. , 1863.
360 p. incl. front.   19 1/2 cm.

10811 Smith, Joseph Emerson.
Oakridge: an old-time story. By J. Emerson Smith ...
Boston, J. R. Osgood and company (late Ticknor & Fields,
and Fields, Osgood & co.) 1875.
415 p.   19 cm.

10812 Smith, Miss M   M
Kick him down hill; or, Ups and downs in business. By
Miss M. M. Smith... New York, United States publishing
company, 1875.
1 p. l. , vi, 312 p.   21 cm.

10813 [Smith, Mrs. Margaret (Bayard)] 1778-1844.
      What is gentility? A moral tale... Washington, D. C.,
      P. Thompson, 1828.
      257 p.   19 1/2 cm.

10814 Smith, Mrs. Mary Stuart (Harrison) 1834-
      Lang syne; or, The wards of Mount Vernon; a tale of the
      revolutionary era, by Mary Stuart Smith. New York, J. B.
      Alden, 1889.
      133 p.   19 1/2 cm.
      CONTENTS. -Lang syne. -The women of the revolution.

10815 [Smith, Richard Penn] 1799-1854.
      The actress of Padua, and other tales. By the author of
      "The forsaken"... Philadelphia, E. L. Carey & A. Hart,
      1836.
      2 v.   18 1/2 cm.

10816 Smith, Mrs. Sara Henderson.
      Alice Singleton; or, The fashion of this world passeth
      away. By Mrs. S. Henderson Smith. New York, J. Wiley,
      1850.
      2 p. 1. , 86 p.   19 cm.

10817 [Smith, Seba] 1792-1868.
      John Smith's letters, with 'picters' to match. Containing
      reasons why John Smith should not change his name; Miss
      Debby Smith's juvenile spirit; together with The only authen-
      tic history extant of the late war in our disputed territory...
      New-York, S. Colman, 1839.
      139 p. front. , plates.   18 cm.
      A collection of humorous letters first published in the New
      York mirror.
      Not included under Seba Smith's works in Williamson's
      Bibliography of Maine, but attributed to Seba Smith by M. A.
      Wyman in her Two American pioneers, p. 87-88 and 236,
      and by Sabin, Bib. amer. , v. 20, p. 563-564.

10818 [Smith, Seba] 1792-1868.
      Letters written during the President's tour, 'down East,'
      by myself, Major Jack Downing, of Downingville... Down
      East [Cincinnati, Stereotyped by J. A. James] 1833.

69 p.   incl. front.   15 1/2 cm.

10819 [Smith, Seba] 1792-1868.
    The life and writings of Major Jack Downing [pseud.] of
Downingville, away down East in the state of Maine.
Written by himself... Boston, Lilly, Wait, Colman, &
Holden, 1833.
    xii, [13]-260 p. front. , plates.   19 cm.
    "Originally pub. in the Portland daily courier, Jan. 18,
1830-1833."-Allibone.

10820 [Smith, Seba] 1792-1868.
    May-day in New York; or, House-hunting and moving:
illustrated and explained in letters to Aunt Keziah. By
Major Jack Downing [pseud.] New York, Burgess, Stringer
and company, 1845.
    xxviii, [29]-120 p.   19 1/2 cm.
    Illustrated t. -p.

10821 [Smith, Seba] 1792-1868.
    My thirty years out of the Senate. By Major Jack
Downing [pseud.]... New York, Oaksmith & company, 1859.
    458 p. incl. illus. , plates. front.   19 cm.
    Half-title illustration: Major Jack Downing's letters.
Preface signed: Seba Smith.

10822 [Smith, Seba] 1792-1868.
    The select letters of Major Jack Downing [pseud.] of the
Downingville militia, away down East, in the state of Maine.
Written by himself... Philadelphia, Printed for the publisher, 1834.
    xi, 212 p. incl. front.   17 1/2 cm.
    "In this edishon I have put in my last letters... Contains
many important letters on the great consarns of the nashon,
sent to the Portland curier, and my friend Dwight of New
York," - Pref.

10823 Smith, Stephe R
    Romance and humor of the road: a book for railway men
and travelers. By Stephe R. Smith. Author's edition.
Chicago, Horton & Leonard, Railroad printers, 1871.
    219 p. illus.   22 1/2 cm.

10824 Smith, Thomas Lacey, 1805-1875.
Chronicles of Turkeytown; or, The works of Jeremy
Peters [pseud.] 1st ser. Containing the history of a dread-
ful catastrophe, the amours of Dr. Post and Mrs. Peweetle,
and the history of a tatterdemalion... Philadelphia, R. H.
Small, 1829.
238 p.   19 cm.

10825 [Smith, William B   ]
Egypt Ennis; or, Prisons without walls. A novel. By
Kelsic Etheridge [pseud.] New York, The Authors' publishing company, 1876.
iv, 5-97 p.   23 1/2 cm.   (On cover: Satchel
series, no. 2)

10826 [Smythe, James M   ]
Ethel Somers; or, The fate of the Union. By a Southerner.
Augusta, Ga., H. D. Norrell, 1857.
382 p.   19 1/2 cm.

10827 [Snelling, William Jospeh] 1804-1848.
Tales of the Northwest; or, Sketches of Indian life and
character. By a resident beyond the frontier... Boston,
Hilliard, Gray, Little, and Wilkins, 1830.
viii, 288 p.   16 cm.
CONTENTS.-The captive.-The Hohays.-The devoted.-
Payton Skah.-Charles Hess.-The Bois Brûlé.-Weenokhen-
chah Wandeetcehak.-La Butte des Morts.-Pinchon.-The
lover's leap.

10828 [Somerby, Frederic Thomas] 1814-1871.
Hits and dashes; or, A medley of sketches and scraps,
touching people and things. By "Cymon" [pseud.] Whilom
published in divers news-prints of the day... Boston,
Redding & co., 1852.
2 p. 1., [vii]-viii, [9]-152 p.   18 1/2 cm.

10829 Southworth, Mrs. Emma Dorothy Eliza (Nevitte) 1819-1899.
Allworth abbey. By Mrs. Emma D. E. N. Southworth
... Philadelphia, T. B. Peterson & brothers [c1865]
2 p. 1., 21-421 p.   19 cm.

10830 Southworth, Mrs. Emma Dorothy Eliza (Nevitte) 1819-1899.
        The artist's love. By Mrs. Emma D. E. N. Southworth...
        and stories by her sister, Mrs. Frances Henshaw Baden...
        Philadelphia, T. B. Peterson & brothers [c1872]
        2 p. 1., 21-479 p.   19 cm.

10831 Southworth, Mrs. Emma Dorothy Eliza (Nevitte) 1819-1899.
        The bride of Llewellyn. By Mrs. Emma D. E. N. South-
        worth... Philadelphia, T. B. Peterson & brothers [c1866]
        2 p. 1., 21-550 p.   19 cm.

10832 Southworth, Mrs. Emma Dorothy Eliza (Nevitte) 1819-1899.
        The broken engagement; or, Speaking the truth for a
        day. By Mrs. Emma D. E. N. Southworth... Philadelphia,
        T. B. Peterson and brothers [1862]
        1 p. 1., 19-92 p.   24 cm.

10833 Southworth, Mrs. Emma Dorothy Eliza (Nevitte) 1819-1899.
        The changed brides. By Mrs. Emma D. E. N. South-
        worth... Philadelphia, T. B. Peterson & brothers [1869]
        2 p. 1., 21-503 p.   19 cm.

10834 Southworth, Mrs. Emma Dorothy Eliza (Nevitte) 1819-1899.
        The Christmas guest. A collection of stories. By Mrs.
        Emma D. E. N. Southworth; and her sister, Mrs. Frances
        Henshaw Baden... Philadelphia, T. B. Peterson & brothers,
        1870.
        2 p. 1., 19-338 p.   19 cm.

10835 Southworth, Mrs. Emma Dorothy Eliza (Nevitte) 1819-1899.
        The coral lady; or, The bronzed beauty of Paris... by
        Mrs. Southworth... Philadelphia, C. W. Alexander, c1867.
        1 p. 1., 19-78 p. incl. plates.   23 1/2 cm.

10836 Southworth, Mrs. Emma Dorothy Eliza (Nevitte) 1819-1899.
        Cruel as the grave. By Mrs. Emma D. E. N. South-
        worth... Philadelphia, T. B. Peterson & brothers (c1871]
        1 p. 1., 19-372 p.   19 cm.

10837 Southworth, Mrs. Emma Dorothy Eliza (Nevitte) 1819-1899.
        Hickory Hall; or, The outcast. A romance of the Blue
        Ridge. By Mrs. Emma D. E. N. Southworth... Phila-

delphia, T. B. Peterson and brothers [c1861]
    2 p. l., 21-136 p.   24 cm.

10838 Southworth, Mrs. Emma Dorothy Eliza (Nevitte) 1819-1899.
         The lady of the isle. A romance from real life. By Mrs.
       Emma D. E. N. Southworth... Philadelphia, T. B. Peterson
       and brothers [1859]
         1 p. l., 23-598 p. front.   18 1/2 cm.

10839 Southworth, Mrs. Emma Dorothy Eliza (Nevitte) 1819-1899.
         The lost heir of Linlithgow. By Mrs. Emma D. E. N.
       Southworth... Philadelphia, T. B. Peterson & brothers
       [c1872]
         1 p. l., 21-570 p.   18 1/2 cm.

10840 Southworth, Mrs. Emma Dorothy Eliza (Nevitte) 1819-1899.
         A noble lord. The sequel to "The lost heir of Linlith-
       gow." By Mrs. Emma D. E. N. Southworth. Philadelphia,
       T. B. Peterson & brothers [c1872]
         1 p. l., 19-428 p.   19 cm.

10841 Southworth, Mrs. Emma Dorothy Eliza (Nevitte) 1819-1899.
         Old neighbourhoods and new settlements, or, Chritsmas
       evening legends. By Emma D. E. N. Southworth...
       Philadelphia, A. Hart, 1853.
         3 p. l., 17-370 p.   front. (port.)   19 cm.
         Added t.-p., engr.
         CONTENTS.-The better way; or, The wife's victory.-The
       married shrew; a sequel to "The better way."-The thunder-
       bolt to the hearth.-Neighbours' prescriptions.-The tempta-
       tion.-Across the street; a New Year's story.-The Irish
       refugee.-New Year in the little rough-cast house.-Winny.
       -The fine figure.

10842 Southworth, Mrs. Emma Dorothy Eliza (Nevitte) 1819-1899.
         The prince of darkness. A romance of the Blue Ridge. By
       Mrs. E. D. E. N. Southworth... Philadelphia, T. B. Peterson
       & brothers [c1869]
         1 p. l., 19-370 p.   19 cm.
         CONTENTS.-The prince of darkness.-The broken en-
       gagement.-Winny.-The thunderbolt to the hearth.

10843 Southworth, Mrs. Emma Dorothy Eliza (Nevitte) 1819-1899.
        Self-raised; or, From the depths. A sequel to Ishmael; or,
    In the depths. By Mrs. Emma D. E. N. Southworth... Phila-
    delphia, T. B. Peterson & brothers [1876]
        2 p. 1., 23-658 p.   front.   19 cm.

10844 Southworth, Mrs. Emma Dorothy Eliza (Nevitte) 1819-1899.
        The spectre lover. By Mrs. Emma D. E. N. Southworth
    ... And other stories by her sister Mrs. Frances Henshaw
    Baden... Philadelphia, T. B. Peterson & brothers [1875]
        2 p. 1., 21-416 p.   19 cm.

10845 Southworth, Mrs. Emma Dorothy Eliza (Nevitte) 1819-1899.
        Tried for her life. A sequel to "Cruel as the grave." By
    Mrs. Emma D. E. N. Southworth... Philadelphia, T. B.
    Peterson & brothers [1871]
        1 p. 1., 19-356 p.   19 cm.
        On cover: Peterson's uniform edition of the Complete
    works of Mrs. Emma D. E. N. Southworth.

10846 Southworth, Mrs. S   A
        Hester Strong's life work; or, The mystery solved. By
    Mrs. S. A. Southworth... Boston, Lee and Shepard, 1870.
        1 p. 1., 5-453 p.   17 cm.

10847 Southworth, Mrs. S   A
        The inebriate's hut; or, The first fruits of the Maine law.
    By Mrs. S. A. Southworth... Boston, Phillips, Sampson,
    and company, 1854.
        2 p. 1., 7-240 p. front., plates.   19 1/2 cm.

10848 Spangler, Helen King.
        The physician's wife. A novel. By Helen King Spangler
    ... Philadelphia, J. B. Lippincott & co., 1875.
        305 p.   18 1/2 cm.

10849 Speculation; or, Making haste to be rich. The story of William
    Wilson, the whistling shoemaker. Boston, George W. Light,
    1840.
        80 p.   12 mo.

18050 [Spencer, Mrs. Bella Zilfa] 1840-1867.

Ora, the lost wife. Cincinnati, P. C. Browne, 1863.
384 p.   20 cm.

10851 Spencer, Mrs. Bella Zilfa, 1840-1867.
Tried and true; or, Love and loyalty: a story of the great
rebellion. By Mrs. Bella Z. Spencer. Springfield, Mass.,
W. J. Holland, 1866.
xvi, [17]-394 p. front. (port.) plates.   20 1/2 cm.

10852 Sperry, J   Austin.
Fothergill; or, The man of enterprise. By J. Austin
Sperry... Cincinnati, Printed at "the Great West" office,
1850.
1 p. 1., [11]-118 p.   23 1/2 cm.

10853 Spofford, Mrs. Harriet Elizabeth (Prescott) 1835 -1921.
Azarian: an episode. By Harriet Elizabeth Prescott ...
Boston, Ticknor and Fields, 1864.
1 p. 1., [5]-251 p.   17 1/2 cm.

10854 Spofford, Mrs. Harriet Elizabeth (Prescott) 1835-1921.
New-England legends. By Harriet Prescott Spofford...
Boston, J. R. Osgood and company, 1871.
4 p. 1., 40 p.   illus.   24 cm.
CONTENTS.-The true account of Captain Kidd.-Charles-
town.-Salem.-Newburyport.-Dover.-Portsmouth.

10855 [Spofford, Mrs. Harriet Elizabeth (Prescott)] 1835-1921.
Sir Rohan's ghost. A romance. Boston, J. E. Tilton
and company, 1860.
2 p. 1., [vii]-viii p., 2 1., [11]-352 p.   19 cm.
Published anonymously.

10856 Spofford, Mrs. Harriet Elizabeth (Prescott) 1835-1921.
The thief in the night. By Harriet Prescott Spofford...
Boston, Roberts brothers, 1872.
1 p. 1., 217 p.   17 cm.

10857 Sproat, P   W
The savage beauty, a satirical allegorical novel... By
P. W. Sproat... Philadelphia, Printed by S. Roberts, 1822.
136 p.   18 cm.

10858 [Stabler, Mrs. Jennie Latham] d. 1882.
      Left ot herself. By Jennie Woodville [pseud.] Phila-
delphia, J. B. Lippincott & co., 1872.
      311 p.   18 1/2 cm.
      Published later under title: Edith's mistake.

10859 Stanley, Harvey.
      Pilate and Herod: a tale illustrative of the early history
of the Church of England, in the province of Maryland...
By Rev. Harvey Stanley... Philadelphia, H. Hooker, 1853.
      2 v.   20 cm.

10860 Starbuck, Caleb.
      Hampton Heights; or, The spinster's ward. By Caleb
Starbuck. New York, Mason brothers, 1856.
      xii, [13]-504 p.   18 cm.

10861 [Starnes, Ebenezer] 1810-1868.
      The slaveholder abroad; or, Billy Buck's visit, with his
master, to England. A series of letters from Dr. Pleasant
Jones [pseud.] to Major Joseph Jones, of Georgia... Philadelphia, J. B. Lippincott & co., 1860.
      xii, 13-512 p.   front., plates.   19 cm.
      Authorship attributed by Cushing to William Tappan
Thompson.

10862 [Stebbins, George Stanford]
      My satchel and I; or, Literature on foot. By Ikabod Izax
[pseud.] Illustrated by Louis A. Roberts... Springfield,
Mass., D. E. Fisk and company [c1873]
      326 p. incl. front., illus.   18 1/2 cm.

10863 Steele, James William, 1840-1905.
      The sons of the border. Sketches of the life and people of
the far frontier. By James W. Steele. ("Deane Monahan")
Topeka, Kan., Commonweslth printing company, 1873.
      260 p.   22 cm.
      CONTENTS.-Introduction.-The sons of the border.-Chuck.
-New Mexican common life.-The scout's mistake.-Copper-
distilled.-Jack's divorce.-A harvest-day with the Pueblos.
-Brown's revenge.-A day with the padres.-Joe's pocket.
-Woman under difficulties.-The reunion of the ghosts.

Coyotes. -The priest of El Paso. -La señorita. -Peg. -Captain
Jinks. -Jornado del muerto.

10864 Stell, Charles.
        The life of a reprobate... New York [etc.] F. Tennyson
        Neely [c1899]
            265 p.   20 cm.

10865 Stephens, Mrs. Ann Sophia (Winterbotham) 1813-1886.
        Bertha's engagement. By Mrs. Ann S. Stephens...
        Philadelphia, T. B. Peterson & brothers [c1875]
            2 p. l., 21-552 p.   19 cm.

10866 Stephens, Mrs. Ann Sophia (Winterbotham) 1813-1886.
        The curse of gold. By Mrs. Ann S. Stephens... Phila-
        delphia, T. B. Peterson & brothers [c1869]
            2 p. l., 21-406 p.   18 cm.

10867 Stephens, Mrs. Ann Sophia (Winterbotham) 1813-1886.
        The heiress of Greenhurst: an autobiography... By
        Mrs. Ann S. Stephens... New York, Edward Stephens,
        1857.
            430 p.   20 cm.

10868 Stephens, Mrs. Ann Sophia (Winterbotham) 1813-1886.
        Lord Hope's choice. By Mrs. Ann S. Stephens... Phila-
        delphia, T. B. Peterson & brothers [c1873]
            2 p. l., 21-312 p.   18 1/2 cm.
            Sequel: The old countess

10869 Stephens, Mrs. Ann Sophia (Winterbotham) 1813-1886.
        Mary Derwent [a novel] By Mrs. Ann S. Stephens...
        Philadelphia, T. B. Peterson and brothers [c1858]
            1 p. l., v-viii, [9]-408 p.   19 cm.

10870 Stephens, Mrs. Ann Sophia (Winterbotham) 1813-1886.
        A noble woman. By Mrs. Ann S. Stephens... Philadel-
        phia, T. B. Peterson & brothers [c1871]
            1 p. l , 19-479 p.   18 1/2 cm.

10871 Stephens, Mrs. Ann Sophia (Winterbotham) 1813-1886.
        The old countess; or, The two proposals. By Mrs. Ann

S. Stephens... A sequel to "Lord Hope's choice." Philadelphia, T. B. Peterson & brothers [c1873]
    1 p. l. , 21-321 p.   18 1/2 cm.

10872 Stephens, Mrs. Ann Sophia (Winterbotham) 1813-1886.
        Palaces and prisons. By Mrs. Ann S. Stephens...
    Philadelphia, T. B. Peterson & brothers [c1871]
        1 p. l. , 19-592 p.   18 1/2 cm.

10873 Stephens, Mrs. Ann Sophia (Winterbotham) 1813-1886.
        Phemie Frost's experiences. By Ann S. Stephens... New
    York, G. W. Carleton & co. [etc. , etc.] 1874.
        3 p. l. , [9]-408 p.   18 cm.

10874 Stephens, Mrs. Ann Sophia (Winterbotham) 1813-1886.
        The soldier's orphans. By Mrs. Ann S. Stephens...
    Philadelphia, T. B. Peterson and brothers [c1866]
        1 p. l. , 19-330 p.   18 1/2 cm.

10875 Stephens, Mrs. Ann Sophia (Winterbotham) 1813-1886.
        The wife's secret. By Mrs. Ann S. Stephens... Philadel-
    phia, J. B. Peterson & brothers [c1864]
        2 p. l. , 21-480 p.   19 1/2 cm.

10876 Stephens, Harriet Marion (Ward) 1823-1858.
        Hagar the martyr; or, Passion and reality, a tale of the
    North and South. New York, W. P. Fetridge and Co. [c1854]
        360 p.   22 cm.

10877 Stephens, Robert Neilson, 1867-1906.
        The continental dragoon; a love story of Philipse manor-
    house in 1778, by Robert Neilson Stephens... illustrated by
    H. C Edwards... Boston, L. C. Page and company, 1898.
        4 p. l. , 11-299 p.   front. , 5 pl.   19 cm.

10878 Stephens, Robert Neilson, 1867-1906.
        An enemy to the king, from the recently discovered
    memoirs of the Sieur de la Tournoire... Boston, L. C.
    Page and co. , 1897.
        459 p.   illus.   20 cm.

10879 Stephens, Robert Neilson, 1867-1906.

Philip Winwood; a sketch of the domestic history of an
American captain in the war of independence... written by
his enemy in war, Herbert Russell... Presented anew by
Robert Neilson Stephens... illustrated by E. W. D.
Hamilton. Boston, L. C. Page & company, 1900.
    412 p. incl. front. (port.) 5 pl.   19 1/2 cm.

10880 Sterling, Charles F
    Buff and blue; or, The privateers of the revolution. A
    tale of Long island sound. By Charles F. Sterling... New
    York, W. H. Graham, 1847.
    128 p.   24 cm.

10881 Sterling, Charles F
    The Red Coats; or, The sack of Unquowa. A tale of the
    revolution. By Charles F. Sterling... New York, Williams
    brothers, 1848.
    111 p.   25 cm.

10882 [Stimson, Alexander Lovett] 1816-
    Poor Caroline; the Indiaman's daughter. Or, All's well
    that ends well. A tale of Boston and our own times. Boston,
    Pub. by the author, 1845.
    1 p. l., [5]-62 p.   23 1/2 cm.
    Published anonymously.

10883 [Stimson, Alexander Lovett] 1816-
    Waifwood. A novel. By the author of "Easy Nat"...
    Boston, W. V. Spencer, 1864.
    iv, 472 p.   18 cm.

10884 [Stimson, Frederic Jesup] 1855-1943.
    The crime of Henry Vane; a study with a moral, by J. S.
    of Dale... New York, C. Scribner's sons, 1884.
    2 p. l., 206 p.   18 cm.

10885 Stimson, Frederic Jesup, 1855-1943.
    King Noanett; a story of old Virginia and the Massa-
    chusetts bay, by F. J. Stimson (J. S. of Dale)...
    [Illustrations by Henry Sandham. 2d ed. with map] Boston
    and New York, Lamson, Wolffe, and company [etc., etc.]
    1896.

xv, 327 p. incl. front. , illus. plates, map.
20 1/2 cm.

10886 Stockton, Frank Richard, 1834-1902.
   A bicycle of Cathay; a novel, by Frank R. Stockton...
illustrated by Orson Lowell. New York and London, Harper
& brothers, 1900.
   v, [1] p. , 1 1. , 239, [1] p. front. , illus. , plates.
19 1/2 cm.

10887 Stockton, Frank Richard, 1834-1902.
   The casting away of Mrs. Lecks and Mrs. Aleshine...
New York, The Century co. [c1886]
   130 p.   20 cm.
   The Dusantes (1888) is a sequel.

10888 Stockton, Frank Richard, 1834-1902.
   The girl at Cobhurst, by Frank R. Stockton. New York,
C. Scribner's sons, 1898.
   vii, 408 p.   19 cm.

10889 Stockton, Frank Richard, 1834-1902.
   The great stone of Sardis; a novel, by Frank R. Stockton;
illustrated by Peter Newell. New York and London, Harper
& brothers, 1898.
   vii, 230 p. front. , plates. 18 1/2 cm.

10890 Stockton, Frank Richard, 1834-1902.
   The hundredth man, by Frank R. Stockton... New-
York, The Century co. [c1887]
   1 p. 1. , 432 p.   20 cm.

10891 Stockton, Frank Richard, 1834-1902.
   A jolly fellowship; a novel, by Frank R. Stockton...
New York, Charles Scribner's sons, 1880.
   298 p.   19 1/2 cm.

10892 Stockton, Frank Richard, 1834-1902.
   The lady, or the tiger? and other stories, by Frank R.
Stockton. New York, C. Scribner's sons, 1884.
   v, 201 p. 17 1/2 cm.
   CONTENTS. -The lady, or the tiger ?-The transferred

ghost. -The spectral mortgage. -Our archery club. -That
same old 'coon. -His wife's deceased sister. -Our story. -Mr.
Tolman. -On the training of parents. -Our fire-screen. -A
piece of red calico. -Every man his own letter-writer.

10893 Stockton, Frank Richard, 1834-1902.
The late Mrs. Null, by Frank R. Stockton... New York,
Charles Scribner's Sons, 1886.
2 p. 1., 437 p.   18 cm.

10894 Stockton, Frank Richard, 1834-1902.
Mrs. Cliff's yacht, by Frank R. Stockton; illustrated by A.
Forestier. New York, C. Scribner's sons, 1896.
vii, 314 p.   8 pl. (incl. front.)   18 1/2 cm.

10895 Stockton, Frank Richard, 1834-1902.
The Squirrel inn. By Frank R. Stockton... New York,
The Century co., 1891.
viii p., 1 1., 222 p. incl. front., illus.   20 cm.
Illustrated by A. B. Frost.

10896 Stockton, Frank Richard, 1834-1902.
A story-teller's pack. By Frank R. Stockton. Illustrated
by Peter Newell, W. T. Smedley, Frank O. Small, Alice
Barber Stephens, and E. W. Kemble. New York, C.
Scribner's sons, 1897.
viii p., 1 1., 380 p.   16 pl. (incl. front.)
19 1/2 cm.
CONTENTS. -A few words to begin with. -The magic egg.
-The staying power of Sir Rohan. -The widow's cruise. -Love
before breakfast. -The Bishop's ghost and the printer's baby.
-Captain Eli's best ear. -As one woman to another. -My
well and what came out of it. -Stephen Skarridge's Christmas.
-My unwilling neighbor.

10897 Stoddard, Charles Warren, 1843-1909.
A troubled heart, and how it was comforted at last, by
Charles Warren Stoddard. Notre Dame, Ind., J. A. Lyons,
1885.
178 p.   17 3/4 cm.

10898 Stoddard, Charles Warren, 1843-1919.

The wonder-worker of Padua, by Charles Warren
Stoddard. Notre Dame, Ind., The Ave Maria, 1896.
187 p.   17 cm.

10899 Stories and sketches by our best authors. Boston, Lee and
Shepard, 1867.
3 p. 1., 9-307 p.   19 1/2 cm.
CONTENTS.-The skeleton at the banquet. Seeley Regester.
-Let those laugh who win. Samuel W. Tuttle.-The proper use
of grandfathers. Fitz Hugh Ludlow.-At eve. Gertrude Brode.
-Broken idols. Richmond Wolcott.-Dr. Huger's intentions.
Louise Chandler Moulton.-The man whose life was saved.
*****.-The romance of a western trip. J. L. Lord.-The
ghosts of New London turnpike. Mrs. Galpin.-Down by the
sea. Hattie Tyng Griswold.-Why Mrs. Radnor fainted. *****.
-Under a cloud. William Wirt Sikes.-Coming from the front.
Richmond Wolcott.-A night in the sewers. Chas. Dawson
Shanly.

10900 Stories from real life; comp. with a view to the moral improvement of all classes. Fitchburg, Mass., S. & C.
Shepley, 1848.
3 p. 1., [5]-158, [1] p. front., illus.   11 1/2 cm.
Added engr. t.-p. has imprint: Worcester, J. Grout, jr.

10901 Story, James P.
Choisy. A novel. By James P. Story... Boston, J. R.
Osgood and company, 1872.
131 p.   23 cm. (On cover: Osgood's library of novels,
no. 20)

10902 [Stowe, Mrs. Harriet Elizabeth (Beecher)] 1811-1896.
The chimney-corner. By Christopher Crowfield [pseud.]...
Boston, Ticknor and Fields, 1868.
2 p. 1., 311 p.   18 cm.
Originally published in the Atlantic monthly, January 1865
to September 1866. Order of numbers changed; included also
the papers published under title "Little foxes," here omitted.

10903 Stowe, Mrs. Harriet Elizabeth (Beecher) 1811-1896.
Dred; a tale of the great Dismal Swamp. By Harriet
Beecher Stowe... Boston, Phillips, Sampson and company,

1856.
    2 v.   19 1/2 cm.

10904 Stowe, Mrs. Harriet Elizabeth (Beecher) 1811-1896.
        The Mayflower; or, Sketches of scenes and characters among
the descendants of the Pilgrims. By Mrs. Harriet Beecher
Stowe, New York, Harper & brothers, 1843.
        xvii, [19]-324 p.   16 cm.
        First edition.
        CONTENTS.-Love versus law.-The tea-rose.-Trials of
a house-keeper.-Little Edward.-Let every man mind his
own business.-Cousin William.-Uncle Tim.-Aunt Mary.
-Frankness.-The Sabbath.-So many calls.-The canal-boat.
-Feeling.-The sempstress.-Old Father Morris.

10905 Stowe, Mrs. Harriet Elizabeth (Beecher) 1811-1896.
        The minister's wooing. By Harriet Beecher Stowe. New
York, Derby and Jackson; Boston, Brown, Taggard, and
Chase, 1859.
        2 p. 1., 578 p.   19 cm.

10906 Stowe, Mrs. Harriet Elizabeth (Beecher) 1811-1896.
        My wife and I; or, Harry Henderson's history. By
Harriet Beecher Stowe... New-York, J. B. Ford and
company, 1871.
        viii, 474 p.   front., plates.   18 1/2 cm.

10907 Stowe, Mrs. Harriet Elizabeth (Beecher) 1811-1896.
        Oldtown folks. By Harriet Beecher Stowe... Boston,
Fields, Osgood & co., 1896.
        viii, 608 p.   19 1/2 cm.

10908 Stowe, Mrs. Harriet Elizabeth (Beecher) 1811-1896.
        Poganuc people; their loves and lives. New York, Fords,
Howard, & Hulbert [1878]
        1 p. 1., vi, 7-375, [3] p. plate.   18 1/2 cm.
(19 1/2 cm: Copy 2)
        Publisher's advertisements: preliminary leaf and [3] p.
at end.
        Red cloth cover, design in black (Copy 1); green cloth
cover, design in black (Copy 2).
        Foley, p. 280.

10909 Stowe, Mrs. Harriet Elizabeth (Beecher) 1811-1896.
        Sam Lawson's Oldtown fireside stories. By Harriet Beecher
     Stowe... Boston, Houghton, Osgood [1871]
        2 p. 1., 216 p. front., plates.   19 cm.
        CONTENTS.-The ghost in the mill.-The Sullivan looking-
     glass.-The minister's housekeeper.-The widow's bandbox.
     -Captain Kidd's money.-"Miss Elderkin's pitcher."-The
     ghost in the Cap'n Brown house -Colonel Eph's shoe-buckles.
     -The bull-fight.-How to fight the devil.-Laughin' in meetin'.

10910 Stowe, Mrs. Harriet Elizabeth (Beecher) 1811-1896.
        Uncle Sam's emancipation; Earthly care, a heavenly dis-
     cipline; and other sketches. By Mrs. Harriet Beecher
     Stowe... With a sketch of Mrs. Stowe's family. Philadel-
     phia, W. P. Hazard, 1853.
        124 p.   19 cm.
        CONTENTS.-Account of Mrs. Beecher Stowe and her
     family, by an Alabama man.-Uncle Sam's emancipation.
     -Earthly care, a heavenly discipline.-A scholar's adven-
     tures in the country.-Children.-The two Bibles.-Letter
     from Maine, no. 1.-Letter from Maine, no. 2.-Christmas,
     or The good fairy.

10911 Stowe, Mrs. Harriet Elizabeth (Beecher) 1811-1896.
        We and our neighbors; or, The records of an unfashion-
     able street. (Sequel to "My wife and I.") A novel. By
     Harriet Beecher Stowe... New York, J. B. Ford & company,
     [1875]
        v, [1], [7]-480 p. front., plates.   19 cm.

10912 Stratton, Ned.
        A romantic tale of high American life; or, Excursion to
     Montauk. First and last time. By Ned Stratton... Providence,
     J. F. Moore, printer, 1847.
        32 p. incl. plates.   22 cm.

10913 Subdued southern nobility; a Southern ideal. By one of the
     nobility. New York, Sharps publishing company [c1882]
        392 p.   19 cm.

10914 [Suddoth, Mrs. Harriet Almaria Baker]
        An orphan of the Old Dominion. Her trials and travels.

Embracing a history of her life, taken principally from her journals and letters. By Lumina Silvervale [pseud.]... Philadelphia, J. B. Lippincott & co., 1873.

viii, 9-390 p.   19 1/2 cm.

10915 [Sutherland, Thomas Jefferson]
Loose leaves, from the port folio of a late patriot prisoner in Canada. New York, W. H. Colyer, printer, 1840.

iv, [5]-216 p.   15 cm.

10916 Swell life at sea; or, Fun, frigates, and yachting; a collection of nautical yarns. From the log-book of a youngster of the mess. New York, Stringer & Townsend, 1854.

2 p. l., [iii]-iv p., 1 l., [7]-432 p.   19 1/2 cm.

CONTENTS.-Gould, J. W. Cruise of a guineaman.-Hannay, J. Fitz-Gubin; or, The admiral's pet.-Homeward bound.-An aquatic expedition from Gibraltar to Barcelona. -Hannay, J. Mr. Snigsby's yacht.-The death shot; a tale of the coast guard.

10917 Swift, John Franklin.
Robert Greathouse. An American novel. By John Franklin Swift... New York, Carleton [etc., etc.] 1870.

1 p. l., [v]-vi, [7]-573 p.   19 cm.

T

10918 Talbot, Mary Elizabeth.
Rurality. Original desultory tales. By Miss Mary Elizabeth Talbot... Providence, Marshall and Hammond, printers, 1830.

196 p.   19 cm.

10919 Tales for you: a collection of original and selected literature, from celebrated English and American authors. Philadelphia, J. J. Sharkey, 1841.

240 p.   17 1/2 cm.

CONTENTS.-The lover's leap.-The merchant's daughter.

-The threefold destiny. -Kate Connor. -The mountain of the
two lovers. -The knight of Sheppey. -The wood demon. -
Married by mistake. -The spectre's voyage. -The Wyandot's
story. -An incident at Algiers. -A legend of Charlemagne.
-The abbey garden. -First love. -Reconciliation.

10920 Tales of the Emerald isle; or, Legends of Ireland. By a lady
of Boston, author of "Tales of the fireside," and "Stories
for children"... New York, W. Borradaile, 1828.
2 p. l., 258 p.   20 cm.

10921 Tales of the fireside. By a lady of Boston... Boston, Hilliard,
Gray, Little and Wilkins, 1827.
225 p.   20 cm.
CONTENTS. -The fortune teller. -The house on the heath.
-The miniature picture. -The battle of Monmouth. -Rose
Bradshaw. -The emigrants.

10922 [Taliaferro, H   E   ]
Fisher's river (North Carolina) scenes and characters, by
"Skitt" [pseud.] "who was raised thar". Illustrated by John
M'Lenan. New York, Harper & brothers, 1859.
viii p., 1 l., [13]-269 p. incl. front., plates.   18 1/2
cm.

10923 Tarkington, Booth, 1869-1946.
The gentleman from Indiana, by Booth Tarkington. New
York, Doubleday & McClure co., 1899.
viii p., 1 l., 384 p.   20 1/2 cm.

10924 Tarkington, Booth, 1869-1946.
Monsieur Beaucaire, by Booth Tarkington; illustrated by
C. D. Williams. New York, McClure, Phillips & co., 1900.
6 p. l., 3-127, [1] p. incl. front., plates.   19 cm.

10925 Tartan, pseud.
Philadelphia malignants. Typographed... By Tartan.
Philadelphia, Weir & co., 1863.
1 p. 1 , [5]-28 p.   18 1/2 cm.
A satirical pamphlet, written in Biblical style, dealing
with Philadelphia politics before and during the civil war.
Autograph letter from Jno. A. McAllister inserted, giving

378

key to the characters mentioned in the book.

10926 Taylor, Bayard, 1825-1878.
Hannah Thurston, a story of American life... New York,
G. P. Putnam, 1863.
464 p.   20 cm.

10927 Taylor, Bayard, 1825-1878.
John Godfrey's fortunes; related by himself. A story of
American life. By Bayard Taylor. [1st ed.] New York,
G. P. Putnam, Hurd and Houghton, 1864.
viii, 511 p.   18 1/2 cm.

10928 Taylor, Bayard, 1825-1878.
Joseph and his friend: a story of Pennsylvania. By Bayard
Taylor... New York, G. P. Putnam & sons [etc., etc.] 1870.
vi, 361 p.   18 1/2 cm.

10929 Taylor, James Wickes, 1819-1893.
The victim of intrigue. A tale of Burr's conspiracy. By
James W. Taylor... Cincinnati, Robinson & Jones, 1847.
1 p. 1., [xv]-xvi p., 1 1., [17]-120 p.   23 cm.
Imprint on cover: Philadelphia, T. B. Peterson; Cincinnati,
Robinson & Jones.

10930 Taylor, Joseph.
A fast life on the modern highway; being a glance into the
railroad world from a new point of view. By Joseph Taylor
... New York, Harper & brothers, 1874.
220 p. incl. front., illus. plates, tab., diagr.   19 cm.

10931 Tefft, Benjamin Franklin, 1813-1885.
The shoulder-knot; or, Sketches of the three-fold life of
man. A story of the seventeenth century. By B. F. Tefft...
New York, Harper & brothers, 1850.
3 p. 1., [xvii]-xxiii, [25]-305 p.   19 1/2 cm.

10932 Ten years of torture; or, Sutten's death-bed confession of
how he married Miss Martha Morton, an accomplished
young lady of Baltimore, with the hellish design of torturing
her to death... By Bishop Williams, who says he never in
all his life listened to such a recital as he heard from Sutten's

dying lips. Published by special request of the author...
Philadelphia, C. W. Alexander [1871]
   76 p. incl. plates.   23 cm.

10933 [Tenney, Mrs. Tabitha (Gillman)] 1762-1837.
       Female quixotism: exhibited in the romantic opinions and
       extravagant adventures of Dorcasina Sheldon... Boston,
       J. P. Peaslee, 1829.
          2 v. fronts.   15 1/2 cm.
          Added t.-p., engraved.

10934 [Terhune, Mrs. Mary Virginia (Hawes)] 1830-1922.
          Alone. By Marion Harland [pseud.]... 5th ed. Richmond,
       A. Morris, 1854.
          384 p.   19 1/2 cm.

10935 [Terhune, Mrs. Mary Virginia (Hawes)] 1830-1922.
          At last. A novel. By Marion Harland [pseud.]... New
       York, Carleton [etc., etc.] 1870.
          1 p. l., v-vi, [7]-360 p.   18 1/2 cm.

10936 [Terhune, Mrs. Mary Virginia (Hawes)] 1830-1922.
          The Christmas holly, by Marion Harland [pseud.] New
       York, Sheldon & co., 1867.
          vii p., 1 l., [11]-86, [1] p. front., plates.   22 cm.
          Title-page illustrated.
          CONTENTS.-Nettie's prayer.-A Christmas talk with
       mothers.

10937 [Terhune, Mrs. Mary Virginia (Hawes)] 1830-1922.
          Dr. Dale; a story without a moral, by Marion Harland
       [pseud.] and Albert Payson Terhune. New York, Dodd,
       Mead and company, 1900.
          vi, 408 p.   19 1/2 cm.

10938 [Terhune, Mrs. Mary Virginia (Hawes)] 1830-1922.
          The empty heart; or, Husks. "For better, for worse."
       By Marion Harland [pseud.]... New York, Carleton [etc.,
       etc.] 1871.
          2 p. l., [7]-353 p.   19 cm.
          The empty heart published in 1863 under title: Husks.
       "For better, for worse": p. [245]-353.

10939 [Terhune, Mrs. Mary Virginia (Hawes)] 1830-1922.
   From my youth up. By Marion Harland [pseud.] New
Your, G. W. Carleton & co [etc., etc.] 1874.
   3 p. l., [9[-390 p.   18 1/2 cm.

10940 [Terhune, Mrs. Mary Virginia (Hawes)] 1830-1922.
   Helen Gardner's wedding-day; or, Colonel Floyd's wards.
A battle summer. By Marion Harland [pseud.] New York,
Carleton [etc., etc.] 1870.
   1 p. l., [5]-382 p.   18 1/2 cm.
   Published in 1863 under title: Colonel Floyd's wards.

10941 [Terhune, Mrs. Mary Virginia (Hawes)] 1830-1922.
   The hidden path, by Marion Harland [pseud.] author of
"Alone." New York, Derby & Jackson, 1858.
   435 p.   20 cm.

10942 [Terhune, Mrs. Virginia (Hawes)] 1830-1922.
   Moss-side. By Marion Harland [pseud.]... New York,
Derby and Jackson, 1857.
   450 p.   19 1/2 cm.

10943 [Terhune, Mrs. Mary Virginia (Hawes)] 1830-1922.
   My little love. By Marion Harland [pseud.] New York,
G. W. Carleton & co. [etc., etc.] 1876.
   4 p. l., [11]-396 p.   18 1/2 cm.

10944 [Terhune, Mrs. Mary Virginia (Hawes)] 1830-1922.
   Nemesis; a story of social and domestic life. By Marion
Harland [pseud.] New York, Derby and Jackson, 1860.
   499 p.   20 cm.

10945 [Terhune, Mrs. Mary Virginia (Hawes)] 1830-1922.
   Phemie's temptation. A novel. By Marion Harland
[pseud.]... New York, Carleton; London, S. Low, son &
co., 1869.
   2 p. l., [7]-396 p.   19 cm.

10946 [Terhune, Mrs Mary Virginia (Hawes)] 1830-1922.
   Ruth Bergen's limitations: a modern auto-da-fe, by
Marion Harland [pseud.] New York, Chicago [etc.] F. H.
Revell company, 1897.

3 p. 1., 9-123 p.   18 1/2 cm.

10947 Teuffel, Blanche Willis (Howard) von, 1847-1898.
       Dionysius the weaver's heart's dearest, by Blanche Willis
       Howard... New York, C. Scribner's sons, 1899.
       2 p. 1., 375 p.   20 cm.

10948 Teuffel, Blanche Willis (Howard) von, 1847-1898.
       Tony, the maid, a novelette, by Blanche Willis Howard...
       New York, Harper & brothers, 1887.
       3 p. 1., 166 p.   front., plates.   17 1/2 cm.

10949 Thayer, Mrs. Carolin Matilda (Warren) d. 1844.
       The gamesters; or, Ruins of innocence. An original novel,
       founded in truth. By Caroline Matilda Warren... Boston,
       J. Shaw, 1828.
       iv, 300 p.   13 cm.
       Published also under title: Conrade, or The gamesters.
       London, 1806.

10950 Theodore and Matilda; or, The fatal plot, and foul deeds
       detected: in which are displayed the triumphs of virtue,
       and the punishment of vice; a touching and thrilling history.
       To which is added, Cruelty disarmed, and The lonely man...
       Boston, Dow and Jackson, 1845.
       29 p.   front.   27 cm.

10951 [Thomas, Frederick William[1806-1866.
       Howard Pinckney. A novel. By the author of "Clinton
       Bradshaw"... Philadelphia, Lea and Blanchard, 1840.
       2 v.   19 cm.

10952 Thomas, Frederick William, 1806-1866.
       John Randolph, of Roanoke, and other sketches of character,
       including William Wirt. Together with tales of real life. By
       F W. Thomas... Philadelphia, A. Hart, late Carey and
       Hart, 1853.
       viii, [13]-375 p.   19 cm.

10953 Thomas, Frederick William, 1806-1866.
       Sketches of character, and tales founded on fact. By F. W.
       Thomas... Louisville, Pub. at the office of the Chronicle of

Western literature and art, 1849.
4 p. 1. , 117 p.   18 1/2 cm.
CONTENTS. -Boarding-school scenes: or, A frolic among the lawyers. -The unsummoned witness. -William Wirt. -The last of the pioneers. -Simon Kenton. -Mary McIntire has arrived. -John Randolph.

10954 [Thomas, Martha McCannon] 1823-
Life's lesson. A tale. New York, Harper & brothers, 1854.
2 p. 1. , [13]-398 p.   18 1/2 cm.
Published anonymously.

10955 [Thompson, Clara M   ]
The chapel of St. Mary. By the author of "The rectory of Moreland"... Boston, J. E. Tilton and company, 1861.
viii, [9]-396 p.   19 1/2 cm.
Attributed by Cushing and Boston Public Library to Mary Evans.

10956 [Thompson, Mrs. Clara M   ]
The rectory of Moreland: or, My duty... Boston, J. E. Tilton and company, 1860.
1 p. 1. , 339 p.   19 1/2 cm.
First published under the title "Mary Evans".
Attributed by Boston Public Library to Mary Evans.

10957 [Thompson, Daniel Pierce] 1795-1868.
Centeola; and other tales, by the author of "Green mountain boys"... etc. New York, Carleton, 1864.
2 p. 1. , [ix]-xii, [13]-312 p.   19 cm.
CONTENTS. -Centeola. -The starving settlers. -The unfathomable mystery. -The rustic financiers. -The counterfeiter.

10958 [Thompson, Daniel Pierce] 1795-1868.
The doomed chief; or, Two hundred years ago. By the author of "The Green mountain boys"... etc. , etc. Philadelphia, J. W. Bradley, 1860.
1 p. 1. , 5-473 p.   19 1/2 cm.

10959 Thompson, Daniel Pierce, 1795-1868.

May Martin; or, The money diggers, a Green mountain tale.
By D. P. Thompson... Canandaigua, N. Y., H. Underhill,
1849.
171 p.   15 1/2 cm.

10960 [Thompson, George] novelist.
Jack Harold; or, The criminal's career: a story with a
moral. Tracing a life of villainy from the cradle to the
gallows; and showing the awful effects of crime, the consequences of vice, the power of beauty, the seductive influ-
ences of voluptuousness, the blighting results of passion and
the mysteries of city life. By Greenhorn [pseud.]... Boston,
W. Berry & co. [1850]
1 p. 1., [7]-201 p.   illus.   22 1/2 cm.
Sequel: The criminal.

10961 Thompson, James Maurice, 1844-1901.
Alice of old Vincennes... by F. C. Yohn. Indianapolis,
The Bowen-Merrill company [1900]
419 p. illus.   20 cm.

10962 [Thompson, William Tappan] 1812-1882.
John's alive; or, The bride of a ghost, and other sketches.
By Major Jones [pseud.] of Pineville, Ga. ... Ten original
full-page illustrations, by H. T. Cariss. Philadelphia, D.
McKay, 1883.
xi, 17-264 p. incl. front., 9 pl.   19 cm.
Collected and published by the author's daughter, Mrs. May
A. Wade.

10963 [Thorpe, Thomas Bangs] 1815-1878, supposed author.
The master's house; a tale of Southern life. By Logan
[psued.]... New York, T. L McElrath & co. [etc., etc.]
1854.
301 p.   front., plates.   19 1/2 cm.

10964 Thorpe, Thomas Bangs, 1815-1878.
The mysteries of the backwoods; or, Sketches of the South-
west: including character, scenery, and rural sports. By
T. B. Thorpe... Illustrations by Felix O. C. Darley.
Philadelphia, Carey and Hart, 1846.
1 p. 1., 5-190 p. front., illus., plates.   19 cm.

10965　The thrilling and romantic story of Sarah Smith and the Hessian.
An original tale of the American revolution.　To which is
added, Female heroism exemplified, an interesting story
founded on fact.　Together with Mr. Keith's captivity among
the American Indians...　Philadelphia, 1844.
24 p.　illus.　22 1/2 cm.

10966　[Tiernan, Mrs. Frances Christine (Fisher)] 1846-1920.
Carmela, by Christian Reid [pseud.]...　Philadelphia,
H. L. Kilner & co. [c1891]
371 p.　19 cm.　(On cover: Catholic Library)
Reprinted from the "Ave Maria."

10967　[Tiernan, Mrs. Frances Christine (Fisher)] 1846-1920.
A comedy of elopement, by Christian Reid [pseud.]　New
York, D. Appleton and company, 1893.
1 p 1., 261 p.　18 1/2 cm.　(On cover: Appleton's
Town and Country Library, no. 108)

10968　[Tiernan, Mrs. Frances Christine (Fisher)] 1846-1920.
Ebb-tide, and other stories.　By Christian Reid [pseud.]
...　New York, D. Appleton and company, 1872.
2 p. 1., [7]-166 p.　front., plates.　23 cm.
CONTENTS -Ebb-tide.-Miss Inglesby's sister-in-law.
-The story of a scar.-A doubt.

10969　Tiernan, Mrs. Frances Christine (Fisher) 1846-1920.
A gentle bell.　A novel.　By Christian Reid [pseud.]　New
York, D. Appleton and company, 1879.
142 p.　24 cm.

10970　[Tiernan, Mrs. Frances Christine (Fisher)] 1846-1920.
Hearts and hands.　A story in sixteen chapters.　By
Christian Reid [pseud.]...　New York, D. Appleton and
company, 1875.
99 p.　23 1/2 cm.　(On cover: Appletons' library of
American fiction [no. 13])

10971　[Tiernan, Mrs. Frances Christine (Fisher)] 1846-1920.
Mabel Lee.　A novel.　By the author of "Valerie Aylmer",
"Morton house", etc. ...　New York, D. Appleton and company,
1895.

162 p   front., plates.   23 1/2 cm.

10972 [Tiernan, Mrs. Frances Christine (Fisher)] 1846-1920.
      A question of honor. A novel. By Christian Reid [pseud.]
New York, D. Appleton and company, 1875.
      iv, 501 p.   20 cm.

10973 [Tiernan, Mrs. Frances Christine (Fisher)] 1846-1920.
      Valerie Aylmer. A novel. By Christian Reid [pseud.]...
New York, D. Appleton and company, 1870.
      221 p.   24 cm.

10974 [Tiernan, Mrs. Mary Spear (Nicholas)] 1836-1891.
      ... Homoselle... Boston, J. R. Osgood and company,
1881.
      iv, 367 p.   17 1/2 cm.   (On cover: Round-robin series)
Series title also at head of t.-p.

10975 Tiernan, Mrs. Mary Spear (Nicholas) 1836-1891.
      Jack Horner; a novel, by Mary Spear Tiernan... Boston
and New York, Houghton, Mifflin and company, 1890.
      iv., 347 p.   18 1/2 cm.

10976 Tiernan, Mrs. Mary Spear (Nicholas) 1836-1891.
      Suzette; a novel, by Mary Spear Tiernan... New York,
H. Holt and company, 1885.
      1 p. 1., 306 p.   17 cm.

10977 Tiffany, Osmond, 1823-
      Brandon; or, A hundred years ago. A tale of the American
colonies. By Osmond Tiffany... New York, Stanford &
Delisser, 1858.
      xii, 9-285 p.   18 1/2 cm.

10978 [Tilden, Catherine]
      The first patient: a story, written in aid of the fair for the
"Channing home"... Boston, J. Wilson and son, 1859.
      63, [1] p.   18 cm.

10979 Tilton, Theodore, 1835-1907.
      Tempest-tossed: a romance... New York, Sheldon &
company, 1874.

606 p.   20 1/2 cm.

10980 [Tilton, Warren]
Trifleton papers. By Trifle and the Editor [pseuds. of
Warren Tilton and Wm. A. Crafts] Boston, Whittemore,
Niles and Hall; Milwaukie, A. Whittemore & co., 1856.
vi, [7]-310 p.   18 1/2 cm.

10981 Tincker, Mary Agnes, 1833-
Two coronets, by Mary Agnes Tincker... Boston and
New York, Houghton, Mifflin and company, 1889.
523 p.   20 cm.

10982 Titan Agonistes; the story of an outcast. New York, G. W.
Carleton & co. [etc., etc.] 1867.
8, [11]-544 p.   18 1/2 cm.

10983 [Todd, Charles W   ]
Woodville; or, The anchoret reclaimed. A descriptive
tale. Knoxville, Tenn., Printed by F. S. Heiskell, 1832.
1 p. l., ii, 278 p.   18 cm.

10984 Todd, John, 1800-1873.
Summer gleanings; or, Sketches and incidents of a pastor's
vacation. By John Todd, D. D., collected and arranged by
his daughter. Northampton, Hopkins, Bridgman, & co.,
1852.
vi, [7]-281 p. front.   19 cm.

10985 Tomlin, John.
Tales of the Caddo. By John Tomlin... Cincinnati,
Printed at the office of "The Great West," 1849.
2 p. l., [11]-110 p.   23 1/2 cm.

10986 [Torrey, Elizabeth R   ]
Theognis: a lamp in the cavern of evil, by Catius junior
[pseud.]... Boston, Wentworth and company, 1856.
xxiv p., 1 l., 27-346 p.   17 1/2 cm.

10987 Torrey, Mrs. Mary (Ide) 1817-1869.
City and country life; or, Moderate better than rapid gains.
By Mrs. Mary Ide Torrey... Boston, Tappan & Whittemore;

Milwaukie, A. Whittemore & co. [etc., etc.] 1853.
iv, [5]-318 p.   18 1/2 cm.

10988 Tourgée, Albion Winegar, 1838-1905.
Black ice, by Albion W. Tourgée... New York, Fords,
Howard, & Hulbert, 1888.
435 p.   18 1/2 cm.

10989 Tourgée, Albion Winegar, 1838-1905.
Bricks without straw; a novel, by Albion W. Tourgée...
New York, Fords, Howard, & Hulbert [etc., etc.c1880]
6 p. 1., [7]-521 p.   front.   18 cm.

10990 Tourgée, Albion Winegar, 1838-1905.
Button's inn. By Albion W. Tourgée... Boston, Roberts
brothers, 1887.
x, 418 p.   18 cm.
A story of Mormonism in the early part of the century.

10991 Tourgée, Albion Winegar, 1838-1905.
Hot plowshares. A novel, by Albion W. Tourgée... New
York, Fords, Howard, & Hulbert, 1883.
5 p. 1., 7-610 p.   front.   18 1/2 cm.   (On cover:
Tourgée's American historical novels)

10992 Tourgée, Albion Winegar, 1838-1905.
John Eax and Mamelon; or, The South without the shadow,
by Albion W. Tourgée... New York, Fords, Howard, &
Hulbert [c1882]
3 p. 1., [iii]-ix, [9]-300 p.   17 1/2 cm.
Story of the reconstruction period.

10993 Tourgée, Albion Winegar, 1838-1905.
Murvale Eastman, Christian socialist, by Albion W.
Tourgée. New York, Fords, Howard, & Hulbert [etc.,
etc., c1890]
2 p. 1., viii, [9]-545 p.   19 cm.

10994 Tourgée, Albion Winegar, 1838-1905.
Out of the sunset sea, by Albion W. Tourgée; illustrations
by Aimée Tourgée. New York, Merrill & Baker [c1893]
462 p.   illus.   20 1/2 cm.

10995 Tourgée, Albion Winegar, 1838-1905.
An outing with the queen of hearts, by Albion W. Tourgée;
decorated by Aimée Tourgée. New York, Merrill & Baker,
1894.
1 p. 1., 133 p.   19 cm.
Marginal illustrations.

10996 [Tourgée, Albion Winegar] 1838-1905.
Toinette. A novel. By Henry Churton [pseud.]... New
York, J. B. Ford and company, 1874.
vi, [7]-510 p.   19 cm.
Published in 1881 under title: A royal gentleman.

10997 Townsend, Edward Waterman, 1855-
"Chimmie Fadden"; Major Max; and other stories, by
Edward W. Townsend... New York, Lovell, Coryell &
company [c1895]
iv p., 2 1., 3-346 p. plates.   20 cm.

10998 Townsend, Edward Waterman, 1855-
Near a whole city full. By Edward W. Townsend... illustrated by F. A. Nankivell. New York, G. W. Dillingham
& co., 1897.
260 p. incl. front., illus.   18 1/2 cm.

10999 [Townsend, Frederic]
Fancies of a whimsical man. By the author of "Musings
of an invalid." 4th ed. New York, J. S. Taylor, 1852.
iv, [9]-281 p.   19 cm.
With autograph of George Townsend.

11000 [Towsend, Frederic]
Fun and earnest. By the author of "Musings of an invalid,"
"Fancies of a whimsical man," etc. New-York, J. S. Taylor,
1853.
v, [13]-274 p.   19 cm.

11001 [Townsend, Frederic]
Ghostly colloquies. By the author of "Letters from Rome,"
"Clouds and sunshine," etc. New York, D. Appleton and
company, 1856.
267 p.   17 1/2 cm.

11002 [Townsend, Frederic]
Mutterings and musings of an invalid. New York, J. S.
Taylor, 1851.
1 p. l. , [9]-281 p.   20 cm.

11003 [Townsend, Frederic]
Spiritual visitors. By the author of "Musings of an invalid,"
"Clouds and sunshine," etc. New York, J. S. Taylor, 1854.
4 p. l. , [xi]-xii, [13]-346 p.   19 1/2 cm.
"The following dialogues... appeared originally in the
Bizarre."

11004 Townsend, George Alfred, 1841-1914.
The entailed hat; or, Patty Cannon's times, a romance by
George Alfred Townsend "Gath." New York, Harper &
brothers, 1884.
2 p. l. , [4], 565 p.   17 1/2 cm.

11005 Townsend, George Alfred, 1841-1914.
Lost abroad... By Geo. Alfred Townsend. Hartford,
Conn. , S. M. Betts and company; Chicago, Gibbs & Nichols,
1870.
xii, [13]-594 p. front.   19 cm.

11006 Townsend, Virginia Frances, 1836-
The battle-fields of our fathers. By Virginia F. Townsend.
New York, J. Bradburn (late M. Doolady)1864.
3 p. l. , [3]-368 p.   19 cm.

11007 Townsend, Virginia F[rances] 1836-
Darryll Gap; or, Whether it paid. By Virginia F. Townsend
... Boston, W. V. Spencer, 1866.
456 p.   19 1/2 cm.

11008 Townsend, Virginia Frances, 1836-
Janet Strong. By Virginia F. Townsend... Philadelphia,
J. B. Lippincott & co. , 1865.
314 p.   19 cm.

11009 Trammell, William Dugas.
Ça ira. A novel. By Wm. Dugas Trammell. New York,
United States publishing company, 1874.

358 p.   19 1/2 cm.

11010 Tremayne, Mrs. S   C   H
        Florence Dalbiac, and other tales. By Mrs. S. C. H.
        Tremayne... New York, Printed by S. W. Benedict, 1840.
        234 p.   19 cm.
        CONTENTS. - Florence Dalbiac. - The Lexington. - The
        three widows. - A sail in sight. - The escape.

11011 Troubetzkoy, Amélie (Rives) Chanler, 1863-1945.
        According to St. John, by Amelie Rives... New York,
        J. W. Lovell Company [1891]
        3 p. 1., [3]-352 p.   front. (port.) 15 pl.   19 cm.

11012 Troubetzkoy, Amélie (Rives) Chanler 1863-1945.
        A damsel errant, by Amélie Rives (Princess Troubetzkoy)
        Illustrated by Violet Oakley. Philadelphia, J. B. Lippincott
        company, 1898.
        211 p. front., 3 pl.   16 1/2 x 29 cm. (On cover:
        The lotos library)

11013 Troubetzkoy, Amélie (Rives) Chanler, 1863-1945.
        The quick or the dead? A study... Philadelphia, J. B.
        Lippincott company, 1889.
        255 p.   front.   20 cm.

11014 Troubetzkoy, Amélie (Rives) Chanler, 1863-1945.
        The witness of the sun. By Amélie Rives... Philadelphia,
        J. B. Lippincott company, 1889.
        248 p. incl. front. (port.)   19 cm.

11015 Trowbridge, John Townsend, 1827-1916.
        Coupon bonds, and other stories. By J. T. Trowbridge
        ... Boston, J. R. Osgood and company, 1873.
        v p., 1 1., 411 p. front., plates.   19 1/2 cm.

11016 Trowbridge, John Twonsend, 1827-1916.
        Lucy Arlyn. By J. T. Trowbridge... Boston, Ticknor
        and Fields, 1866.
        564 p.   19 1/2 cm.

11017 Truman, Ernest.

Leander; or, Secrets of the priesthood. By Ernest Truman
... Philadelphia, Claxton, Remsen and Haffelfinger, 1869.
iv p. , 2 1. , [9]-76 p.   23 cm.

11018 Trumbull, Annie Eliot, 1857–
Rod's salvation, by Annie Eliot Trumbull... with ...
illustrations by Charles Copeland. New York, A. S. Barnes
and company, 1898.
5 p. 1. , 285 p. front. , 3 pl.   18 cm.
CONTENTS. -Rod's salvation. -Decline and fall. -Uneffectual
fire. -The Chevalier Saint Agar.

11019 [Tucker, Nathaniel Beverley] 1784-1851.
The partisan leader; a tale of the future. By Edward
William Sidney [pseud.]... Printed for the publishers, by
J. Caxton, 1856 [i.e. Washington, Printed by D. Green,
1836]
2 v.   19 1/2 cm.
Secretly printed in 1836 with a fictitious imprint and date
of 1856. cf. Allibone, Crit. dict. of Eng. lit.

11020 Tuckerman, Henry Theodore, 1813-1871.
Isabel; or, Sicily. A pilgrimage... By Henry T. Tuckerman... Philadelphia, Lea and Blanchard, 1839.
230 p.   20 cm.

11021 Tuckerman, Henry Theodore, 1813-1871.
The Italian sketch book... By an American. Philadelphia,
Key & Biddle, 1835.
xii, [13]-216 p.   20 1/2 cm.
Published anonymously. Later editions published under
author's name.

11022 Tuckerman, Henry Theodore, 1813-1871.
Rambles and reveries. By Henry T. Tuckerman... New-
York, J. P. Giffing, 1841.
3 p. 1. , [v]-vi, 436 p.   18 1/2 cm.

11023 Tuel, John E
The prisoner of Perote. A tale of American valor and
Mexican love. By J. E. Tuel. Boston, F. Gleason, 1848.
1 p. 1. , [5]-50 p. incl. pl.   23 cm.

11024 [Tuel, John E   ]
　　　St. Clair; or, The protegé, a tale of the federal city. By
　　J. E. T. ... New York, Philadelphia [etc.] W. Taylor &
　　co. , 1846.
　　　viii, 142 p.　　　23 1/2 cm.

11025 [Tufts, Marshall] 1802-1855.
　　　Shores of Vespucci; or, Romance without fiction. Lexing-
　　ton, Ms. [!] M. Tufts, 1833.
　　　240 p.　　　18 cm.

11026 Turnbull, Charlotte.
　　　The Lawrences: a twenty years' history. By Charlotte
　　Turnbull... New York, The American news company
　　[c1872]
　　　x, 498 p.　　　18 1/2 cm.

11027 Turnbull, Francese Hubbard (Litchfield) "Mrs. Lawrence
　　Turnbull," d. 1927.
　　　The catholic man, a study, by Mrs. Lawrence Turnbull...
　　Boston, D. Lothrop company [c1890]
　　　3 p. 1. , 311 p.　　　19 1/2 cm.
　　　"The chief character is a study of Sidney Lanier, the
　　poet. " - Who's who in America, 1906-07, p. 1814.

11028 Turnbull, Francese Hubbard (Litchfield) "Mrs. Lawrence
　　Turnbull," d. 1927.
　　　The golden book of Venice; a historical romance of the
　　16th century, by Mrs. Lawrence Turnbull... New York,
　　The Century co. , 1900.
　　　6 p. 1. , 399 p.　　　19 1/2 cm.

11029 Turnbull, Francese Hubbard (Litchfield) "Mrs. Lawrence
　　Turnbull," d. 1927.
　　　Val-Maria. A romance of the time of Napoleon I. By
　　Mrs. Lawrence Turnbull... Philadelphia, J. B. Lippincott
　　company, 1893.
　　　2 p. 1. , 3-200 p.　　front.　　　19 cm.

11030 Turner, Bessie A
　　　A woman in the case. A story, by Miss Bessie Turner...
　　New York, G. W. Carleton & co. [etc. , etc.] 1875.

288 p. incl. front. (port.)   19 cm.

11031 Turner, William Wilberforce, 1830-
         Jack Hopeton; or, The adventures of a Georgian. By Wm.
       W. Turner... New York, Derby & Jackson, 1860.
         364 p.   18 1/2 cm.

11032 Turnover, a tale of New Hampshire. Boston, J. French [etc.]
       1853.
         86 p.   19 x 11 cm.

11033 Tuthill, Mrs. Louisa Caroline (Huggins) 1798-1879.
         Reality; or, The millionaire's daughter. A book for young
       men and young women. By Mrs. L. C. Tuthill... New York,
       C. Scribner, 1856.
         vi, 7-310 p.   19 cm.

11034 Twells, Mrs. Julia Helen (Watts)
         The mills of the gods. A novel. By Mrs. J. H. Twells.
       Philadelphia, J. B. Lippincott & co., 1875.
         366 p.   18 1/2 cm.

11035 Tyler, Mrs. M   W
         A book without a title; or, Thrilling events in the life of
       Mira Dana By Mrs. M. W. Tyler... Boston, Printed for
       the author, 1855.
         viii, [9]-260 p.   19 cm.

11036 [Tyler, Royall] 1757-1826.
         The Algerine captive; or, The life and adventures of Doctor
       Updike Underhill [pseud.] six years a prisoner among the
       Algerines... Two volumes in one. Hartford: Printed by
       Peter B. Gleason and co. ..... 1816.
         vii, [9]-252 p.   14 1/2 cm.

11037 [Tyler, Royall] 1757-1826.
         The Yankey in London, being the first part of a series of
       letters written by an American youth, during nine months'
       residence in the city of London... vol. I. New-York:
       Printed and published by Isaac Riley, 1809.
           ix p., 180 p.   19 cm.
         No more published.

"Judge Tyler never crossed the Atlantic, his description of scenes in London being entirely imaginary." - Gilman Bibl. of Vermont. p. 282.

U

11038 [Underhill, Edward Fitch] 1830-1898.
    The history and records of the Elephant club; comp. from authentic documents now in possession of the Zoölogical society. By Knight Russ Ockside, M. D. [pseud.] and Q. K. Philander Doesticks, P. B. [pseud.] New York, Livermore & Rudd, 1856.
        4 p. 1., [vii]-x, 11-321 p. illus.   18 1/2 cm.
        Added t.-p., engraved.

11039 The unveiled heart; a simple story. By the author of Early impressions, etc., etc. Boston, J. Allen and co., 1835.
        viii, [9]-262 p.   17 cm.

11040 Upton, George Putnam, 1834-1919.
    Letters of Peregrine Pickle [pseud.] by George P. Upton ... Chicago, The Western news company, 1869.
        3 p. 1., [v]-x, 340 p.   19 cm.
    Originally appeared in the Chicago tribune, 1866-69, in the form of weekly letters, "devoted to matters of gossip and interest in the world of amusement". cf. Pref.

11041 Urbino, Levina (Buoncuore) "Mrs. S. R. Urbino"
    Sunshine in the palace and cottage; or, Bright extremes in human life. By L. B. Urbino. Boston, Heath and Graves, 1854.
        2 p. 1., [iii]-vi, [7]-239 p. front., plates.   18 1/2 cm.

11042 The victims of gaming. Being extracts from the diary of an
American physician. Boston, Weeks, Jordan & Company,
1838.
172 p.   8 vo.

11043 [Victor, Mrs. Metta Victoria (Fuller)] 1831-1885.
Miss Slimmens' window, and other papers. By Mrs.
Mark Peabody [pseud.]... New York, Derby & Jackson,
1859.
312 p. incl. front., illus.   18 1/2 cm.
CONTENTS.-Miss Slimmens's window.-The Tallow family
in America.-Lucy in the city.-Mr. Fitz Foom in the country.

11044 Victor, Mrs. Metta Victoria (Fuller) 1831-1885.
... The senator's son; or, The Maine law; a last refuge;
a story dedicated to the law-makers. By Metta Victoria
Fuller. 2d ed. Cleveland, O., Tooker and Gatchel, 1853.
vii, 291 p.   19 cm.
At head of title: Fourth thousand.

11045 Victor, Mrs. Metta Victoria (Fuller) 1831-1885.
Who was he? A story of two lives. By Mrs. M. V. Victor.
New York, Beadle and company [c1866]
83 p. front.   22 1/2 cm.

11046 Vidi, pseud.
Mr. Frank, the underground mail-agent. By Vidi.
Illustrated with designs by White. Philadelphia, Lippincott,
Grambo & co., 1853.
2 p. l., iii-viii, 9-238 p. front., plates.   19 cm.
Added t.-p., engraved.
Caption title: The underground mail-agent.

11047 Vincent, Ellerton.
The artist's dream. By Ellerton Vincent. New York, G.
W. Carleton & co.; London, S. Low, son & co., 1868.
1 p. l., [9]-374 p.   19 cm.

11048 [Vingut, Mrs. Gertrude (Fairfield)]

Irene; or, The autobiography of an artist's daughter. And other tales. Boston, Damrell and Moore, 1853.
3 p. 1., [5]-383 p. front. (port.) 23 1/2 cm.
CONTENTS.-The vice president's daughter. By Miss G. G. Fairfield.-The wife of two husbands. By Miss G. G. Fairfield.-Irene; or, The autobiography of an artist's daughter. By Miss Gertrude Fairfield.

W

11049 Waisbrooker, Lois.
Helen Harlow's vow. By Lois Waisbrooker... Boston, W. White and company; New York, The American news company, 1870.
290 p. 19 cm.

11050 Waisbrooker, Lois.
Nothing like it; or, Steps to the kingdom. By Lois Waisbrooker... Boston, Colby & Rich, 1875.
336 p. 19 1/2 cm.

11051 [Waldo, James Curtis] 1835-1901.
Mardi gras; a tale of ante bellum times. By Tim Linkinwater... New Orleans, P. F. Gogarty, 1871.
131, [1] p. 23 1/2 cm.
Old St. Patrick's: last page.

11052 [Wallace, Horace Binney] 1817-1852.
Stanley; or, The recollections of a man of the world...
Philadelphia, Lea & Blanchard, 1838.
2 v. 20 cm.
Published anonymously.
Ascribed to William Landor by Edgar Allan Poe in Graham's American monthly magazine, 1841, v. 19, p. 231.

11053 Wallace, Lewis, 1827-1905.
The fair god; or, The last of the 'Tzins. A tale of the conquest of Mexico. By Lew Wallace... Boston, J. R.

Osgood and company, 1873.
xiv, 586 p. 19 cm.

11054 Wallace, Lewis, 1827-1905.
The prince of India; or Why Constantinople fell, by Lew
Wallace... New York, Harper & brothers, 1893.
2 v. 17 1/2 cm.

11055 Wallace, M   A
Well! Well! A tale, founded on fact. By M. A. Wallace
... [2d ed.] ... New York, Boston [etc.] D. & J.
Sadlier & co., 1863.
viii, [v]-x, [7]-312 p. 19 1/2 cm.

11056 [Waln, Robert] 1794-1825.
The hermit in America on a visit to Philadelphia. Contain-
ing some account of the beaux and belles... of that famous
city... Edited by Peter Atall, esq. [pseud.] Philadelphia:
Published by M. Thomas, (Johnson's Head) No. 52, Chesnut
Street. 1819-21.
2 v. in 1. 18 cm.
[Vol 2] title reads: The hermit in Philadelphia. Second
series... Philadelphia, J. Maxwell and M. Thomas; New
York, Haely and Thomas, 1821.

11057 Walsingham, Charlotte, pseud. ?
Annette; or, The chronicles of Bellevue. By Charlotte
Walsingham. Philadelphia, Claxton, Remsen & Haffelfinger, 1875.
1 p. l., ix-xii, 13-374 p. 19 cm.

11058 Walworth, Mrs. Jeannette Ritchie (Hadermann) 1837-1918.
Against the world. By Jeanette R. Hadermann... Boston,
Shepard and Gill, 1873.
334 p. 18 1/2 cm.

11059 Walworth, Mrs. Jeannette Ritchie (Hadermann) 1837-1918.
Dead men's shoes. A romance. By Jeannette R.
Hadermann... Philadelphia, J. B. Lippincott & co., 1872.
2 p. l., vii-viii, 9-420 p. 19 cm.

11060 Walworth, Mrs. Jeannette Ritchie (Hadermann) 1837-1918.
Forgiven at last. By Jeannette R. Hadermann. Philadelphia,

J. B. Lippincott & co. , 1870.
viii, 9-333 p.   19 cm.

11061 Walworth, Mansfield Tracy, 1830-1873.
Beverly; or, The white mask. A novel. By Mansfield
Tracy Walworth... New York, G. W. Carleton & co.
[etc.] 1872.
2 p. l. , [7]-422 p.   18 1/2 cm.

11062 Walworth, Mansfield Tracy, 1830-1873.
Delaplaine: or, The sacrifice of Irene. A novel. By
Mansfield Tracy Walworth. New York, G. W. Carleton &
co. , 1871.
2 p. l. , 7-300 p.   19 cm.

11063 Walworth, Mansfield Tracy, 1830-1873.
Hotspur. A tale of the old Dutch manor. By Mansfield
T. Walworth... New-York, Carleton, 1864.
1 p. l. , [5]-324 p.   18 1/2 cm.

11064 Walworth, Mansfield Tracy, 1830-1873.
Lulu. A tale of the National hotel poisoning. By Mansfield Tracy Walworth. New York, Carleton, 1863.
1 p. l. , [v]-vi, [7]-367 p.   19 cm.

11065 Walworth, Mansfield Tracy, 1830-1873.
The mission of death; a tale of the New York penal laws.
By M. T. Walworth. New York, Boston [etc.] D. & S.
Sadlier & co. , 186[3?]
iv, [5]-281 p.   16 1/2 cm.

11066 Walworth, Mansfield Tracy, 1830-1873.
Stormcliff. A tale of the highlands. By Mansfield T.
Walworth... New York, Carleton, 1866.
2 p. l. , [7]-387 p.   19 cm.

11067 Walworth, Mansfield Tracy, 1830-1873.
Warwick; or, The lost nationalities of America, a novel
by Mansfield Tracy Walworth. New-York, G. W. Carleton;
London, Low, son & co. , MDCCCLXIX.
470, 8 p.   18 1/2 cm.

11068 Ward, Mrs. Elizabeth Stuart (Phelps) 1844-1911.
          Beyond the gates. By Elizabeth Stuart Phelps... Boston,
       New York, Houghton, Mifflin and company, 1883.
          196 p.   18 1/2 cm.

11069 Ward, Mrs. Elizabeth Stuart (Phelps) 1844-1911.
          Come forth! By Elizabeth Stuart Phelps and Herbert D.
       Ward. Boston and New York, Houghton, Mifflin and
       company, 1891.
          iv, 318 p.   18 cm.

11070 Ward, Mrs. Elizabeth Stuart (Phelps) 1844-1911.
          Donald Marcy, by E. S. P. Boston and New York,
       Houghton, Mifflin and company, 1894.
          2 p. 1., 242 p.   18 cm.
          "Copyright, 1893."

11071 Ward, Mrs. Elizabeth Stuart (Phelps) 1844-1911.
          The gates ajar. By Elizabeth Stuart Phelps... Boston,
       Fields, Osgood, & co., 1869.

11072 Ward, Mrs. Elizabeth Stuart (Phelps) 1844-1911.
          The gates between, by Elizabeth Stuart Phelps... Boston
       and New York, Houghton, Mifflin and company, 1887.
          1 p. 1., 222 p., 1 1.,   18 cm.

11073 Ward, Mrs. Elizabeth Stuart (Phelps) 1844-1911.
          Hedged in. By Elizabeth Stuart Phelps... Boston, Fields,
       Osgood, & co., 1870.
          iv, 295 p.   18 cm.

11074 Ward, Mrs. Elizabeth Stuart (Phelps) 1844-1911.
          The master of magicians, by Elizabeth S. Phelps and
       Herbert D. Ward... Boston and New York, Houghton
       Mifflin and company, 1890.
          2 p. 1., 324 p.   18 cm.

11075 Ward, Mrs. Elizabeth Stuart (Phelps) 1844-1911.
          Men, women, and ghosts. By Elizabeth Stuart Phelps...
       Boston, Fields, Osgood, & co., 1869.
          3 p. 1., 334 p.   18 cm.
          CONTENTS. -No news. -The tenth of January. -Night-

watches.-The day of my death.-"Little Tommy Tucker."
-One of the elect.-What was the matter?-In the Gray Goth.
-Calico.-Kentucky's ghost.

11076 Ward, Mrs. Elizabeth Stuart (Phelps) 1844-1911.
          A singular life, by Elizabeth S. Phelphs... Boston, and
       New York, Houghton, Mifflin and company, 1895.
          2 p. l., 426 p.   18 cm.

11077 Ward, Mrs. Elizabeth Stuart (Phelps) 1844-1911.
          The silent partner. By Elizabeth Stuart Phelps...
       Boston, J. R. Osgood and company, late Ticknor & Fields,
       and Fields, Osgood, & co. [etc., etc.] 1871.
          1 p. l., [v]-viii, [9]-302 p.   17 1/2 cm.

11078 Ward, Mrs. Elizabeth Stuart (Phelps) 1844-1911.
          The story of Avis. By Elizabeth S. Phelps... Boston,
       J. R. Osgood and company, 1877.
          2 p. l., 7-457 p.   18 1/2 cm.

11079 Ward, Mrs. Elizabeth Stuart (Phelps) 1844-1911.
          The supply at Saint Agatha's, by Elizabeth Stuart Phelps;
       with illustrations by E. Boyd Smith and Marcia Oakes
       Woodbury. Boston, and New York, Houghton, Mifflin and
       company, 1896.
          1 p. l., 88 p. front., plates.   20 cm.

11080 Ward, Herbert Dickinson, 1861-
          The burglar who moved paradise, by Herbert D. Ward.
       Boston and New York, Houghton, Mifflin and company,
       1897.
          x p. 1 l., 226 p. front.   18 1/2 cm.
       Note by Elizabeth Stuart (Phelps) Ward.

11081 [Ware, Henry] 1794-1843.
          The recollections of Jotham Anderson, minister of the
       gospel... Boston, The Christian register office, 1824.
          118 p.   20 cm.
       Originally printed in the Christian register.

11082 Ware, William, 1797-1852.
          Aurelian:, or Rome in the third century. In letters of

Lucium M. Piso [pseud.] from Rome, to Fausta the daughter
of Gracchus, at Palmyra. By William Ware... New York,
C. S. Francis & co.; Boston, J. H. Francis, 1848.
    2 v in 1.   18 cm. (Half-title: Francis & co.'s cabinet
library of choice prose and poetry)
    Originally published in 1838, under title: "Probus"; later
republished abroad, and also in this country, by approval of
the author, under above title.
    Sequel to "Letters of Lucius M. Piso, from Palmyra".

11083 [Ware, William] 1797-1852.
    Julian; or, Scenes in Judea. By the author of Letters from
Palmyra and Rome... New York, C. S. Francis; Boston,
J. H. Francis, 1841.
    2 v.   19 1/2 cm.

11084 [Ware, William] 1797-1852.
    Letters of Lucius M. Piso [pseud.] from Palmyra, to his
friend Marcus Curtius, at Rome. Now first translated and
published... New York, C. S. Francis; Boston, J. H.
Francis, 1837.
    2 v.   19 cm.
    Running title: Letters from Palmyra.
    The first 9 letters appeared in the Knickerbocker maga-
zine.
    Published later under title: Zenobia.
    Sequel: Aurelian.

11085 [Warner, Anna Bartlett] 1827-1915.
    Dollars and cents. By Amy Lothrop [pseud.]... New
York, G. P. Putnam, 1852.
    2 v.   19 cm.
    A novel.

11086 Warner, Anna Bartlett, 1827-1915.
    Miss Tiller's vegetable garden and the money she made
by it. By Anna Warner... New York, A. D. F. Randolph
& company [c1873]
    140 p.   17 1/2 cm.

11087 Warner, Anna Bartlett, 1827-1915.
    My brother's keeper. By A. B. Warner... New York

[etc.] D. Appleton & company, 1855.
    385 p.   18 1/2 cm.

11088 Warner, Charles Dudley, 1829-1900.
    The golden house. A novel. By Charles Dudley Warner
    ... Illustrated by W. T. Smedley. New York, Harper &
    brothers, 1895.
    1 p. 1., 346 p. front., plates.   19 1/2 cm.

11089 Warner, Charles Dudley, 1829-1900.
    That fortune. A novel. By Charles Dudley Warner...
  New York & London, Harper & brothers, 1899.
    2 p. 1., 396, [1] p.   19 1/2 cm.

11090 Warner, Charles Dudley, 1829-1900.
    Their pilgrimage, by Charles Dudley Warner; illustrated
  by C. S. Reinhart. New York, Harper & brothers, 1887.
    vii, 363 p.   illus.   19 1/2 cm.

11091 [Warner, Eliza A   ]
    Our two lives; or, Graham and I. By A.H.K. [pseud.]
  New York, A.D.F. Randolph & company [c1873]
    1 p. 1., 233 p.   18 cm.

11092 Warner, Fannie.
    Beech Bluff, a tale of the South. By Fannie Warner.
  Philadelphia, P. F. Cunningham, 1870.
    332 p.   19 cm.

11093 [Warner, Susan] 1819-1885.
    Daisy. Continued from "Melbourne House." By the
  author of "Wide, wide world," "Queechy"... Philadelphia,
  Lippincott & company, 1868-69.
    2 v.   18 cm.

11094 Warner, Susan, 1819-1885.
    The end of a coil. By the author of "The wide, wide
  world"... New York, R. Carter and brothers, 1880.
    viii, [7]-718 p.   19 cm.

11095 [Warner, Susan] 1819-1885.
    The hills of the Shatemuc. By the author of the "Wide,

wide world"... New York, D. Appleton and company, 1856.
iv, 516 p.   19 cm.

11096 Warner, Susan, 1819-1885.
Nobody, by the author of the "Wide, Wide world"... New
York, R. Carter and brothers, 1883.
2 p. 1., 7-695,   19 cm.

11097 [Warner, Susan] 1819-1885.
Queechy. By Elizabeth Wetherell [pseud.]... New York,
G. P. Putnam, 1852.
2 v.   18 1/2 cm.

11098 [Warner, Susan] 1819-1885.
Say and seal. By the author of "Wide, wide world", and
the author of "Dollars and cents"... Philadelphia, J. B.
Lippincott & co., 1860.
2 v.   18 1/2 cm.
Preface signed by Elizabeth Wetherell [pseud.] and Amy
Lothrop [pseud.]

11099 Warner, Susan, 1819-1885.
Wych Hazel, by Susan and Anna Warner... New York,
G. P. Putnam's sons, 1876.
iv, 528 p.   18 1/2 cm.
Sequel: The gold of Chickaree.
"Copyright, 1876."

11100 Warren, Ebenezer W   b. 1820.
Nellie Norton; or, Southern slavery and the Bible. A
Scriptural refutation of the principal arguments upon which
the abolitionists rely. A vindication of southern slavery
from the Old and New Testaments. By Rev. E. W. Warren.
Macon, Ga., Burke, Boykin & company, 1864.
208 p.   22 cm.

11101 [Warren, Nathan Boughton] 1815-1898.
The lady of Lawford, and other Christmas stories. By the
author of "The holidays". (With illustrations by F. O. C.
Darley)... Troy, N. Y., H. B. Nims and company [c1874]
viii p., 1 1., [11]-346 p. front., 14 pl.   19 cm.
CONTENTS.-The lady of Lawford.-Lawford hall.-Parson

Ingram. -Hidden treasure.

11102 [Warriner, Edward Augustus] 1829?-1908.
Victor La Tourette. A novel. By a broad churchman...
Boston, Roberts brothers, 1875.
406 p.   18 cm.

11103 [Washburn, Charles Ames] 1822-1889.
Gomery of Montgomery: a family history. By the author
of "Philip Thaxter"... New York, Carleton, 1865.
2 v.   19 cm.

11104 [Washburn, Mrs. Katharine Sedgwick]
Ina [a novel] By Katherine Valerio. Boston, J. R. Osgood
and company, 1871.
1 p. l., 133 p.   23 1/2 cm.

11105 Washburn, Mrs. Katharine Sedgwick.
The Italian girl [a novel] By Katharine Sedgwick Washburn... Boston, Lee and Shepard; New York, Lee, Shepard
and Dillingham, 1874.
1 p. l., [7]-390 p.   18 cm.

11106 [Washburn, William Tucker] 1841-1916.
Fair Harvard: a story of American college life... New
York, G. P. Putnam & son [etc., etc.] 1869.
vi, 309 p.   18 cm.

11107 Waterhouse, Benjamin, 1754-1846.
A journal, of a young man of Massachusetts, late a
surgeon on board an American privateer, who was captured
at sea by the British... and was confined first, at Melville
island, Halifax, then at Chatham, in England, and last, at
Dartmoor prison. Interspersed with observations, anecdotes and remarks, tending to illustrate the moral and
political characters of three nations. To which is added,
a correct engraving of Dartmoor prison, representing the
massacre of American prisoners. Written by himself...
Boston: Printed by Rowe and Hooper, 1816.
228 p. fold. front.   18 1/2 cm.
"A novel founded on fact." - Allibone, Dict. of authors.

11108 Waters, Clara (Erskine) Clement, 1834-1916.
        Angels in art, by Clara Erskine Clement... Boston,
    L. C. Page and company, 1898.
        267 p. incl. front. , 33 pl.   19 1/2 cm.

11109 [Watmough, Edmund Carmick] 1796-1848.
        Scribblings and sketches, diplomatic, piscatory, and
    oceanic. By a fisher in small streams. 2d ed. , with
    additions. Philadelphia, C. Sherman, printer, 1844.
        viii, [9]-189 p.   20 cm.
    Erroneously ascribed to William Linn Brown, also to
    Edward Coxe Watmough.

11110 Watson, James V   1814-1856.
        Tales and takings, sketches and incidents, from the
    itinerant and editorial budget of Rev. J. V. Watson...
    New York, Carlton & Porter, 1857.
        1 p. 1. , [5]-466 p.   19 1/2 cm.

11111 We, by us; that is to say, James Yellow and John Blue: their
    travails, by them. New York, Baker, Godwin & co. ,
    printers, 1854.
        196 p.   18 1/2 cm.

11112 [Webb, Charles Henry] 1834-1905.
        John Paul's book: moral and instructive: consisting of
    travels, tales, poetry, and like fabrications. By John
    Paul [pseud.] ... With several portraits of the author,
    and other spirited engravings... Hartford, Conn. , and
    Chicago, Ill. , Columbian book company, 1874.
        xv, [16]-621 p.   front. , plates.   22 cm.
    Added t. -p. , engraved.

11113 Webb, Charles Henry, 1834-1905.
        Liffith Lank; or, Lunacy. By C. H. Webb. Illustrations
    by Sol. Eytinge, jr. Quotations by various authors... New-
    York, Carleton, 1866.
        48 p. illus.   17 cm.
    A travesty of Charles Reade's "Griffith Gaunt".

11114 Webb, Charles Henry, 1834-1905.
        St. Twel'mo; or, The cuneiform cyclopedist of Chatta-

nooga. By C. H. Webb... Illustrations by Sol Eytinge, jr.
... New York, C. H. Webb, 1867.
59 p. illus. 17 cm.

11115 Webber, Charles Wilkins, 1819-1856.
Old Hicks, the guide; or, Adventures in the Camanche
country in search of a gold mine. By Charles W. Webber.
New York, Harper & brothers, 1848.
2 p. 1., [ix]-x p., 1 1., [13]-356 p. 19 cm.
Sequel: The gold mines of the Gila.

11116 Weld, Horatio Hastings, 1811-1888.
Corrected proofs, by H. Hastings Weld. Boston, Russell,
Shattuck & co., 1836.
261, [1] p. 19 1/2 cm.
Title vignette.
"Selections from the contributions of the author to different
periodicals... principally ... to the Boston galaxy, and
Boston pearl." - p. 8.

11117 Weld, Horatio Hastings, 1811-1888.
Jonce Smiley, the Yankee boy who had no friends. By
Ezekiel Jones, esq. [pseud.]... Ed. by H. Hastings Weld.
New York, Philadelphia, E. Ferrett and company, 1845.
75 p. 23 1/2 cm. (On cover: Library of American
novels, no. 3)
Cover-title: Jonce Smiley, the Yankee boy who had no
friends. By H. Hastings Weld.

11118 Wellmont, Emma.
Uncle Sam's palace; or, The reigning king. By Emma
Wellmont. Illustrated by Billings. Boston, B. B. Mussey
and company, 1853.
308 p. front., plates. 18 cm.

11119 Wells, David Ames, 1828-1898.
Robinson Crusoe's money; or, The remarkable financial
fortunes and misfortunes of a remote island community. By
David A. Wells... With illustrations by Thomas Nast...
New York, Harper and brothers, 1876.
118 p. incl. front., illus., 3 pl. 24 cm.

11120 Wells, David Dwight, 1868-1900.
　　　　Her ladyship's elephant, by David Dwight Wells. New
　　York, H. Holt and company, 1898.
　　　　vi, 234 p.　　19 1/2 cm.

11121 Welty, Mrs. E　　　A
　　　　Self-made; or, Living for those we love. By Mrs. E. A.
　　Welty... New York, Sheldon and company; Boston, Gould
　　and Lincoln, 1868.
　　　　280 p.　　19 1/2 cm.

11122 [Wentz, Sara A　　　　　]
　　　　Amy Denbrook. A life drama. By the author of "Woman
　　and marriage"... New-York, J. O'Kane [c1867]
　　　　2 p. l., [7]-482 p.　　19 cm.

11123 Wentz, Sara A
　　　　Smiles and frowns. By Sara A. Wentz... New York,
　　D. Appleton and company, 1857.
　　　　376 p.　　20 cm.

11124 Westcott, Edward Noyes, 1846-1898.
　　　　David Harum, a story of American life. By Edward
　　Noyes Westcott. New York, D. Appleton and company,
　　1900.
　　　　viii, 392 p.　　19 cm.

11125 Westcott, Margaret Jane Cook
　　　　Bessie Wilmerton; or, Money, and what came of it. A
　　novel. By Margaret Westcott. New York, G. W. Carleton
　　& co. [etc., etc.] 1874.
　　　　384 p.　　18 1/2 cm.

11126 Western border life; or, What Fanny Hunter saw and heard
　　in Kansas and Missouri. New York, Derby & Jackson;
　　Cincinnati, H. W. Derby & co., 1856.
　　　　xii, [13]-408 p.　　19 1/2 cm.
　　　　A novel, dealing with the struggle to make Kansas a free
　　state.

11127 Westmoreland, Mrs. Maria Elizabeth (Jourdan) b. 1815.
　　　　Clifford Troup: a Georgia story. By Maria Jourdan

Westmoreland... New York, G. W. Carleton & co. [etc.,
etc.] 1873.
>3 p. 1., [9]-338 p.   18 1/2 cm.
>Published in 1880 under title: Drifted together.

11128 Westmoreland, Mrs. Maria Elizabeth (Jourdan) b. 1815.
>Heart-hungry: a novel. By Maria Jourdan Westmoreland.
>New York, G. W. Carleton & co., 1872.
>3 p. 1., [ix]-x, [11]-332 p.   19 cm.

11129 [Weston, Maria D   ]
>Kate Felton; or, A peep at realities. By an American
>lady... Boston, E. P. Weston, 1859.
>vi, 444 p.   front.   20 cm.

11130 Wharton, Edith Newbold (Jones) 1862-1937.
>The touchstone [a story] by Edith Wharton... New
>York, C. Scribner's sons, 1900.
>2 p. 1., 155, [1] p.   20 cm.

11131 [Wharton, George M   ]
>The New Orleans sketch book. By "Sthal" [pseud.]...
>Philadelphia, A. Hart, 1853.
>7, viii, 21-202 p.   front.   19 cm.
>Added t.-p., illustrated.

11132 Wharton, Thomas Isaac, 1859-1896.
>A latter day saint: being the story of the conversion of
>Ethel Jones. Related by herself. New York, Henry Holt
>and company, 1884.
>200 p.   19 cm.

11133 [Wheeler, A   O   ]
>Eye-witness; or, Life scenes in the Old North State,
>depicting the trials and sufferings of the unionists during
>the rebellion. By A. O. W. ... Boston, B. B. Russell
>and company: Chicago, S. S. Boyden, 1865.
>276 p.   front., 2 pl.   19 cm.

11134 Wheeler, Andrew Carpenter, 1835-1903.
>The iron trail. A sketch. By A. C. Wheeler, (the "Nym
>Crinkle" of the N. Y. World.)... New York, F. B. Patter-

son, 1876.
    46 p. illus.   19 1/2 x 16 1/2 cm.
    Account of a visit to Kansas and Colorado, written in
the style of fiction.

11135 Which, the right or the left... New-York, Garrett & co.,
    1855.
    3, iv, [5]-536 p.   19 cm.

11136 Whitcher, Mrs. Frances Miriam (Berry) 1811-1852.
    Widow Spriggins, Mary Elmer, and other sketches. By
    Mrs. F. M. Whitcher... Edited, with a memoir, by Mrs.
    M. L. Ward Whitcher. With comic illustrations. New
    York, G. W Carleton & co.; London, S. Low, son & co.,
    1867.
    378 p. incl. front.   plates.   19 cm.

11137 White, Eliza Orne, 1856-1947.
    The coming of Theodora [a novel] by Eliza Orne White...
    Boston and New York, Houghton, Mifflin and company, 1895.
    2 p. 1., 304 p.   18 cm.

11138 White, Eliza Orne, 1856-1947.
    A lover of truth... Boston, Houghton, Mifflin and
    company, 1898.
    319 p.   18 cm.

11139 White, Eliza Orne, 1856-1947.
    Miss Brooks; a story. By Eliza Orne White. Boston,
    Roberts brothers, 1890.
    283 p.   18 cm.

11140 White, Eliza Orne, 1856-1947.
    Winterborough, by Eliza Orne White... Boston and New
    York, Houghton, Mifflin and company, 1892.
    2 p. 1., 350 p.   18 cm.

11141 White, Homer.
    The Norwich cadets: a tale of the rebellion. By Rev.
    Homer White... St. Albans, Vt., A. Clarke, 1873.
    136 p.   20 1/2 cm.

11142 [White, Mrs. Rhoda Elizabeth (Waterman)]
　　　Mary Staunton; or, The pupils of Marvel hall. By the
　　author of "Portraits of my married friends." New York
　　[etc.] D. Appleton and company, 1860.
　　　2 p. l., 398 p.　　20 cm.

11143 [White, Mrs. Rhoda Elizabeth (Waterman)]
　　　Portraits of my married friends; or, A peep into Hymen's
　　kingdom. By Uncle Ben [pseud.] New York [etc.] D.
　　Appleton & co., 1858.
　　　343 p. front., plates.　　20 1/2 cm.

11144 [White, Richard Grant] 1821-1885.
　　　The adventures of Sir Lyon Bouse, bart., in America
　　during the civil war. Being extracts from his diary.
　　New York, The American news company, 1867.
　　　1 p. l., 64 p.　　19 cm.

11145 [White, Richard Grant] 1821-1885.
　　　The chronicles of Gotham. By the author of "The new
　　gospel of peace." Book first. New York, G. W. Carlton
　　& co. [etc., etc.] 1871.
　　　1 p l., [5]-43 p.　　18 1/2 cm.
　　　In Biblical language.

11146 [White, Richard Grant] 1821-1885.
　　　The fall of man; or, The loves of the gorillas. A popular
　　scientific lecture upon the Darwinian theory of development
　　by sexual selection. By a learned gorilla. Ed. by the
　　author of "The new gospel of peace." New York, G. W.
　　Carleton & co. [etc., etc.] 1871.
　　　48 p.　illus.　　18 1/2 cm.

11147 White, Richard Grant, 1821-1885.
　　　The fate of Mansfield Humphreys, with the episode of Mr.
　　Washington Adams in England, and an apology. By Richard
　　Grant White... Boston, New York, Houghton, Mifflin and
　　company, 1884.
　　　4 p. l., 446 p.　　18 cm.
　　　"A few chapters of this book appeared in 'The Atlantic
　　monthly' magazine; and the first three were published in
　　Edinburgh, with the title 'Mr. Washington Adams in
　　England' " cf. Advertisement.

11148 [White, Richard Grant] 1821-1885.
    The new gospel of peace, according to St. Benjamin. New York, S. Tousey [1863-66]
    4 v. in 1.   19 1/2 cm.
    Imprint varies: v. 1-2, New York, S. Tousey [1863] - v. 3. New York, American news agency [1864] - New York, The American news company [1866]

11149 [Whiting, M   H   ]
    Faith White's letter book. 1620-1623. Plymouth, New England... Boston, H. Hoyt [c1866]
    365 p.   front.   18 cm.

11150 Whitman, William Edward Seaver, 1832-
    The ship-carpenter's family. A story for the times. By William E. S. Whitman. New York, H. Long and brother [c1855]
    viii, [9]-399 p.   19 1/2 cm.

11151 Whitney, Mrs. Adeline Dutton (Train) 1824-1906.
    Ascutney street; a neighborhood story, by Mrs. A. D. T. Whitney. Boston and New York, Houghton, Mifflin and company, 1890.
    1 p. 1., 259 p.   19 cm.

11152 Whitney, Mrs. Adeline Dutton (Train) 1824-1906.
    Hitherto: a story of yesterdays. By Mrs. A. D. T. Whitney... Boston, Loring [c1869]
    473 p.   19 1/2 cm.

11153 Whitney, Mrs. Adeline Dutton (Train) 1824-1906.
    Patience Strong's outings. By Mrs. A. D. T. Whitney ... Boston, Loring, 1869.
    1 p. 1., v-vi, 7-233 p.   19 cm.

11154 [Whittier, John Greenleaf] 1807-1892.
    Leaves from Margaret Smith's journal in the province of Massachusetts bay. 1678-9. Boston, Ticknor, Reed and Fields, 1849.
    3 p. 1., 224 p.   17 1/2 cm.

11155 Whittier, John Greenleaf, 1807-1892.

Legends of New-England... By John G. Whittier. Hartford, Harmer and Phelps; Boston, Carter, Hendee & Babcock [etc., etc.] 1831.
    iv p., 1 l., [7]-142 p.   18 cm.
    In prose and verse.
    First book published by the author.

11156 Whittlesey, Sarah Johnson Cogswell, 1825-1896.
    Bertha the beauty; a story of the Southern revolution.
By Sarah J. C. Whittlesey... Philadelphia, Claxton,
Remsen & Haffelfinger, 1872.
    xii, 13-382 p.   18 1/2 cm.
    Laid in Virginia, 1850-1865.

11157 Wiggin, Kate Douglas (Smith)1856-1923.
    A cathedral courtship, and Penelope's English experiences,
by Kate Douglas Wiggin. With five illustrations by Clifford
Carleton. Boston and New York, Houghton, Mifflin and
company, 1893.
    4 p. l., 164 p. front., plates.   18 cm.
    "Penelope's English experiences": p. [51]-164.

11158 Wiggin, Kate Douglas (Smith) 1856-1923.
    Penelope's progress; being such extracts from the commonplace book of Penelope Hamilton as relate to her experiences in Scotland, by Kate Douglas Wiggin. Boston and
New York, Houghton, Mifflin and company, 1898.
    3 p. l., 268 p., 1 l.   18 cm.

11159 Wiggin, Kate Douglas (Smith) 1856-1923.
    Penelope's English experience, by Kate Douglas Wiggin,
with fifty-three illustrations by Charles E. Brock. Boston
and New York, Houghton, Mifflin & company, 1900.
    xi, 176 p. incl. front., illus.   19 1/2 cm.
    Cover-title: Penelope's experiences. England. v. 1.

11160 Wiggin, Kate Douglas (Smith) 1856-1923.
    Polly Oliver's problem, a story for girls, by Kate
Douglas Wiggin. Boston and New York, Houghton, Mifflin
and company, 1894.
    3 p. l., 212 p., 1 l.   18 cm.

11161 Wiggin, Kate Douglas (Smith) 1856-1923.
      Timothy's quest, a story by Kate Douglas Wiggin...
Boston and New York, Houghton, Mifflin and company,
1893.
      3 p. 1. , 201 p. , 1 l.   18 cm.

11162 Wiggin, Kate Douglas (Smith) 1856-1923.
      The village watch-tower, by Kate Douglas Wiggin...
[13th thousand] Boston and New York, Houghton, Mifflin
and company, 1895.
      4 p. 1. , [3]-218 p.   18 cm.
      CONTENTS.-The village watch-tower.-Tom o' the
Blueb'ry Plains.-The nooning tree.-The fore-room rug.
-A village Stradivarius.-The eventful trip of the Midnight
cry.

11163 Wilcox, Mrs. Ella (Wheeler) 1855-1917.
      An ambitious man by Ella Wheeler Wilcox... Chicago,
E. A. Weeks & company [c1896]
      197 p. incl. front. (port.)   17 1/2 cm.

11164 [Wiley, Calvin Henderson] 1819-1887.
      Alamance; or, The great and final experiment... New
York, Harper & brothers, 1847.
      viii, [9]-151 p.   24 1/2 cm.

11165 [Wilkes, George] 1820?-1885.
      The lives of Helen Jewett and Richard P. Robinson. By
the editor of the New York National police gazette, author of
"Murrell", "Lives of the felons", &c. &c. New York [1849]
      132 p. incl. front. , illus.   25 cm.
      Imprint on cover: Philadelphia, W. B. Zeiber.
      On cover: By the editor of the New York National police
gazette, author of "Life of John A. Murrell," "Joseph T.
Hare," "Colonel Monroe Edwards," etc. etc.
      Copyrighted 1849 by George Wilkes, who was one of the
editors of the National police gazette at that time.
      "The life and adventures of Joseph T. Hare" has been
ascribed to H. R. Howard. cf. Cushing; Sabin; Stonehill.

11166 [Willett, Edward] 1830-
      The Shawnee scout; or, The death trail. By J. Stanley

Henderson [pseud.] New York, Beadle and Adams [1870]
98 p.   16 1/2 cm.

11167 Williams, Mrs. Anna Vernon (Dorsey)
        Betty; a last century love story, by Anna Vernon Dorsey
    ... New York, J. W. Lovell company [1889]
        246 p. front., plates.   19 1/2 cm. (On cover:
    American authors' series, no. 10)

11168 Williams, Mrs. Catherine Read (Arnold) 1790-1872.
        Annals of the aristocracy; being a series of anecdotes of
    some of the principal families of Rhode-Island. By Mrs.
    Williams... 1st[-2d] no. ... Providence, B. T. Albro,
    printer, 1845.
        2 v. in 1.   25 1/2 cm.
    No more published.

11169 Williams, Mrs. Catherine Read [(Arnold)] 1790-1872.
        Aristocracy; or, The Holbey family: a national tale... By
    Mrs. C. R. Williams... Providence, Printed by J. Knowles,
    1832.
        viii, [9]-312 p.   18 1/2 cm.

11170 [Williams, Mrs. Catherine Read (Arnold)] 1790-1872.
        Fall River, an authentic narrative. By the author of
    "Tales, national, revolutionary," &c. ... Boston, Lilly,
    Wait & co; Providence, Marshall, Brown & co., 1833.
        198 p. front.   16 1/2 cm.
    An account of the circumstances leading to the trial of the
    Rev. Ephraim K. Avery for the murder of Sarah M. Cornell
    in Fall River in December 1832.

11171 Williams, Mrs. Catherine Read (Arnold) 1790-1872.
        The neutral French; or, The exiles of Nova Scotia. By
    Mrs. Williams... 2d ed. Providence, The author [1841]
        2 v. in 1.   19 cm.

11172 Williams, Mrs. Catherine Read (Arnold) 1790-1872.
        Religion at home; a story, founded on facts... By Mrs.
    Williams. 2d ed. Providence, Printed by B. Cranston
    & co., 1837.
        vi, [7]-312 p.   19 cm.

11173 Williams, Mrs. Catherine Read (Arnold) 1790-1872.
        Tales; national and revolutionary. By Mrs. C. R. Williams
    ... Providence, H. H. Brown, printer, 1830-35.
        2 v.   15 1/2 cm.
        Vo. 2 printed by Cranston & Hammond.
        CONTENTS. -[I] Preface. Narrative of Rosanna Hicks.
Life of Capt. Oliver Read. The blind sisters. The king's
ship. Providential escape. Loyalty. Scott's pond thirty
years ago. - II. Preface. Life of Judge C - a tale of the
West. To an infidel [a poem]. The last of the Dinsmores.
A sketch of the Brown's. The cholera at Quebec.

11174 [Willis, Charles W   ] 1864-
        "Buckra" land. Two weeks in Jamaica. Details of a
voyage to the West Indies, day by day, and a tour of Jamaica,
step by step. With appendix; by Allan Eric [pseud.]...
Boston, Bangor, Me., The Journal publishing co., 1896.
        89, [6] p. incl. front., 1 illus., plates.   22 cm.

11175 [Willis, John R   ]
        Carleton, a tale of seventeen hundred and seventy-six.
Philadelphia, Lea & Blanchard, 1841.
        2 v.   18 cm.
        Published in London under title: Carleton; or, Duty and
patriotism... By John R. Willis...

11176 Willis, Nathaniel Parker, 1806-1867.
        Dashes at life with a free pencil. By N. P. Willis...
New York, Burgess, Stringer & co., 1845.
        4 pt. in 1 v.   26 1/2 cm.
        CONTENTS. -pt. I. High life in Europe, and American
life. -pt. II. Inklings of adventure. -pt. III. Loiterings of
travel. -pt. IV. Ephemera.

11177 Willis, Nathaniel Parker, 1806-1867.
        Fun-jottings; or, Laughs I have taken a pen to, by N.
Parker Willis. New-York, C. Scribner, 1853.
        vi, [7]-371 p.   19 1/2 cm.

11178 [Willis, Nathaniel Parker] 1806-1867.
        Inklings of Adventure, by the author of "Pencillings by
the way"... London, Saunders and Otley, 1836.

3 v.   19 cm.

11179 Willis, Nathaniel Parker, 1806-1867, ed.
        The legendary, consisting of original pieces, principally
        illustrative of American history, scenery, and manners.
        Ed. by N. P. Willis... Boston, S. G. Goodrich, 1828.
            2 v.   18 1/2 cm.

11180 Willis, Nathaniel Parker, 1806-1867.
        Life, here and there; or, Sketches of society and adven-
        ture at far-apart times and places. By N. P. Willis.
        New York, Baker & Scribner, 1850.
            vii, 377 p.   18 1/2 cm.

11181 Willis, Nathaniel Parker, 1806-1867.
        Paul Fane; or, Parts of a life else untold. A novel.
        By N. Parker Willis. New York, C. Scribner; Boston, A.
        Williams & co. [etc., etc.] 1857.
            viii, [9]-402 p.   18 1/2 cm.

11182 Willis, Nathaniel Parker, 1806-1867.
        People I have met; or, Pictures of society and people of
        mark, drawn under a thin veil of fiction. By N. Parker
        Willis. New York, Baker and Scribner, 1850.
            xiv, 357 p.   18 1/2 cm.

11183 [Willis, Nathaniel Parker] 1806-1867.
        Romance of travel, comprising tales of five lands, by the
        author of Pencilings by the way. New York, S. Colman,
        1840.
            5 p. 1., [15]-300 p.   19 cm.
            CONTENTS.-Lady Ravelgold.-Paletto's bride.-Violanta
        Cesarina.-Pasquall, the tailor of Venice.-The bandit of
        Austria.-Oonder hoofden, or, The undercliff.-The picker
        and piler.-Stratford-on-Avon.-Charlecote.

11184 Wilmer, Lambert A   1805?-1863.
        The confessions of Emilia Harrington. Baltimore, L. A.
        Wilmer, 1835.
            96 p.   17 cm.

11185 [Wilson, Mrs. Augusta Jane (Evans)] 1835-1909.

Macaria; or, Altars of sacrifice. By the author of "Beulah"
... 2d ed. Richmond, West & Johnston, 1864.
183 p.   23 1/2 cm.

11186 Wilson, Mrs. Augusta Jane (Evans), 1835-1909.
St. Elmo, a novel, by Augusta J. Evans... New York,
Carleton, pub. , ; London, S. Low, son and Co. , 1867.
571 p.   19 cm.

11187 Windle, Mary Jane, 1825-
Life at the White Sulphur Springs; or, Pictures of a
pleasant summer. By Mary J. Windle... Philadelphia,
J. B. Lippincott and co. , 1857.
4 p. 1. , [13]-326 p.   19 cm.
CONTENTS. -[Life at White Sulphur Springs] Pen and ink
sketches. -The lady of the rock. -Pocahontas. A legend of
Virginia. -Grace Bartlett. An American tradition.

11188 Windle, Mary Jane, 1825-
Truth and fancy: tales legendary, historic, and descriptive.
By Mary J. Windle. Philadelphia, C. Sherman, printer, 1850.
viii p. , 2 1. , [13]-303 p.   20 1/2 cm.
A later, enlarged edition has title: A legend of the
Waldenses, and other tales.
CONTENTS. -The Huguenot. -Florence de Rohan. -The
lady of the rock.

11189 [Winsor, Henry]
Pebblebrook, and the Harding family. Boston, B. H.
Greene, 1839.
vii, 207 p.   19 1/2 cm.
Published anonymously.

11190 Winston, James.
Cora O'Kane; or, The doom of the Rebel guard. A story
of a great rebellion. Containing incidents of the campaign
in Missouri under Generals Fremont and Sigel, and the
thrilling exploits of the Unionists under Major Zagonyi. By
Sergt. J. Winston. [Claremont, N. H.] Pub. by an
association of disabled soldiers, 1868.
84 p.   32 1/2 cm.

11191 Winterburn, Florence Hull, 1858–
      Southern hearts, by Florence Hull Winterburn... New York, The F. M. Lupton Publishing company, 1900.
      406 p.   front.   19 cm.
      CONTENTS.–When love enslaves.–The wife of Lothario.–Peter Weaver.–A halt at dawn.–Pink and black.–Mrs. May's private income.–The laziest girl in Virginia.–An awakening.–Apples Blossoms.

11192 Winthrop, Theodore, 1828–1861.
      Cecil Dreeme. By Theodore Winthrop. Boston, Ticknor and Fields, 1861.
      iv, [5]–360 p.   18 1/2 cm.
      "Biographical sketch of the author. By George William Curtis": p. [5]–19.

11193 Winthrop, Theodore, 1828–1861.
      Edwin Brothertoft. By Theodore Winthrop... 3d ed. Boston, Ticknor and Fields, 1862.
      2 p. 1., [7]–369 p.   18 cm.

11194 Winthrop, Theodore, 1828–1861.
      Life in the open air, and other papers. By Theodore Winthrop... Boston, Ticknor and Fields, 1863.
      iv p., 2 1., [3]–374 p.   front. (port.) pl.   19 cm.
      CONTENTS.–Life in the open air. Katahdin and the Penobscot.–Love and skates.–New York Seventh regiment. Our march to Washington.–Washington as a camp.–Fortress Monroe.–Brightly's orphan. A fragment.–"The heart of the Andes."

11195 Wise, Henry Augustus, 1819–1869.
      Captain Brand, of the "Centipede". A pirate of eminence in the West Indies: his loves and exploits, together with some account of the singular manner by which he departed this life. By Harry Gringo, (H. A. Wise, U. S. N.)... New York, Harper & brothers, 1864.
      299 p. incl. front., plates.   24 cm.

11196 Wise, John Sergent, 1846–1913.
      Diomed; The life, travels, and observations of a dog, by John Sergent Wise; illustrated by J. Linton Chapman. Boston,

London and New York, Lamson, Wolffe and company, 1897.
vi p., 1 1., 330 p.   illus.   20 1/2 cm.

11197 Wood, Benjamin, 1820-1900.
        Fort Lafayette; or, Love and secession. A novel, by
        Benjamin Wood. New York, Carleton, 1862.
        2 p. 1., 7-300 p.   18 cm.

11198 [Wood, Charlotte Dunning] 1858-
        ... Cabin and gondola, by Charlotte Dunning [pseud.]...
        New York, Harper & brothers, 1886.
        cover-title, 203 p.   18 1/2 cm.   (Harper's handy
        series, no. 48)
        CONTENTS.-Pam.-Mrs. Brayfield.-Told between the
        acts.-In a cracker's cabin.-Decker's second wife.-The soul-
        sisters.-Annina.-At the Maison Dobbe.-Whither curiosity
        led.-By Parna's grave.-"Mees."

11199 Wood, George, 1799-1870.
        Future life; or, Scenes in another world. By George Wood
        ... New York, Derby & Jackson, 1858.
        xiv, 15-359 p.   18 cm.
        Reissued later, under title: The gates wide open.

11200 Wood, George, 1799-1870.
        Modern pilgrims: showing the improvements in travel,
        and the newest methods of reaching the celestial city...
        By George Wood... Boston, Phillips, Sampson & co.;
        New York, J. C. Derby, 1855.
        2 v.   19 cm.
        The plan of the book was suggested by Hawthorne's
        allegory, "The celestial railroad".

11201 [Woodruff, Mrs. Julia Louisa Matilda (Curtis)] 1833-1909.
        Holden with the cords, by W. M. L. Jay [pseud.]...
        New York, E. P. Dutton & company, 1874.
        vi, [7]-517 p.   19 cm.

11202 [Woods, Caroline H   ]
        The diary of a milliner. By Belle Otis [pseud.] New York,
        Hurd and Houghton, 1867.
        viii, 200 p.   18 cm.

11203 Woods, George Bryant, 1844-1871.
     Essays, sketches, and stories, selected from the writings of
George Bryant Woods. With a biographical memoir. Boston,
J. R. Osgood and company, 1873.
     xxii, 399 p.   19 1/2 cm.
     "In memoriam" signed: H. A. C[lapp].

11204 Woodworth, Samuel, 1785-1842.
     The champions of freedom, or, The mysterious chief, a
romance of the nintheenth century, founded on the events of
the war, between the United States and Great Britain, which
terminated in March, 1815... By Samuel Woodworth...
New York: Printed and published by Charles N. Baldwin,
Bookseller, No. 49 Division-street. 1816.
     2 v.   17 1/2 x 10 cm.

11205 Woolson, Constance Fenimore, 1840-1894.
     Castle Nowhere: lake-country sketches. By Constance
Fenimore Woolson. Boston, J. R. Osgood and company,
1875.
     2 p. l., [7]-386 p.   19 cm.
     Originally appeared in the Atlantic monthly, Scribner's
monthly, and other magazines.
     CONTENTS. -Castle Nowhere. -Peter the parson. -Jean-
nette. -The old agency. -Misery Landing. -Solomon. -
Wilhelmina. -St. Clair flats. -The lady of Little Fishing.

11206 Woolson, Constance Fenimore, 1846-1894.
     For the major, a novelette, by Constance Fenimore
Woolson... New York, Harper & brothers, 1883.
     2 p. l., 208 p.   front., 5 pl.   17 1/2 cm.

11207 Woolson, Constance Fenimore, 1838-1894.
     Rodman the keeper: southern sketches. By Constance
Fenimore Woolson... New York, D. Appleton and company,
1880.
     339 p.   18 cm.
     Originally published in the Atlantic monthly, Appletons'
journal and other periodicals.
     CONTENTS. -Rodman the keeper. -Sister St. Luke. -Miss
Elisabetha. -Old Gardiston. -The South Devil. -In the cotton
country. -Felipa. -"Bro."-King David. -Up in the Blue Ridge.

11208 [Wright, E M .]
    Behind the scenes: a story of the stage. By Verity Victor
   [pseud.] Boston, New England news company, 1870.
    284 p. 17 1/2 cm.

11209 Wright, Edmund, pseud.
    Narrative of Edmund Wright: his adventures with and
   escape from the Knights of the golden circle... Cincinnati,
   J. R. Hawley, 1864.
    vi, [15]-150 p. front. , plates. 24 cm.

11210 Wright, Mrs. Julia (MacNair) 1840-1903.
    Almost a priest. A tale that deals in facts. By Mrs. Julia
   McNair Wright... Philadelphia, McKinney & Martin, 1870.
    432 p. front. , plates. 18 cm.

11211 Wright, Mrs. Julia (MacNair) 1840-1903.
    Circled by fire. A true story. By Julia McNair Wright
   ... New York, National temperance society and publication
   house, 1879.
    91 p. front. 16 cm.

11212 Wright, Mrs. Julia (MacNair) 1840-1903.
    John and the demijohn; a temperance tale. By Mrs.
   Julia McNair Wright... Boston, H. Hoyt [c1869]
    3 p. 1. , [9]-408 p. front. , plates. 18 1/2 cm.

11213 Wright, Mrs. Julia (MacNair) 1840-1903.
    Jug-or-not. By Mrs. J. McNair Wright... New York,
   National temperance society and publication house, 1870.
    2 p. 1. , [iii]-vi, 7-346 p. front. , pl. 17 1/2 cm.
    Added t. -p. , illustrated.

11214 [Wright, Mrs. Julia (MacNair) 1840-1903.
    Moth and rust. A very plain tale. Boston, H. Hoyt
   [c1870]
    4 p. 1. , 7-394 p. front. , plates. 17 1/2 cn. (Half-
   title: Prize book)
    Title-page in colors, within ornamental border.

11215 Wright, Mrs. Julia (NacNair) 1840-1903.
    Nothing to drink. A temperance sea story. By Julia

McNair Wright... New York, National temperance society
and publication house, 1873.
    399 p.   front., plates.   17 1/2 cm.

11216 Wright, Mrs. Julia (MacNair) 1840-1903.
    Our Chatham street uncle; or, The three golden balls.
By Mrs. J. McNair Wright... Boston, H. Hoyt [c1869]
    345 p.   front., plates.   18 cm.

11217 Wright, Mrs. Julia (MacNair) 1840-1903.
    Secrets of the convent and confessional: an exhibition of
the influence and working of papacy upon society and republican institutions. By Mrs. Julia M'Nair Wright...
With an introduction, by Rev. Daniel March... Cincinnati,
O. [etc.] National publishing company; Chicago, Ill., Jones
brothers and company, 1872.
    xi, [13]-622 p.   front., 15 pl.   20 1/2 cm.

11218 Wright, Mrs. Julia (MacNair) 1840-1903.
    Under the yoke, and other tales. By Mrs. J. McNair
Wright... Cincinnati, Western tract and book society,
1871.
    216 p. front.   19 cm.
    CONTENTS.-Under the yoke.-Making a proselyte.-The
lay sister.

11219 Wright, Sarah Ann.
    The gem of the lake. A novel. By Mrs. Sarah A. Wright
... New York, American news company, 1868.
    vi, 3-60 p.   23 1/2 cm.

11220 Wright, Sarah Ann.
    The golden ladder; or, The stolen jewel. By Mrs. Sarah
A. Wright... New York, American news company, 1871.
    6, [vii]-viii, [7]-377 p.   front. (port.) pl.   19 cm.

Y

11221 The Yankee in London; or, A short trip to America...

Philadelphia, J. Carson, 1826.
107 p.   15 cm.

11222 The Yankee traveller: or, The adventures of Hector Wigler...
Concord: Published by George Hough. Sold at the Concord
Book-Store, wholesale and retail. 1817.
107 p.   16 cm.
Caption title: The adventures of Hector Wigler.

11223 Young, Samuel, b. 1821.
The orphan, and other tales. Pittsburgh, Printed by A. A.
Anderson, 1844.
107 p.   19 cm.

11224 Young, Samuel, b. 1821.
The smoky city, a tale of crime. Pittsburgh, Printed by
A. A. Anderson, 1845.
204 p.   22 cm.

11225 Young, Samuel, b. 1821.
Tom Hanson, the avenger, a tale of the backwoods:
embracing the history, legends, and romance of the
"country around the head of the Ohio" ... By Samuel
Young... Pittsburgh, J. W. Cook, 1847.
2 p. 1., [iv]-vii, [9]-199 p.   22 1/2 cm.

8489 Alden, Isabella (Macdonald) "Mrs. G. R. Alden," 1841-
Missent; or, The story of a letter, by "Pansy" (Mrs.
G. R. Alden)... Boston, Lothrop publishing company, 1900.
175, [1] p. front.   19 cm.